THE
MARTIAL ARTS
ENCYCLOPEDIA

JENNIFER LAWLER

MASTERS PRESS

NTC/Contemporary Publishing Group

Library of Congress Cataloging-in-Publication Data

Lawler, Jennifer, 1965–.
    The martial arts encyclopedia / Jennifer Lawler.
        p.   cm.
    Includes index.
    ISBN 1-57028-068-1
    1. Martial arts—Encyclopedias.   I. Titles.
GV1101.L39   1996
796.8'03—dc20   95-53692
                                           CIP

Published by Masters Press
A division of NTC/Contemporary Publishing Group, Inc.
4255 West Touhy Avenue, Lincolnwood (Chicago), Illinois 60712-1975 U.S.A.
Printed in the United States of America
International Standard Book Number: 1-57028-068-1

7 8 9 0 VLP VLP 0 5 4 3 2 1

TABLE
OF
CONTENTS

PREFACE

The Martial Arts Encyclopedia is intended to serve as a general reference tool for beginning martial artists, advanced practitioners and those who are simply interested in learning more about martial arts. The Encyclopedia covers all aspects of the martial arts, with seven different sections: general martial arts information; schools and styles; forms and techniques; literature; biography; weapons; and countries of origin. A pronunciation guide is included, along with appendices for selected readings and an index. For ease of use, the names of schools, styles and techniques are listed by their most commonly used name in the United States. However, since there can be an enormous variety in the names and spellings used for any one technique, school, etc., other variants are cross-referenced. The book is designed to be a general reference to all styles of martial arts, providing a brief but complete picture of each aspect of each martial art. For further information, consult the suggested readings in the back for specialized books.

Several people assisted in the completion of this book, and I would not wish them to go unacknowledged. Sean Edinger, technical instructor of Ryobu-kai Karate (Lawrence, Kansas), kindly spoke at length with me about Karate-do and allowed me to photograph pictures of his class. Bill Wiswell, manager and C.E.O of Ryukyu Martial Arts Supply (Shawnee, Kansas) was gracious enough to allow me to photograph his extensive weapons collection, and discussed the uses and construction of many of those weapons. Dena Freisen supplied the drawings and a number of excellent ideas, as well as moral support, so she deserves special thanks. Great appreciation must be extended to my sa beum nim, Mr. Donald Booth and Mrs. Susan Booth, for setting me on the path and giving me the gifts of discipline and unqualified encouragement. I cannot express the significance of my martial arts training under these fine instructors, nor can I express how seriously I have learned to view the tenets of Tae Kwon Do, as the Booths have taught them to me. Affection and appreciation and thanks is owed also to the black belts and other students at New Horizons Black Belt Academy of Tae Kwon Do, who have become my second family. Most importantly, I thank my husband, Bret Kay, who helps me on the way with love, generosity and unfailing support. He has long been my model of the complete martial artist, with his patience, humor, spiritual calm and spectacular jump spinning wheel kick.

Jennifer Lawler
Lawrence, Kansas
October 19, 1995

Below are charts indicating the approximate pronunciation of words in Korean, Japanese and Chinese.

JAPAN:
"i" as in "marine"
"o" as in "no"
"u" as in "fool"
"e" as in "step"
"g" as in "grapes"
"ae" as in "may"
"ai" as in "smile"
"ei" as in "bet"
"ts" as in "zoo"

Therefore, the phrase "age-tsuki" is pronounced "ah-gee-zoo-key."

CHINA:
"ai" as in "sign"
"ao" as in "blue"
"e" as in "met"
"ei" as in "aim"
"g" as in "gate"
"ie" as in "saw"
"ng" as in "sing"
"ou" as in "show"
"tz" as in "zip"

Therefore, the phrase "T'ai Chi" is pronounced "tie-chee."

KOREA:
"a" as in "father"
"o" as in "boat"
"i" as in "gift"
"e" as in "let"
"ae" as in "day"
"yu" as in "unique"
"wa" as in "when"
"eu" as in "true"
"g" as in "kite"

Therefore, the phrase "ja yu dae ryun" is pronounced "jaw-you-day-re-youn."

GENERAL SECTION

ACUPRESSURE

In this process, the channels through which chi, or life energy, flows are opened by putting pressure on or massaging certain areas of the body. There are 14 major channels, called meridians, and at certain places along these meridians, gentle pressure will stimulate the organs, dispersing the chi energy and helping to reduce pain or cure disease. The points to which pressure is applied are those that vital point attacks target. This process is similar to acupuncture. It is called Shiatsu. It is also used in the process of resuscitation, called kappo or kuatsu.

ACUPUNCTURE

Similar to acupressure, this process opens up the channels in the body through which chi, or life energy, flows. Points in the body are stimulated with a needle. This stimulation helps the chi move more smoothly and easily through the body. Various organs respond by decreasing pain or even curing disease. This method is more precise than acupressure. It is a vital part of Chinese Healing art. See Acupressure.

AI

See Harmony.

AIKI-HA

A theory that suggests that non-resistance works to defeat an opponent. The opponent's own momentum and movement works against him or her, and as a result, the opponent is responsible for his or her own defeat. The Chinese call the energy that can be turned against the opponent "jing." See Strategy.

AIKIDOJI

See Uniforms.

AIKIKAI

An important martial arts training hall for traditional Aikido, located in Tokyo. Students travel from all over the world to train at the Aikikai, where the headquarters of the Aikido Federation are also located .

AIR SHIELD

See Training Equipment.

AM

Same as Yin. See Yin-Yang.

AM-DUONG

Same as Yin-Yang. See Yin-Yang.

AN

Variation of Am. Same as Yin. See Yin-Yang.

AN-DUONG

Variation of Am-Duong. Same as Yin-Yang. See Yin-Yang.

ANGLES OF ATTACK

A concept of defending against attack according to the angle at which an attack is delivered, as opposed to defending against a specific technique. For instance, if the opponent attacks to the left side of the head, the appropriate counter is one that protects the left side of the head, for instance a high block. It does not matter whether the opponent is attacking with a roundhouse kick or a hook punch, the appropriate response is the same. Some systems see eight angles of attack while others count twelve. See Arnis in the Schools and Styles section.

ARMOR

Refers to both the armor worn by feudal warriors as well as the various kinds of protective gear used by martial artists. The latter is commonly called gear, protective gear or sparring equipment. It goes by the name bogu in Korean. Soldiers have always used some form of armor to help protect themselves, often made of metal, as in chain mail. The kind and amount of armor was determined by the status of the soldier. This was true in the East as well as the West. In Asia, the earliest known armor was used in the fifth century A.D., but some form of protection, perhaps leather, was probably used even earlier. Most armor was made of steel, and since it was cumbersome, could actually hinder the warrior. In the eighteenth century, this problem was partly resolved by the introduction of lacquered bamboo armor (mune-ate) which was created by Nakanishi Chuta. This armor became extremely popular and was more durable than it sounds. In Japan, o-yoroi or kachu armor covered the whole body and was worn by high-ranking warriors while haramaki covered the chest only, and was for ordinary warriors, including the foot soldiers. The complete armor worn by high-ranking samurai included a helmet (kabuto), often highly decorated, usually with a moveable visor. A mesh face mask (men) could be attached to the helmet. This mask was later adopted by Kendo practitioners, as were other pieces of armor. The body was protected by a chest plate (do), shoulder guards (sode), and arm guards (kote). Full body armor usually included leg guards (sune-ate) and a thick skirt that protected the thighs and abdomen (hae-date). The armor worn in the East tended to be lighter and easier to put on than the armor favored in the West (in which the entire body was sheathed in steel), but the lighter armor was also less protective, and was especially vulnerable to arrows. On the other hand, it meant that the warrior was mobile and could more easily defend himself from attack. See Sparring Equipment. See Armor, Kendo.

ARMOR, HORSE

Iron, steel or leather armor protected the head of the horse in the manner of a helmet. Leather armor, sometimes padded, sometimes lacquered, sometimes both, protected the body of the horse. It was decorated with gilding, as were the leather squares that covered the hindquarters. Horse armor was not as heavy or confining in Asia as in Europe, in keeping with the general preference for mobility and agility.

ARMOR, KENDO

Kendo practitioners wear an adapted version of classical Japanese body armor. A helmet with a steel mesh face mask (men), is worn. The helmet has padded flaps to protect the neck from the shinai, or bamboo sword, used by practitioners. The body protector (do) is a large cushioned pad that covers the body from neck to waist. Padded gloves (te) are worn to protect the hands. Male competitors wear the kinteki-ate, the groin protector. The whole is adapted from classical Japanese samurai warrior armor.

ART

As in martial art. See Do. See Martial Art.

ARTS OF COMBAT

The arts of combat are different from the ways of combat (budo). Arts of combat (bugei) focus on the most expedient method to kill or injure an opponent in a real fighting situation. These were practiced by the samurai using various weapons, and included rules for the ethical behavior of warriors. The spiritual or sport aspect of martial arts is not emphasized. See Bugei. See Budo. See Techniques of Combat.

Fig. 1.1 : Kendo armor.

ASA-GEIKO

Same as Asa-keiko. See Training (Morning).

ASA-KEIKO

See Training (Morning).

ATEMI

Vital points. See Vital Points.

BACHDAI

See Ranking Systems.

BAKUFU

This term means "government from the hut," that is, direct military rule. In Japan, this military rule lasted from the twelfth to the nineteenth century. In 1868, the emperor was restored and assumed direct control of the government. Under bakufu, the imperial family had mostly figurative power and simply named a shogun or military ruler to govern the country. In turn, the imperial rulers were allowed to keep their nominal rights. Succeeding dynasties of military families assumed direction of the government, often after bloody wars. Each family had different political and military aims, and relied on warriors, samurai, to help them achieve their aims. Shogun, which is the word that is more familiar to Westerners, is the military ruler, and the shogunate is the military government. See Shogun.

BALANCE

Maintaining balance is essential to martial artists. This balance includes physical balance, plus harmony between the mental and the physical. Balance is manifested in the proper relation of opposites. In martial arts, balance is important especially when executing movements. For instance, when one punches with one fist, one must pull with the other. Each action has a reaction and the reaction must be compensated for. Through the understanding of this concept, the martial artist maintains balance, which is essential, and generates speed and power. A martial artist who has balance can defeat an opponent. When one loses one's balance because of the failure to compensate for the opposing reaction, it is called hando-no-kuzushi. Balance is also fundamental to correct posture and stances. A person who has "strong" stances is exhibiting excellent balance. Balance is also associated with harmony, as it is shown in the concept of yin-yang. In martial arts which rely on throwing or grappling, breaking the opponent's balance — that is, off-balancing the opponent — is essential to the correct execution of techniques. Conversely, the martial artist who wishes to avoid being thrown must maintain correct balance at all times. See Strategy. See Yin-Yang.

BANZUKE

Sumo rank. See Ranking Systems.

BARO

Korean command meaning to finish and return to starting position. See Commands.

BEGIN

Command meaning to start, applied either to a sparring match or to the performance of a form. See Commands.

BELT

Most modern martial arts schools award belts of different colors to practitioners. These indicate rank or the level of skill. Traditionally, the darker the belt, the higher the rank. Thus, a black belt indicates the highest level of proficiency. Occasionally, both the highest and lowest ranks in an art are given a white belt to indicate the completion of a circle. Some Wushu stylists wear sashes as opposed to belts, but they have the same meaning. The colors used to indicate rank vary among martial arts system, styles and schools. Such colored belts were first used in Judo. The term "belt" is often used to designate various groups of students. "Senior belts," for instance, are higher ranking students who are accorded special respect. A "low belt," or "under belt" is a student whose rank is at the beginner level. In some schools, students are addressed by their belt color instead of their names, a practice that focuses the students on the group and the training, and not on individuals. See Ranking Systems.

BENG CHUAN

Chinese term meaning "crushing fist." It refers to the explosive power cultivated in some styles of Wushu.

BOGU

See Sparring Equipment.

BONNO

Loss of focus, which can be dangerous for the martial artist. See Mental Awareness.

BOWING

In martial arts, the practice of bowing is the same as shaking hands or, in the military, saluting an officer. It is a sign of respect with little or no religious symbolism remaining. Students usually bow to the shomen, the front of the room, as they enter it. The bow is often directed toward a specific place, such as flags, or a picture of the style's founder. Martial artists also bow to higher-ranking students (called senior belts) and the instructor. Some bows are executed from a standing position and others from a kneeling position. Kneeling bows are sometimes called seated bows. In sword arts, the practitioners often bow to their swords as well. "Rei" means bow, "zarei" refers to seated bows, and a "shinzen no rei" is a bow to the front of the room. See Etiquette. See Kamiza.

BOXER

A Chinese martial artist. Usually refers to Shaolin temple monks. The so-called Boxer Rebellion was named after the martial artists who fought in it. See Boxer Rebellion.

BOXER REBELLION

In 1900, Chinese nationalists rebelled against foreign rule and were subsequently put down by an international army. Secret martial arts societies trained members for this rebellion; some of these secret societies are still in existence. Because of the threat of death, many people involved in the Boxer Rebellion fled to the United States, where they settled mostly in California.

BRAHMAN

The highest caste in Hinduism. Brahmins are keepers of sacred knowledge. The members of this caste make up the Hindu priesthood. See Hinduism.

BREATHING EXERCISES

See Techniques Section.

BU

War or combat. The word is often used to form the name of a martial art, such as Bu-jutsu, or as part of a martial art term, for instance, budo. Combat in this sense refers to the physical actions of attack, defense, counter-attack and simple evasion, plus military strategy.

BUDDHA

A term meaning "enlightened one," given to Buddhists who have achieved the highest state of understanding. It is a title of respect that was given to Siddhartha Gautama, the founder of Buddhism, who brought this religion to Asia. Though it is a title, not a name, it is commonly used to designate Gautama himself.

BUDDHISM

A religion and philosophy founded in the sixth century B.C. by Siddhartha Gautama, who is known by the title "buddha," meaning "enlightened one." This eastern religion posits that suffering is inherent in life, but that one can achieve tranquillity by certain mental and moral practices. The Four Noble Truths are the basis of Buddhism. They are that birth, sickness, death and frustration are painful; that pain comes from desire; that the pain will stop if the desire is also stopped; and that the way to stop desire is to follow the Eightfold Path. The Eightfold Path is the way taken by followers of Buddhism. This concept suggests that appropriate conduct in life will lead to a deliverance from suffering. The Eightfold Path consists of having right views, right purpose, right speech, right conduct, right vocation, right effort, right awareness, and right concentration.

BUDO

A term referring to those martial arts that have more than a combat or martial dimension. Unlike the so-called combat arts (bugei or bujutsu), "martial way" arts or "budo" emphasize the growth and development of the individual's spiritual and physical well-being. Personal growth, not just self-defense, is the primary purpose of such arts. Budo arts are derived from the combat arts; they did not develop independently of them. Through long practice and training, the martial artist who practices a budo style will achieve spiritual, mental and emotional peace. Budo arts are those that include the word "do" or "way," in their name, such as in Aikido, Judo and Iaido, plus others.

BUDO-SEISHIN

The martial spirit inherent in one who follows a way of combat (budo). See Way of the Warrior.

BUDOKA

The term for any practitioner of a budo ("martial way" or "do") art. More generally, anyone who practices a martial art is given this designation. A martial artist who follows a specific system is also referred to by that system's name: for instance, a "karateka" or "judoka" is one who follows the practices of Karate or Judo.

BUDOKAN

A large hall constructed for the 1964 Olympic Games held in Tokyo. The hall is used for all Japanese martial arts systems, with many different martial arts styles being taught. Thousands of students travel from around the world to be instructed at the Budokan. The name refers to "the place of martial way arts." See Kodokan.

BUGEI

Martial arts that emphasize the fighting aspect as applied to combat or battle. Such martial arts are mostly concerned with weapons use. Same as Arts of Combat. See Art of Combat. See Budo.

BUJUTSU

Another word for Bugei. See Techniques of Combat.

BUJUTSU-RYU HA

A tradition of combat arts; any classical style incorporating weapons and warfare methods, such as battlefield practice, sword and staff, plus healing.

BUKE

The Japanese warrior class that was responsible for developing combat techniques. From these techniques derive many Japanese martial arts.

BUSHI

A Japanese word meaning warrior, which is what the samurai called themselves. Others classes called them samurai, which means "attendant" or "servant." Bushi refers to those of the warrior class as distinct from members of the aristocracy. The Bushi were a powerful force in the government of Japan, and the ruling class was derived from these families for many centuries. See Samurai.

BUSHI NO NASAKE

See Gentleness of the Warrior.

BUSHIDO

An ethical code followed by the samurai, much like the celebrated chivalric code of medieval Europe. The term was coined in the late-19th century by a writer, Inazo Nitobe. See Way of the Warrior.

CAP

See Ranking Systems.

CARNATION EYEBROWS SOCIETY

One of many secret political or military factions that existed in China throughout its history. Its participants trained in Chinese boxing. See Secret Societies.

CENTERLINE

A concept that, while important to many martial arts, is fundamental to Wing Chun. An imaginary line is drawn from the practitioner's solar plexus to the opponent's chin. This line is the centerline. As long as it is in proper alignment — that is, directly in front of an opponent — the practitioner can attack in the straight charge that is practiced in Wing Chun. On another level, it refers to the basic understanding of the position of the practitioner's body in relationship to the opponent's body.

CEREMONY

See Tea Ceremony. See Tournaments.

CHALLENGES

In Asia, in particular China, this was the central part of a martial arts master's life. Any individual could challenge to fight a master, hoping to prove prowess and skill. The master could not refuse a challenge, though sometimes a senior student would be asked to accept the challenge in the place of the master. This was done not so much to protect the master, but to discourage untested, unskilled people from making such demands on the master. The challenger would chose the weapons, which is the reason martial arts masters were skilled in a variety of weapons, and the challenger also specified death or defeat; that is, whether the match would conclude when one admitted defeat (or was clearly bested) or only when one participant was killed. A defeated master was disgraced and would lose students, who sometimes followed the victor. Thus, a martial artist looking for students would sometimes wander the country, challenging others until finding a master who could be defeated.

CHAN

Same as Zen. See Zen.

CHA-NO-YU

See Tea Ceremony.

CHAREYHET

The Korean term for "attention." Students are expected to assume the attention stance. See Command.

CHASHI

See Training Equipment.

CHEN

Same as Zen. See Zen.

CHI

Chi refers to the life force or vital energy of life. In China, this concept is called qi or chi and in Korea and Japan, it is called ki. Chinese, Korean and Japanese ideas regarding the chi are nearly identical. The Indian term, prana or pranja, has some connection to the idea of the soul. This life force is located in the abdomen (the hara) where it is controlled by the breath. Thus, the proper use of the chi is one of the reasons why correct breathing is fundamental to the proper exercise of the martial arts. Some styles, such as Wushu, emphasize breathing more than others. Chi is the essential force that unites all things. In this way, it is more than just personal energy. As a creative and active force, it can be summoned through the shout or kiai. It can make a person more powerful than physical strength alone can. It is thought that one's chi can be seen in one's personality, and in all outward actions. It somehow reflects the inner person. Strong chi is therefore the equivalent of good character. Chi is an important concept in the Asian philosophies that underlie the martial arts, which is why it is a principle central to so many martial arts styles. See Ji-gong.

CHI-CHI

In China, vital point attacks. See Vital Points.

CHIKARAISHI

See Training Equipment.

CHING

Ching is controlled chi, or life energy. Ching refers to the physical power that derives from the internal energy of chi. Chi and ching work as complements to each other, much as yin and yang do.

CHU GYO NIM

See Teacher.

CHUAN BI

Vietnamese phrase meaning "ready." Students are expected to stand in ready stance or position. See Commands.

CHUMBEE

Same as Chunbee. See Chunbee.

CHUNBEE

Korean term for "ready." Students assume a ready stance. See Commands.

CIRCULAR MOTION

Movements and techniques using an indirect approach, as in Aikido. The technique does not move directly toward the target but instead finds a circular path. These movements are generally characterized as passive or soft, evasive and defensive as opposed to offensive and direct. Usually used by internal schools. The opposite of linear. See Linear Motion.

COACH

See Teacher.

COMMANDS

Terms used to tell students what to do. Ordinarily, they are given in the language of the country in which the martial art originated, and are therefore unfamiliar to western practitioners. The more common commands designate "begin," "ready," and "attention"; the latter two require the student to assume specific stances while awaiting the next command. The attention command requires that the student focus on the instructor, perhaps while being quizzed. The ready command requires that the student prepare for the demands that will follow.

COMPETITION RULES

See Tournaments.

CONFUCIANISM

Relating to the teaching of Confucius. This is a system of philosophy, not a religion. It became codified and systematized during the Han Dynasty (206 B.C. to 220 A.D.), soon becoming the dominant philosophy of China, though it competed with Taoism and Buddhism with which it had much in common. Sometimes it was connected with religious rituals, but Confucianism was never intended to be a religious doctrine. It is a philosophy that is concerned with goodness, piety, and virtues that produce peaceful relationships among humans. See the Literature section for more information regarding the writings of Confucian philosophers. See Confucius in the Biography section.

CONTESTS

See Tournaments.

CONTROL

See Uniforms.

COSTUME

See Uniforms.

COURTESY

See Etiquette.

COURTESY THROW

A throw in martial arts practice which the opponent does not try to prevent. The lower-ranked practitioner allows the higher-ranked practitioner to throw him or her; sometimes courtesy throws are conducted in turns, as an aid to training.

CUONG NHU TUONG THOI

Vietnamese principles of Yin-Yang. See Yin-Yang.

DAI-SENSEI

See Teacher.

DALYEUN-JU

Same as Makiwara. See Training Equipment.

DAMPATSU SHIKI

See Hair Cutting Ceremony.

DAN

See Ranking Systems.

DANG

See Ranking Systems.

DANSHA

See Ranking Systems.

DANTIAN

The location of chi energy in the abdomen. See Hara.

DAO

Same as Tao. See Tao.

DAU

Vietnamese term meaning "begin." See Commands.

DAYANG

See Ranking Systems.

DEGREE

A black belt rank. See Ranking Systems.

DELAYED DEATH TOUCH

The ability of a martial artist to cause death by touching an opponent in a certain way, on a certain area of the body. The death would take place at some future time. Though it is possible to injure or even kill an individual by striking a vital point with enough force, a simple touch is not sufficient. Those techniques that are thought to cause immediate death are known as poison finger or poison hand techniques. It is thought that perhaps the legendary illnesses or deaths that supposedly resulted from delayed death touch are actually owing to one attcker poisioning the other. Also known as Dim Mak.

DERO DOHRAS

Korean term meaning "turn around." Students are expected to turn away from the instructor while adjusting their uniform or while being judged after a performance in competition and in certain other situations.

DHYANA

Indian word for meditation. See Mental Awareness. See Zen.

DIM MAK

See Delayed Death Touch. See Poison Finger Techniques.

DISTANCE

The area that separates two opponents. It is also called range. A number of distance or ranges are acknowledged by martial artists, usually including far, long, medium and close. At a far distance, opponents cannot reach each other. Such an opponent who is out of range is called toi. At long distance, opponents can touch. At medium distance, opponents can strike to the head or body. At close range, opponents are within a few inches of each other. The martial artist must determine what distance or range is most desirable and to his or her best advantage. He or she must also have some technique for "closing the gap," that is, covering the distance to the opponent. This judgment is called ma-ai. See Strategy.

DISTANCE DEATH

A superstitious belief that certain martial artists could cause death even if they did not touch the opponent, using supernatural abilities. Sometimes this skill was connected with the ability to control chi. By sending one's breath or chi to the opponent, one could defeat him or her while remaining unseen. A similar belief posited the ability of a skilled martial artist to cause death merely by touching an opponent. These are called poison finger techniques. If death did not immediately occur, the skill was called delayed death touch.

DO

Japanese word for the "Way," used to define the path that one follows. In relation to the spiritual or philosophical, the "way" is a fundamental basis of Taoism. Thus, the path is all-encompassing. When "do" refers to a style of the martial arts, it means a martial way that leads to self-understanding, as opposed to a primarily combat art. See Taoism. Also, in Kendo, a chest plate or protector. See Armor, Kendo.

DOBOK

See Uniforms.

DOCES PARES SOCIETY

In the Philippines, a secret society made up of skilled Arnis practitioners. See Arnis in the Schools and Styles section.

DOGI

See Uniforms.

DOGU

See Uniforms.

DOHRAS

Same as Dero Dohras. See Dero Dohras.

DOHYO

Literally, "clay and rice bales," which refers to the materials originally used to construct a Sumo ring. See Training Hall.

DOHYO-IRI

The "entering the ring" ceremony performed before a Sumo contest. See Tournaments, Sumo.

DOJANG

See Training Hall.

DOJO

See Training Hall.

DOJO DEFEAT

An event that occurred when the master and students of one martial arts school (dojo=training hall) challenged the members of another school. The master who was defeated in such a contest lost face, and his methods and abilities would be in doubt. His students would leave and join the school of the winner. Today, such challenges are friendly, and usually take place in a tournament setting. Students now would not ordinarily leave their schools regardless of who "won" such events. Also called Dojo Tempest or Dojo Destruction.

DOJO OATH

Sometimes called a dojo pledge or code. A statement of ethical behavior for use in the training hall and daily life made by a martial artist. Students promise to train hard and to follow the way. Many schools have such oaths. Often, upon earning the black belt, a student will sign an oath promising to uphold the dignity of the school and agreeing not to teach the methods of the school without the consent of the master instructor.

DUONG

Same as Yang. See Yin-Yang.

EIGHT DIRECTIONS OF MOVEMENT, THE

The directions in which one can move to attack or evade an attack. These include, of course, forward and backward and to the left and the right, but also consist of moving forward in a diagonal direction toward the left or right, and moving backward diagonally to either the left or right. Trigram Boxing uses this theory as a basis of movement. Footwork is designed so that the practitioner can move in any one of the eight directions at any given time.

EIGHTEEN WEAPONS, THE

The traditional weapons used in Chinese martial arts since the 13th century, including sword, spear, halberd, long rod, iron bar, trident, tiger (or horse) fork (also called forked staff), hook, tapered rod, ring, saber, crutches, axe, whip, sai, hammer, short staff, and pestle. The weapons differ for each era after the Sung Dynasty in which they originated. See Weapons section.

EIGHTFOLD PATH, THE

Sometimes called the Eightfold Way. In Buddhism, the steps necessary to reach enlightenment and to live correctly. The eight elements are right views, right purpose, right speech, right conduct, right vocation, right effort, right awareness, and right concentration. See Buddhism.

EMPTY HAND

Refers to martial arts styles that do not use weapons and rely on the body (hands, feet, etc.) for self-defense.

ENRYO

Indifference to death. Even more, a mental attitude that death is beneath notice. The warrior who despises death is nearly invincible in battle. It is also an essential element in seppuku, or ritual suicide. See Mental Awareness.

ETIQUETTE

The practice of showing proper respect to the martial arts master, the other students, the training hall and the martial art itself. For instance, bowing to the front of the room when entering or leaving and bowing to senior belts and instructors is an almost universal sign of respect. When an instructor enters the room students are expected to stop what they are doing, stand and greet the teacher. Proper etiquette also consists of addressing higher ranking belts as "Mr." or "Ms." or in the case of a master, "Master," plus the person's last name. Some teachers prefer the use of titles such as "sensei." Students also must wear the school uniform for all practices, classes and workout sessions, and the uniform must be kept clean and mended. Some schools expect students to wear a patch or emblem on the uniform that identifies the school they attend. Students are expected to use their martial arts knowledge only if absolutely necessary. One who fights unnecessarily may be dismissed from the school or demoted in rank. Students are also expected to refrain from teaching others without their instructor's permission. Since all behavior reflects on the school, students must be polite and helpful even when they are not in the training hall. Schools have varying levels of etiquette, with some taking it quite seriously and others being more relaxed. Other rules of etiquette vary from school to school.

EXAMINATIONS

In order to promote in rank, martial arts practitioners must periodically undergo public testing. Their knowledge of techniques, forms, appropriate terminology and sometimes breaking will determine whether they pass or fail. Judges look for good form, power, speed and accuracy. Physical control is also important. In some styles, technical skill is weighed more heavily than fighting skill. Some styles also take the examinee's character and confidence into consideration. Some martial art schools have a required number of hours of instruction before one is eligible to take the exam. Requirements increase in complexity as the practitioner promotes through the ranks. A diploma (gaku) is sometimes awarded. See Ranking Systems. See Menkyo System.

FIVE ANIMALS, THE

An important concept to Chinese martial arts, which often incorporate the qualities and movements of animals. The five animals are traditionally the dragon, snake, leopard, crane and tiger, though other variations exist. The most common variation is bird, deer, monkey, bear and tiger. Each animal symbolizes certain qualities and actions. The tiger, for instance, might indicate power, clawing techniques and courage. These are also associated with the Five Elements of wood, fire, earth, metal and water. See Five Elements. See Twelve Animals.

FIVE ELEMENTS, THE

In Chinese philosophy, the five elements are wood, fire, earth, metal and water. These elements influence martial arts for they have special qualities that martial artists are encouraged to develop. Fire, for instance, is quick and aggressive, which can be good for a martial artist. But fire can be quenched by water, which is passive and yielding, so the quick and aggressive martial artist must be aware of this counter. Balance, as in all things, is essential. The elements interact in the following way: wood makes fire, fire makes earth, earth makes metal, metal makes water, and water makes wood. But wood destroys earth, earth destroys water, water destroys fire, fire destroys metal, and metal destroys wood. The Five Elements are also identified with the Five Animals. Fire is identified with the bird, earth with the monkey, wood with the deer, water with the bear, and metal with the tiger.

FIVE SCHOOLS, THE

The most famous swordmaking smiths during the classical age of the Japanese sword. See the Weapons section.

FIVE WAYS OF KUNG-FU, THE

According to Bruce Lee, the methods that could be used against an opponent. These included strikes, kicks, joint locks, throws and weapons.

FOCUS

The ability to concentrate only on one's goal, whether to perfect a technique or score a point or win a contest, is fundamental to success as a martial artist. When one loses one's focus, even for a moment, one can be defeated. This loss of concentration is called "bonno" or "suki"; that is, "disturbed feeling." See Mental Awareness.

FORM

See Forms and Techniques section.

FOUR CORNERS

Indicates the boundary for using techniques in Wing Chun. The target includes the area from eyebrow to groin and from shoulder to shoulder.

FOUR POISONS OF KENDO

Mental, emotional or intellectual difficulties that interfere with success in Kendo. Through training these difficulties — fear, doubt, surprise and confusion — can be controlled. Though specific to Kendo, the concept underlies most martial arts, especially those that practice and encourage free-style sparring matches, such as Karate and Tae Kwon Do.

FUDO-NO-SEISHIN

See Fudoshin.

FUDOSHIN

Unchangeable or strong at heart; that is one who has the ability to be calm and detached at all times. When one is calm and detached, the difficulties in life are unthreatening. Small problems as well as large ones can be approached with this attitude. Regarded as of primary importance by the famous warrior Miyamoto Musashi, it is fundamental to all warrior philosophy. Sometimes called fudo-no-seishen. The stance of the warrior who has cultivated fudoshin is called fudotachi. See Mental Awareness.

FUDOTACHI

See Fudoshin.

FUNDOSHI

See Uniforms.

GAKKO

A term which means school, as in an actual physical building or training hall, not a martial arts style. See Training Hall. See School.

GAKU

A certificate given upon successful completion of a rank promotion examination. See Examination. See Ranking Systems.

GEIKO

Same as Keiko. See Training.

GENTLENESS OF THE WARRIOR

A tenet of Bushido, the Way of the Warrior. Called "bushi no nasake," the concept emphasizes that even the strongest, most powerful individuals should be sympathetic and fair toward everyone, not just equals or superiors. Further, martial arts should be used unselfishly, for the benefit of all. This is equivalent to the chivalric virtues of charity and compassion prized by Europeans in the Middle Ages. This ideal was promulgated to counteract the tendency of the lower classes to fear and criticize the conduct of samurai. See Way of the Warrior.

GI

See Uniforms.

GO

A Japanese word meaning hardness and action, the opposite of ju, related, in effect, to yin-yang. It is a concept that led to the development of hard striking styles of the martial arts, such as Karate.

GOHO

See Method of Hardness.

GOKYU

See Ranking Systems.

GOMAN

A Korean term for "finish and return to starting position." See Commands.

GRADES

See Ranking Systems.

GRAPPLING

Techniques for holding and wrestling with an opponent instead of using kicks and punches to strike. Many grappling techniques are intended to throw the opponent to the ground, or, as in the case of Sumo, to force the opponent out of the ring. Once on the ground, joint locks and immobilizations are used to defeat the opponent. Many martial arts systems use wrestling and groundwork techniques and do not rely solely on striking methods. Judo, Sumo and Jujutsu are considered grappling arts since they rely primarily on grappling techniques; other systems simply make use of grappling techniques. Styles that emphasize striking and avoid grappling are of course called striking styles.

GUP

See Ranking Systems.

GURU

A spiritual teacher or wise person. See Teacher.

HA

A branch of a school of martial arts. Also, one of the three stages of development. See Three Stages of Development.

HACHIMAKI

See Uniforms.

HAE-DATE

A protective skirt worn with armor. See Armor.

HAIR CUTTING CEREMONY

On their retirement from the sport, top-ranked Sumo practitioners participate in a retirement ceremony that consists of cutting their top knot. The elaborate hair styles of Sumo wrestlers indicate their status and skill level. When one is no longer an active participant, one can no longer wear the Sumo hairstyle. The act of retirement itself is called intai-zumo. The hair-cutting ceremony is called Dampatsu-shiki.

HAJIME

The Japanese word meaning "begin." See Commands.

HAKAMA

See Uniform.

HAKUDA

Refers to a general period of martial arts training, often in preparation of a contest or tournament. See Training.

HAND CONDITIONING

Like other methods of hardening the body, hand conditioning had a more useful function in feudal warrior days than it does now. Essentially, hand conditioning causes scar tissue to form on the hand, usually as a result of striking hard surfaces. This causes the scarred area to become callused and insensitive to pain. It was an important part of training when empty-handed martial artists might have to break through an enemy's armor or shield to cause injury. It is used today by certain martial artists to aid in board or brick breaks, though it has no other real use. Such martial artists are said to have an iron palm or iron hand. Thai boxers use a similar method to condition their shins to deliver and block devastating shin kicks.

HANDO NO KUZUSHI

See Balance.

HANSHI

Literally, "Master." Reserved for high-ranking black belts. See Teacher.

HAORI

See Uniforms.

HARA

The part of the body, usually equated with the abdomen, where the chi, or life energy, is located. Since chi is essential to the performance of the martial arts, locating this spot is a technique practiced by many martial artists. Attention to the hara will increase one's ability to call on one's chi when necessary, which will increase power. The art of calling up this energy is called haragei. The hara is also called tanden, dantian, and tan tien. See Tao. See Aiki. See Chi.

HARA-KIRI

Ritual suicide. See Seppuku.

HARAGEI

Essentially, the ability to locate and use one's chi. These are techniques that use hara, or the energy of chi, the life force. See Chi. See Hara.

HARD STYLES

Those martial arts that use striking, linear techniques, as opposed to soft styles that use evasive, circular movements. Such arts are often called striking arts and do not rely heavily on grappling techniques. See Method of Hardness. See Go.

HARMONY

A basic principle of martial arts, it is the balance of two opposites. The idea of two opposites resting in harmony is called "ai." In Asian philosophy, harmony is a principle of the universe. Humans and nature must be in balance. Harmony also means the intuitive connection between the universe, humans and nature. See Yin-Yang.

HATSU GEIKO

A special period of training that starts on New Year's Day and ends a few days later with a tournament. The objective is to help participants begin the New Year appropriately — that is, with sufficient attention paid to the martial arts, to the exclusion of other concerns. This creates the appropriate mindset for martial arts practice throughout the year. See Training.

HEAVY BAG

See Training Equipment.

HEIJO-SHIN

A calm but focused state of mental awareness that a warrior must have during battle. It is characterized by a relaxed and confident attitude. Anger or fear may cause the warrior to lose concentration, or may cause him to be blinded to the opponent's strategy, so it is necessary to be sharply focused, but equally calm. It is necessary to have cultivated fudoshin, detachment, for this mental state to be possible. See Mental Awareness.

HET

Vietnamese word for kiai or shout. See Shout.

HEYA

A "stable" of Sumo wrestlers, equivalent to a martial arts school. See Stables, Sumo.

HIDDEN TEACHINGS

Those techniques not taught to all students. At first, the need for security made it paramount for a master to "hide" some techniques or abilities. A master would not teach all of his or her techniques to a student because the student might betray the teacher and try to defeat him or her in a challenge. Over time, this need for security evolved into a rite of initiation, in that those advanced and trusted students whom the master considered to have the most potential would be taught the hidden teachings. Such students had access to the complete martial art. These hidden teachings were sometimes special techniques, or perhaps specialized knowledge of medicine or resuscitation methods, or even spiritual matters. Other, uninitiated students remained unaware of the existence of these teachings. Those who were shown the hidden teachings were called the inner circle; those who were not were called the outer circle. This is not to be confused with secret school or secret teachers, who merely made access to their school or teachings difficult; once one was admitted, one was taught all that the master knew, though one had to promise not to reveal any of the knowledge thus gained.

HI-GI

An inquiry into the development of the spiritual. Only the highest ranking students are permitted to undertake this study, and only certain martial arts styles pursue such discussions and studies.

HINDUISM

The dominant religion of India. It emphasizes meditation, contemplation and asceticism. What is sought is the "one reality." The doctrine of rebirth is fundamental to Hinduism. One is reborn after death, either at a higher station or a lower one. Karma is the spiritual matter, negative or positive, that accumulates throughout one's life and determines how one will be reborn in the next life. The escape from the necessary rebirth, through correct living and attainment of enlightenment, is considered salvation. The caste system that resulted from Hinduism is hereditary and cannot be changed. The caste system is a rigid social hierarchy that determines everything from what one can eat to whom one may marry. Each caste has a different social function. At the top of the hierarchy are the brahmins, who are the keepers of religious learning and who make up the members of the priesthood. The Kshatriyas are the warriors and the members of the ruling class. Vaisyas are merchants and artisans, Sudras are servants, and the lowliest of all are the Panchamas who are called the untouchables. Then there are various tribal groups that have not been assimilated into Hindu society. Vedic literature is the authority of Hindu practices and belief, which basically have to do with a number of gods who are at war with demons. The gods are strengthened through the sacrificial fire ritual, which only Brahmin can perform, thus making the brahmin, in a sense, almost as powerful as the gods. See India in the Countries section.

HO-GOO

See Sparring Equipment.

HOGU

Same as Ho-goo. See Sparring Equipment.

HONTAI

Readiness. The martial artist is alert and prepared for any event. Thus, nothing will come as a surprise and the martial artist will not be confused and uncertain as to his or her course of action. Such awareness is dulled by caffeine, alcohol, and other drugs, plus mental and emotional preoccupations. See Mental Awareness.

HUYET

See Vital Points.

HYOHO

See Method of Strategy.

IHRU

See Chi.

IKKYU

See Ranking Systems.

IMMOVABLE ELBOW THEORY

A central concept in Wing Chun Wushu. While one's hands and forearms can move anywhere, in any position, one's elbow should always remain in the same position, about three inches in front of the body. This protects one's centerline and contributes to good balance.

IN

Same as Yin. See Yin-Yang.

INNER CIRCLE

Those trusted, privileged students who have been hand-picked by the master to learn the hidden teachings of a school. See Hidden Teachings. See Outer Circle.

IN-YO

Same as Yin-Yang. See Yin-Yang.

IPPON

One full point in competition. See Tournaments.

IRON PALM

A method in which chi or life force is used to develop so much power that a mild slap with a relaxed, open hand could seriously injure an opponent. See Hand Conditioning.

JING

A term used in Chinese martial arts to refer to energy, force, especially as the martial artist can use it. This is related to chi, but it is not chi. There are different kinds of this energy. Tien jing, for instance, is listening jing, a kind of energy or force that allows one to develop sensitivity to another. One's sense of touch is developed so that one can anticipate the opponent's movements. Listening jing is coupled with dong jing, which is understanding force; fa jing, which is dissolving force; and fat jing, which is using one's own force against an opponent.

JU

A word meaning softness and yielding, referring to the flexibility of both mind and body. Turning the opponent's own momentum against him or her, and allowing the opponent to defeat him or herself is the essence of ju. Passive resistance thus is preferred to active resistance and was especially prized by monks who did not wish to permanently injure or kill anyone. Ju is the opposite of go, or hardness and action, and exists in a yin-yang relationship to it. See Method of Softness.

JUDGES

See Tournaments.

JUDO-SHUGYOSHA

The traditional name for a Judo practitioner below the fourth dan (degree) black belt.

JUDOGI

See Uniforms.

JUDOJO

See Training Hall.

JUHO

See Method of Softness.

JUKYO

See Ranking Systems.

JUN DANG

See Training Hall.

JURU

A term that refers to the parts of the body, such as hands, feet, knees, elbows, shins, and so on.

JUTSU

A term that indicates a style or school of the martial arts that emphasizes force and combat effectiveness. These styles often use weapons and try to imitate "real" combat or fighting situations. These are combat arts or arts of war (bugei) rather than those martial arts that emphasize sport aspects or personal growth. Aiki-jutsu and Jujutsu are just two examples of so-called combat arts. Modern "way" arts stem from jutsu arts. See Bugei. See Budo.

KA

A suffix meaning practitioner. A karateka is one who practices Karate; a judoka is one who practices Judo, and so on.

KABUKI

Classical Japanese heroic theatre that developed from Noh theatre. The scenery is more elaborate and more extensive. The movements and costumes are as stylized as in Noh. The stories often concern samurai and frequently display martial arts techniques. See Noh.

KABUTO

A helmet. See Armor.

KACHU

Armor. See Armor.

KAGURA

The religious ritual conducted before a Sumo contest, which stems from the time when Sumo was still used for Shinto divination. See Shinto. See Sumo in the Styles and Schools section.

KAIDEN

See Menkyo System.

KAME

See Training Equipment.

KAMI

In ordinary use, the spirits, divinities and deities of Shinto, a major Japanese religion. The kami guide their followers. Often these spirits are ancestors, but the word also refers to objects in the natural world as well as inanimate objects. In its less usual sense, it means anything sublime, as in an exceptional being or an impressive object. See Spiritual Awareness.

KAMIDANA

An altar to the kami — spirits and deities — that is placed in the front of the room in a training hall. An additional altar to the ancestors is sometimes placed at the front of the room as well. As a gesture of respect, martial artists bow to the kamidana.

Fig. 1.2 : A kamidana. The Japanese character means chi.

KAMIKAZE

Though most often identified with Japanese pilots on suicide missions in World War II, the term, meaning "divine wind," actually refers to an unquenchable spirit, the lack of concern about personal well-being and a strong regard for the situation of others. It was used in this sense as early as the thirteenth century.

KAMIZA

This word means "the place of the spirits." It refers to the bow that martial artists make to the front of the room and to the objects representing the traditions of the art that are kept there. These objects might include a picture of a particular style's founder, an altar, or other relics of importance. See Kamidana.

KAN-GEIKO

Also Kan-keiko. See Training (Winter).

KAN-KEIKO

See Training (Winter).

KAN-SHU

See Training Equipment.

KAPPO

A special system of acupressure used for resuscitation. The knowledge of such techniques was once considered extremely important for a martial arts master, since his students might suffer injury or loss of consciousness during practice. Now, martial arts practice is less dangerous and the likelihood of getting knocked out during a class is relatively slim. For this reason, many of the techniques of kappo are being lost. The study of resuscitation techniques is usually reserved to black belts and is only taught in some schools. Also called Kuatsu. See Acupressure.

KARMA

A Hindu belief. The spiritual force generated by a person's actions, which can be positive or negative, and which determines the nature of the individual's next life. See Hinduism.

KEIKO

Training in general, but with the intention of continually trying to improve, whether through repetition, practice, or study of other techniques and theory. See Training.

KEIKO-GI

See Uniforms.

KEIKOBA

See Training Hall.

KENDOGI

See Uniforms.

KENDOGU

See Uniforms.

KENSEI

A silent kiai or shout to focus the chi or life energy. Kensei is used when it is not practical to shout out loud; for instance, when mental or emotional demands, rather than physical ones, are placed on the practitioner, and the practitioner is not in the training hall.

KEROJAK

In Pentjak-Silat, an Indonesian martial art, this contest is used to test the practitioner's skill. Multiple opponents, both armed and unarmed, attack the single defender.

KESHO-MAWASHI

See Uniforms.

KEUP

Also called gup. See Ranking System.

KEUPSO

See Vital Points.

KHI

Same as Chi. See Chi.

KI

Same as Chi. See Chi.

KIAI

See Shout.

KI-HAP

Korean word for kiai or shout. See Shout.

KI-O-TSUKETE

A Japanese term that means "attention"; students assume attention stance. See Commands.

KIHOP

Same as Ki-hap. Korean word for kiai or shout. See Shout.

KIME

The ability to focus single-mindedly on an immediate goal, and execute whatever action must be taken to successfully complete the goal. The samurai who seemed undefeatable in battle demonstrated kime. See Focus.

KINTEKI-ATE

Groin protector. See Armor, Kendo.

KIRISUTE GOMEN

Literally, "killing and going away." Japanese warriors were accorded the privilege of killing disrespectful commoners with no penalty, which they considered an entitlement of their position. The commoners saw it differently and frequently accused the samurai of "sword-testing murder," that is, murdering a person merely to test the edge of a sword.

KODANSHA

See Ranking Systems.

KODOKAN

Literally, "hall for teaching the way." The first Judo school in existence, opened in 1882 by Kano Jigoro, the founder of Judo. It soon became world famous, drawing students and teachers from all over the world. Later it was replaced by the Budokan, a training hall for all martial arts. Kodokan Judo is considered the "official" version of traditional Judo.

KODOKAN JOSHI-BU

The women's section of the Kodokan. It was opened in 1926 by Kano Jigoro.

KOKORO

Essentially, heart or spirit. A martial arts practitioner can understand techniques and can possess great talent, but if he or she does not also possess kokoro, he or she is not a true martial artist. Kokoro requires complete commitment to the martial art. It is perseverance, dedication and the willingness to continue striving even after failure or defeat.

KOKUGIKAN

The national center for Sumo, a large stadium located in Tokyo. Sumo contests are held and instruction is given. Nearly all traditional martial arts have a central institute for the study and practice of the martial art.

KOTE

Forearm guards. See Armor.

KRU

A master in Muay Thai boxing. See Teacher.

KUATSU

Resuscitation techniques. Like kappo, the use of acupressure to revive an injured person. Kuatsu has the wider meaning of using therapeutic acupressure for many injuries, not just those that cause the loss of consciousness. The study of Kuatsu, which is declining, is reserved for black belts in certain martial arts. See Kappo. See Acupressure.

KUJI-KIRI

Mystical hand and finger symbols used in particular by the Ninja. See Nine Symbols.

KUK-KI-WON

The international headquarters of Korean martial arts, built in 1972, located in Seoul. It houses the headquarters of the World Tae Kwon Do Federation. It is devoted to unifying the various styles of Tae Kwon Do, and offers Tae Kwon Do training, contests, black belt promotions and teaching certification.

KURAI

A flexible, passive state of mind cultivated by practitioners of soft-style martial arts. By developing such a mental state, one can respond to an attacker by using his or her own force against him or her. Thus it is an especially important state of mind for arts like Aikido.

KUZURE NO JOTAI

Loss of balance. See Balance.

KUZUSHI

"Breaking" the opponent's balance — that is, off-balancing the opponent to make a throw easier to effect, as in Judo. See Balance.

KWAN

Korean term for school. See School.

KWAN JANG

Korean term for the head master of a martial art school or style. See Teacher.

KWOON

Chinese term for school. See School.

KYOGEN

A style of Japanese theatre. It was said that because Noh was so boring, Kyogen was created. It is the antithesis of the dramatic, stylized movements and stories of the Noh theatre. Kyogen performs comic plays that follow the manner of the burlesque.

KYOSHI

See Ranking Systems.

KYU

See Ranking Systems.

KYUBA-NO-MICHI

See the Way of Bow and Horse.

KYUDAN

Refers to the entire system of classifying martial artists according to belt rank. See Ranking Systems.

KYUSHO

See Vital Points.

LAKAN

See Ranking Systems.

LEI-TEI

A platform on which martial arts are performed for spectators, particularly in China. Unlike a boxing ring, which it otherwise resembles, this platform has no ropes, and participants can fall off the platform. Usually when this happens, the participant loses points or may even forfeit the entire contest.

LINEAR MOTION

Those techniques and movements that are direct, delivered in a straight line to the target. These are usually offensive striking techniques, or powerful blocking strikes. The opposite of circular or indirect movements. See Circular Motion.

MA-AI

A judgment of the distance between the practitioner and the opponent and the time it will take to cover the distance or "close the gap." Thus, ma-ai is a part of timing; one must be aware of one's own speed and skill to bridge the distance effectively. An understanding of ma-ai is essential to the martial artist. See Distance. See Strategy.

MACHI-DOJO

See Training Hall.

MAKIWARA BOARD

A striking post used to improve hand techniques. See Training Equipment.

MANABU

The traditional method of martial arts instruction, in which the student attempts to imitate the movements of the instructor, with little verbal instruction given. This contrasts with most modern methods of teaching martial arts, in which the student is routinely given information, instructions and is otherwise taught, even to the point of having his or her techniques physically corrected by the instructor.

MARMAN

In India, vital points. See Vital Points.

MARTIAL ARTS

Denotes the various Asian fighting systems that teach combat techniques. Those skills, abilities, and techniques that are martial in nature but do not benefit the practitioner and his or her community are generally not considered martial arts. The component of mutual benefit must exist. Some fighting systems emphasize weaponless techniques while others teach the use of weapons such as the staff or sword. Weaponless systems use hand, arm, foot, shin and knee striking and blocking techniques. Martial arts have been practiced since at least 2000 B.C. Folklore recounts mythical creatures called Tengu who practiced martial arts and passed them on to humans. Founders of martial arts who wanted to give their methods the aura of legitimacy would often claim that the Tengu had taught them the art. Martial arts are thought to have originated in India and made their way through China and across the rest of Asia. Legend says that Bodhidharma, the Buddhist monk who brought Zen to China from India, also brought the martial arts. The best known martial arts are Aikido, Judo, Jujutsu, Karate, Tae Kwon Do and Wushu (Kung Fu). For contemporary artists, the martial arts are practiced for self-defense, fitness, sport and law enforcement as well as spiritual benefits. Not all activities designated as martial arts are martial or artistic. Some developed from warrior combat. Others developed as a means for physical and spiritual development. Not all forms of self-defense are actually martial arts. Some historians and artists insist that unless warriors used a fighting system in actual combat, it is not a martial art. In addition, there is a difference between martial art and martial sport; the sport application of a combat system is not a martial art. Strictly defined, martial arts are combat arts, methods for killing an opponent in battle. Martial ways, that is, those arts that have a spiritual component, go beyond combat effectiveness. See Bugei and Budo for further information regarding martial arts and martial ways. See Shaolin Temple. See Bodhidharma in the Biography section.

MASTER

Title of respect given to a high-ranking black belt. See Teacher.

MATAWARI

See Stretching.

MATTE

See Tournaments.

MAWASHI

See Uniforms (Sumo).

MEDITATION

Techniques for focusing one's thoughts; reflecting and pondering over philosophical or religious issues. Many Asian religions and philosophies encourage the use of meditation for achieving enlightenment. Zen, which considers meditation essential to spiritual enlightenment, recognizes seven common methods of meditation: 1. Meditation through breathing. 2. Meditation by focusing thoughts on one point. 3.

Fig. 1.3 : Karate practitioner meditating before training.

Meditation through reading, seeing or hearing literature, art or music. 4. Meditation through repeating a word or sound. 5. Meditation through praying. 6. Meditation through philosophy. 7. Meditation through martial arts performance. See Spiritual Awareness.

MEI HWA-CHUANG

"Plum Flower Stumps." See Training Equipment.

MEN

A mesh face mask. See Armor.

MENKYO SYSTEM

A ranking system used by the combat arts, the bugei. A teaching certificate, called kaiden, is given to the student when he or she has mastered the art. It is essentially a license to teach the art, and so is awarded only to those who show an aptitude for teaching as well as a thorough understanding of the martial art. No colored belts are used to indicate rank. The only distinction is occasionally the one where the students wear white belts and the instructor wears a black belt. See Ranking Systems.

MENTAL AWARENESS

This refers to the states of mind a warrior or martial artist should cultivate in order to remain aware and to achieve detachment. These states of mind are essential to success.

Method of strategy is the phrase used by the famous warrior Miyamoto Musashi to refer to the state of mind necessary to fight. One must see the relationship between mind and technique. The concept is similar to Tao.

Seishi-o-choetsu, indifference to life or death, depends on the ability to sacrifice oneself for the greater good.

Seishin is a state of mind reached after a period of ascetic living that creates the conviction that any difficulty encountered can be adequately responded to. Ordinarily, this state of mind is reached through training in a martial art.

Mizu-no-Kokoro is a mental state in which one is in harmony. This makes one able to anticipate an attack.

Muga is the focus which nothing can interrupt or interfere with.

Muga mushin is literally, "no self, no mind." The concept posits that if the martial artist puts aside all thoughts, in particular selfish thoughts, such as the desire to win, one can defeat the opponent. Without conscious will on the part of the practitioner, the power of the art can work through him or her. Any conceit, ego, or selfishness will interfere with and disrupt this process.

Mushin is an open mind, one that is not concerned with appearances.

Nyunan-shin is a mindset that allows a martial artist to accept the teachings of the master with humility out of a thirst for knowledge and a respect for the master's skill.

Enryo is an attitude of contempt for death, related to *seishi-o-choetsu*, indifference to life and death.

Focus, the ability to concentrate only on one's goal, whether to perfect a technique or score a point or win a contest, is fundamental to success as a martial artist. When one loses one's focus, even for a moment, one can be defeated. This loss of concentration is called "bonno" or "suki"; that is, "disturbed feeling."

Fudoshin is a mental state in which one is calm, detached and unthreatened. This principle was developed by Miyamoto Musashi, and is fundamental to all warrior philosophy.

Heijo-shin is a calm but focused state of mental awareness that a warrior must have during battle. *Hontai* is a similar state of alert readiness maintained by a warrior.

Kurai is a yielding, passive state of mind. One bends with the attacker's force and uses it against him or her.

Sutemi is the warrior's awareness of his need for self-sacrifice, even to the death. Japanese culture embraces the ideal of the sacrifice and of the temporary, even transient, nature of human life.

Zanshin is complete awareness and alertness, anticipation of success in combat.

MESTRE

A "master" of the Brazilian martial art Capoeira. See Teacher.

METHOD OF HARDNESS

Called "goho," this method advocates the aggressive use of offensive attacks and counter attack techniques, and using powerful strikes and blows. Most strikes are linear and direct and rely on speed and power. It is the opposite of method of softness.

METHOD OF SOFTNESS

Called "juho," this method advocates the use of evasive and defensive techniques. Blocks, deflections and redirections depend on the attacker's momentum. It is the opposite of method of hardness, and relies on the principle of ju, or flexibility and yielding.

METHOD OF STRATEGY

The famous warrior-philosopher Miyamoto Musashi used the word hyoho or method of strategy to describe the state of mind necessary to fight successfully. To achieve this mental state when it is needed requires an understanding of the connection of the mind to martial art techniques. One must be aware of how the mind influences the outcome of a martial art contest. To be prepared to fight on demand requires long training, but the ability to do so creates self-confidence. As in Tao, a practitioner seeks to become one with what he or she practices. See Tao. See Strategy.

METSUKE

Eye contact or position. During sparring matches, keeping eye contact with the opponent is advantageous, both psychologically and strategically. During the performance of forms and the practice of techniques, the position of one's eyes is extremely important.

MICHI

Path or way. See Tao.

MIZU-NO-KOKORO

A mental state in which one is at harmony. This harmony or peace makes one aware of and attuned to all others and thus can anticipate an attack. See Mental Awareness.

MOK YAN JING FAT

Training Dummy. See Training Equipment.

MOKU-SO

Achieving spiritual discipline through meditation, especially meditation practiced in the training hall before or after a martial arts training session. See Spiritual Awareness.

MON FAT JOONG

Training Dummy. See Training Equipment.

MONDO

A meeting between a teacher and a student or group of students with conversation regarding the martial arts. Occasionally, spiritual matters are addressed. In some schools, such meetings occur regularly, usually restricted to the higher ranked students.

MONTSUKI

See Uniform.

MOOK JONG

A wooden dummy used in Wing Chun and other martial arts for training in blocking, striking and trapping techniques. See Training Equipment.

MORNING TRAINING

See Training (Morning).

MU-CHUANG

Training Dummy. See Training Equipment.

MUDRA

Mystical hand movements. See Nine Symbols.

MUGA

The ability to focus so completely on the act at hand that nothing can interfere with its completion. See Mental Awareness.

MUGA MUSHIN

Literally, "no self, no mind." The concept that if the martial artist puts aside all thoughts, in particular selfish thoughts (such as the desire to win), one can defeat the opponent. Without conscious will on the part of the practitioner, the power of the art can work through him or her. Any conceit, ego, or selfish desire will interfere with and disrupt this process. See Mental Awareness.

MUNE-ATE

Bamboo Armor. See Armor.

MUSCLE CONTROL

Usually called simply "control." This is the ability to execute a technique with such skill that even at full speed, the technique can be stopped a fraction of an inch before the target. This makes it possible to have no contact matches between martial arts practitioners, yet still helps the practitioner develop excellent physical skills. Control also refers to the ability to maintain little or medium contact when sparring, as opposed to always operating at full contact or full speed. Certain exercises are performed to build muscle control, but practice, of course, is essential.

MUSHIN

A word meaning "no mind," part of Muga-mushin, "no self, no mind." This is an open mind, one that is not concerned with appearances. See Muga-mushin. See Mental Awareness.

MUSHOTOKU

The same principle as muga-mushin, in which self-gratification is not the reason for acting. See Muga-mushin. See Mental Awareness.

MUTO

The principle that an opponent can be defeated without physical force; that is, one can always avoid combat if one wishes to.

NEKODE

Metal "cat's claws" designed to grip hard surfaces. Used by Ninjas to scale walls. See Ninjutsu in the Schools and Styles section.

NIKYU

See Ranking Systems.

NINE SYMBOLS

Mystical hand or finger movements that allegedly give practitioners special powers. Such hand or finger movements have no real practical application, though certain martial arts schools incorporate these symbols into their practice to aid in fighting. Such symbols are used in some Buddhist sects during meditation or prayer and were thus adopted by certain martial arts styles. Called Kuji-kiri or Mudra.

NINE TEMPLE EXERCISES

Tai Chi Chuan exercises designed to help cultivate chi, life energy, and to improve muscle tone and condition. These exercises were developed not so much as a martial art or system of self-defense, but as a way to combat the harmful physical effects of the quiet contemplative life of monks and nuns. The exercises consist of simple calisthenics. See Stretching in the Forms and Techniques section.

NOH

Classical Japanese theatre that relies on heroic themes, stylized dance movements and highly symbolic scenery and costumes. It reached its height in the seventeenth century, though it is still studied and practiced today.

O-SENSEI

See Teacher.

O-YOROI

A kind of armor. See Armor.

OBI

Japanese word for belt. See Belt.

OKUDEN

Japanese word for "hidden teachings." See Hidden Teachings.

OMOTE

Same as Yang. See Yin-Yang.

ORGANIZATIONS

There are literally hundreds of martial arts associations, federations and organizations. Those that might be of specific interest follow:

Action International Martial Arts Association
All-European Karate Federation
All-Japan Eishin-Ryu Traditions Association
All-Japan Iaido Federation
All-Japan Karatedo Association
All-Japan Kempo Federation
American Aikido Federation
American Amateur Karate Federation
American Bando Association
American Hapkido Federation
American Karate Association
American Kendo Federation
American Martial Arts Federation
American Tae Kwon Do Association
American Tae Kwon Do Federation
American Tae Kwon Do Union
Choi Kwang Do Martial Art International
Choson-Do Society
European Judo Union
European Karate Union
Global Tae Kwon Do Federation
Gospel Martial Arts Union (The)
International Aikido Federation
International Amateur Karate Federation
International Bando Association
International Combat Hapkido Federation
International Isshin-ryu Karate Association
International Judo Federation
International Karate Association
International Kendo Federation
International Kenpo Karate Association
International Martial Arts Association
International Martial Arts Boxing
International Martial Arts Federation
International Shootfighting Association
International Tae Kwon Do Association
International Tae Kwon Do Federation
Japan Karate Association
Japan Karate Federation
Ki Society
Korea Kum Do Association
Korea Tae Kwon Do Association
KoreAmerica Tae Kwon Do Union
Korean Hapkido Federation
National Karate League
National Tai Chi Chuan Organization
North American Tae Kwon Do Union
Pan American Tae Kwon Do Union
Pan American Tang Soo Do Federation
Police Martial Arts Association
Shotokan Karate of America
Shotokan Karate International
Traditional Wushu Association
United Fighting Arts Federation
United Karate Federation
United Martial Artists Association
United States Judo Association

United States Chung Do Kwan Association
United States Karate Association
United States Kum Do Association
United States Judo Federation
United States Martial Arts Development Foundation
United States Shim Shin-Do Martial Arts Federation
United States Soo Bahk Do Moo Duk Kwon Federation
United States Tae Kwon Do Association
United States Tae Kwon Do Federation
United States Tae Kwon Do Union
Universal Tae Kwon Do Association
Universal Tae Kwon Do Federation
World Black Belt Bureau
World Chung Do Mu Sool Won Association
World Han Mu Do Association (The)
World Hapkido Federation
World Karate Association
World Karate Union
World Martial Arts Association
World Moo Duk Kwan Tang Soo Do Federation
World Moosul Kwan Federation
World Oriental Martial Arts Federation
World Professional Karate Organization
World Sin Moo Hapkido Association
World Tae-Keuk-Do Association
World Tae Kwon Do Federation
World Tang Soo Do Association

O-SEKI
Same as ozeki. See Ranking Systems.
OUTER CIRCLE
Those students not picked to learn the hidden teachings of a school. See Hidden Teachings. See Inner Circle.
OZEKI
See Ranking Systems (Sumo).
PA-KUA
The eight trigrams used in I-Ching fortune-telling. The symbols for yin-yang are used. Yin is indicated by a broken line, and yang is indicated

by a solid line. Each trigram consists of a combination of the symbols for yin and yang in a different order. See Yin-yang. See Book of Changes in the Literature section.
PANDEKAR
In Indonesia, a martial arts teacher. See Teacher.
PAO
See Training Equipment.
POISON HAND TECHNIQUES
Same as Poison Finger Techniques. See Poison Finger Techniques.
POISONED FINGER TECHNIQUES
The ability to kill another person just by touch. Though it is possible that a sufficient strike to a vital point could injure or even kill a person, a simple touch could not cause great harm. Perhaps the term derives from applying poison to an opponent, the poisoner having first developed an immunity to the poison, as the Ninja were known to do. See Delayed Death Touch.
POWER TRAINING
See Training.
PRACTICE MURDER
See Sword Testing Murder
PRAJNA
An Indian term related to chi, or life energy. See Chi.
PROMOTIONS, RANK
See Ranking Systems. See Examinations.
PUNCHBAG
See Training Equipment.
QI
See Chi.
RANDORI KYOGHI
See Tournaments, Aikido.
RANGE
See Distance.
RANK
The level of mastery a martial arts practitioner has achieved and has been recognized for is his or her rank. In the modern "do" or "way" schools, this is denoted by belts of various colors from white to black. The combat schools use the menkyo

system, and simply give a teaching certificate to those students who have mastered the system. See Ranking Systems. See Menkyo System.

RANKING SYSTEMS

Martial arts styles rank students and instructors according to their mastery of the skills and techniques of the school, as well as their contributions to the art. In ancient Asian fighting arts, no ranks were recognized other than master and student. Usually, a student simply earned a certificate of mastery (kaiden) that enabled him or her to teach. See Menkyo System. Today the most common ranking system is the grade/class, called dankyu, system, whereby non-black belts promote through a series of colored belts. The colored belts are called gokyu, kyu, gup or keup. The black belt ranks are called "dan" in the Japanese, Okinawan and Korean martial arts, "dang" in Vietnamese martial arts. The word "degree" is popularly used to indicate a black belt rank. Earning a black belt requires several years of continuous study. Usually, at least 1000 hours of instruction are required to become a first dan black belt. In some schools, a minimum age, usually 17, is also required.

Certain titles of respect are accorded practitioners who have earned a black belt. One who has earned a black belt is called "dansha." A practitioner at the fifth dan and above is called "kodansha." One who is at the 6th or 7th dan is "kyoshi." See also Teacher.

A white belt usually indicates a beginner, while a red or brown belt is frequently used to indicate an advanced rank, often the rank before black belt. A black belt indicates expert level. Many systems use blue, yellow, orange, green and purple belts to indicate intermediate levels. A colored belt awarded in one school or system cannot be compared with that earned in another system. In some systems belts are awarded solely through competition: winners are promoted, losers are not. In other systems, promotion is achieved by demonstration of technical skill or through formal examinations. Skills, plus knowledge of the art's history and culture, are routinely the basis on which public examinations are given. In many systems, the higher black belt ranks are given based on contributions to the art. Promotions and demotions, however, can be made at the discretion of the teacher. See Examinations. The colors often take on meanings: white signifies innocence; yellow, gold or orange, the earth from which the "plant" (i.e., the martial artist) takes root; green is the martial artist's growth; blue symbolizes the heavens towards which the martial artist reaches; brown is a sign of danger; while black, as the opposite of white, indicates the wearer's skill and mastery over fear. The "black belt" is sometimes dark navy, sometimes black with red markings. Sometimes the master wears a white belt as well, to indicate that he or she has come full circle. The non-black belt levels often consist of ten classes or ranks. The following are colors often given to indicate different levels:

10th class — white belt
9th class — white, yellow, orange
8th class — white, yellow, orange
7th class — white, yellow, orange, green
6th class — yellow, green, blue
5th class — yellow, green, blue
4th class — yellow, green, blue, brown
3rd class — green, brown, red
2nd class — brown or red
1st class — brown or red

After this, the practitioner earns a black belt.

In Judo, the basic principle is the darker the color, the higher the grade. Rank structures differ from country to country. Japanese schools usually have fewer ranks than European schools, for instance. Fifth dan black belts are honorary. Tenth dan is the highest that has been awarded, of which there have been seven, though there are none now. There is a provision for 12th dan, but it has never been reached. The dan, or adult black belt, has different colors at various levels. First dan through 5th dan is a black belt; 6th through 8th dan is a red and white belt; while 9th and 10th dan are red belts.

For kyu classes (adult):

10th white
9th yellow
8th orange
7th orange
6th green
5th green
4th blue
3rd blue
2nd brown
1st brown

For junior grades, called "mon," students move from 1st to 18th, instead of in descending order.

1st white belt plus one red bar
2nd white belt plus two red bars
3rd white belt plus three red bars
4th yellow belt plus one red bar
5th yellow belt plus two red bars
6th yellow belt plus three red bars
7th orange belt plus one red bar
8th orange belt plus two red bars
9th orange belt plus three red bars
10th green belt plus one red bar
11th green belt plus two red bars
12th green belt plus three red bars
13th blue belt plus one red bar
14th blue belt plus two red bars
15th blue belt plus three red bars
16th brown belt plus one red bar
17th brown belt plus two red bars
18th brown belt plus three red bars

In Kyudo, there are two non-black belt levels and then ten black belt levels. No indication of rank is usually worn.

In Bersilat, there are four non-black belt levels: white, green, red and yellow. The practitioner then earns a black belt.

In Kenpo Karate, there are fifteen grades, with corresponding belts: white, yellow, yellow with an orange tip, orange, orange with a purple tip, purple, purple with a blue tip, blue, blue with a green tip, green, green with a brown tip, brown, and brown with up to three stripes. There are ten levels of black belt.

In Sumo, ranking evolved from the number of rows that could be printed on a program, as developed in the early 18th century. Sumo wrestlers were known as, for instance "second row" and "third row." Because four is not auspicious in Japan, as it means death, the fourth row was known as the second row up from the bottom. Now, however, these terms are used, in descending order:

yokozuna (champion wrestler)
ozeki
sekiwake
komusubi
maegashira
juryo
makushita
sandamme
jonidan
jonokuchi
banzaukegai (beginner)

The three highest ranks below champion (ozeki, sekiwake, and komushubi) are collectively known as sanyaku. These, plus the maegashira and juryo ranks, are known as sekitori wrestlers. The last are unpaid contestants. The first four ranks receive many special privileges. After each tournament the banzuke, rankings, are revised and wrestlers are promoted or demoted. The champion, yokozuna, cannot be demoted. To be promoted to yokozuna, a wrestler must have won two or more tournaments while holding the rank of ozeki. The rank of a wrestler determines the styles in which his long hair is dressed. The higher the rank, the more elaborate the hair style.

In Karate, the color of belt worn by kyu grades (below black belt) varies from style to style, with only the white belt always used for beginners. Most styles also use the brown belt for the rank just before black. In the class grades, the progression is from highest to lowest, tenth being the beginner and first being more advanced. The kyu grades are:

jukyu=10th
kyukyu= 9th
hachikyu=8th
shikyu=7th
rokkyu=6th
gokyu=5th
yonkyu=4th
sankyu=3rd
nikyu=2nd
ikkyu=1st

The in-between colors vary from style to style. The most common colors used are yellow or orange, purple, blue, green and brown. In traditional Japanese styles, the black belts have special titles which denote levels of achievement.

shodan=1st degree black belt
nidan=2nd
sandan =3rd
yodan=4th
godan=5th
rokudan=6th
schichidan=7th
hachidan=8th
kudan=9th
judan=10th

In Tae Kwon Do, the ranking system is similar to Karate. Ten non-black belt levels are usually acknowledged, with nine levels of black belt. In Tae Kwon Do, the belt is usually thicker than in other styles. The colors vary from school to school, but a common formulation is white, first and second gold, first and second green, first and second blue, and first through third brown. For the black belt ranks, the following names are given:

1st dan=illdan or chodan
2nd dan=yeedan or eadan
3rd dan=samdan
4th dan=sahdan or sadan
5th dan=ohdan
6th dan=yookdan or yukdan
7th dan=childan
8th dan=paldan
9th dan=koodan or kudan.

In Sambo, a ranking system was only established in 1979. Sambo belts are determined exclusively by competition. Belt rankings are:

1st degree=white
2nd degree=yellow
3rd degree=green
4th degree=blue
5th degree=red
6th degree=black
7th degree=black with national color
8th degree=bronze with federation symbol
9th degree=silver with federation symbol
10th degree=gold with federation symbol
11th degree=gold with federation symbol plus honor band.

The first three belts are awarded by local instructors. The fourth and fifth are awarded by regional coaches. The sixth degree is awarded by national coaches. The seventh degree is awarded only to national Sambo champions. The eighth degree is awarded to wrestlers who have placed third in a world championship. The ninth degree is awarded to those placing second in a world championship and the tenth to world cup winners and world champions. The eleventh degree is given exclusively to international masters of Sambo. Coaches can be awarded belts based on the performance of their wrestlers.

In Arnis, belts are awarded according to gender. The dayang are black belts given to female students, and the lacan are black belts given to male students. Requirements for each are the same; thorough understanding of the basic techniques plus some teaching and competition experience. Ranks are:

1st degree: dayang-isa or lacan-isa
2nd degree: dayang-dalawa or lacan-dalawa
3rd degree: dayang-tatlo or lacan-tatlo
4th degree: dayang-apat or lacan apat
5th degree: dayang-lima or lacan-lima
6th degree: dayang-anim or lacan-anim
7th degree: dayang-pito or lacan-pito
8th degree: dayang-walo or lacan-walo
9th degree: dayang-siyam or lacan-siyam
10th degree: dayang-sampu or lacan-sampu

Belts are fringed with red through the fifth degree and with orange thereafter. See Belt.

READY COMMAND

See Commands.

REFEREES

See Tournaments.

REI

A ceremonial bow. See Etiquette.

RELIGION AND PHILOSOPHY

Religious and philosophical beliefs have had a profound impact on martial arts. See Hinduism, Taoism, Shinto, Buddhism, Zen, and Confucianism. See Spiritual Awareness.

RENSHI

A title meaning master. See Teacher.

RESOLUTE IN FIVE RESPECTS

A Japanese belief that all athletes should follow certain teachings. The belief is called Wu-kuo-ying, and consists of these five concepts: Athletes should firmly believe in the philosophy of their school. They should stay fit regardless of personal circumstances. They must be committed to mastering the skills they have undertaken to learn. They must be willing to participate in difficult training. They must do their best in competition. These five commitments are fundamental to successful martial arts training.

RHYTHM

See Broken Rhythm in the Techniques section.

RI

One of the three stages of development. See Three Stages of Development.

RIGHTEOUS FISTS SOCIETY

One of many political secret societies in China whose members trained in Chinese Boxing. The members of this group took part in the famous Boxer Rebellion. See Secret Societies.

RING CEREMONY

A Sumo ceremony that has links to its early use as a Shinto divination ritual. On the morning before the day a tournament begins, three referees consecrate the ring, asking the gods to prevent injuries. They kneel in front of seven wands which represent the gods of creation and the four seasons and say a blessing. A wand is placed at each corner of the mat and good luck symbols are buried in the center of the ring. Attendants arrive with drums and circle the ring. One of the drums is used to signal the end of each day's contests.

ROKKYU

See Ranking Systems.

RONIN

Samurai without masters. Though they were highly suspicious and disreputable for they had either failed to protect their master from death or they were driven from their master's ranks, they often became well-respected martial arts teachers and body guards for members of other classes. A famous story tells of the revenge of samurai whose master was wrongfully forced to commit seppuku, ritual suicide, causing them to become ronin. Eventually, they were able to avenge themselves. The story is called The Forty-Seven Ronin. See The Forty-Seven Ronin in the Literature section.

RYU

Means "school." See Schools.

RYUSHA

The follower or practitioner of a particular "ryu" or school.

SA BEUM NIM

See Teacher.

SA BUM NIM

Same as Sa Beum Nim. See Teacher.

SACRED CIRCLE

A dohyo or Sumo ring. See Training Hall. See Tournaments (Sumo).

SALUTES

In martial arts etiquette, the martial artist shows respect for his or her teachers, senior belts and others by saluting them using various techniques, usually some form of a bow. See Etiquette. See Salutation Techniques in Techniques section.

SAM

See Uniforms.

SAMURAI

The word is taken from the Japanese verb "to serve as an attendant." Samurai were Japanese warriors who were in the service of the great warrior class families. They felt the sword and the soul were intertwined and thus followed an ethical code, called the Way of the Bow and Horse, later called Bushido, the Way of the Warrior. Samurai referred to themselves as "bushi," or "warrior," whereas the other classes called them samurai, "attendant."

SAN PU-PA CHING SHEN
See Three No Fear Spirit, The.

SANKYU
See Ranking Systems.

SASH
Some martial arts styles use sashes instead of belts. See Belts. See Ranking Systems.

SASHI
See Training Equipment.

SATORI
An epiphany or enlightenment that illuminates the essence of the universe and the interrelationship of all elements of the universe. This transitory experience is an aim of Zen meditation.

SATSUMA REBELLION
In 1877, thousands of samurai using traditional weapons fought the modern Japanese army, which had assumed a Western style. The fighting lasted eight months and only ended when the samurai leader, Saigo Takamori, committed ritual suicide during a battle. This ended the direct influence of the samurai on Japanese life, and shortly thereafter, samurai were forbidden to wear the sword. The Satsuma, for which the rebellion was named, were an important warrior class family.

SCARF
The lapel of a Judo uniform, useful for grabbing. See Uniforms.

SCHOOLS
During the feudal era, swordfighting was a highly valued skill and therefore instructors were in great demand in Japan. Since the warrior families employed the samurai, they also employed the instructors for the samurai under their maintenance. These "employers" attempted to hire the best martial arts instructors, and rewarded them well.

Skilled, ambitious warriors sought such positions. This arrangement led to the development of different schools, "ryu," of swordsmanship. Each school had a special method and a founder or head instructor. A son or a talented follower would serve as successor. Each system of martial arts, such as Tae Kwon Do, Karate, and so on, has many schools, some of which are further divided into branches. Today, over one thousand different schools of martial arts exist in Japan. Similar numbers exist in other countries world wide.

SCIENCE OF SOFTNESS
See Method of Softness.

SECRECY
In the past, martial arts instructors kept certain techniques or even entire martial arts schools secret. For some of these schools, the word "private" is more appropriate, in the sense that the public might know about the instructor and his or her school, but that the instruction was not available to simply any member of the general public. Occasionally, schools were kept secret because for one reason or another the government banned the study of martial arts. Sometimes it was simply tradition, as was the case for many arts handed down through families. Sometimes the secrecy was for purposes of effectiveness — the students were thought to appreciate it more; in addition, it was an established principle in Zen tradition to "never tell too plainly." All of these elements contributed to an aura of mystery or secrecy around the martial arts. On occasion, a school might be kept secret merely because the teacher was inadequate and did not wish to be challenged or was perhaps mean-tempered and not willing to share. Many systems died out because of this insistence on secrecy.

SECRET SOCIETIES
In China, the decline of the Ching Dynasty brought revolutionary feelings among many individuals. These individuals banded together into secret societies, sometimes called Wushu societies because they studied and practiced Chinese Boxing (Wushu) but had political aims. These secret

societies led the aptly named Boxer Rebellion in 1900 A.D., which was put down. Many of those involved fled China to avoid imminent death by torture and arrived in California and other mining areas. Some of the better known secret Wushu societies include the Carnation Eyebrows, Righteous Fists, Society of Red Spears, White Lotus Society and the Yellow Turbans.

SEISHI-O-CHOETSU

The ability and willingness to sacrifice the self owing to an indifference to both life and death. See Mental Awareness.

SEISHIN

A state of mind reached after a period of ascetic living or severe privation that creates the conviction that any difficulty encountered can be adequately responded to. Ordinarily, this state of mind is reached through continued practice of a martial art. See Mental Awareness.

SEKITORI

See Ranking Systems (Sumo).

SEKIWAKE

See Ranking Systems (Sumo).

SELF-DEFENSE

The idea of protecting oneself, one's property and one's family from an enemy. Martial arts are often studied for the purpose of self-defense. See Martial Arts.

SEMPAI

See Teacher.

SEN

Taking control of a combat — or in fact any problematic — situation, through the application of strategy. Sen, when correctly used, can lead to quick and simple victory. Incorrectly applied, it can cause one's own defeat. See Strategy.

SENSEI

Japanese word for teacher. See Teacher.

SEPPUKU

More commonly known as hara-kiri, seppuku is the ritualized suicide expected of a samurai who had brought disgrace upon himself or his master. Contrary to popular thought, the samurai usually did not kill himself in isolation. In fact, seppuku was often performed in front of the person who had ordered it, if it had been ordered, or in front of a peer. The samurai did slit his belly, but instead of disemboweling himself and dying a painful and protracted death, the peer, called a second, would perform a decapitation once the samurai had indicated his wish to die. Schools of swordsmanship actually taught methods of assisting at seppuku. The wives of samurai committed seppuku by cutting their throats, usually using the women's weapon, the kaiken.

SESSHIN

See Seishin.

SEVEN STARS

According to Bruce Lee, the opponent's seven weapons that must be avoided — hands, feet, elbows, knees, shoulders, thighs and head. Also, a style of Praying Mantis Wushu.

SEVEN WAYS OF GOING

These were the essential disguises that all Ninja were taught to duplicate. Such disguises allowed a Ninja to escape unnoticed from the scene of a criminal action. He could choose to disguise himself as a traveling actor, as an itinerant priest, a mountain priest, a Buddhist priest, a traveling entertainer, a farmer, or a merchant. Of course, there were other disguises available to the Ninja, but these were the most convenient, convincing and easiest to procure.

SEVERE TRAINING

See Training.

SHIAI

Judo contest. See Tournaments.

SHAOLIN TEMPLE

Popularly considered the birthplace of Asian martial arts, this Buddhist monastery was originally located in the Sung-Shan mountains in Hunan province, China. It was built late in the fifth century in honor of the Indian monk Bodhiruchi. In the sixth century, the Indian monk Bodhidharma traveled from India to the Shaolin Temple, bringing with him Zen Buddhism and the martial arts, or at least some principles of self-defense or physical fitness. Many martial arts claim to trace their origins to this first martial art. Two styles of martial arts are credited as having developed at the Shaolin Temple; those that are hard and linear, relying on strikes and aggressive action and those that are soft, relying on evasive actions. The temple was the focus of government interest over the years for a number of reasons, including the fact that it gave refuge to dissidents and rebels. The temple was destroyed several times; it was finally moved to the south, to Fukien province. This Shaolin Temple, often called the Fukien Shaolin Temple or the Second Shaolin Temple, was also destroyed. The scattered nuns and monks are credited with teaching their martial arts skills to the general population. Five main styles are thought to have developed from Shaolin. These are the Hung-gar, Ts'ai-gar, Li-gar, Mo-gar and Liu-gar. The name Shaolin, meaning "small forest" derives from the temple's location in a copse of trees. Many martial arts styles are named after either "shaolin" or "trees" in order to honor this heritage.

SHAOLIN TEMPLE WUSHU GUAN

A Chinese martial arts training hall built in 1988 to train foreigners in Wushu techniques. It has multiple training areas, auditoriums, and dormitories.

SHIAI-JO

Same as dojo. See Training Hall.

SHIATSU

Japanese term for acupressure, or more commonly known to Westerners as a method of massage. See Acupressure.

SHICHI-HO-DE

See Seven Ways of Going.

SHICHIKYU

See Ranking Systems.

SHIKIRI

See Tournament (Sumo).

SHIKONA

The assumed name taken by martial artists, especially in Sumo. It is common practice for the Sumo wrestler to change his name yet again after he retires.

SHINKEN SHOBU

A fighting contest. Originally, mortal combat, now official competition. See Tournaments.

SHINOBI SHOZOKU

Ninja Uniform. See Uniforms.

SHINOBI WARRIOR

Means "the stealer in," and is an early name for the Ninjas. From this word, the name "Ninjutsu" evolved.

SHINPAN

Referee. See Tournaments.

SHINTO

A nature religion that most Japanese belong to. Shinto does not preclude belief in other religions. It is considered a form of ancestor worship. One prays to personal gods belonging to the family and the community. As might be imagined, the number of such deities is incalcuable. Kami (spirits) are seen in everything. The spirit of even inanimate objects is appreciated. Through appropriate prayers, actions and offerings, it is hoped that the deities will bring good fortune. Shinto priests are secular individuals chosen by the community. Their duties are limited to the care of holy places. They also are present at and participate in religious rites, such as the ring consecration that takes place before Sumo contests, at certain archery contests, and at other ceremonies. Shinto is simply a celebration of life and an expression of respect for nature. A state of spiritual awareness occurs in Shinto, called sumikiri, when the mind is clear and the body is pure. This state is sought by martial artists.

SHITAGI

Undergarment. See Uniforms.

SHOGUN

A Japanese military ruler, one who ruled by "permission" of the emperor. Actually, martial combat determined who and what families would rule. Three different warrior class families supplied most of the shoguns; their periods of influence were called shogunates, or more correctly, bakufu. The Kamakura ruled from 1185 to 1333. The Ashikaga family, also called Muromachi, ruled from 1336 to 1573 and the Tokugawa family, whose era is also called Edo (Tokyo) for the city that served as capital, ruled from 1603 to 1868. See Bakufu. See Minamoto no Yoritomo in the Biography section.

SHOMEN

The front of the room, which is bowed to upon entering the training hall. The kamidana (altar to the spirits and the ancestors) if present, is located there. See Kamidana.

SHOUT   KYA

In the martial arts, a shout is made at the moment of attack, at certain points during the performance of a form, and just before breaking a board or a brick. It is the vocalization of chi, or vital energy, and it serves to surprise an opponent, allowing an extra moment for attack. It also serves to summon energy and to focus a person's thoughts and energy. The ability to perform an adequate shout depends on appropriate breathing techniques. The Vietnamese term is het. In Korea it is a kihop, or kihap, and in Japan it is a kiai. See Hara. See Chi.

SHU

One of the three stages of development. See Three Stages of Development, The.

SHUAI-JIAO

A Chinese term for physical training, especially weightlifting. See Training.

SHUGYO

A period of difficult training designed to improve one's character and push one's limits. See Training.

SI GUNG

The title of one's instructor's instructor, the "grandfather" of the school.

SI JAK

Korean command meaning "begin." See Commands.

SIFU

See Teacher.

SIJO

The founder of the martial arts style or school being practiced.

SIX RULES OF KARATE-DO

Regulations conceived by Funakoshi Gichin, the founder of modern Karate. These rules are similar to the Resolute in Five Respects concept which is encouraged in all martial arts. Funakoshi's list includes the caveats to be serious about training; to concern oneself with training and not with theory, to try to be self aware and self perceptive; and to be morally and ethically responsible in all areas of life.

SIX TOOLS FOR TRAVELING, THE

These were indispensable tools carried by the Ninja whenever they traveled: a short length of bamboo, rope, hat, towel, stone pencil, and medicine.

SOCIETY OF RED SPEARS

During one of the most chaotic periods in Chinese history, this labor group sprang up. Like other such secret societies, members were often trained in Chinese Boxing, and participated in the Boxer Rebellion. See Secret Societies.

SODE

Shoulder (literally, "sleeve") guard. See Armor.

SOFT STYLES

Those martial arts that rely on the internal method, that emphasize passive, evasive movements and focus on the use of the opponent's own power against him or her, as evidenced in Aikido. Often, circular, not linear, motion is taught. It is the opposite of hard style.

SOHEI

An elite cadre of Japanese warrior priests, followers of a sect of militant Buddhism. They were among the first to systematize the use of the bo (staff) and the jo (sticks). As warriors, they became increasingly involved in conflicts with the warrior class, or samurai. Their monasteries were actually constructed with stone walls and moats, more like castles or forts than religious structures. In 1571, Oda Nobunaga, the famous warlord and military leader who overthrew the Ashikaga family, challenged them and destroyed them and their monasteries. The Sohei Buddhist order never recovered from this attack. See Oda Nobunaga in the Biography section.

SON

See Zen.

SPARRING EQUIPMENT

Protective padding used during free sparring exercise in martial arts training and in some tournaments. Such padding can consist of forearm guards, shin guards, fist or hand guards, chest protector, foot guards, groin cup, headgear and mouthpiece, or some combination of these. This equipment is sometimes made of padded cotton and sometimes of rubber-like foam. The name "ho-goo" (hogu) refers to protective sparring gear developed by the Korean Tae Kwon Do Association. Bogu refers to protective equipment used for practice and competition in some styles of Karate. Similar in purpose is the armor worn in Kendo. See Armor, Kendo.

Fig. 1.4 : Sparring equipment. Fist guards, shin guards, foot guards and head gear.

SPEED TRAINING

See Training.

SPIRITUAL AWARENESS

In the martial arts, certain religious and philosophical concepts are necessary for a complete understanding of the meaning of an art and how it can affect personal growth. Certain essential concepts include chi, hara, ching, haragei, hi-gi, karma, muto, shushin ho, meditation and zazen meditation. For further information on specific religions and philosophies, see Taoism,

Buddhism, Confucianism, Hinduism, Shinto, and Zen. One of the most important concepts in martial arts, *chi*, refers to the life force or vital energy of life. In China, this concept is called qi or chi and in Japan, it is called ki. The Indian term, prana or pranja, is connected to the idea of the soul. This vital force is located in the abdomen, the hara, where it is connected with breathing. Thus, chi is one of reasons why correct breathing is fundamental to the proper exercise of the martial arts. Chi is the essential energy that unites all things. *Ching* is simply properly cultivated chi, or rather, the product of chi, which is power. It is sometimes used to mean force, particularly physical force. The two are directly related, in the way that yin and yang are related. *Hara* is the center of the body, located in the abdomen, which is also where the chi is thought to reside. The art of calling up this energy is called *haragei*. Hi-gi is the philosophical study of the spiritual. This study is reserved for the highest ranking students. *Karma* is a concept generally associated with Hinduism, but it is relevant to Buddhism as well. This is the spiritual force generated by a person's actions, which can be positive or negative, and which determines the nature of the individual's next life. *Muto* is a spiritual doctrine that suggests one can always avoid combat if one wishes to. *Shushin-ho* suggests the achievement of self-improvement, with the goal of self-perfection, through the study of martial arts. The martial arts also emphasize techniques of meditation, which are methods for focusing one's thoughts; reflecting and pondering over philosophical or religious issues. Many Asian religions and philosophies encourage the use of meditation for achieving enlightenment. *Zazen meditation* is a kind of meditation in which one merely tries to control and stop all thoughts, trying to attain an empty, harmonious mind. In true meditation, a mental exercise, the goal is more on the achievement of enlightenment. *Satori* is the term used for the sudden enlightenment that is the goal of meditation in Zen. See Mental Awareness.

STABLES, SUMO

These are training halls for Sumo wrestlers, where they live and practice. There are about 40 stables, mostly in Tokyo. The ten most powerful are probably the following: Dewanoumi, Futagoyama, Hanakago, Isegahama, Kasugano, Kataonami, Nishonoseki, Sadogatake, Takasago, and Tokitsaukaze. Each emphasizes different techniques and styles of fighting, just as the various school of other martial arts do. See Training Hall.

STRATEGY

All martial artists are concerned with strategy, with devising techniques and tactics that will defeat the opponent. The basics of strategy include the following:

Closing the gap. This is determining the distance or range that one wishes to fight from, and then moving there without being stopped or interfered. A footwork pattern that allows one to advance quickly on an opponent is essential, for it works by bringing the opponent into attacking range, whether that range is close, middle or long. Judging this distance is called ma'ai.

Evasion. This is the ability to execute techniques of dodging, ducking, or retreating at any angle from the opponent through specifically patterned

Fig. 1.5 : Two Tae Kwon Do practitioners working on strategy.

footwork. It can be as simple as moving out of range or as complex as staying in range but avoiding any attack.

Feints. This is the ability to string together a series of physical techniques that trick the opponent into taking an action that leads to his or her defeat. Such methods include movements based on timing and counter attacking, and require the practitioner to carefully feel the opponent out to determine what his or her reactions will be.

Trapping the opponent. This is intercepting or redirecting the opponent's attacks and using a series of techniques that lead up to such a trap. The opponent can then be immobilized or at least controlled.

Blocking and countering. Using physical techniques such as deflecting, blocking, plus arm and leg strikes to resist the opponent's attack; also using mental awareness and practical skills to anticipate attacks that one can then block and counter immediately, even before the attack is fully launched.

Reading the opponent. Judging the opponent and probing for weaknesses that will eventually lead to the opponent essentially defeating him or herself.

This requires sensitivity training. Concepts such as the centerline, rhythm, method of strategy and others also allow one to create and control a situation in which the opponent is defeated through superior strategy, regardless of his or her skill level otherwise.

STRETCHING EXERCISES

See Forms and Techniques section.

STYLE

Usually means the martial art, in general, that one practices, for instance Judo or Tae Kwon Do. Within those styles are various schools that practice methods and techniques that differ to varying degrees from one another. In Karate and a few other styles, however, the word style usually refers to the school in which one practices. Partly this stems from the vast differences between Karate schools. Therefore, those who are engaged in the practice, for example, of Shotokon or Goju-ryu often refer to their "style" of Karate, as opposed to their "school" of Karate. The word system, on the other hand, refers to larger groups of martial arts styles. Wushu, for instance, is a system, since it is a collection of a number of different styles of martial arts, many with few similarities among them. See Schools. See Schools and Styles section.

SUKI

A Japanese term for "loss of focus." See Focus. See Mental Awareness.

SUMOTORI

Name given to Sumo practitioner.

SUNE-ATE

Leg guards. See Armor.

SUTEMI

The warrior's awareness and acceptance of the need for self-sacrifice, even to the death. Japanese culture embraces the ideal of the sacrifice and emphasizes the temporary, even transient, nature of human life. See Mental Awareness.

SWORD-TESTING MURDER

See Kirisute Gomen.

TABI

Split-toed socks. See Uniform.

TAEGEUG

See Tao.

TAIJI

See Tao.

TE-MERRIAN MARTIAL ARTS INSTITU-TION

A building that houses the ancient and modern African martial arts. Similar to the Budokan in Japan.

TAN TIEN

See Hara.

TANDEN

See Hara.

TAO

A Chinese word meaning "way," as in a spiritual path one follows to achieve enlightenment and self-perfection. The sign that symbolizes Tao is the yin-yang sign, which suggests that the way is of

harmony and balance. The word also indicates the unknowable source, which is a fundamental concept in Taoism. The taiji is the higher entity or the "supreme ultimate." In Japan, it is called "do" or "dao." In Vietnam the term is also "do," and the Korean term is "taegeug." See Yin-Yang. See Taoism.

TAOISM

Following the "way." This philosophy is traditionally accorded to Lao Tzu in the sixth century B.C. It is mainly concerned with the unknowable source, the Tao, and with following a way of life notable for its simplicity and even passivity. It is marked by the emphasis on harmony and balance in human life. It is the dominant Chinese world view, and it asserts that everything is interrelated. The principle of performing an action in harmony with the essence of the action is fundamental to Taoism. This might be expressed as the art of being "at one" with something. In martial arts, this principle is expressed in the idea that the training "becomes" the practitioner and the practitioner "becomes" the training, a state achieved only after tireless practice. After a time, Taoism became a folk religion. Good fortune was sought through magical means. This, however, is at odds with the nature of Taoism. Also called Daoism. See Tao.

TARE

A protective skirt (Kendo). See Uniforms.

TARGET AREA

The parts of a human body that are considered legitimate scoring areas in the martial arts.

In most Karate and Tae Kwon Do

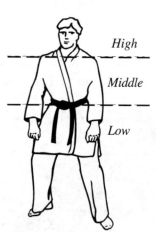

Fig. 1.6 : Target areas for Karate and Tae Kwon Do. Kicks and punches can be aimed at low, middle and high sections, but in contests, it is usually illegal to kick low.

contests, for instance, the head and the torso are considered target areas, whereas the knees and the back are illegal areas and cannot be struck to earn a point. Target areas also include the

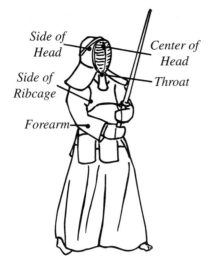

Fig. 1.7 : Kendo target areas.

designations of low, middle and high. In martial arts practice, a practitioner may practice strikes aimed at the different target levels, so that in a fight he or she could strike the area that would do the most damage to the opponent or would be the most likely to stop him or her. The high area is the head and neck, including the face; the middle area is from the shoulders to the hips, including the solar plexus; and the low area is from the thighs to the feet, including the knees and the groin.

In Kendo, the target area is the center of head, the right and left side of the head, both forearms, the throat, and either side of chest. In Kenjutsu, the only legitimate target areas are the top of the head, either wrist, either side and either leg below the knee.

TATAMI
Practice mat. See Training Equipment.
TE
Gloves. See Armor, Kendo.
TEA CEREMONY
A ritual ceremony especially important to Zen Buddhists. A tea master prepares tea according to rigid rules and with highly stylized movements. The tea master uses the ceremony to achieve a mind receptive to enlightenment and participants try to achieve a state of calm during the ceremony. The tea master, who must study for many years, is often a martial artist. Early in its development, it was considered an important component of the practice of combat arts because it allowed the samurai to refresh and renew themselves. The tea ceremony is still used today as a ritual for relaxation and contemplation.

TEACHER
The martial arts instructor can develop a profound relationship with his or her students, becoming like family members. The teacher is treated with respect and courtesy at all times, even in the case of a disagreement. A master is a teacher who has achieved a certain rank or level as a black belt, often the fourth dan. A grandmaster, then, is the master who has taught a master, or has achieved an extremely high rank as a black belt. In Tae Kwon Do, different titles are given to teachers depending on their rank. Chu gyo nim is a teacher who is below fourth dan; sa beum nim (sa bum nim) refers to those who are fourth dan and above.

In Pentjak Silat, the pandekar is the master teacher, who possesses martial arts skills and supernatural powers. The pandekar is frequently a mystic.

In Japan, the name sensei is given to all martial arts teachers, regardless of the style they teach. The sensei may teach multiple martial arts, such as archery, spearmanship, swordsmanship, and Karate, or other unarmed styles. Especially in Japan, the relationship between student and teacher is pronounced. The student is often called a disciple or follower, which indicates a philosophical or religious tie to the instructor. In Karate, the chief instructor for an organization of world-wide status is called Kancho. Instructors who are ranked above 6th dan are known as shihan; black belts from 2nd to 5th dans are sempai (senior). All sempai are expected to be role models for the other students. A hanshi is a master. In most martial arts, those who are at higher ranks are expected to take on teaching duties. In some styles, the student who wishes to promote to black belt must demonstrate a commitment to teaching and to perpetuating the art. Some teachers prefer the simple title "coach."

TECHNIQUES OF COMBAT

Feudal Japanese warriors adopted combat methods designed for use in battle. In the martial arts, these techniques of combat (bugei and bujutsu) are different from the ways of combat, because the techniques of combat emphasize deadly fighting skills as opposed to the ways of combat, which are interested in the development of character or the pursuit of spiritual enlightenment. See Budo.

TENETS OF TAE KWON DO

The five qualities or principles that Tae Kwon Do practitioners strive to cultivate. Every practitioner must discover for him or herself what these tenets mean. They are courtesy, integrity, perseverance, self-control and indomitable spirit.

TENGU

Mythical creatures, similar to European fairy folk, who inhabited the Asian mountains and were skilled in martial arts. They were often credited with teaching the founders of various schools, to give the school legitimacy.

TENUGUI

Cloth band. See Uniforms.

THIEN

Same as Zen. See Zen.

THREE FRONTS, THE

The areas of the body that must be defended: the area in front of one's eyes; the area in front of one's hands; and the area in front of one's legs. See Target Areas.

THREE NO FEAR SPIRIT, THE

The belief, especially in China, that a martial artist should continue training regardless of hardship, pain or fatigue. Called San Pu-pa Ching Shen. See Training.

THREE QUALITIES OF BUSHIDO

The main principles of bushido, fundamental to the way of the warrior. These are loyalty, right conduct and bravery.

THREE STAGES OF DEVELOPMENT, THE

The belief that the martial artist follows three defined stages of development. In the first stage, shu, the martial artist follows the teacher without question. In the second stage, ha, the martial artist attempts to improve the teachings of the school by introducing effective or useful methods from other schools or styles. In the third stage, ri, the martial artist founds a new school, one of his or her own design. The traditional martial arts associations do not approve of the second and third stages.

TI

Korean term for belt. See Belt.

TO

Striking Post. See Training Equipment.

TO-SHIN

In Karate, striking skills in general.

TOBOK

Korean word for uniform. See Uniform.

TOI

An opponent who is out of range. See Distance. See Strategy.

TORI

In Judo, the person who throws. The one who is thrown is uke, receiver.

TORITE

In Aikido and Judo, restraining techniques in general. See Forms and Techniques section.

TOURNAMENTS

Because many styles of martial arts have sport applications, contests or tournaments are often staged for the opportunity to compete. Contests consist of three types: forms, breaking and sparring. Forms competition is simply the judging of the performance of forms that are part of each school's instruction. Practitioners select a form that best showcases their control, power and technique, for which they are evaluated. In forms competitions among multiple styles, the competition is usually divided by hard styles, such as Karate and Tae Kwon Do; soft styles, such as Wushu; and forms that use weapons. Usually, five judges score the form and the highest and lowest scores are discarded. The competitor with the highest number wins. Pair or group forms are also judged at some tournaments. Occasionally forms are done to music. In this case, showmanship and the harmony of the music and form together are judged.

In breaking contests, usually limited to Tae Kwon Do competitions and a few Karate tournaments, competitors are given a specified number of boards to break. Usually these boards are one inch thick. Occasionally brick or tile breaking is done. The competitors choose the techniques with which they will break. In the case of a tie, at the judges' discretion, the referee can determine the technique to be used to break the tie. Five or sometimes six judges award up to ten points, taking into consideration the degree of difficulty, whether the technique was executed correctly, and whether the board broke. The competitor with the highest combined score wins.

Sparring matches in tournaments include Judo and Sumo contests, as well as the traditional sparring matches of Karate and Tae Kwon Do.

In shiai or Judo contests, the participants always begin in a standing position. After performing the appropriate courtesy, they grasp each other's uniforms and begin. The object is to throw the opponent to the ground and pin him or her. The contest area, a mat, is about 10 yards. A referee, two judges and a scorekeeper are required in a Judo match. The referee controls the match and makes calls, though either of the judges can disagree. Disagreements are resolved by simple majority. If at the end of the match the contestants' scores are tied, the judges arrive at a decision (hantei). If the judges cannot agree, the referee makes the final determination. There are no rounds in Judo competition, though national contest matches are from 6 to 10 minutes. In Olympic competition, matches can last 15 or 20 minutes. If either competitor scores a full point (ippon) at any time during the match, the match ends and he or she is declared the winner. A full point is awarded when the opponent is thrown squarely on his or her back with considerable power. A full point can also be earned by immobilizing an opponent for at least

30 seconds or by applying a choke or armlock until the opponent surrenders. Two half points can be added together to make a full point. A half point, waza-ari, occurs when a throw is not quite square, or when an immobilization is not quite thirty seconds. Two other scores can be given: what might be called the almost half point, and the almost almost half point. That is, the yuko is scored if a throw causes the opponent to land only on his or her side, not back, or if an immobilization lasts for only about fifteen seconds. The koka is an almost yuko, that is, for instance, an immobilization that lasts for only a few seconds. These two scores can accumulate throughout a contest and will help the judges make a decision at the end, but they cannot be added together to make a full point. Penalties are assessed as points awarded to the non-penalized, so an individual can win a match merely because of the penalties incurred by his or her opponent. The points thus awarded are based on the severity of the rules infraction. Men, women, children and teenagers compete in different divisions.

In Sambo, which is similar to wrestling and Judo, jackets may be held while executing techniques; submission holds and joint locks are permitted. Takedowns and direct leg attacks are also permitted. A Sambo match consists of two bouts of three minutes each, with a one minute rest. The object of a Sambo contest is to achieve "total victory" which occurs when a perfect throw is performed and the opponent lands squarely on his or her back while the thrower remains standing; or when the opponent surrenders; or when one wrestler earns twelve points more than his or her opponent. There are four types of techniques used to score points or "total victory." These are holddowns (immobilizations); takedowns; submission holds; and throws. The power in the throw is not considered relevant; only the final position of the thrown wrestler is important, as long as the thrower remains standing.

In Sumo, the object of the contest is to push the opponent out of the ring or to force him to touch the ground. Strikes, kicks, and other various techniques are not permitted. Certain approved Sumo techniques are used. There are no weight categories, so Sumo contestants all tend to be heavyweights. Sumo contests are highly ritualized. The dohyo-iri, for instance, is the official presentation of contestants. The wrestlers wear ceremonial aprons and participate in a short ritual. They are presented in groups according to rank. After the final contest of the day, yumitori-shiki is performed. Known as the bow dance, the ceremony stems from the Edo (Tokyo) period when the prize for winning was a bow. Many other rituals are beloved parts of the Sumo contest, including the shikiri, in which the wrestlers work the audience up. Six tournaments are held each year. They continue for fifteen days, and each sumo wrestler fights each day. At the end of the tournament, rank promotions and demotions are announced and special awards are given to participants for the number of opponents defeated, the best fighting spirit and so on.

In Karate, sparring competition takes place between two individuals of equal rank and weight. No contact sparring, which includes most Karate matches, consists of practitioners striking and blocking with hands and legs until a blow comes extremely close to a target area on the opponent's body. This calls for excellent control of techniques. In traditional Japanese systems, if the strike is correctly executed and is not blocked, a full point is awarded. A technique, if not perfectly executed, or if it does not land cleanly, may nonetheless be awarded a half point. The one point system, now rarely used, awards a win to the first person who scores a full point. Among non-traditional styles, usually a full point is awarded for a correct, clean technique, with no award if the technique is blocked or improperly executed. A bout usually lasts between two and three minutes, depending on the contest organizers. Whoever has the most points at the end of this time wins. For black belt grand championships, which are contests between

the winners of all black belt weight divisions to determine the single best contestant, there are usually two bouts with a minute rest between. A referee and judges decide points and fouls. Ordinarily, a contestant is given several warnings before a foul is called; a foul requires either a point deduction or a forfeit. Fouls are usually given for too much contact or for kicks below the target area, though sometimes they are given if a competitor repeatedly steps outside the ring area or frequently turns away to avoid an attack. In some contests, if the sparring match ends in a tie, the person who can break the most boards is declared the winner. Semi-contact Karate, where protective gear is worn and light contact is allowed, has various rules, but it usually follows the accumulated point system with a two-minute match. Excessive contact ends in disqualification. Professional Karate, or full contact, is fought to the knockout. In international competition, teams also compete. There are five people on a team, and the team with the most points wins. In the case of a draw, one contestant is chosen from each team in question and they fight a title bout.

In Wushu, forms and sparring (both are done with and without weapons) are the areas of contest. Competitions take place on mats and the contestants display their skill, with 10 points possible. Four judges and one chief judge decide the score of each contestant while the number of referees varies. Since Wushu styles and schools vary significantly, specific rules are determined and posted at each contest.

In Thai boxing, which like Sumo always begins with rite or invocation, bouts consist of five three-minute rounds with two-minutes between. Two judges and a referee will award a decision, but Thai boxing is usually decided by knockout. Points are awarded for any attack that is legal; this includes most techniques, although certain throws and holds are not permitted.

Tae Kwon Do matches are conducted like Karate matches, with two- or three-minute rounds. Points are called when a correctly executed technique strikes the target unblocked. A blow must cause a visible shock to count. Because all Tae Kwon Do contests allow contact, protective equipment is required. The only legal targets are the front of the body from waist to the base of neck, not including the throat. No hand techniques to the head are allowed, though foot techniques are allowed. All competitions require a referee, and four or five judges. Sometimes the judges score the match independently, sometimes they must agree by majority. Fouls are called when either opponent steps out of bounds on purpose, tries to avoid fighting by turning away, throws the opponent down and for other infringements. These result in point deduction. Knock downs and knock outs earn the most points. Foot techniques are scored higher than hand techniques, jumping techniques are scored higher than standing techniques; a kick to the face is better than a kick to the body. These rules of thumb are used to arrive at a decision.

In Aikido, when competition is allowed, it consists of three kinds of sparring. Ninin-dori is sparring with two participants attacking a third. Tanto-randori is an unarmed opponent against an armed opponent and in randori-kyoghi, two unarmed contestants try to score against each other with skillfully applied techniques.

TRAINING

All martial artists spend considerable time in the practice of the techniques and methods of their art. This daily practice is simply the usual training, and consists of stretching and strengthening exercises, the repetition of basic movements and techniques, the performance of forms, plus sparring of the step or free style variety. In addition, exercises to increase speed and flexibility may form part of the daily training. Training might also include special diet regimens plus weight training to improve power. In addition to this ordinary training, which is called hakuda, other methods are used to increase the martial artist's skills and abilities. These include morning training, known as asa-geiko; winter

training, known as kan-geiko; hatsu geiko; power training; speed training; severe training; and shuai-jiao. Martial artists are expected to develop the three no fear spirit, that is, the ability to continue training regardless of hardship, pain or fatigue. The martial artist must also, according to the famous warrior-philosopher Miyamoto Musashi, train without ceasing in the martial art and its theory in order to achieve self improvement and even self perfection. Morning training, which is actually summer training, is an intense workout in the heat of the summer designed to make the martial artist less vulnerable to the climate. It is done in conjunction with winter training, in which martial artists train outside in the winter and learn to endure the cold and its attendant discomforts. Hatsu-geiko is a special period of training that starts on New Year's Day and ends with a tournament, with the purpose of beginning the New Year in the appropriate frame of mind. Severe training is an intense physical workout that pushes the practitioner's physical, emotional and mental limits. Power training is used to develop muscle strength and may include weight training. Speed training focuses on developing flexibility and quickness through exercises designed to improve accuracy and speed. See also Resolute in Five Respects.

TRAINING EQUIPMENT

Almost all styles of the martial arts use equipment designed to help practitioners improve their skills. Some of this equipment is designed to improve the striking ability of the student. These pieces of equipment include the makiwara board, also called a to, which is a striking post. In Korean arts, this is known as the dalyeun-ju. This post is a thick piece of lumber with padding attached to it, which the practitioner punches to improve the power of the fist, or strikes with other hand techniques to increase the striking skills.

There are a number of variations of this. A striking pad is a pad either attached to a wall or pole or held by a partner and is used for training in punching and kicking. These vary in size and shape depending on whether they are intended to absorb the full force of a blow or are used only as focus pads, to improve the accuracy of a technique. This pad, sometimes called a shield, is named pao. Some pads are filled with air instead of material; these air shields work in the same way. The punchbag or the heavy bag is also used to improve strikes, including kicks.

Wooden dummies, used in Wing Chun and other arts, also increase striking, blocking and trapping skills. The mook jong wooden dummy can be used to practice blocks and counters, as it is equipped with wooden "arms" and "legs." The mon fat jong is another dummy used as a training device. This has springs that recoil so the practitioner can determine the power of a blow. The Mu-chuang is simply a large wooden dummy used for striking practice.

In order to produce powerful blows, the martial artist sometimes feels it is necessary to increase the strength of his or her hands, from the fingertips down. The kan shu conditions the hands. Basically, the practitioner thrusts his or her hands or fingers into a pail filled with abrasive material (such as sand). Over time, this hardens the hands. The material grows harder as the hands grow harder. The kame, weighted jars, are lifted and moved to increase grip strength.

The chashi or sashi is a Chinese training device, a heavy block with a handle that is used much like a barbell. It is used to increase strength in the wrist and forearm. This device is known as "thrusting stones." The chikaraishi is an Okinawan variation in which a stone with handles is used to increase strength. These devices are often carried as the practitioner practices forms and techniques.

To increase leg strength and to condition the legs, Wushu practitioners sometimes use the chi shing chung. Several posts are sunk into the ground. The martial artist kicks the posts with various techniques. Eventually the practitioner can break the posts with a kick.

The jiu shing dorsien chung is another Wushu training device. This time the posts are taller than the practitioner. A group of them is arranged so that they are close to each other. The martial artist must be able to quickly move between them without touching them.

Wushu also uses posts driven into the ground for training in balance. The mei-hwa-chuang, literally "plum flower stumps," consists of posts driven into the ground, on top of which the martial artists train. Certain styles such as White Crane and Hop Gar use these for training and sparring. In the past, the places between the posts were dotted with sharpened spikes, so that a fall would be very serious. Each style places the posts in a different pattern.

The jou sing or "running rope" improves quickness and balance. The practitioner holds onto a suspended rope which supports his or her weight. The practitioner perfects footwork this way and improves his or her ability to be light on the feet.

In Judo, a training ball is used. One sweeps the ball towards a partner, using the same action as a foot sweep throw would require. Practitioners also use a large canvas bag filled with sawdust or rags for solo practice of throws. Shadow throwing is also practiced. Blindfolded sparring is sometimes practiced by experts, as is sparring with shoes or socks on.

TRAINING HALL

Refers to the physical building that houses a martial arts school, and can refer to any place of training, where martial arts are practiced, or where competitions are held. Ordinarily, it is simply a large room with mats or carpets to practice on and equipment that is used to improve techniques. In most martial art styles, the front of the room, shomen, is the place of respect. The kamidana, the altar to the spirits, or other relics of the school, will be found there. National flags are also hung at the front of the room. Students line up with the highest ranks at the front. The training hall is sometimes called the meditation hall, because of its religious roots. Each martial art style has a different name for the training hall: machi-dojo, shiai-jo, zour, dohyo, keikoba, heya, judojo, dojang and so on.

TRIAD SOCIETY

One of the many rebellious secret societies in China whose members were martial artists. This group was allegedly created by monks who escaped from the Shaolin Temple during its destruction by government troops. See Secret Societies.

TWELVE ANGLES OF ATTACK

See Angles of Attack.

TWELVE ANIMALS

In Chinese Wushu, the qualities and characteristic movements of animals are incorporated into the techniques. Often forms are named after the Twelve Animals, who each symbolize different qualities that are admired by Chinese martial artists. The Twelve Animals are related to the Five Animals, a smaller group of animals after which many martial arts styles are modeled. The Twelve Animals are usually considered to be the following: the dragon, tiger, monkey, horse, chicken, falcon, snake, tai bird (a mythical creature), lizard, swallow, eagle and bear. See Five Animals.

UKE

In Judo, the person who is thrown, the receiver. The person who performs the throw is tori.

UM

Same as Yin. See Yin-Yang.

UM-YANG

Same as Yin-yang. See Yin-Yang.

UNIFORMS

All martial arts styles have uniforms or special clothes to wear during training and contests. By far the most common is the "gi," a white jacket and loose fitting trousers worn with slight variations by Karate, Judo and Tae Kwon Do practitioners. In Korean, it is called a dobok, or tobok; in Japanese, it is a dobo, though Karate practitioners sometimes refer to it as keikogi. In the Vietnamese martial arts, it is called vo phuc. The jacket is sometimes called uwagi. A jacket with

Fig. 1.8 : Martial arts uniforms for sale.

wide sleeves is called the haori, and it is commonly worn by Aikido practitioners. A hachimaki, a bandanna or headband, is often worn to keep sweat from dripping into the eyes while practicing.

The uniform worn by Judo practitioners is called a judogi or gi, and the trousers, zubon, usually extend only to the mid calf. The fundoshi, a tight fitting loin cloth, is worn by Judo practitioners to avoid injury. The practitioner might also wear zori, known as Judo slippers, made of rubber or straw.

In Iaido, the practitioners wear a kimono-like blouse that is called montsuki. It is black in winter, white in summer, but at all formal events the black

Fig. 1.9 : Naginata practitioner wears hakama.

montsuki is worn. The Iaido practitioner also wears a pleated skirt called a hakama. This is also worn by Aikido, Kendo, and Kyudo practitioners. Tabi are split-toed socks reserved for senior teachers.

In Sambo, practitioners compete in outfits that combine the wrestling uniform with the Judo uniform. Slippers or light shoes, trunks and a tight fitting jacket known as the kurtka are worn. The Sambo jacket differs from a Judo uniform in that it is tighter and shorter and has epaulets for grabbing. Having jackets in both red and blue is required for competition.

In Bersilat, the students wear a black uniform consisting of a short-sleeved shirt, baggy trousers and a headband.

The Ninja uniform, called shinobe shozoku, is a formfitting outfit resembling a catsuit, usually black but often reversable to another color. A hood covers the head and face, and shoes or boots are split-toed. The uniform has hidden pockets for weapons.

In Kendo, a jacket called a kendogi is worn with the hakama. Beginners wear jackets made of light cotton with black stitching, while the instructor wears a heavier or quilted version, usually in black or dark blue. The hachimaki, a light cotton towel, also called tenugui, can be worn under the Kendo mask. It is additional protection and absorbs perspiration. An apron called tare helps to protect the hips and abdomen. When the Kendo practitioner dons the entire outfit, including the Kendo armor, he or she is wearing "dogu" or "kendogu."

Fig. 1.10 : Ninja uniform.

In Wushu, the sam consists of loose trousers plus a loose fitting jacket that usually buttons up the front and can be made of cotton, silk or satin.

In Aikido, the uniform for black belts consists of a loose fitting blouse or jacket (haori) and hakama. The dogi, like the gi worn in Karate, is a jacket and trousers worn by an Aikido practitioner who is not a black belt.

In Sumo, practitioners wear the mawashi, a loin cloth with a long fringe in front called a sagari. A kesho mawashi is a ceremonial apron worn by high-ranking sumo wrestlers just prior to their bouts, as they are being introduced. They are worn during the ring entering ceremony and are made of silk, and are embroidered and fringed.

In Kyudo, a long blouse called the monpoku is tucked into the hakama. A shooting glove, called a yugake, made of buckskin is worn on the right hand. An attached strap is wrapped around the wrist to hold the glove in place.

URA

Same as Yin. See Yin-Yang.

URA-OMOTE

Same as Yin-Yang. See Yin-Yang.

UWAGI

Uniform jacket. See Uniforms.

VALID TARGETS

See Target Areas.

VITAL POINTS

Areas on the body that are especially vulnerable to injury. These often include areas near joints, which is why joint locks can be extremely painful and very effective. Acupressure and acupuncture techniques manipulate these points to improve the flow of chi, life energy. Martial artists, by attacking these points, can cause serious harm and even death. Called atemi or kyusho.

VO

Vietnamese term meaning "begin." See Commands.

VO PHUC

Vietnamese martial art uniform. See Uniform.

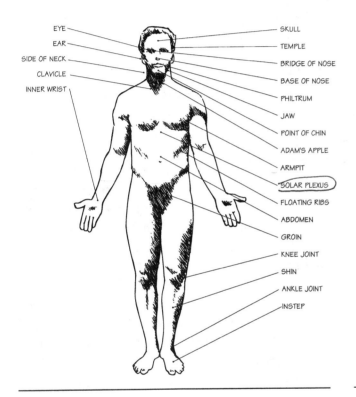

EYE
EAR
SIDE OF NECK
CLAVICLE
INNER WRIST

SKULL
TEMPLE
BRIDGE OF NOSE
BASE OF NOSE
PHILTRUM
JAW
POINT OF CHIN
ADAM'S APPLE
ARMPIT
SOLAR PLEXUS
FLOATING RIBS
ABDOMEN
GROIN
KNEE JOINT
SHIN
ANKLE JOINT
INSTEP

VITAL POINTS
(FRONT)

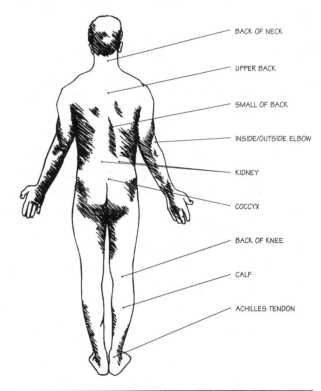

BACK OF NECK
UPPER BACK
SMALL OF BACK
INSIDE/OUTSIDE ELBOW
KIDNEY
COCCYX
BACK OF KNEE
CALF
ACHILLES TENDON

VITAL POINTS
(BACK)

VO SU

A Vietnamese term for martial arts instructor. See Teacher.

VO THUAT

Vietnamese name for techniques of combat. See Techniques of Combat.

WARNING

A reminder given to a contest participant before a foul is called and points are lost. See Tournaments.

WAY OF ARCHERY AND HORSEMANSHIP, THE

See Way of Bow and Horse, The.

WAY OF BOW AND HORSE, THE

A code of ethics, that while neither written nor enforceable, governed the behavior of the samurai. It dates from the thirteenth century, and was eventually replaced with the code of Bushido, or the Way of the Warrior. It emphasized bravery and loyalty as the essential qualities of the samurai. The same as The Way of Archery and Horsemanship. Called kyuba-no-michi. See The Way of the Warrior.

WAY OF THE WARRIOR, THE

Called Bushido. This ethical code governing the behavior of samurai grew from the ideals of The Way of the Bow and Horse, an early ethical or philosophical belief system, an ideal adhered to in thought and writing if not in action. The way of the warrior developed from the 17th century on, when the ethical beliefs of the samurai became the subject of written code, debate, discussion and instruction. Ideal behavior for a samurai included the affectation of contempt for death, plus loyalty and courage. The term Bushido used to characterize this ideal was coined by Nitobe Inazo in his work called *Bushido*. This ideal is similar to the chivalric code celebrated in medieval Europe. See *Bushido* in the Literature section.

WAY OF COMBAT

In contrast to techniques of combat, these are martial ways that emphasize the development of the self while teaching self-defense skills. See Techniques of Combat.

WHITE LOTUS SOCIETY

A powerful secret society that was in existence before 1644. Like other Chinese secret societies, this one sought political ends and its members were trained in the martial arts. See Secret Societies.

WINTER TRAINING

See Training, Winter.

WU-KUO-YING

See Resolute in Five Respects.

YAMA BUSHI

Japanese mountain warriors of legend. They are found in many stories about the various martial arts.

YELLOW TURBANS SOCIETY

A political, rebellious secret society that existed around 170 A.D. Its members were martial arts practitioners. See Secret Societies.

YIN-YANG

Essentially, the nature of the universe. Opposing elements are conflicting but also harmonious, each requiring the other to give it meaning. One cannot exist without the other. Yin is symbolic of the negative and the destructive. It is soft, passive and feminine. Yang, on the other hand, represents the positive and the creative. It is hard, active and masculine. In Chinese philosophy, these two are the origin of life. The concept of yin-yang is essential to Eastern philosophy and the martial arts. The martial artist must be able to combine the hard and the soft to achieve mastery of the art. Yin is called, variously, "ura" and "in" (Japanese); "am" or "an" (Vietnamese); and "um" (Korean). Yang is called "omote" and "yo" (Japanese); "duong" (Vietnamese). Koreans retain the word "yang." In Vietnamese Taoism, the principle of the interaction of yin and yang is expressed in the phrase "cuong nhu tong thoi." See Taoism.

YO

Same as Yang. See Yin-Yang.

YOI

Japanese command meaning "attention." Practitioners assume the attention or ready position. See Commands.

YOKOZUNA

See Ranking Systems.

YONKYU

See Ranking Systems.

YOROI

Armor. See Armor.

YUDANSHA

See Ranking Systems.

ZANSHIN

Mental alertness or awareness that is the ideal of the warrior. Because one is confident of being able to perceive an attack before it is launched, one remains calm. Such calm is acquired with practice. This was the ideal state of mind for the warrior. See Mental Awareness.

ZAREI

See Bowing.

ZAZEN MEDITATION

A kind of meditation in which one assumes a yoga position and merely tries to control or stop all thoughts, trying to achieve a perfectly empty mind. In true meditation, a mental exercise, the goal is more on the achievement of enlightenment.

ZEN

A sect of Buddhism brought to Japan from China, where it is called Chan or Chen. It was brought to China by the meditative Indian sect Dhyana, whose proponent Bodhidharma, according to legend, brought the martial arts with him. The philosophy suggests that one must be detached but still a part of the universe. Followers attempt to achieve enlightenment, which is a state of transcendence. This enlightenment is not intellectual and is not achieved through study, but is intuitive and spiritual, and is achieved through the practice of meditation. Many Zen concepts were adopted by warriors, including the meditative aspects. The practice of zazen, emptying the mind, and other forms of meditation helped the warrior to prepare for his eventual death without expressing fear. These also helped the warrior endure the rigors of military life. Zen complements martial arts for these reasons and because it emphasizes the discipline appropriate to the development of character and self-sacrifice. Zen emphasizes the necessity of the teacher-student relationship, which may have influenced the master-student relationship that developed in the martial arts. It also emphasizes non-reliance on Buddhist writings, that is, it places great importance on the ability to think, experience, and feel for oneself. The relationship of the individual to the higher entity was considered a direct and personal one. Finally, because of the interconnectedness of all things, Zen says the Buddha, the enlightened one, is in everyone. See Meditation.

ZEN BUDDHISM

A meditative sect of Buddhism. See Zen.

ZHANGZHUANA

A form of mediation practiced while standing. See Meditation.

ZOUR

See Training Hall.

ZUBON

See Uniforms.

SCHOOLS AND STYLES

Martial arts consist of a variety of combat methods. Some systems use weapons, while others are empty hand. Some focus on grappling while others emphasize striking. The following are listed by the most common name known to Westerners. Chuan and quan mean the same thing; they are merely different spellings for different dialects. For martial arts masters who invent a school, the usual approach is to give the school the name of the martial arts master's family. Thus, the last name of the master is the name of the school. The words "kwan" and "ryu" simply mean "school."

ABE RYU

A Kendo (sword art) school established in the 17th century, making it one of the earliest schools of Kendo. Also called Abe Tate Ryu.

ABE TATE RYU

See Abe Ryu.

AIKI-KENDO

A recently created martial art style. Sudoh Momoji founded this martial art to improve upon Aikido, which he felt failed because it did not offer a sport aspect and did not develop fighting spirit in its practitioners. Aiki-kendo is thus more aggressive and competitive than traditional Aikido.

AIKIDO

The name Aikido means "the way of harmony with the chi (or life force)." Aikido is a soft style martial art from Japan; it stresses the harmony between mind, body and morality. It emphasizes quick, decisive movements that are designed to use the attacker's force against him or her. This is done through evasive movements and body shifting. An Aikido practitioner does not punch or kick, though he or she may touch the opponent to guide the opponent's body. The techniques of Aikido are designed to help the student overcome physical and psychological barriers and to become more in harmony with the surrounding world. Circular movements without breaks are used. The circle is seen as a symbol of wholeness and unity which can be used against disharmony, disunity and violence. The art developed from the 1930's on.

It emphasizes self-defense, but it is also a way of life. Ueshiba Morihei, the founder, wanted to create a school that was defensive in nature. He wished to do away with harmful martial philosophy. He investigated over 200 martial arts styles, using Aikijutsu as a starting point. Aikido combines spirituality with exercise, sport and martial arts. The style uses some Jujutsu techniques but focuses on those techniques that keep one from close contact with an assailant. These techniques use the attacker's energy against him or her and rely on evasive maneuvers. Two methods of subduing an assailant are important: controlling an opponent and throwing an opponent. Over 700 techniques are possible. Originally presented as a highly dangerous fighting art, Aikido is now perceived as one of the gentlest of martial arts. Currently there is no competition in traditional Aikido. Its methods are practiced in free-style techniques and in forms. As a method of unarmed self-defense, Aikido offers physical fitness, strength and flexibility, discipline with a non-violent attitude, and improved posture and sensory perceptions. The beginning levels emphasize basic techniques and breakfall skills. At the advanced levels, emphasis is placed on self-examination. The training always focuses on improving techniques and increasing awareness of the art as a way of life. Since Aikido developed from Zen philosophy, meditation is used to understand the power of the chi and to develop stronger techniques. Aikido is not a striking or grappling art, emphasizing instead passive circular movement. In 1969, after the death of Ueshiba Morihei, the development of Aikido was taken over by his son, Ueshiba Kisshomaru. For related schools, see Aikijutsu, Kobujutsu, Korindo, Koryu Aikido, Shindo Rokugo ryu, Tomiki Aikido, Yoseikan, and Yoshin.

AIKIJITSU

Also Aikijutsu. See Aikijutsu. See Aikido.

AIKIJUTSU

An unarmed combat system with methods that rely on vital point attacks to the opponent's body.

It was founded during the Kamakura period (1185-1336) in Japan, where it was fully developed by Miyamoto no Yoshimitsu. Also known as Aiki-jujutsu, it originated from Kenjutsu (sword fighting). The word "aiki" means "meeting of the chi." In essence the life energy of opponents meets; the person with the stronger chi will defeat the person with the weaker chi. Thus, the name "harmony art." See related schools: Daito ryu, Daitokan. See Aikido.

AIO-RYU

A martial art school that taught lance techniques (Yari-jutsu) plus those of unarmed combat (Jujutsu).

AMERICAN FREESTYLE KARATE

A name given to an approach to Karate training, not necessarily a distinct Karate school. Dan Anderson, who coined the name, says it suggests a method of instruction, a non-Oriental method. He likens the approach to a boxer training under a certain trainer; all boxers are trained to use the boxing techniques of hook punch, cross punch, and jab, but the trainer, who takes on only a few students at a time, is able to help the fighter capitalize on his or her skills and abilities, instead of forcing him or her into a preconceived mold.

AMERICAN SHAOLIN KENPO

An American school of Karate that emphasizes Jeet Kune Do concepts. Students are trained to be prepared for any situation and to respond in their own way. The school was created by the American Karate master June Castro.

ANZAWA RYU

A Japanese school of the art of the naginata, a halberd-like weapon with a long handle and a shorter curved blade. Mostly women practice this martial art. See Naginata-jutsu.

ARAKI-RYU

A school of classical Kendo (sword art) that used round wooden swords, similar to the shinai, or bamboo sword, later used by all Kendo schools. It is named for its founder, Minamoto Hidetsuna, who changed his name to Araki Mujinsai. The school also taught the techniques of the chigiriki,

a staff with a ball and chain attached, and the kusarigama, a sickle with a length of chain attached.

ARCHERY

See Kyudo.

ARNIS

The word "Arnis" comes from the Spanish phrase, "Arnis de mano," harness of the hand, which was used to describe this combat art. Arnis is considered the mother martial art in the Philippines. The other Phillipine combat arts of Kali and Escrima are thought to have derived from Arnis, but essentially all three arts are the same, though there are dozens of different schools. Kali is practiced in the southern Philippines, Escrima in the central Philippines and Kali in the north. Arnis is one of the most popular martial arts in the Philippines. The art has been practiced for centuries. Arnis techniques are executed empty-handed or with such weapons as a stick or a knife. One form of combat, "espada y daga (sword and dagger)," uses a long wooden sword and a short wooden dagger. Single stick Arnis requires a long stick made of wood or cane. Such sticks are about two feet long. Double stick Arnis, in which each participant wields two sticks, is also taught. Arnis stresses striking and parrying techniques, using the hands. Other parts of the body are not used with much frequency. Like other martial arts, Arnis uses three teaching methods: drills, prearranged sparring, and free style practice. The art also has secret styles. It is a serious form of self-defense, though it is often treated like a sport. As in other arts, in addition to physical skills, the student must learn mental, emotional and spiritual qualities. Training is very physical and arduous, with an emphasis on strategy. Modern Arnis was significantly refined and developed by Remy Presas, who has been called the founder of modern Arnis. Only recently has Arnis been available to students in the United States. See also Escrima and Kali.

ASURA

A form of Indian wrestling in which the only foul is striking below the chest. The first person to fall to the ground loses the match. See Wrestling, Indian.

BA FAN

See White Crane Boxing.

BA GUA QUAN

Same as Pa Kua. See Eight Trigram Boxing.

BA-JI QUAN

A Chinese school of Wushu that emphasizes hand techniques, such as upper cuts and elbow strikes, along with arm holds and locks.

BA-JUTSU

A Japanese term meaning "horsemanship." See Bugei. See Jobajutsu.

BAHKTI NEGARA

See Bhakti Negara.

BAK MEI

See White Eyebrow Style.

BAK-SING CHOY LI FUT

A variation of Choy-Li-Fut which adds together methods from Wushu and original Choy-Li-Fut. As is usual in styles that combine methods, a story is told about the founders, who allegedly fought each other. Being equal in strength and skill, one could never defeat the other, so they became like brothers and combined their martial arts styles to create a new one.

BANDESH

An Indian art of combat that focuses on the use of weapons without killing, in keeping with the Hindu belief in the sacred value of all life. Bandesh is practiced as an important part of any weapons art. Using its techniques, one can perform a joint lock or a headlock, effectively immobilizing an opponent. In Bandesh competition, whoever takes the weapon from the other wins.

BANDO

A martial art of Burma (the country is now called Myanmar). The use of knives is emphasized though the use of the sword and stick is also taught. As with other extensive martial arts systems, different schools have different methods, but all teach the basic footwork, and the basic stances. Techniques are first taught through forms, then with partners and finally in sparring contests. Numerous forms exist for the practice of blocking and parrying; these defensive forms are taught first. Once they have been mastered, offensive (striking) forms are taught. Bando forms incorporate the characteristics of animals and are named after them. Twelve animal forms are commonly taught. Bando stresses combat strategy. Open hand strikes, grappling, and locking techniques are all used. Bando incorporates methods from Chinese Wushu, Karate and Judo. It was introduced in the United States by Dr. Maung Gye who also organized the American Bando Association. Sometimes called Thaing. See Thaing.

BANSHAY

A general term for Burmese weapons use. Both Indian and Chinese sources influenced the development of weapons systems. The sword, staff, and spear are the major weapons. With the sword, the goal is to disarm the opponent. Sword fights are even conducted with the sword still sheathed, since only under extreme conditions will a Burmese swordsman unsheathe his or her sword.

BAT QUAI

See Eight Trigram Boxing.

BATTO-JUTSU

This means "sword drawing art," an earlier name for Iaijutsu. Though the practitioners practice cutting with the blade, it is a type of Iaido (sword drawing) based on defeating the opponent through quickness in unsheathing the sword, not on particular cutting and slashing techniques. See Iaijutsu. See Iaido.

BERSILAT

Literally, "to do fighting," this Malaysian martial art is similar to Pentjak Silat, an Indonesian martial art, which it is thought to have derived from. It is a self-defense system dating from the fifteenth century. There are several schools of Bersilat, each with two branches, one for public display, one for combat. Silat pulat is a dance-like art, usually performed at weddings and other festivities. Silat buah is for combat. Some schools emphasize unarmed combat while others focus on weapons use. Minangkabau is the name of the woman who introduced the art, which imitates the movement of animals like Chinese styles do. Bersilat emphasizes leg techniques, but punches, throws and holds are also important. Students are forbidden to divulge secrets and training is often handed down from family member to family member. The art has both a sport side and a spiritual side. The most important styles of Bersilat are Chekak, Kelantan, Lintan, Medan, Peninjuan, and Terelak.

BHAKTI NEGARA

This major style of Pentjak Silat is taught mostly in Bali where it developed in the modern era.

BINOT

A rarely practiced Indian martial art which pits an unarmed practitioner against an armed opponent. It emphasizes the use of both hands. It is extremely difficult to learn and very dangerous to practice. It is thought to be the oldest of this type of fighting (armed vs. unarmed) extant.

BLACK TIGER

A modern school of Vietnamese martial arts.

BO-JUTSU

This is "staff art." The bo, or long staff, is 5 feet or more in length. It requires a two-handed grip and can deflect and defeat a sword. Although it is generally perceived as a long range weapon, it can be used for in-close fighting as well. Often practitioners train outside, on difficult terrain, much as they might train for sword fighting. This helps them to be prepared for uneven footing and other obstacles. The repetition of forms is the only Bojutsu training method. It can be studied by itself or along with other martial arts such as Kendo and Karate. Japanese feudal warriors studied Bojutsu in great numbers, especially in the 16th century, but the art has been in existence since the 12th, when it was systematized. It was the primary method used by police during the Tokugawa period (1603-1868). Because the Bo is slightly less dangerous to practice with than a blade, the staff and other wooden weapons were used in the military arts schools of the feudal era. In Okinawa,

where the staff is about a foot longer, there exist more than ten arts of the bo. See Bugei.

BONG PO KUEN

See Praying Mantis.

BOX FIGHTING

A style of fighting in Hung Gar, in which matches are conducted in a three-foot-square area to develop techniques of in-close fighting.

BOXE FRANCAIS

Practitioners follow rules similar to other forms of boxing, but kicks are allowed. The sport derived from Savate. See Savate.

BOXING, BURMESE

This hard, offensive style of martial arts is the opposite of the Burmese style of self-defense called Bando. It is also known as Lethwei. Burmese boxing is similar to Thai boxing. Most Burmese boxers are farmers. The Shan dance, called the fight dance, which is still seen today, is really a method of training for actual combat. Burmese boxers train alone or with a partner, but there is no equipment like heavy bags. Practitioners are divided into four categories: youth, novice, intermediate and professional, but there are no weight classifications. Promotion from one category to the next occurs as a result of contest wins. A contest consists of four untimed rounds. A blow that delivers a visible shock or an effective grappling technique will end a round, except for the last round, which goes on until one participant is bloodied, gives up, or is knocked out. Blood must result from a head wound, so most attacks are aimed high.

BOXING, CHINESE

Refers to Chinese martial arts that were originally taught at the Shaolin Temple in China. They are broken into Northern and Southern styles, but all are part of Wushu. See Wushu.

BOXING, CLASSICAL GREEK

An ancient sport which emphasized punching techniques. It began early in Greek history and lasted until late Roman times, when it declined. Hooks, uppercuts, and chops were used, as in modern boxing. Greek boxing is a forerunner of Pankration, Greek wrestling.

BRAZILIAN JUJUTSU

A style of Jujutsu from Brazil that incorporates Capoeira techniques. It uses methods of streetfighting, including striking, kicking and grappling. Participants use head butts, elbow strikes and knee strikes. See Jujutsu.

BUDO

Term meaning "martial way," used to describe martial arts with a spiritual or self-improvement side. This is largely a 20th-century development of Bugei, combat arts that do not emphasize a philosophical or spiritual side. Budo styles of martial arts come from the Bugei styles of martial arts and can exist side by side. An example is Judo, a Budo form of Jujutsu, a Bugei art.

BUGEI

Combat arts that developed from about the 10th century on. This is the name for ancient Japanese combat systems, from which Budo, the "way" or "art" styles developed. Warriors were expected to have a well-developed knowledge of most of the Bugei arts. No complete list of these combat arts exists, but what follows is the martial arts historian Donn Draeger's suggestions:

Ba jutsu: horsemanship

Bojutsu: staff art

Chigiriki-jutsu: techniques for using the chigirki, a ball and chain on short stick

Chikujo-jutsu: techniques of fortification

Fuki-bari: blowing small needles by mouth

Gekigan-jutsu: techniques using ball and chain

Genkotsu: assaulting vital points

Hayagake-jutsu: improving speed in walking and running

Hojojutsu: techniques for tying an enemy

Hojutsu: techniques of gunnery

Iai-jutsu: swordsfighting (defensive)

Jojutsu: short staff or stick art

Jujutsu: unarmed grappling

Jukenjutsu: bayonet art

Jutte-jutsu: techniques using metal truncheon

Karumi-jutsu: techniques to lighten oneself for climbing, jumping

Kenjutsu: swordfighting (offensive)

Kumi-uchi: armor grappling

Kusarigamajutsu: techniques using chain and sickle weapon

Kyujutsu: bow and arrow techniques

Naginata-jutsu: halberd techniques

Noroshi-jutsu: signal fire techniques

Sasumata-jutsu: techniques using forked staff

Senjojutsu: tactics of deployment of warriors

Shinobi-jutsu: techniques of camouflage and disguise

Shuriken-jutsu: throwing bladed weapons

Sodegaramijutsu: techniques using a barbed pole

Sojutsu: spear techniques

Suiei-jutsu: technique of swimming and fighting in water in armor

Suijohokojutsu: technique for crossing water

Sumo: unclad grappling

Tessen-jutsu: techniques using fan

Tetsubojutsu: techniques using long iron rod

Uchi-ne: throwing the arrow by hand

BUJUTSU

General term for combat techniques used by ancient Japanese warriors. Such techniques were prized and were developed only for their use in battle. See Techniques of Combat in General Section.

BÛNO

A Phillipine art of wrestling.

BUSHIDO

Japanese term meaning "the way of the warrior." It was a natural development from centuries of military experience. Bushido is an ethical belief, not a fighting system. By following it, warriors could apply their combat skills in strictly defined right or wrong ways, just as Westerners followed the code of chivalry. Bushido incorporated Shinto and Confucian ideas. The term itself was first used in the twentieth century to describe this ancient ideal.

BYAKURENMONKEN

A style of Kempo originating at the Shaolin temple. See Kempo.

CAMBO

See Sambo.

CAPOEIRA

This African system of unarmed combat is thought to have been created by African slaves in Brazil who developed the movements of ritual dance. The movements of the dance evolved into techniques of self-defense in the 16th century. It is still set to music today and an emphasis is placed on personal expression. As in many unarmed combat systems, the original practitioners could not own weapons and the practice of the art was forbidden. Even after slavery ended, Capoeira practitioners could be imprisoned or deported. This, coupled with the fact that the founders had no freedom and could be bound and chained, influenced its development. It relies primarily on leg techniques and strategy. Defense is supplied mostly by evasion and not by blocking, again because techniques were limited by the amount of physical freedom the practitioner had. An intelligent Capoeirist could seem helpless while at the same time be capable of a devastating attack. Only recently has Capoeira been taught outside of Brazil.

CHA CHUAN

This form of Wushu was established during the Ming dynasty (1368-1644). It is an internal, Northern method, developed by Chamir, a Muslim hero, around the 17th century. The school emphasizes long and fluid techniques. High long leaps are designed to cover distances quickly.

CHA QUAN

See Cha Chuan.

CHAMPAKA PUTIH

A style of Pentjak Silat charaterized by sweeping throws.

CHANG CHUAN

This style of long fist boxing was developed by the martial arts master Kuo I, around the first century A.D. It is perhaps the original Wushu art, spread through China by itinerant teachers. It has many of the characteristics of Northern Shaolin martial arts, and it seems to have been the origin of many other Wushu arts. Its influence on Tai Chi Chuan is clear. It is characterized by strong stances, and a wide variety of techniques. High kicks are practiced, but low kicks are used in fights. Its movements are so graceful and smooth that the Chinese Opera integrates many of its techniques. The style of Wushu has recently become very popular once again, and it is extremely popular in forms competition. Currently, however, many people lump all Chinese boxing styles under this one name, though Chang Chuan is a distinct entity.

CHEKAK

A school of Bersilat in which correct breathing is emphasized. It uses open hand techniques with only an occasional front kick.

CHI KUNG

See Ji Gong.

CHIAO LI

Same as Chiao Ti. See Chiao Ti.

CHIAO TI

An ancient form of Chinese wrestling, meaning "horned strength" from the horned headgear participants wore. See Wrestling, Chinese.

CHIGIRIKI-JUTSU

This is an ancient combat art, techniques of using the chigiriki, a ball and chain attached to a short stick. See Bugei.

CH'I GUNG

See Ji Gong.

CHIH YU HSI

In this form of Chinese wrestling, participants wore horned headgear and butted each other. It was the forerunner of Chiao Ti. See Wrestling, Chinese.

CHIKARA KURABE

An ancient form of strength testing.

CHIKUJO-JUTSU

Techniques of fortification, required knowledge for any warrior who commanded others. See Bugei.

CHINESE GOJU

A Karate style based on the Goju-ryu style of Karate, founded by an American Karate instructor. Like its namesake, it combines hard and soft techniques, but adds methods from other martial arts systems as well.

CHINESE FIST

Called Zhonguo Quan. See Kempo.

CHIN-NA

The art of seizing. A general term for Chinese grappling or wrestling arts. As a specific method of Wushu, it emphasizes the ability to grasp and control the opponent. Techniques are similiar to vital point striking. The purpose is to stop an attack without injuring the opponent.

CHITO-RYU

A school of Karate that synthesizes the techniques of Goju-ryu and Shorin-ryu Karate. Personal growth is encouraged over simple technical skill.

CHO CHIAO

A style of Northern Chinese boxing. It is characterized by high kicks unusual for Wushu styles.

CHOSON-DO

A Korean martial art that relies on palm and hand techniques.

CHOTO-JUTSU

A form of Naginata-jutsu, art of the halberd.

CHOW-GAR

A Southern Wushu style founded by Chow Lung, who adapted the techniques of Hung Gar, which is where the name derives from. He included methods from both the Eight Trigram and Choy styles of Wushu.

CHOY GAR

A style of Southern Wushu founded by Choy Gar kee. One of the five original styles, this relies on long arm techniques, low stances and speed. The emphasis is on developing techniques that will serve dual purposes: a block can be converted to a strike, and vice versa. Circular motion is used to increase force.

CHOY LEE FUT

See Choy Li Fut.

CHOY LI FUT

A style of Wushu that derives from the Shaolin temple. It was founded in 1836 by Chan Heung, who learned it from a monk named Choy Fuk. One of the most popular styles of Wushu, it relies on powerful hand and arm techniques. Four main hand techniques are used, including the straight punch, the backfist, the uppercut and the hook punch. It incorporates oriental medicine and philosophy. The emphasis is on learning through forms practice and many hand and weapons forms are taught, most of which have between one hundred and three hundred movements. Speed, balance, and power are all important elements in this style of Wushu, which also combines hard and soft techniques. Many full contact fighters follow this system.

Practitioners can also learn numerous weapons including the double hook swords and the staff, plus the nine dragon trident, which is exclusive to this style.

CHUAN FA

See Kempo.

CHUAN SHU

A general term meaning "Chinese Boxing."

CHUNG KUO CHUAN

Literally, "Chinese fist." See Kempo.

CHUO-JIAO-QUAN

A style of Wushu that relies on kicking and other leg techniques for both striking and blocking.

CIKALONG

A style of Pentjak Silat. See Pentjak Silat.

CIMADE

A style of Pentjak Silat. See Pentjak Silat.

CIREUM

A term broadly including all Korean wrestling in general, still popularly practiced. These forms of wrestling stem from Chinese grappling. Cireum resembles Sumo, not only because of the formality and ritual, but also because contestants only wear a loin cloth and attempt to push each other out of a ring or down to the ground. There are two types of Cireum. The stance type requires the opponents to wear a cloth strip around their thighs. When opponents grab the left side of the cloth, it is called left stance or left style; when opponents grab the right side of the cloth, it is called right stance or right style. The second type does not require a cloth strip, and is called Tong-cireum.

COMBAT HAPKIDO

A modified version of Hapkido meant to emulate realistic combat or fighting situations. See Hapkido.

COMBAT TAE KWON DO

A modified version of Tae Kwon Do, meant to emulate realistic combat or fighting situations. See Tae Kwon Do.

CRANE STYLE

A style of Wushu that is based on animal qualities. It is a defensive style characterized by one-legged stances. It requires an alert practitioner. Crane stylists do not attack, they counter-attack. Also called Hok. See White Crane Style.

CUONG-NHU

This Vietnamese style of Karate is named after the Vietnamese phrase for yin-yang and combines both hard and soft elements. The founder, Ngo Dong, studied both Karate and Aikido. This art incorporates elements of both.

DAITO-RYU

A famous classical Aiki-jutsu school founded in the twelfth century. It is one of the earliest schools to teach empty-handed techniques. Ueshiba Morihei, who founded Aikido, was a student at this school after it had been renamed Daitokan.

DAITOKAN

See Daito-ryu.

DALETAI

An ancient Chinese martial art combining wrestling and boxing techniques.

DHARANIPATA

An old style of Indian wrestling in which the loser is thrown and pinned to the ground. See Wrestling, Indian.

DI-TANG-QUAN

Same as Ditang Chuan. See Ditang Chuan.

DITANG CHUAN

A Wushu school known for its practitioners' great leaping and tumbling ability. The school emphasizes groundwork and grappling as well.

DRAGON STYLE

A method of Wushu known as "Lung Ying." A series of attacking techniques that do not let up characterizes this style. Speed and offense are essential. It shares similarities with White Eyebrow Style; the founder, Tai Yuk, studied that style before creating his own. Five internal elements (spirit, purpose, endurance, chi and power) are paired with five external elements (eyes, mind, hands, waist and stance) to create power. This style uses forearm and palm strikes plus a form of footwork called slide stepping. Advanced practitioners develop their inner energy or chi to increase their power and force.

DRUNKEN STYLE

General term for Wushu forms, techniques and styles that appear to imitate a drunken practitioner, who lulls the opponent into thinking he or she can easily be overcome, using this strategy to defeat the opponent.

DUMOG

A form of wrestling practiced in the Philippines. Practitioners use various grappling techniques. The object is to throw the opponent. Unlike Judo, where partially successful throws can count in competition, in Dumog, the loser's back must touch the ground squarely for the throw to count. Opponents either grip each other's belts or each other's waists.

E-MEI SHAN PAI

A style of Wushu created at the Shaolin temple.

EAGLE CLAW

A style of Wushu related to the White Crane system. It has highly complicated forms but is beautiful and surprising to watch. The renowned master Lau Fat Mang, who is famous for his drunken sets, is considered responsible for its enormous appeal. It was founded almost nine hundred years ago by Ouk Fay, but it did not become popular until the twentieth century. Practitioners use speed, cleverness and strength, imitating the eagle pursuing its prey. It has some similarities to Jujutsu, with its reliance on joint-locks. It has 108 striking points derived from acupuncture charts. The number 108 is considered in Chinese philosophy to be a fortunate number. Thirty-six of these striking points are thought to be lethal. Ten forms are taught, all empty hand, and all 108 techniques are contained in these forms. Eagle Claw Wushu emphasizes controlling, not injuring or killing, the opponent. It is characterized by the claw hand, "ying jiao," with fingers held partially clenched. The claw hand technique can be used to stop, control or injure an opponent, as necessary. Though kicks are used, they are primarily blocking, not striking, techniques.

EIGHT DRUNKEN IMMORTALS

A northern style of Wushu that relies on the appearance of drunkenness for its effectiveness. The practitioner appears off-balance and can thus take advantage of an unsuspecting opponent. It is interesting to watch but very difficult to learn. Called Tsui Pa Hsien.

EIGHT SECTION BROCADE

An exercise for "cleansing" the inner body by improving the circulation of the chi, or life energy. Without this free circulation, one can easily become ill. See Ji Gong.

EIGHT TRIGRAM BOXING

A style of Wushu belonging to the internal or soft method. It is sometimes called Eight Hexagram or Eight Directions. It is thought to correspond to the Eight Trigrams of the *I-Ching*, or *The Book of Changes*, in which eight trigrams are combined into pairs that make hexagrams, which represent all possible events and action in human life. The name, Pakua (Bo Gua), also refers to the Eight Directions of Movement. Little is known about its origins except that a martial artist, Tung Hai Chuan (1798-1879) learned it during the Ching Dynasty. Later, Tung was challenged by Kuo, the master of Hsing-I or Mind-Body Boxing,

known for his iron palm. Tung defeated Kuo, but only after several days of trying. After this, the two agreed that their students should learn each other's style. The techniques of Eight Trigram Boxing are practiced solo; one executes a series of movements in a circle about three feet in diameter. The techniques so learned can be applied to fighting. The main exercise is called walking the circle, and in it one learns how the body moves and turns. Basically, one walks in a continuous circle, focusing on an imaginary opponent. The techniques include various upright stances, low kicks, and footwork based on the movements of animals such as snake, stork, dragon, hawk, lion and monkey. The name comes from the philosophy of the *The Book of Changes*, in which eight trigrams combined into pairs that make hexagrams represent the possible events and actions in human life. Four main weapons are taught: the double-edged sword, the staff, the broadsword and the spear. Special weapons include the deer horn knife, called lu jyau do, which has two sickle-shaped blades that are crossed, and the pun gung bi, which are six-inch needles, sharp at both ends, which attach to the fingers with rings.

EISHIN RYU

One of the original schools of Iaijutsu (sword-drawing art). Eishin-ryu was founded in the 17th century when it split from the Muso Jikiden Ryu , the earliest known Iaijutsu school. Eishin-ryu uses forms and techniques from Kenjutsu in addition to those from Iaijutsu. See Muso Jikiden-Ryu.

EL CUCHILLO

Mexican knife fighting. Santiago was one of most famous fighters and teachers.

EMMEI-RYU

A school of Kenjutsu (swordfighting) founded by the famous warrior-philosopher Miyamoto Musashi, who taught the cultivation of calmness and serenity of mind under all circumstances. Also called Nito-ryu, the two sword school, or the two skies school. It taught a special technique for crossing two swords to create a defensive wedge which was difficult for an opponent to penetrate.

ESCRIMA

A derivation of Arnis, Escrima was brought to the Philippines by travelers from Indonesia and Malaysia. The Spanish rule of the Philippines led to the evolution of Escrima. The Spanish rapier and dagger system had the greatest impact, leading as it did to the method of Escrima called "daga y espada." Escrima includes twelve areas of study, including projectile weapons, anatomical weapons, and bladed weapons. Escrima is best known for its stick fighting techniques. It is sometimes considered an art of traditional fencing. Sometimes spelled Eskrima. See Kali. See Arnis.

EXTERNAL SYSTEM

A general term referring to any hard and vigorous martial art that relies on linear strikes, such as Karate or Tae Kwon Do. The Chinese call this "wai chia."

FANTZU HAO CHUAN

See White Crane.

FANZI QUAN

Same as Fantzu Hao Chuan. See White Crane.

FIVE ANIMALS

A style of Wushu sometimes called "five frolicking animals" or "five animals play." It was based on the movements of animals, as is most traditional Chinese Wushu, and was devised around 200 A.D.

FIVE ELDERS

A style of Wushu, this also refers to the five legendary monks who escaped the burning of the original Shaolin temple. They spread throughout China, teaching the martial arts. The system is based on the movements of the Five Animals, as many Wushu styles are. Also called Hung Chia Chuan.

FONG NGAN

See Phoenix Eye.

FOREST SCHOOLS

These are the three branches of the Shorin-ryu (Shaolin) school of Karate, called "small forest," "young forest" and "pine forest" school. See Shobayashi-ryu, Kobayashi-ryu and Matsubayashi-ryu.

FU-CHIAO PAI

See Tiger Style.

FUKI-BARI

Techniques of blowing small needles by mouth at attackers or pursuers. Such weapons are easily concealed. See Bugei.

FULL CONTACT KARATE

A style of American Karate. As the name implies, strikes are performed with full power, instead of the little or no contact found in ordinary Karate matches. It has few of the restraints of ordinary Karate competition. The goal is to knock out the opponent; in the event of no knock-out, the opponents abide by the judges' decision. It was co-founded by Mike Anderson and Jhoon Rhee in the early 1970s. No forms exist and all terminology is in English. It is strictly a sport contest. It differs from boxing mainly in that participants must deliver a certain number of kicks in each round.

FULL-NUNCH

See Full-Nunchaku.

FULL-NUNCHAKU

A type of sport Karate that uses the nunchaku. Opponents deliver full power strikes and attempt to knock each other out. Participants wear protective gear but the sport is nevertheless quite dangerous.

GASSAN-RYU

A 19th-century school that taught the use of the naginata, a halberd-like weapon with a long wooden handle and a shorter curved blade usually handled by women. See Nagingata-jutsu.

GEKIGEN-JUTSU

Techniques using a ball-and-chain weapon. See Bugei.

GENJI NO HEIHO

The collective martial arts of the celebrated Minamoto warrior family (who were also called the Genji). Their school included all the traditional arts of the Bugei.

GENKOTSU

Vital point attacks. See Bugei.

GI-GONG

See Ji Gong.

GO-TI

An early style of Chinese wrestling practiced in the Chou Dynasty (1027 B.C. to 256 B.C.). See Chiao Ti.

GOJU-RYU

A Karate school founded in the early-1930s. The style is a combination of hard ("go") and soft ("ju") techniques, which work together like the traditional yin and yang elements. Therefore, linear motion is combined with circular motion. Forms are practiced with slow movements and with an emphasis on correct breathing. The techniques have a spiritual component as well. Miyagi Chojun, the founder, actually adopted techniques of Okinawan Karate and Chinese Kempo. Goju-Ryu has influenced many other Karate styles.

GONG FU

Same as Kung Fu. See Wushu.

GOSHIN-DO

In Judo and Karate, a form of self-defense that has practical instead of sport applications or methods. Practitioners learn to defend against staff, knife and gun.

GOSHIN-JUTSU

Also known as Tanaka Goshin-Jutsu. A style of Jujutsu developed by Tanaka Tatsu. Like Kano Jigoro, Tanaka felt that traditional Jujutsu was extremely dangerous, so he created a safer version which relies primarily on grappling techniques. The art resembles Judo in some respects.

GOSOKO RYU

A Karate style that depends on speed, power and defense. The school relies on free-style sparring to increase the effectiveness of the training. The methods are derived from a combination of other styles.

GRACIE JUJUTSU

A modern style of Brazilian Jujutsu created by the Gracie family, which relies primarily on ground work techniques and joint locks. See Brazilian Jujutsu.

GUNG-FU

Same as Kung Fu. See Wushu.

GUOSHO

Same as Kuoshu, a general Chinese term meaning "national sport." See Wushu.

HAC HO

See Black Tiger.

HADAKO

A style of Chinese Kempo. See Kempo.

HADE

Same as Hadako, a form of Kempo. See Kempo.

HAKKO-RYU

A modern school of Jujutsu created by Okuyama Yoshiji, it became the source for Shorinji Kempo. The school teaches defense by vital point striking. Traditional kicks and punches are rarely used. Flexibility is preferred over muscular strength. Students are expected to master the principle hand techniques first and then move onto foot techniques, footwork, and body movement.

HANBO-JUTSU

A martial art that teaches the use of the bo, the staff.

HAO PAI

A style of Wushu. See Heron Style.

HAPKIDO

Literally, "the way of coordinated power." Name given to the traditional Korean art of Yu-Sol, after its techniques were developed and refined by Choi Yong Shul in the 1930s. He added Aikido elements to Korean methods. All techniques are used for their practical self-defense purposes. Since the style is predominately defensive, a practitioner generally allows an attacker to make the first move, thereby committing him or herself. Originally a grappling and throwing art, it now includes a variety of strikes and kicks. Hapkido was introduced in the United States in the 1960s, and it has grown in popularity since.

HARIMAU SILAT

See Tiger Silat.

HASAKU-BO

Staff art using a spear-length staff.

HAYAGAKE JUTSU

Techniques for improving one's walking and running speed. See Bugei.

HEIKI RYU

Founded in the fourteenth century by Heiki Danjo, it is an early Japanese school of combat archery. Techniques were extremely accurate.

HERON STYLE

A style of Wushu based on the postures of the heron, using the fingers and hand in the shape of the bird's beak to attack. Called Hao Pai.

HIKIDA-RYU

A Kendo (sword art) school founded by a famous swordsman named Hikida Bungoro (1537-1606). The school used a forerunner of the shinai or bamboo sword.

HOJO-JUTSU

One of the arts of the Bugei; techniques for tying up an opponent. See Bugei.

HOJUTSU

A 16th century school of martial arts that taught the use of the arquebus, a heavy, crude gun. It is also called Ka-jutsu, techniques of gunnery. See Bugei.

HOKI-RYU

Iaido: a style of Iaido (sword drawing art) founded by Katayama Hokinokami Hisayasu and recognized by the All Japan Iaido Federation.

Kyujutsu: a school of Kyujutsu (archery) created in the 10th century.

HOKUSAI-RYU

Ancient school that emphasized Hojo-jutsu, or the art of tying the enemy. See Bugei.

HOKUSHIN ITTO-RYU

A style of Kenjutsu (swordfighting) founded in the Edo (Tokyo) period. It focused on sword training as a spiritual discipline rather than a martial discipline. Participants used a sword similar to the shinai or bamboo sword used in Kendo. Practitioners competed against women using the naginata, a halberd-like weapon with a long wooden handle and a shorter curved blade.

HOP GAR

A style of Wushu emphasizing combat effectiveness. The style is based on Lion Roar Wushu, which originated during the Tang Dynasty and was taught to many generations of monks. It finally reached the Lama, from which the style derived its nickname, Lama Wushu. The name was changed to Hop Gar early in the twentieth century. Hop Gar teaches both short and long range techniques and uses both empty hand and weapons techniques. Footwork is practiced on top of the so-called plum flower stumps, posts of various heights driven into the ground. Practitioners train on them to develop balance and other skills. Technique and form are rigorously taught, but once the practitioner has mastered the method, he or she adapts the techniques to meet his or her needs.

HOSHIN-RYU

A school that teaches the art of the naginata, a halberd-like weapon with a long wooden handle and a shorter curved blade. The school emphasized spiritual and mental awareness in its followers, who were mostly women. See Naginata-jutsu.

HOU CHUAN

See Monkey Style.

HOZO-IN-RYU

A school of Kendo (sword art) that was founded by a Buddhist monk in the fifteenth century, who taught it to other monks. It languished in obscurity for some years before being made famous by Takeda Sokaku Minamoto Masayoshi in the late 19th century.

HSIANG PU

Term used in Tang Dynasty China to refer to Chinese wrestling. Literally, "mutual beating."

HSING-I CHUAN

See Mind-Body Boxing.

HSING-I LU HO CHUAN

See Mind-Body Boxing.

HSING-YI

See Mind-Body Boxing.

HUNG CHIA CHUAN
See Five Elders.

HUNG FUT
A style of Wushu that is three hundred years old. It derived from Hung Gar and other styles. It emphasizes evasion, and teaches both short and long strikes. The tiger claw is the hand technique most frequently used. It is characterized by its left-handed strikes; the first strike the practitioner delivers is with the left hand. Since most people strike with the right hand, it is confusing and surprising to the opponent. The style also has a famous form, called Iron Cloth Form, in which the practitioner uses his or her own shirt as a whip-like weapon.

HUNG GAR
A style of Wushu based the qualities of animals. The Hung Gar fighter at close range imitates the hard movements of the tiger; at long range, he or she imitates the elusive movements of the crane. The style was founded by Hung Hei Gune. It emphasizes external strength, powerful muscles, and low stances. It teaches the nunchaku, unusual for a Chinese art. It is one of five original forms of Wushu from Fukien Shaolin, and it remains one of the most popular styles of Wushu.

HWARANG-DO
One of the oldest Korean arts of combat. Hwarang-do means "the way of the flower of manhood," since it was originally taught in a youth organization. Originating almost 2,000 years ago, it is the Korean martial art from which many others stem. It was founded by a Buddhist monk, Bopsa Won Kwang, to educate aristocratic youths in martial arts and philosophy. These young adults were called "Hwarang" and in the Silla Dynasty they developed a reputation as the most feared warriors. Practitioners of Hwarang-do were expected to develop several principle qualities common to all martial artists: loyalty, courage and fairness. Like most "do" arts, Hwarang-do relies on the concept of yin-yang, or um-yang as it is called in Korea, for it focuses on the spiritual and personal growth of the individual, balanced by development of the mind and body.

Eventually the power of the Hwarang dissipated. The art was driven underground during the Yi Dynasty, where it remained for many years. In 1960, two brothers who had been students of Hwarang-do for many years opened the first modern public school. The art has spread to other countries, where it is often taught in combination with Tae Kwon Do.

HYODO
The term for Japanese martial arts of the early-18th century, sometimes called heiho or "military way."

I-CHUAN
See Mind-Body Boxing.

IAIDO
A method of sword fighting that derived from Kenjutsu and Iaijutsu, more accurately called sword drawing art because the primary goal of the practitioner is to be able to draw quickly enough to cut or block the opponent before he or she can act. The practitioner practices the skill of drawing the sword for many hours daily. The art is now more of a spiritual discipline than a self-defense method, combining elements of Zen, Shinto, Buddhism and Confucianism. It is part of the Japanese Kendo Federation. Though it is not a style of Kendo, it is often taught with Kendo. Unlike Iaijutsu, which was used in real combat and originated around 1560, it is primarily a spiritual and mental discipline. It is done at a slow, controlled pace, and consists of twenty movements for drawing, each slightly different, and fifty movements for cutting and slicing, again, each slightly different. The forms practiced in Iaijutsu are practiced in a slightly modified version in Iaido. Important schools include Hoki-ryu, Ichiden-ryu, Mugai-ryu, Omori-ryu, Tamiya-ryu, and Toyama-ryu.

IAIJUTSU
A defensive style of swordfighting that with Kenjutsu, an offensive, aggressive style of swordfighting, comprise the basic principles of classical swordsmanship. Its defensive basis distinguishes it from Kenjutsu, and it emphasizes fluid, quick motion. In Iaijutsu, how the

practitioner draws the sword is as important as how he or she strikes with it. Most methods employ drawing and striking in the same movement. This emphasis probably derives from the ancient practice of Tachi-gake, or sword-drawing techniques. Over time, as peace ensued, martial arts techniques, not combat tactics, influenced the development of Iaijutsu. Practitioners still trained exhaustively, practicing hundreds of techniques a day. When live enemies could not be found, sword techniques were tried out on the corpses of executed criminals. Or, as peasants claimed, on the unsuspecting members of the lower class. Eventually the techniques of Iaijutsu developed into Iaido. In both Iaijutsu and Iaido, four phases of each technique are practiced. They include drawing the sword (nukisuke), cutting with the sword (kiritsuke), removing the blood from the sword (chiburi), and, finally, resheathing the sword (noto). Each stage has many different methods, taking into account a variety of possible situations (obstructions that might prevent quick removal of sword from sheath, for instance). Techniques are performed from standing, crouching, and kneeling positions. Iaijutsu is also known as Batto-jutsu. The most famous schools include Eishin-ryu, Katori-ryu, Mizuno Shinto-ryu, Muso-ryu, Muso Jikiden-ryu, Nakamuru-ryu, and Tachi-gake-ryu. See Bugei. See Iaido. See Kenjutsu.

IGA-RYU

One of the main branches of Ninjutsu. It was developed and handed down in the Iga region. See Ninjutsu.

INTERNAL SYSTEM

Any of the Chinese Wushu styles emphasizing the development of chi, or life energy. Can refer to any martial art that makes use of soft and circular movements. Called Nei Chia.

ISSHINRYU

A style of modern Okinawan Karate, founded by the Shimabuku Tatsuo in 1954. It combines techniques and methods from Shorin-ryu and Goju-ryu. It emphasizes simple low kicks and short stances. The goal is for Isshinryu to be useful for streetfighting. Participants follow a code that incorporates the fundamental principles of the system, including an emphasis on harmony and awareness of one's surroundings. The school teaches the kusarigama, a weapon that consists of a sickle with a chain attached.

ISSHIN SHORINJI

A style of Okinawan Karate.

ITATO

Name for Okinawan Karate.

JEET KUNE DO

A modern style of Wushu created by the renowned martial artist Bruce Lee. The name means, literally, "Way of the Intercepting Fist," and the most famous tenet is "absorb what is useful, reject what is useless, add what is specifically your own." The style emphasizes simplicity. No forms are taught, nor are set techniques designed to counter other techniques. Instead, the style attempts to take a problem solving approach. The essentials are to preserve the center line, a concept Lee learned from Wing Chun Wushu, which he studied; to maintain a constant rhythm, and to begin sparring immediately. The simplicity of approach is also evident in the central idea of blocking and attacking at the same time. No set of rules or codified techniques exist for this art. Jeet Kune Do uses methods and techniques from all styles, not just empty hand systems, but weapons systems as well. Whatever is effective can and should be used in self-defense. Jeet Kune Do is seen by its practitioners as a road to self-discovery and self-examination. Its followers consider Jeet Kune Do to be a point of view rather than a school or style of martial art. To this end, Lee was against setting up systematic methods of instruction, for once more than a few students enrolled in a school, the techniques and instruction would have to become codified and the result would be that the students would undergo repetitious drills, forms practice and prearranged sparring, to the detriment of developing the ideal awareness of what Jeet Kune Do really attempts to do. It is up to the student to gather the necessary experience and develop his or her own reportoire. Instead of confining oneself to sparring only other Jeet Kune Do students, the practitioner should pursue opportunities to spar any kind of fighter and learn what he or she can from the experience. The study of different fighting systems could aid in the development of proper Jeet Kune Do perspective, but only if the student devoted time to studying the strengths and weaknesses of any system, and deciding what he or she could use from each system. In this way, Jeet Kune Do is heavily reliant on experience and theory.

JI DO KWAN

A school of Tae Kwon Do founded by Gae Byang Yun in Korea in 1953.

JI GONG

A style of Wushu that has been practiced for over three hundred years. Its purpose is to tap internal energies and help with the correct circulation or movement of chi, or life energy throughout the body. Practitioners believe it can prevent and heal physical injuries and disease. The art, which consists of meditation and easy movement, is related to Tai Chi Chuan and is even taught with Tai Chi. Eighteen exercises comprise the essential techniques. Ji Gong conferences are held annually, with the presentation of scientific research and the performance of forms.

JIANDAO

An ancient art of Chinese swordfighting.

JIAODISHU

A name for Kempo. See Kempo.

JIAOLI

A military sport, a kind of wrestling, popular in China during the Chou Dynasty.

JIGEN-RYU

A school of Kenjutsu (swordfighting) created by Togo Shigekura Bizen no Kami in Japan during the 16th century. This offense-centered style was the martial art of choice for the Japanese warriors of the powerful Satsuma clan. A separate school of Kenjutsu that developed on Okinawa goes by the same name.

JIJITSU

See Jujutsu.

JIJUTSU

See Jujutsu.

JIKAKU RYU

A 16th-century school that emphasized the art of the arquebus, a crude gun. Other techniques of gunnery include Ka-jutsu.

JIKISHIN KAGE-RYU

A school of Kenjutsu (swordfighting) created by Yamada Heizaman. This school taught the use of the shinai, the bamboo sword used in Kendo.

Also, a school of the art of naginata (halberd) for women. One of the three modern "do" or art schools of the naginata. The other two are Tendo and Toda Buko. In this school, the circle is the essential concept. Basics are studied and then practiced against a partner with a sword, since the naginata is used to defend against the sword. When the student has mastered these basics, she or he moves onto forms practice. The school teaches twenty-five techniques of the naginata.

JIKISHIN RYU

An important school of Jujutsu that used empty hand techniques entirely and used the term "Judo," to refer to non-lethal techniques.

JITE-JUTSU

Techniques for using a metal truncheon. See Bugei.

JIUJITSU

See Jujutsu.

JIUJUTSU

See Jujutsu.

JOBAJUTSU

Essentially, the techniques of horsemanship. Though not necessarily taught in a systemized way, horsemanship is one of the arts of the bugei although very few warriors were ever mounted. Sometimes called Bajutsu.

JODO

"The way of the stick." It developed from the classical art of Jujutsu (the art of the stick), which was founded more than 400 years ago by Muso Gunnosuke. Jodo is the form of stickfighting currently practied. The short staff or long stick measures about four feet long, and its techniques include strikes, blocks, thrusts and parries among others. It is frequently used in training against the sword. Forms practice is the main method of teaching, and strict teaching guidelines are followed. See Jojutsu.

JOJUTSU

This combat art of stick fighting was developed in the sixteenth century, though stone sticks may have been used for self-defense many centuries earlier. Jojutso derives from Bojutsu, the art of the staff, which, since it was practiced by monks throughout Asia, has a decidedly Chinese flavor, though it reached its greatest development in Japan. Like Bojutsu, Jojutso was taught as part of the swordfighting curriculum in Iaijutsu and Kenjutsu schools. The style of Bojutsu taught by Izasa Ienao in the 14th century is the root of Jojutsu. The 12 techniques of his school form the basic techniques of Jojutsu. According to legend, Muso Gunnosuke, a highly proficient staff (bo) master, was defeated by the famous swordsman, Miyamoto Musashi. This embarrassed him so that he spent years in exile, training and preparing for another encounter with Miyamoto Musashi. During this period of reflection and training, Muso Gunnosuke developed the jo (stick) and adapted the basic techniques of the bo (staff) to it. Once he had perfected this art, he challenged the master swordsman again, this time defeating him. The modern study of the jo is known as Jodo. Jojutsu for police purposes is referred to as Keibosoho; police use a nightstick instead of a long stick or staff. See Bugei.

JUDO

"The Way of Gentleness" is a defensive martial art that was created in 1882. Like Aikido, this soft grappling style is based on the techniques of Jujutsu. Judo emphasizes upsetting an opponent's balance, using various throwing techniques. Also like Aikido, Judo techniques include those that control an attacker in additional to those that throw an attacker. However, Judo also relies on a wide variety of grappling techniques, including those to immobilize an attacker. Joint locking and strangulation techniques are taught. No weapons are practiced. The founder, Kano Jigoro, adapted what he felt were the valuable Jujutsu techniques, though he abhorred the brutality of Jujutsu. Students attempt to defeat the opponent as efficiently as possible thus fulfilling one of Kano Jigoro's concepts (the concept of maximum efficiency with minimum effort). While Judo uses the throws, strangulations and joint-locks of Jujutsu, the use of these techniques is strictly controlled, which distinguishes Judo the sport from Jujutsu the combat art. This fulfills the other of Kano Jigoro's concepts, the concept of mutual welfare and benefit. From 1889 on, Kano travelled throughout the world, promoting Judo. Though many people did not distinguish it from Jujutsu at first, Kano was vigorous in insisting on the distinctions. His was a gentle art. It was also, he said, "a training for life." Though many considered it an ideal sport for competition, or as a way to keep in shape, or as a method of self-defense, Kano felt it was a holistic art, used to improve mental, emotional and spiritual health, in addition to physical health. Though Kano discouraged

Fig 2.1: Judo practitioners.

67

competition, Judo has become more and more sport-oriented. The first world championship competition was held in 1956. Judo was made an Olympic sport in 1964. In 1980, the first women's world championship competition was held. Unlike other martial arts, there are no different schools and styles; Judo is Judo. It is taught through forms, which are prearranged series of throws, and randori, which is the equivalent of sparring. Shiai, or competition, is now extremely important to Judo practitioners. Because Judo is taught in a similar fashion all over the world, a clear sequence of instruction has been established. Breakfalls — that is, how to fall correctly so that injuries will not occur — are taught first. Because Judo is a form of clothed wrestling, clothing grips are essential. The basic clothing grips are taught once the student no longer fears falling. Correct stances are taught, then footwork and only then do students begin the study of Judo proper, including foot, leg and hip throws, ground techniques which include strangulations, locks, immobilizations and holds; and finally, vital point attacks are learned, in which strikes are directed at vulnerable parts of the body, though in competition locks are restricted and vital point attacks are never permitted.

JUJITSU
See Jujutsu.

JUJUTSU

A general name meaning "science of softness" that is applied to many schools of unarmed and hand-to-hand combat. The earliest schools were created during the twelfth through fourteenth centuries in Japan. The soft grappling style was intended to help disarmed soldiers to fight against still armed enemies. The basic principle was to defeat the enemy in any way possible, using the least amount of force necessary. Jujutsu emphasizes turning an attacker's own force against him or herself. The opponent is put off balance and immobilized. Jujutsu also emphasizes certain grappling moves and striking to vital areas. The proficient Jujutsu practitioner

is expected to know how to gauge the force of an opponent's attack and use that force against the opponent; know how to evade an attack; know how to use leverage against an opponent; and know how to attack in case the vulnerable areas of the opponent's body are not open to attack. Over the centuries, the basic techniques have been improved upon by many important martial artists. Techniques from Chinese and Okinawan martial arts systems have also been incorporated. Some schools use small weapons, but the techniques consist primarily of anatomical weapons, with some schools favoring hitting and kicking like Karate, and others favoring throws and groundwork like Judo. Samurai, in particular those without masters, established many schools of Jujutsu. From this unruly beginning, the style developed a disreputable quality. Ninja and peasants began to use the art, and so it was associated with non-noble individuals, which did not enhance its prestige. The art became more and more ruthless with dangerous, even fatal, results. Schools tested their efficiency in contests with other schools. These contests, though dangerous and even deadly, could enhance the status of a particular school or instructor, and also helped improve the techniques. The close combat methods used in the armed forces are taken from Jujutsu. These are schools of interest: Brazilian Jujutsu, Goshin Jujutsu, Gracie Jujutsu, Hakko-ryu, Hogu-jutsu, Ho Kusai-ryu, Kito-ryu, Koryo Katam Kushin-ryu, Sekiguchi ryu, Shin no Shindo-ryu, Shindo Yoshin-ryu, Sosuichi-ryu, Sosui Shitsu-ryu, Taijutsu, Takenouchi-ryu, Tanaka Goshin-jutsu, Tenjin Shin-Yo Jujutsu, Yawara, and Yoshin-ryu. See Bugei.

JUKEN-JUTSU

A martial art that developed in Japan after the introduction of the rifle. A proficient practitioner can use the bayonet to slash, hook, trap or block, but the primary technique is a simple thrust. Over time, this martial art developed into Jukendo. See Jukendo.

JUKENDO

The way of the bayonet, a sport with spiritual elements. Participants wear Kendo armor, and use a wooden rifle with a blunted tip to represent the bayonet. They attempt to score a thrusting attack on predetermined target areas. This martial art is based on Juken-jutsu.

JUN FAN

A school of Wing Chun Wushu created by Bruce Lee. He founded this school before his ideas were more fully realized in Jeet Kune Do. In Jun Fan, he attempted to make the stances and footwork more fluid while at the same time also more direct. He added kicks to fill in where his short range hand techniques could not work. This became a style of kickboxing. Though later he moved away from all codified, systematized martial arts, the elements of Lee's martial arts philosophy are already developed in Jun Fan. See Jeet Kune Do.

KABAROAN

A style of Kali. See Kali.

KAGE RYU

A school of Kenjutsu (swordfighting) founded by Aizu Iko (1452-1538). It became the basis of many other schools of swordfighting. Such kage or "shadow" schools emphasize the skill of perceiving what the attacker intends to do. Practitioners claimed that the attacker's expression and body movement could reflect his or her intentions as clearly as a mirror.

KAIKO

An early name for Kempo. See Kempo.

KAJUTSU

The techniques of gunnery and explosives, especially as used by the Ninja in Japan.

KAKUTO BUGEI

Term meaning "fighting martial arts." The phrase is given to a group of techniques involving the use of weapons. Unarmed techniques are not included. See Bugei.

KALARI PAYAT

An ancient Indian martial art, "the way of the field of battle," which incorporates empty hand techniques and weapons techniques, including the use of daggers, clubs and lances. According to legend, this is the same martial art that the Bodhidharma brought to China from India. It reached the height of its popularity in the 16th century but with the introduction of firearms into warfare, it, like other combat arts, lost most of its functional value. Now it serves as a means of self-defense and physical fitness, though elaborate etiquette is still demanded of the student. Techniques that are taught include controlled breathing, vital point attacks, plus calisthenics and other conditioning exercises. As in other martial arts that teach both weapons and empty-hand techniques, the practitioner first learns the use of weapons and then moves onto empty-hand techniques. Forms and prearranged sparring are used to improve skills. The student finally progresses to learning unarmed defense against an armed opponent.

KALI

This martial art of the southern Philippines is essentially the same as Arnis and Escrima, the two other major arts of the Philippines. It has existed since before the ninth century, but its modern form was greatly influenced by the arrival of the Spanish in the 16th century. As in other systems, Kali practitioners first learn to use weapons and adapt what they have learned to empty hand techniques. There are several methods of weapons use. One is "espada y daga," a kind of sword and knife fighting based on Spanish fighting methods. A wood stick and a dagger are usually used. The single stick method uses one stick about 30-inches long. The double stick method requires two sticks. Kicks are done with various parts of the leg as well as the foot. Arm and hand techniques include palm strikes and elbow strikes. When the Spanish authorities banned the practice of Kali early in the 18th century, it was practiced in secret and managed to flourish. Kali was brought to the United States, where it was called Escrima, in the early-20th century. It was not until 1964 when the first U.S. school opened. See Arnis. See Escrima.

KAPU LUILUA

A Hawaiian martial art that incorporated many Asian martial arts, relying on vital point attacks. According to historians, martial art schools were established throughout the Hawaiian islands, under the supervision of priests who specialized in martial arts. Most of the fighting techniques are lost, but one form of Kenpo comes from Hawaii. See Kenpo.

KARATE

The "art of the empty hand." This hard-style martial art takes some of its techniques from both Chinese and Japanese martial art systems. It is based on centuries old methods that use bare hands and feet, though weapons use is also part of the training. Karate weapons include nunchaku, which are flails, and tonfa, which are similar to nightsticks. Such weapons have traditional weapons forms that teach their use.

The origins of Karate began when the Chinese occupiers of Okinawa, one of the Ryukyu islands off the coast of Japan, forbade the natives from owning weapons of any kind. Later, Japanese occupiers enforced the same ban. Thus, fighting techniques were developed by Okinawan residents to help them defend themselves against troops, thieves and other rascals. The weapons ban explains why Karate weapons are so unusual; they are based on farming implements that could double as weapons when needed.

Originally, the combat arts of China were brought to other countries, including Okinawa, by settlers and itinerant monks and priests. Unarmed combat already existed in Okinawa, where it was called "te." Later, influenced by Chinese Wushu, te developed into an early form of Karate. The word "Karate" was first translated as "T'ang hand" or "China hand" to indicate its Chinese origin. In the 20th century, however, the founder of modern Karate, Funakoshi Gichin, changed the meaning of "Karate" by using a different set of characters. He advocated the translation "empty hand." Funakoshi was fundamental in spreading Karate from Okinawa to Japan and from there through

out the world. In the last few decades, Karate has become the most widely practiced of all Asian martial arts.

There are numerous schools and styles of Karate and many martial arts syles that are not Karate call themselves Karate for the name recognition. Students are graded and promoted on their execution of form, power, speed and accuracy, plus character, self-confidence and control. Karate, unlike arts such as Judo or Aikido, is not a grappling or wrestling art. It relies primarily on hand and leg strikes and blocks. Most styles use both circular and linear movements, but will emphasize one over the other. Beginners learn stances and basic punches, kicks and blocks, usually working solo. Then the student begins working with partners in prearranged sparring and free-style sparring to improve technique and timing. The large number of styles in Karate are basically divided into Okinawan and Japanese styles. The most widely practiced ones include American Freestyle, American Shaolin Kenpo, Chinese Goju, Chito ryu, Cuong Nhu, Full Contact, Full Nunchaku, Goju-ryu, Gossoko-ryu, Itato, Isshinryu, Isshin Shorinji, Karate-jutsu, Karate-shinto, Kenpo, Kenshikan, Kenshin-ryu, Koei-kan, Kobayashi-ryu, Kong Soo Do, Matsubayashi-ryu, Motojo, Nagamine, Nambu-do, Nippon Kenpo, Okinawa-te, Okinawan Goju-ryu, Okinawan Kenpo, Okinawan Shorin-ryu, Renbukan, Ryobu-kai, Sankukai, Seikidoho, Shindon Shizen-ryu, Shinto-ryu, Shito-ryu, Shobayashi-ryu, Shorei-ryu, Shoreiji-ryu, Shorin-ryu, Shorinji-ryu, Shorinji Kenpo, Shotokai, Shotokan, Shukokai, Tomari-te, Uechi-ryu, Wado-ryu and Washin ryu.

KARATE-DO

Style of Karate that combines fighting techniques and Zen Buddhist philosophy. Funakoshi Gichin, the founder of modern Karate, originally used this term to mean Karate as a way of life and a means for building character. Later, certain elements of philosophy were added that made Karate-do a discipline distinct from traditional Karate.

KARATE-JUTSU

In Okinawa, an early style of Karate, the style Funakoshi Gichin, the founder of modern Karate, brought to Japan. Only later did he drop the "jutsu" in favor of "do."

KARUMI-JUTSU

Techniques to lighten oneself for climbing, jumping and dodging. See Bugei.

KATORI RYU

A school of Iaijutsu (sword drawing art). This school is distinct from others because of its grip method. Many styles use a grip in which the thumb is held on the handguard. The Katori school, however, considers this dangerous, for an opponent could pull the scabbard off, unsheathing the blade and causing a wound. In Katori, the hand grips the lateral edge of handguard. The sword is drawn with a twisting action. This method also allows a longer reach, which is harder to block and parry.

In Karate, a school that uses four naginata (halberd) techniques that are considered the deadliest, most effective methods. It also teaches grappling methods and certain Ninjutsu techniques.

KATORI SHINTO RYU

A school of Kenjutsu (swordfighting) that incorporates other techniques from other schools, including weapons other than the sword. Founded in the early-15th century by Iizasa Choisai, it emphasizes the spiritual as well as the martial.

KAZEI RYU

A school of Jujutsu developed by Saka No Ueutamoro, using elements of the Koden-ryu style.

KELANTAN

A style of Bersilat that focuses on locks and grappling techniques.

KEMPO

A Chinese empty-hand martial art meaning "way of the fist," sometimes called "Chinese fist." Called Quan Fa or Chuan Fa in China, where it originated as early as the seventh century. By 1600, it had spread throughout Asia. It has been known by the names of Jiaodishu, Kaiko and Kenyu. It emphasizes self-defense and self-improvement similar to Karate, with a focus on Buddhist philosophy. Other arts are taught as well, including archery and sword fighting. Some of the schools of Kempo are Byakurenmonken, Hadako, Okinawan Kempo, and Shorinji Kempo.

KEN FAT

Same as Kempo. See Kempo.

KENBU

The art of sword dancing. This is not so much a martial art as a theatre performance. Dancers re-enact famous battles fought by legendary samurai; the samurai themselves took part in the performance. It is still widely practiced in Japan.

KENDO

This school of sword art, known as "the way of the sword," is a highly stylized sport derived from Kenjutsu (swordfighting). As in Judo, skill and technique is more important than size or strength. For this reason, men and women can compete against each other without any unfair advantage. Practitioners use the shinai, a bamboo sword. Sometimes the bokken, a wooden sword, is used in practice. The art developed most quickly after wearing the sword became illegal in Japan, when the practice of Kenjutsu or swordfighting was also declared illegal. Over time, Kendo grew into one of the most accepted martial disciplines. Often it is taught in conjunction with Iaido, which is the art of drawing the sword. Practitioners wear samurai dress, including the hakama and jacket, with protective equipment. The techniques taught are limited to a few blows and thrusts. The target area is restricted to the head, the side of the body, the throat and the wrists. Practitioners learn grips and stances, and are taught the importance of eye contact and the kiai, or shout. Forms are practiced, usually using a live blade. Some of the important schools of Kendo include Abe-ryu, Araki-ryu, Hikida-ryu, Hozan-ryu, Ken-no-michi, Kum Do, Nen-ryu, Oishi Shinkage ryu, Ono-ha-itto ryu, and Shinden Munen-ryu. See Armor. See Kenjutsu.

KENJUTSU

Kenjutsu (swordfighting) along with Iaijutsu, comprise the basic principles of swordsmanship. Kenjutsu is the offensive, aggressive art of the sword, whereas Iaijutsu is more defensive in nature. Kenjutsu is the forerunner of Kendo; it was outlawed in 1876, when wearing swords was banned. Schools of Kenjutsu flourished from the ninth century on. Ten centuries later, hundreds of Kenjutsu schools were still in operation. Masters and students continually attempted to improve their techniques, adapting the methods of other schools if they proved effective. As might be expected, numerous personal battles were fought among students and teachers of different schools, to prove whose method was superior. Of all the sword arts, Kenjutsu is the one that most closely resembles European fencing, emphasizing as it does cuts, thrusts and parries. There are also clear target areas. To wound an opponent in a non-target area was considered unworthy. Over time, Kenjutsu developed into the art of Kendo.

Today, only a few schools remain of the original hundreds. Some of the more important schools include Emmei-ryu, Gan-ryu, Hasegawa, Hokushin Itto-ryu, Itto-ryu, Jigen-ryu, Jikishen Kage-ryu, Kage-ryu, Kanemake-ryu, Katori-ryu, Kumi-tachi, Muji Shinden, Muto-ryu, Nakanishi-ha-itto-ryu, Nikaido-ryu, Okuyama-ryu, Shingen-ryu, Taisha-ryu, Tomita-ryu, Yagyu-ryu and Yoshin-ryu. See Kendo. See Bugei.

KENPO

A style of Karate developed in the West. It deviates from traditional Karate in several important respects. First, the terms used are in the language of the country in which it is being taught. Japanese is not the language of instruction. Also, students are encouraged to change and adapt the techniques. The school emphasizes vital point attacks using punches, strikes and kicks. Throws are also important. The art was originally introduced in Hawaii by James Mitose, near the start of World War II.

Later, William Chow, one of his students, adapted Mitose's approach and "Americanized" the art. Ed Parker, who is probably the most famous practitioner, was a student of Chow's and further adapted the methods so that they would prove practical in an actual fight. He created a logical organization for the basic Kenpo techniques, dividing them into eight categories, such as stances, blocks, punches and so on. These are taught in forms, in self-defense practice, and in free-style sparring.

KENSHIKAN

A style of Karate similar to Shito-ryu. It emphasizes forms practice and practical self-defense applications of techniques.

KENYU

A form of Kempo. See Kempo.

KEUPSO CHIRIGI

The Korean art of attacking vital points.

KIAIJUTSU

A martial art that uses the kiai, or shout, to harm opponents. Legends are told of martial artists who could injure or kill with a shout, but actually, very little is known about this art. It is clear that the kiai, and its origin, the chi, are essential to success in the martial arts.

KICKBOXING

An American fighting method that is not actually a martial art, though the boxers use both hands and feet, as in Karate. It combines Karate and Thai Boxing elements and because it is a realistic, practical method of fighting, it is a popular sport. The goal is to knock out the opponent, so strikes are delivered full force. In this way it is similar to Full Contact Karate.

KILIRADMAN

A style of Kali practiced by the Visayans in the Philippines.

KITO RYU

A Jujutsu school that was founded in the 17th or 18th century. The techniques and methods of this school were codified by the Buddhist priest Takuan. Though its origins are cloudy, it is an adaptation of a Jujutsu style to a "do" or "way of life" art form. The founder is unknown.

KNOCK-DOWN KARATE

See Full Contact Karate.

KOBAYASHI-RYU

An Okinawan school of the Shorin-Ryu style of Karate, one of three branches. Its name refers to its origins, which were believed to derive from Shaolin temple teachings.

KOBU-JUTSU

A style of Okinawan Karate. Its most striking characteristic is the enormous array of weapons it teaches, including the traditional Okinawan weapons, such as the nunchaku, plus variations on them, such as the one-tined sai. The style centers on the practice of forms as a method for perfecting techniques. Also known as Ryukyukobu-jutsu.

In Aikido, a group of self-defense techniques derived from Aikido methods.

KODEN RYU

A school of Jujutsu founded in the seventh century by Fujiwara Kamatori. Some techniques are thought to be from Korea.

KODOKAN JUDO

The so-called "authorized" version of Judo, which includes the teachings of unbalancing the opponent, breakfalls, throwing, grappling, self-defense and so on. See Judo. See Kodokan in the General section.

KOEI-KAN

A modern school of Karate founded by Onishi Eizo. As in other "do" arts, personal growth is encouraged. Techniques are taught through drills, forms and sparring, which is done full contact. Students are expected to adapt the techniques that best suit them, using those that work best for them and discarding those that do not work well.

KOGA-RYU

One of the two main styles of Ninjutsu. The other is Iga-ryu. See Ninjutsu.

KONG-SOO DO

A Korean martial art, meaning "empty hand." It is a style of Karate.

KOREAN KARATE

In the United States, a name given to Tae Kwon Do in its early years, before it reached its current popularity, to help potential students identify its purpose.

KORINDO

A school of Aikido created by Hirai, a follower of Ueshiba Morihei, the founder of Aikido. This school deals only with self-defense techniques.

KORYU AIKIDO

Also known as Koryu-goshin-no-kata, this is a strictly self-defense form of traditional Aikido founded by Nobuyoshi Higashi. It teaches the fifty most effective techniques of Jujutsu and Aikido.

KOSHI-NO-MAWARI

Original name for Tai Jutsu. See Tai Jutsu.

KRABI-KRABANG

The art of sword and staff fighting in Thailand. This weapons system is hundreds of years old. Its weapons are made of wood such as rattan. In contests, opponents attack and defend in turn, like prearranged or step sparring, but contact is frequently made. The art combines Chinese, Japanese and Indian martial arts techniques with indigenous Thai methods.

KUK SOOL WON

A contemporary Korean martial art that emphasizes the effectiveness of techniques over power. It blends methods of Chinese, Japanese, and Korean martial arts.

KUKI-SHIN RYU

A secret martial art practiced by ascetic monks. Ueshiba Morihei, the founder of Aikido, studied this art.

KUM DO

Korean art of the sword that follows Japanese Kendo, though it has its own associations and governing bodies. See Kendo.

KUMI-UCHI

A style of Sumo that could be applied against an opponent no matter how he or she was dressed. It concentrated on offensive technique which required strong legs and hips. Its main focus was on armor grappling. See Bugei.

KUNDAO

See Kuntao Silat.

KUNG FU

This term means "human effort" and is incorrectly applied to all Chinese martial arts, which are more correctly called "Wushu." Kung fu, when it means "martial art," refers to the hundreds of styles of martial arts in China, which are all different. Some are hard, linear styles emphasizing kicks and punches. Others are soft, circular styles that do not seem useful for combat. Some schools resemble Karate while others resemble modern dance. Grappling methods are generally not used, so Kung Fu arts are usually considered striking styles, but again, not all styles use strikes. Weapons are used in some schools, but not all. These run the gamut from sword to staff.

Kung Fu gained popularity in the 1960s and '70s because of Bruce Lee's movies and the David Carridine television show, "Kung Fu." In the decades since, it has lost some of its popularity. All Kung Fu schools teach stances, guards, plus attacking and defending methods. The schools are classified into Northern and Southern styles. Northern styles are thought to rely heavily on foot techniques and Southern styles are thought to rely heavily on hand techniques, though this is not necessarily the case. A further distinction is made between internal and external schools. The former emphasizes the inner force, chi, as well as vital points and philosophy. Such schools are characterized by defensive, soft, circular motion. External schools focus on force and speed. For many years, Chinese martial arts were not taught to non-Asians. By the 1960s, however, more and more Chinese teachers began teaching non-Asian students, though many of the arts remain secret today. See Wushu.

KUNG-LI

A rare Northern style of Chinese Wushu, it emphasizes low horse stances, which beginning students spend years learning to master.

KUNG SOOL

The art of archery in Korea. The Koreans always preferred the bow and arrow to the sword, and they were experts in mounted and foot archery. Kung Sool training is arduous. To warm up, the practitioner draws and releases the bow string without arrows over 300 times to improve stance and techniques. Then, the archer begins actual practice using arrows and a target. The archer shoots at least 1,000 arrows. The exercise is repeated every day. Eventually, the archer uses moving targets. Today, this is a style of sport archery instead of a combat art.

KUNTAO SILAT

A name given to a number of combat arts in Indonesia which have their origin in Chinese Wushu. They were mostly learned in the Chinese communities in Indonesia, under strict vows of secrecy. They are defensive techniques, which stress the circular, soft style, and are based, like many Chinese martial arts, on the movements of animals. The main teaching method consists of drills in stances, blocks, strikes, and kicks. All schools of Kuntao Silat are banned by the Indonesian government.

KUNTOW KUNG FU

See Kuntao Silat.

KUOSHU

A Chinese term meaning "national sport." It refers to all forms of Chinese marital arts. Also called Guosho. See Wushu.

KUSARIGAMA-JUTSU

A martial art that teaches the use of the kusarigama, a sickle with a ball and chain attached that is used as a weapon. See Bugei.

KWON BOP

Same as Kwonpup. See Kwonpup.

KWONPUP

A style of Korean empty hand fighting, similar to Tae Kwon Do but not the same.

KYOKUSHIN-KAI

A style of Karate based on power and strength, founded by Oyama Masutatsu in the 1950s. It was greatly influenced by Chinese Kempo and Goju-ryu Karate. Stances are natural, not forced or difficult, and techniques are performed in multiple combinations, as quickly as possible. Many of its techniques are not used in Karate, because they are dangerous, but are taught in this school because they are useful in a real fight. Students wear protective gear and engage in full-contact sparring to overcome the fear of being struck. The school emphasizes breathing exercises. Zen philosophy underlies its concepts. Breaking techniques are also emphasized. Before students can promote in rank, they must prove their ability to break boards.

KYUBA

The way of archery on horseback. This is an art that teaches both archery and horsemanship. See Kyudo.

KYUBA NO MICHI

The Way of Archery and Horsemanship, also called the Way of the Bow and Horse. See The Way of the Bow and Horse.

KYUDO

A style of classical archery that is an effective method of physical and mental training. Kyudo derived from Kyujutsu, the art of archery practiced for war. Kyudo is used in Zen training and emphasizes the unity of mind, bow and body. The Kyudo bow is more than seven feet long and is asymmetrical in design. Since arrows are three or more feet long, the equipment is cumbersome and the mechanics of shooting are difficult. Shooting

Fig 2.2 : Kyudo practitioner.

is divided into eight distinct stages, including holding, steadying and raising the bow, plus others. Because Kyudo emphasizes the spiritual, it also emphasizes the ritual of archery. The vibrating string is thought to have supernatural qualities that can drive evil spirits away. Special arrows are used in rituals and ceremonies. As with many "do" arts, it is the manner in which it is done that counts. See Kyujutsu. See Kyudo Techniques in the Forms and Techniques section.

KYUJUTSU

Classical archery as used in war. It was a primary art in feudal Japan, one that samurai needed to know as much as they needed to know sword fighting, for in battle, bow and arrow were used first, then sword and spear. When Kyujutsu is practiced on horseback, it is called Kyuba No Michi, the Way of the Bow and Horse. The bow and arrow have existed in Japan since the fifth century A.D., so it is an ancient art. The art became Kyudo after the end of the 16th century, when firearms made the bow and arrow no longer relevant to combat. Training required an archer to shoot hundreds of arrows each day. Unlike Kyudo, in which one kind of bow is used, the warrior who trained in Kyujutsu had to be able to handle many types of bows and arrows. See Kyudo. See Bugei.

LAMA KUNG FU

See Hop Gar.

LANGKA SILAT

A Malaysian style of Bersilat. See Bersilat.

LAU GAR

Founded by Lau Soam Ngan, one of the five original Fukien Shaolin Wushu styles. It uses middle range fighting techniques.

LEOPARD STYLE

A style of Wushu that relies on quick, pouncing movements. The ideal qualities of the leopard are captured, especially strength and offensive techniques. Practitioners display a great deal of feinting. Footwork and strategy are emphasized. Called Pao.

LETHWEI

A Burmese style of boxing, not truly a martial art. See Boxing, Burmese.

LI CHIA CHUAN

Same as Li Gar. See Li Gar.

LI GAR

A southern style of Wushu. One of the five original Fukien Shaolin styles. It is characterized by strong stances and techniques, including slapping, pushing and trapping techniques, and works best in the medium range. Emphasis is on mobility of stances and quick footwork. It is named for its founder Li Yao San. It is also called Li Chia.

LIAM I

Literally, "two instruments boxing," an internal method of Chinese boxing. It stresses the use of chi, or life force, plus upper body energy and double impact strikes, that is, simultaneous blows.

LIANGONG

A series of exercises designed to prevent and heal physical problems. These exercises focus on the neck, shoulder, back, hips, and legs and can also resolve internal disorders.

LIEN CHUAN

A Northern method of Chinese boxing.

LINTAN

See Bersilat.

LION ROAR

A style of Chinese Wushu founded during the Ming Dynasty. The monk Daidot was enlightened one day and fell to the ground, roaring like a lion. The style is the basis for Hop Gar. It is composed of eight fist techniques, eight stances (steps), eight finger or hand techniques, eight grips and eight kicks.

LIU-CHIA CHUAN

A Southern method of Chinese Boxing.

LO-HAN CHUAN

A style of Chinese Wushu that developed around the end of the fifth century A.D., meaning "Buddha style," or "Buddha's disciples." The style comes from the Shaolin tradition and it developed both Northern and Southern schools, which vary slightly in emphasis.

LONG BOXING

Term referring to those types of Chinese boxing that use long-range hand techniques. Also called long hand or long fist.

LUNG YING

See Dragon Style.

MA SOOL

A style of Korean archery performed on horseback. It was popular during the Koguryo kingdom. A Chinese short bow was used. When the Mongols under Genghis Khan attacked with armies of mounted archers, the Koreans quickly adopted these methods. The art died out when bow and arrow was no longer necessary in battle. It is no longer practiced even as a sport.

MALLA-KRIDA

A style of early Indian wrestling. See Wrestling, Indian.

MALLAVIDJA

See Science of Combat.

MALLAVIDY

See Science of Combat.

MALLAYUDDAH

A style of early Indian wrestling. See Wrestling, Indian.

MANIWA-NEN-RYU

A school of martial arts founded over 400 years ago, still in existence, which teaches Jujutsu, Kenjutsu and sickle techniques, but emphasizes resolving problems without fighting. It is primarily known for its techniques of using the sword to defend against archery.

MATSUBAYASHI-RYU

This school is one of three branches of Shorin-ryu, Okinawan Karate. Its name alludes to its origin in Shaolin temple styles.

MATSUMURA ORTHODOX

A minor branch of Shorin ryu Karate, this style has few adherents.

MEDAN

See Bersilat.

MEI HUA CHUAN

A Northern style of Wushu, literally "plum flower boxing." It was developed by Pai Chin Tou in the 17th century.

MEN OF STEALTH, THE

See Ninjutsu.

MI-TSUNG-I

A Northern style of Wushu, "lost track fighting," founded in the tenth century. As the name implies, practitioners engage in body shifting, make sudden changes in direction, and make quick and sudden turns, designed to confuse the opponent. The style uses both hard and soft techniques.

MIEN CHUAN

A Northern school of Chinese Wushu that emphasizes the soft, internal system.

MIND-BODY BOXING

Also called Form and Will Boxing. The idea is that thought and action are unified. It originated in the 17th century, founded by Ji Long Feng. A Northern school of Chinese Wushu, it emphasizes the internal method, but has a linear aspect. The philosophy is that the fight should end as quickly as it started. Direct techniques are used, with the striking weapon moving straight to the target. Five basic attacks are based on the Five Elements; the Five Elements correspond to body parts and fighting techniques. Three main hand methods are used: the closed fist, the open hand and the phoenix eye. It contains short forms, which are based on the Twelve Animals (dragon, tiger, monkey, horse, chicken, falcon, snake, tai bird, lizard, swallow, eagle and bear). The style also teaches the use of the knife and the sword.

Three levels of teaching exist. At the beginner level, one develops one's chi and the basic techniques. At the intermediate level, one begins to train the mind, which can defeat the enemy. At the advanced level, one begins to meditate, and to learn to anticipate the opponent.

Also goes by the names Hsing-i Chuan, Hsing-i lu ho chuan, I-chuan, Hsing yi, Xingyi quan. Three main schools exist, the Shansi, which is the original

and is relatively rare now; the Hopei, which is the most common; and the Honan. Each uses different forms and techniques.

MIZUNO SHINTO-RYU

A school of Iaijutsu (sword fighting) founded in the late-16th century. Sword fighting was combined with unarmed combat.

MO-CHIA CHUAN

A Southern method of Chinese boxing.

MOK GAR

A school of Wushu founded by Mok Ching Giu. It has strong kicks and is a short range school. It is one of the five original styles to come from the Fukien Shaolin temple.

MONKEY STYLE

A style of Wushu based on the characteristic movements of monkeys. According to legend, the founder, Kou-tze, was imprisoned. The gates were guarded by fighting monkeys whom he watched, then imitated. This style relies on tumbling, rolling techniques plus confusing footwork. The opponent's attack is deflected, and the practitioner uses feints and unpredictable movements to defeat the opponent. The style consists of five sets of exercises, each designed to develop a different skill. These exercises are named lost monkey, drunken monkey, tall or standing monkey, stone monkey, and wood monkey. According to the legend, this is because each monkey the founder watched had its own style. They show basic fundamentals such as self defense, broken rhythm, power and so on. A student is introduced to the most appropriate one of these. Not all five are taught to any one practitioner. Also called Tai Sing Rek Kwar or Ta Sheng Men.

MU TAU

A modern version of Pankration, Greek wrestling.

MUAI THAI

See Thai Boxing.

MUAY THAI BOXING

See Thai Boxing.

MUGAI RYU

A style of Kenjutsu (swordfighting) founded by Tsuji Mugai Gettan, a peasant, in the late-17th century. He taught the principles of Zen, plus an appreciation of the humanities.

MUJI SHINDEN

A school of Kenjutsu (swordfighting), meaning "of no abiding mind." The discipline stressed spirituality, not harming people.

MUKI BOXING

A style of Indian boxing, more than 300 years old. At one time, group fist fights were held.

MUSO JIKIDEN EISHIN-RYU

See Muso Jikiden-ryu.

MUSO JIKIDEN-RYU

A school of Iaijutsu (sword drawing art) founded in the 16th century. The name of the overall system created by Hojo Hayashizaki Jinsuke Shigenobu is Muso Shinden-ryu. After more than ten generations, the Muso Shinden-ryu and the Eishin-ryu split and are considered distinct styles. Throughout its history, when the teachings and techniques of the school were modified, the school took on a new name. It has been called Muso Jikiden Eishin-ryu and Muso Shinden-ryu Battojutsu. Now it is called Muso Shinden-ryu or Muso Jikiden-ryu. The perfection of technique is achieved through the practice of forms, of which there are many. The school is the origin of many other schools of Iaijutsu and Iaido.

MUSO RYU

See Muso Jikiden-ryu.

MUSO SHINDEN RYU

See Muso Jikiden-ryu.

MUSO SHINDEN RYU BATTOJUTSU

See Muso Jikiden-ryu.

MUSTI-YUDDAH

A style of Indian boxing.

NABAN

A style of Burmese wrestling, not really a martial art. See Wrestling, Burmese.

NABOOT

Techniques of long pole stick fighting.

NAGAO RYU

A school of Jujutsu founded in the 17th century by a samurai who taught a variety of non-noble weapons emphasizing combat effectiveness. He taught mostly commoners and peasants.

NAGINATA-DO

A classical Japanese martial art, the way of the naginata (halberd) is one of the most difficult martial arts to learn, but it is appreciated for teaching respect for traditional etiquette. It is also an effective method of spiritual training. Naginata-do is popular among women. Although the various schools and styles practice their own forms, a standard competition system has been developed. The target area is limited to the face, the top of the head, the forearms, chest or shins, similar to the target areas in Kendo. The schools of Naginata-do include Anzawa-ryu, Gassan-ryu, Hoshin-ryu, Masaki-ryu, Naginata-jutsu, Seni-ryu, Tendo-ryu, Tento-ryu, and Toda-ryu.

Fig 2.3 : Naginata-do practitioner.

NAGINATA-JUTSU

A martial art using the naginata (halberd). Combat methods were practiced in forms and sparring. It became popular for women, who used it to protect their homes from attack. They participated in contests with men, pitting the naginata against the sword. Eventually Naginata-jutsu became Naginata-do. See Naginata-do. See Bugei.

NAHA-TE

One of the original schools of Okinawan "te," the martial art that was the forerunner of Karate.

NAKAMURA-RYU

A style of Iaijutsu (swordfighting) in which the sword techniques are performed in a standing position only. Ordinarily, swordfighting is also taught from the seated and half-seated position as well.

NAMBU-DO

A style of Karate recently founded by Nambu Yoshinao, based on the principles of yin-yang and Tao, with emphasis on the interrelatedness of everything. Nambu-do discourages the idea of competition. Breathing, as in Ji gong, is emphasized.

NEI CHIA

Chinese term for internal method martial arts. See Internal Method.

NEN-RYU

A school of Kendo (sword art) founded in 1350. It was taught until the 18th century by the Higuchi family, but has since disappeared.

NGA MI PHAI

A Vietnamese style of Shaolin. See E-mei Shan Pai.

NINJUTSU

Legendary martial arts system of the Ninja, the assassins and spies of feudal Japan. It originated in the ninth century and flourished throughout the history of Japan, but especially so around the beginning of the 15th century. Ninjutsu embraces many martial techniques. The style is Japanese but it was influenced by Chinese methods. The Minamoto family relied on Ninjutsu to overthrow the rival Taira family. During a later period, the art and its practitioners became disreputable and were forced to leave the courts and warrior ranks and to live as farmers. Because of their function, the Ninja developed martial techniques with minimal equipment and developed a wide variety of skills. The most famous Ninja were from the Iga and Koga areas; thus derive Iga-ryu and Koga-ryu, the two most famous schools of Ninjutsu, though their methods are still relatively unknown. Training in Ninjutsu began at five- or six-years-old. Endurance, weapons, map making, common disguises, and techniques for escaping were all learned. Because of their skills, legend gives the Ninja magical powers. Using special equipment and techniques, they could climb walls and swim silently (even in armor). They used non-noble weapons, such as daggers, and poison. Like other martial arts, Ninjutsu was passed down from generation to generation through family networks. It is thought to have originated as a means for mountain families to defend themselves as a result of the interminable religious and territorial wars, especially during the feudal period. Ninjas were greatly feared and invariably tortured and killed when caught. In many ways, they were the exact opposite of the samurai. Ninjas did not stop at arson, sabotage or assassination. The practice was banned in the 17th century, but in recent years, interest in Ninjutsu techniques has revived. See Bugei.

NITEN-ICHI-RYU

School of Two Swords, created by Miyamoto Musashi. See Emmei-Ryu.

NIYUDDAH-KRIDE

A style of early Indian wrestling. See Wrestling, Indian.

NOROSHI-JUTSU

Signalling techniques. See Bugei.

NORTHERN SYSTEM

Refers to Wushu styles practiced in northern China, a belief that Northern styles are substantially different from Southern styles. Northern styles are thought to rely on leg techniques, as opposed to Southern system schools, which are thought to rely on hand techniques. An examination of Northern and Southern schools shows that this distinction cannot legitimately be made.

OGASAWARA-RYU

A school of Kyudo (archery). It conforms to the traditional rules of etiquette, which cover all areas of life. It teaches a scientific shooting method.

It is also the name of a school of Kyuba (archery and horsemanship) that developed in the 12th and

13th centuries and which is still practiced today. Archers ride on horses and as they gallop past targets, release their arrows.

OH DO KWAN

A school of Tae Kwon Do founded by Hong Hi Choi and Tae Hi Nam in Korea in 1953.

OISHI SHINKAGE-RYU

A Kendo (sword art) school in which students used a long bamboo sword held in one hand, rather than with the usual two-handed grip. The school used a hard, external method.

OKINAWA-TE

Name given to all early martial arts techniques coming from Okinawa. These were also called "tode." The "te" styles developed from Shaolin Wushu. The "te" styles are considered the forerunner of modern Karate.

OKINAWAN GOJU-RYU

A Karate school founded in the late-1920s, one of the four major styles of Okinawan Karate. The name means hard ("go") and soft ("ju"), the only Okinawan style that teaches both methods. There are fourteen forms, in which all the techniques are contained. See Goju-ryu.

OKINAWAN KENPO

A style of Okinawan Karate. See Kenpo.

OKINAWAN KEMPO

A style of Kempo. The two founders first learned Okinawa-te and then studied other styles, especially Chinese Wushu. They founded Okinawan Kempo on the belief that full-contact sparring was essential to true understanding and mastery of martial arts. Under the name of Okinawan Kempo-ryu Karate-do, the school continues to operate.

OKINAWAN SHORIN-RYU

A style of Karate. See Shorin-ryu.

OTSUBO-RYU

An school of Bajutsu (horsemanship). It developed in the 15th century and was devoted to techniques for fully armed and armored warriors.

PA CHI CHUAN

A Northern method of Chinese Wushu.

PA CHUAN

Also called Eight Fists, a basic southern method of Chinese Wushu.

PA KUA CHUAN

See Eight Trigram Boxing.

PAI CHANG

The name for Chinese wrestling during the Sung Dynasty. These traditional schools of Chinese martial arts were associated with secret societies and teach the use of weapons such as the Chinese sword. Such schools are called Phai in Vietnam.

PAI SCHOOLS

See Pai Chang.

PAKCHIGI

An informal system of Korean fighting in which the head is used to butt the enemy.

PAKWA

Same as Pakua. See Eight Trigram Boxing.

PANANANDATA

A style of Arnis practiced by the Tagalog tribes in the Philippines. Speed, timing and distancing are essential.

PANANTUKAN

A style of kickboxing popular in the Philippines.

PANCRASE

Same as Pankration. See Pankration.

PANGAI NOON

"Half-hard, half soft style." See Uechi-ryu Karate.

PANKRATION

A style of Greek wrestling that dates before the seventh century B.C. It used methods from earlier forms of boxing and wrestling, such as Classical Greek Wrestling. Kicking techniques were used in addition to throws and joint locks. It led to widely divergent fighting methods, including modern wrestling. Connections with Asian martial arts may exist, but these have not been established.

PAO

See Leopard Style.

PAO CHUOI CHUAN

Literally, "cannon striking boxing," a style of

Chinese Wushu that developed in the Hunan province in the tenth century.

PAO HAO

See White Crane Boxing.

PATH OF THE FIELD OF BATTLE, THE

See Kalari Payat.

PENCHAK-SILAT

See Pentjak Silat.

PENTJAK SILAT

A martial art of Indonesia and Malaysia. According to legend, a peasant woman in Sumatra invented it from watching animals as they fought. It was influenced by Indian and Chinese methods. Both hands and feet are used to strike, and vital point attacks are common. Strikes using all parts of the body are taught, as are stances, footwork, body shifting, and formal etiquette. Weapons used include the kris, which is practically the national weapon, plus sword, stick, chain and the tjabang, a weapon that is similar to the Okinawan sai. All styles of Pentjak Silat are based on the use of weapons and are not empty-hand styles, except in the sense that hand and foot techniques are also learned. More than four hundred schools exist, using Indonesian and Malaysian terminology. Though Pentjak-Silat was known for centuries, it surged in popularity during the late-1940s, when feelings against the Dutch colonists increased. Native interest in the martial arts quickened the development of the combat arts. The term Pentjak refers to the practice of forms, whereas Silat is more like free-sparring. One wishing to train must bring five specific gifts to a master and must be prepared to swear oaths of loyalty and secrecy on the Koran. Of the numerous styles, some are more important. In Sumatra, they are Pauh, Strelak, Lintow, and Kumango. In West Java, Tjimande, Tjikalong, Tjiandur, Mustika Kwitang, and Tjinkrik. In Central Java, Setia Hati, Perisai Sahkti, Tapak Suji, and in East Java, Perisai Diri. On Madura, Pamur is the style. In Bali, Bhakti Negara and Tridharma. Other styles include Bagalombangdua Bilas Silat, Baru Silat, Budoja Indonesia Matarm, Champaka Putih, Cikalong, Cimade, Delima, Eka Sentosa Setiti (also called "Essti"), Ende, Jokuk, Kendari Silat, Langka Tiga Silat, Paraiman Silat, Patai Silat, Persatrian Hati, Putmandi Silat, Sandang Silat, Serah, Silat Makassar, Sisemba Sulat, Sundra Silat, Tapu Silat, Tiger Silat, Tjampur, Tjatji, Tjinwaringin, Tunggal Hati, and Undukayam Silat.

PHAI

See Pai Chang.

PHAI SCHOOLS

See Pai Chang.

PHOENIX EYE

Called Fong Ngan in China, it is a style of Wushu named after the phoenix eye fist that is its main hand technique. The fist is made with one knuckle protruding; with the force of the blow focused on this area, the phoenix eye fist can be quite injurious. Because the system relies on hand techniques, it teaches close-in fighting and many evasive techniques.

POC KHEK

A modern form of Wushu. Practiced mostly in Malaysia, it is based on the internal methods of Tai Chi Chuan, which is called Thau Khek. It is combined with the traditional Malaysian martial art teachings found in Kun-Tao.

POKULAN

See Pukulan.

PRAYING MANTIS

A northern Chinese Wushu system founded by the martial artist Wong Long near the end of the Ming Dynasty. It consists of lightning quick techniques. Several styles have developed, but they all rely on a ferocious characteristic technique, the mantis hand, which makes a grabbing motion using the power of the wrist and forearm. The style adapted many of the techniques of Hung Gar and of Monkey style. Like the praying mantis the style is named for, the practitioner attempts to be quick, wary and alert. The quick, balanced footwork stems from Wong Long's observation of monkeys. The style uses both straight and circular techniques. Four important hand methods are used: the mantis claw, the downward palm strike, the open hand grab and the upward or high block. The original style is called "seven stars," for the footwork pattern that resembles a constellation. The hands are shaped like hooks and strike quickly and forcefully. The style is also called Chi Hsing Tang Lang (or Tong Lung) and Mei Hwa Tang Lang, that is, plum flower praying mantis. Two other main styles are taught, Six Harmonies and Eight Steps. Both are closer to the internal method and both rely on open hand techniques more than the characteristic hooked hand. The six harmonies style is so named because its founder, Wei San, thought that the six elements of the body (eyes, hands, body, spirit, chi and soul) should work together to feel the opponent's next movement. The eight steps style, developed by Chun Hua Lung, places more emphasis on footwork and close range fighting. The most recent development is Tai Chi Praying Mantis, called Tai Mantis. The techniques are adapted to the practitioner's size, ability and skill. Big people use power techniques; small people use speed techniques.

PRAYING MANTIS, SOUTHERN

This style developed during the Ming Dynasty. It was originally called "Jew Gar" or "royal family Wushu." The name was changed when the Ching Dynasty came to power and persecuted practitioners of Jew Gar. It was thought that the name change would confuse the enemies. It bears no resemblance to the Northern style of Praying Mantis. An unremitting attack until the opponent gives up characterizes this style. Speed is essential; the stances change little and the opponent is given no opportunity to strike. Palm strikes, vital point attacks and the phoenix eye fist are heavily relied on.

PRISAI SAKTI

An Indonesian martial art, unusual in its connection to Christianity as opposed to eastern philosophy. Its name, "Holy Shield," emphasizes this connection.

PUKULAN

An Indonesian term that describes indigineous Indonesian martial arts. Essentially the same as Pentjak Silat. See Pentjak Silat.

QI GONG

See Ji Gong.

QUAN-FA

See Kempo.

QUAN-FU

Same as Kung fu. See Wushu.

QUANSHU

See Chinese Fist. See Kempo.

QWAN-KI-DO

Literally, "the way of the fist and the energy." This Vietnamese martial art is similar to Karate. It was founded by Pham Xuan Tong, who taught empty-hand methods plus the Vietnamese sword. The Taoist philosophy underpinning is considered important. Meditation, forms, and breathing are all emphasized. France has the most students who follow this system.

RENBUKAI

A Karate style that was founded by a group of martial artists from various styles, who at first gathered simply to discuss the martial arts. After some years, their discussions developed into a martial art style that exists predominately in Japan, though its founders were Korean. It is a full contact school.

ROKUSHAKUBO

An Okinawan Karate school that teaches halberd art. The school is based on Chinese principles.

RYUGO-RYU

An early Japanese martial art school that taught the lance and the halberd.

RYUBO-KAI

A style of Karate that practices Jujutsu techniques as well. The founder, Konishi Yasuhiro, practiced Okinawa-te and created this system over a period of time in the 1920s and 1930s. Konishi learned Karate from Funakoshi Gichin, Chojun Miyagi and others. In addition he studied Aikido under Ueshiba Morihei as well.

RYUKYUKOBU JUTSU

See Kobujutsu.

SADO MU SOOL

A Korean martial art that may have been practiced as early as 2000 B.C. Its weapons were of the stone variety. During this period, martial arts contests between the tribes took place during festivals each spring and autumn. Though stone weapons gave way to iron and steel weapons, this martial art continued to be practiced by a small number of artists. In the tenth century, the use of weapons was outlawed, which increased interest in unarmed combat methods. Sado Mu Sool also increased in popularity when the Japanese invaded in 1592. For a long time, it was taught only in monasteries. It developed into Koong Joong Mu, then became Kuk Sool Won.

SAI-JUTSU

The art of using the sai, a special dagger with tines. It is used defensively to trap a sword or to block an attack. These weapons are usually used in pairs. Training in the art of the sai also improves the practitioner's upper body strength.

SAIDE

Another name for Kenjutsu. See Kenjutsu.

SAMBO

A modern style of Russian wrestling that was influenced by Eastern wrestling and other sports. The goal is to immobilize the opponent through a jointlock. Throws and takedown techniques are also important. Anatoly Kharlampfiev devised its ground rules. He thought of Sambo as a method of empty hand self-defense rather than the sport it has become. It is also called Cambo or Sombo.

SANDA

A form of kickboxing popular in China. Free-style fighting is emphasized. It is performed on a platform; if one participant is knocked off, the opponent is awarded five points. Kicks below the belt count; spinning techniques are especially prized. The main kick is the front leg side kick. The rules are similar to kickboxing, with no groin strikes or throat strikes permitted, while almost anything else is acceptable.

SANG MOO KWAN

See Song Moo Kwan.

SASUMATA-JUTSU

Techniques of using the forked staff to hold a person. See Bugei.

SAVATE

A French style of full-contact, empty-hand fighting. It developed as a method of streetfighting adopted from Asian martial arts. In the 19th century, the system caught the attention of the upper classes and soon became a popular method of self-defense. Rank is indicated by a colored band worn on the gloves. Savate has been modified over the years and now includes modern boxing techniques with kicking techniques.

SCHOOL OF THE GREEN DRAGON, THE

A Vietnamese martial art called Thanh Long.

SCHOOL OF THE WAY OF HARMONY, THE

See Wado-ryu.

SCIENCE OF COMBAT

A style of Indian wrestling performed by a caste of professional wrestlers. It is also called Mallavidya or Vajramushti. It was developed during the tenth century and has a religious significance. A weapon, similar to brass knuckles, is worn on the right hand to improve the power of a blow. Contests are brutal and participants are sometimes killed. Some of the techniques were adapted by Kalari Payat. It is still practiced in India.

SCIENCE OF CONCORD

See Wa-jutsu.

SCIENCE OF THE EIGHT LIMBS

See Thai Boxing.

SCIENCE OF SOFTNESS, THE

See Jujutsu.

SEIKIDOJO

A full-contact Karate style with elements of both Japanese and Okinawan Karate.

SEKIGUCHI-RYU

A school of Jujutsu founded by Sekiguchi Ujishin in the 17th century, based upon the ideals of correct samurai conduct.

SENI-RYU

An ancient school of naginata (halberd), a weapon used mostly by women. See Naginata-jutsu.

SENJO-JUTSU

Techniques for army strategy. See Bugei.

SERAK

A style of Pentjak Silat, an Indonesian martial art. Very similar to Chinese Kempo in its hand techniques.

SETIA-HATI TERATE

An Indonesian style of Pentjak Silat, originally a secret art, developed by monks who emphasized ilmu, or life energy, which is similar to chi.

SHADOW WARRIORS, THE

See Ninjutsu.

SHADOWS OF DARKNESS, THE

See Ninjutsu.

SHANG-PU

Name for Chinese wrestling in the T'ang Dynasty. See Wrestling, Chinese.

SHAOLIN TEMPLE BOXING

Originally a specific style of Chinese Boxing, but now the term refers to all styles that are part of the external system. Many boxing styles developed from this original style, which is thought by some to be the one that Bodhidharma brought with him from India. Sometimes called Shaolin Chuan. The original style is often thought to have been Chang Chuan or a forerunner of it. See Long Fist, Lohan Chuan, Chin'na.

SHIN NO SHINDO-RYU

A school of Jujutsu founded during the Tokugawa era (1600-1867). It emphasized joint locks, and was based on principles of suppleness and flexibility.

SHINAI-GEIKO

An 18th century school of Kenjutsu (swordfighting) that used the shinai, or bamboo sword, which was adopted by Kendo. Routine forms practice was de-emphasized and sparring with partners was emphasized. This practice was also adopted by Kendo.

SHINDEN FUDO-RYU

A school that taught lance and axe techniques as well as the naginata (halberd). It was founded in the 15th century, but the techniques were never revealed.

SHINDO MUSO-RYU

A school founded by Muso Gunnosuke Katsuyoshi in the late-16th century. It taught staff techniques. Twelve basic techniques are demonstrated in 64 forms. See Jojutsu. See Jodo.

SHINDO ROKUGO-RYU

A school of Aikido, founded by Noguchi Senryuken, which practices self-defense techniques only.

SHITO RYU

An Okinawan Karate style founded by Mabuni Kenwa. He combined the methods of Naha-te and Shuri-te, two Okinawan pre-Karate systems, into one system.

SHOBAYASHI RYU

One of three branches of the famous Shorin-ryu style of Karate named after the Shaolin temple style from which it ultimately derived.

SHOOTFIGHTING

A modern fighting method that combines Thai boxing techniques with Judo grappling techniques.

SHOOTKICKING

A form of kickboxing that incorporates some wrestling moves.

SHOOTWRESTLING

A form of grappling that includes the use of kicks.

SHOREI-RYU

An Okinawan Karate style. A Chinese influence is evident in the use of the traditional five animals whose qualities and actions the Shorei-ryu practitioner strives to emulate. The animal actions include striking, clawing, kicking, jumping, and so on. In addition, traditional Okinawan weapons are taught including the bo (staff), sai (dagger), nunchaku (flail), tonfa (stick), and kama (sickle). The school is unusual in that it recognizes almost twenty different stances. The school encourages the study of philosophy and classical martial arts texts.

SHOREIJI RYU

A style of Okinawan Karate based on schools of southern Chinese Wushu.

SHORIN RYU

One of the oldest original Okinawan Karate styles, literally "Shaolin way." It developed three branches: Shobayshi-ryu, Kobayashi-ryu and Matsubayashi-ryu. A fourth branch, called Matsumura Orthodox, is rarely practiced. The name refers to the Shaolin temple, which is considered its place of origin. This school emphasizes the practice of forms over all other methods of training.

SHORINJI KEMPO

A modern school of Karate created by So Doshin based on Karate, Aikido and Judo methods. The name means Shaolin Kempo, or Shaolin Chinese Fist, because the founder studied martial arts in China. The founder says the forms and techniques are all based on the traditional Shaolin teachings. Later So Doshin learned more about Kempo. The school teaches the unity of mind and body, and Buddhist philosophy informs the school. It is this combination of religion, philosophy and martial art that makes Shorinji Kempo a religious sect. The techniques include body shifting in addition to blocks and strikes. Vital point attacks are also taught. The focus is on defense. Students are taught to evade; thus the emphasis on displacement and body shifting. There are at least a million members throughout Japan and hundreds of branches exist in other countries. In the 1970s, Japanese courts forced So Doshin to change the name of his school. It is now called Nippon Shorinji Kempo.

SHOSHO RYU

A style of classic Jujutsu that developed from the teachings of the Koden-ryu, a seventh century school.

SHORINJI-RYU

A Japanese style of Karate with significant Chinese influence.

SHOTOKAI

Style of Shotokan Karate, created by one of the sons of Funakoshi Gichin, the father of modern Karate. The school emphasizes the Karate as a way of living, even an art of living. Time is spent trying to achieve various mental states of calmness and awareness.

SHOTOKAN

The "authorized" Japanese style of Karate, founded by Funakoshi Gichin, the father of modern Karate. When he combined some of the Okinawan systems of empty hand fighting into one system of Karate, his students called it Shotokan, Shoto being a pseudonym Funakoshi had adopted. Although Funakoshi never finished adapting and developing his form of empty-hand fighting, it has, since his death, become more rigidly codified. The essence of the teaching philosophy is to master a few techniques completely, by training with dedication. An incomplete understanding of numerous techniques is discouraged. See Karate.

SHOUBO

An ancient Chinese art of shadow boxing.

SHUAI-CHIAO

In China, the contemporary name for wrestling, though Chinese wrestling itself goes back nearly three thousand years. It resembles both Karate and Judo, for it uses both striking and grappling methods. It was similar to archery in importance to the classical warrior, and, exported to Japan, was a powerful influence on the development of Jujutsu.

SHUAI-GO

A style of Chinese wrestling popular during the Ming and Ching Dynasties. It may have influenced the development of Jujutsu.

SHUI LI FU

See Choy Li Fut.

SHUKOKAI

A style of Karate called "the way for all." The style emphasizes speed, agility and movement, and its techniques are adapted to suit this focus. The school was founded in 1948 by Tani Chojiri, and it is based on the Goju-ryu school. Most techniques are delivered in a direct, linear manner. Later teachers developed its artistic potential.

SHURIKEN-JUTSU

The art of the throwing weapon. See Bugei.

SILA-BUAH

See Bersilat.

SILA-PULAT

See Bersilat.

SILAMBAM

An Indian martial art using sticks and staffs.

SILAT-BUAH

See Bersilat.

SILAT-PULAT

See Bersilat.

SINAWALLI ESCRIMA

A style of Escrima (also called Arnis) practiced by two participants. Each has one or two Escrima sticks. Instead of direct strikes and blocks, Sinawalli emphasizes more circular blocking and attacking.

SIU LUM

A term used in Canton meaning "Shaolin." It refers to a specific style of Wushu, not just to the Shaolin temple. This internal method relies on jabs and distracting techniques.

SIX HARMONIES STYLE

See Praying Mantis.

SNAKE STYLE

A form of Wushu emphasizing the animal qualities of grappling and the development of chi, or life energy.

SODEGARAMI-JUTSU

The techniques for using the sodegarami, a barbed pole. See Bugei.

SOJUTSU

Lance or spear fighting techniques. See Bugei.

SOMBO

See Sambo.

SONG MOO KWAN

A school of Tae Kwon Do founded by Byung Chik Ro in Korea in 1953. Also called Sang Moo Kwan.

SOSUICHI-RYU

A school of Jujutsu founded in the mid-17th century. The name means "school of pure water." It followed the techniques and teachings of Takenouchi-ryu. See Takenouchi-ryu.

SOUTHERN SYSTEMS

See Northern Systems.

SPLASHING HANDS

A style of Wushu that combines characteristic Wushu techniques with streetfighting methods.

SSI-REUM

See Cireum.

STEALERS IN, THE

See Ninjutsu.

STICKBOXING

A style of Escrima and Jeet Kune Do using various kicks, hand and arm techniques, locks and takedowns. Each opponent is also armed with a stick.

SUBAK

An ancient Korean martial art, the forerunner of modern Tae Kwon Do. It seems to have reached its greatest development and level of achievement during the 12th century. Eventually it was introduced to Okinawa. In Korea, those interested in pursuing government careers learned Subak, as it was one of the subjects on the examination. During the Yi Dynasty, the art lost popularity and became a sport and entertainment for the public. Because Subak was frequently suppressed, it was studied in secret and passed from family member to family member.

Also called Soo Bahk Do, which survives to the present.

SUIEI-JUTSU

A technique of swimming and even fighting in water while in armor. See Bugei.

SUIJOHOKO-JUTSU

A technique for crossing water. See Bugei.

SUMAI

The original name for Sumo, meaning "struggle." This was the combat form of the great wrestling art.

SUMO

A style of Japanese wrestling which is possibly derived from Korean or Mongolian wrestling. Originally a Shinto divination rite, it is still performed during festivals as a religious ritual. In this respect, it is over one thousand years old. When used in religious ceremony, it is called Shinji-zumo or "god-service Sumo." A children's wrestling contest is also performed during festivals. An ancient Japanese proverb says that a crying child will thrive, and in children's wrestling contests, the first child to cry wins. Sometimes a ring and other sumo accouterments are supplied. Sumo has also been practiced by women, but this was outlawed as being lewd and immoral.

In Sumo itself, which has only been practiced as a martial art since the late-17th century, the goal is to force the opponent out of the ring by using throws and holds. A wrestler can also win if he forces the opponent to touch the ground with any part of his body other than his feet. Each participant grips the opponent's belt. Often, contests last no more than a few seconds. There are no weight limits, so wrestlers tend to be of gigantic size. Great ritual and ceremony surrounds each Sumo contest. In the pre-contest ring ceremony, referees consecrate the ring, asking for the blessing of the gods. Wrestlers are presented in a special ceremony and special events mark the close of each contest day. There are about one thousand professional Sumo wrestlers today, ranked in eleven different levels. Ranks are won through contest; six tournaments are held each year.

TA CHENG CHUAN

A style of Chinese Wushu meaning "great achievement." Founded by Wang Yu Seng, this school concentrates mostly on sparring. It combines the methods of the Mind-Body school with others.

TA SHENG

See Hou Chuan.

TACHI GAKE

A method of drawing the sword, considered the forerunner of Iaijutsu.

TACHI UCHI SHIA

Earliest known systematic method of sword fighting in Japan.

TAE KWON

A style of Korean empty hand fighting similar to Tae Kwon Do, but not the same.

TAE KWON DO

The Korean "art of hand and foot fighting." The term "tae" refers to the foot and the low area; "kwon" refers to the hand and the middle area, and "do" refers to the mind and the high area. In the United States, it was called Korean Karate for a number of years, since it uses many techniques similar to Karate, which is a more widely recognized art. The style represents a way of life as well as a method of self-defense. The development of the student's mental, ethical and spiritual nature is important.

Techniques include strikes using the hand in various positions, plus a wide variety of kicking techniques. Throwing and takedowns are important

Fig. 2.4 : Sumo wrestlers.

in some schools. Correct breathing is essential. Tae Kwon Do also emphasizes breaking techniques and is best known for its showy high jumping or flying kicks. Basically a kicking art, with a wider variety of kicks than most martial arts, many kicks are aimed at high targets so flexibility and leg strength are important.

Tae Kwon Do was created in 1955 from the old Korean training system of martial arts, called Subak. This style of combat was eventually taught to the Hwarang, a group of noble youths, where it developed into Hwarang-do. Under the Japanese occupation in the early- 20th century, the study of Korean martial arts was banned. Karate and Kempo were allowed and this influenced the development of Tae Kwon Do. It comprises the linear methods of striking common to Karate with the circular movements of Wushu, plus the all-important Korean kicking techniques. General Choi is generally given credit as the father of Tae Kwon Do, for he led the drive to consolidate the various styles of Korean martial arts and he systematized and codified the techniques and forms of Tae Kwon Do. Jhoon Rhee is the martial arts master who introduced Tae Kwon Do to the United States. Tae Kwon Do, Tang Soo Do and Hapkido are the major martial arts in Korea. Three important schools of Tae Kwon Do that developed in Korea are Ji Do Kwan, Oh Do Kwan and Song Moo Kwan. See Hwarang-do. See Subak.

TAE KWON PUP

A style of Korean empty hand fighting similar to Tae Kwon Do, but not the same.

TAE KYON

Also spelled Tae Kyun, it is the same as Subak. See Subak.

TAI CHI

See Tai Chi Chuan.

TAI CHI CHUAN

This name means "grand ultimate fist." Tai Chi is one of the oldest martial arts in the world. It is so old that its origins are lost. Little is known about its early history, though its foundation is credited to the Taoist Chang San Feng (Chang Zhangfeng) more than eight hundred years ago. This soft style originated in China. It consists of slow, connected movements that are practiced to reduce tension, to slow breathing and to clear the mind. Moving correctly and allowing the chi to circulate freely is the goal. Students learn to yield so that the attacker is overcome by his or her own force. Tai Chi also has weapons, principally a double-edged straight sword. It is a method for achieving physical fitness and serenity of mind. It is not ordinarily regarded as a practical self-defense system, though the movements have self-defense applications, and practitioners can achieve great power in their techniques.

In China, it is very popular. It is practiced by individuals and groups. Chen is the original style, which indicates to some historians that the Chen family in the Hunan province must have developed it. Other important schools included Yang, which developed directly from Chen and is the most widespread; Wu and Sun, which derived from Yang style, plus Cheng, a more philosophical version. Fu, practiced mostly in China, is less well-known. Others include Li, Hao and Hsu.

The underlying theory of Tai Chi is that the mind, body and spirit must be unified for wholeness and complete health. Opponents can be people, but also illness of mental or physical origin. All must be combatted. The art is practiced alone in forms, and with partners. The forms include the famous Long Form, which can take more than half an hour to complete, and the Short Form, a modified version that can be performed in less than ten minutes. The principle of yin-yang is important, and a complete understanding of such harmony is emphasized. Its original concepts are still intact: it teaches continuous movement, relaxation, solid stances, a straight body and the movement of chi from inside the body to outside. Each arm protects half the body and the hands never reach farther forward than the toes. Tai Chi is one of the five Chinese accomplishments thought to make a superior person, along with painting, poetry, calligraphy, and music. Breathing exercises for health, Ji Gong, are often taught with Tai Chi. See Ji Gong.

TAI-JUTSU

A method of empty-hand self-defense. It is thought to be extremely old, perhaps the forerunner of all others, including Jujutsu. Ninja practiced some of these methods, and in the 16th century, a samurai modified the system, but its original teachings are unknown.

TAI MANTIS

A style of Chinese Wushu that combines the techniques and methods of Tai Chi Chuan with Praying Mantis styles. It is the most recent Praying Mantis style to develop. It is mostly defensive, forcing the opponent to strike and commit him or herself. The practitioner then deflects the blow and delivers a more powerful counterattack.

TAI SING PEKWAR

See Monkey Style.

TAIHO-JUTSU

Japanese police method to restrain offenders. It was created in 1947, using the most effective techniques of the major martial arts. This system is constantly adapted to deal with new conditions of streetfighting. The chief weapon is the keibo, a short police baton.

TAIJI QUAN

See Tai Chi Chuan.

TAKENOUCHI-RYU

A school of Jujutsu, which used some weapons, principally the naginata (halberd) and the short sword. It also emphasized close range methods of attack and defense with short daggers, plus unarmed methods of defense, including immobilizations by tying up the enemy. It included grappling and even Sumo techniques. The school was founded in 1532 by Takenouchi Hisamori, who was allegedly taught by the unidentified ghost of a samurai. About a quarter of the school's techniques have survived, and it influenced other schools of Jujutsu.

TAKISHIMA RYU

A school that taught the art of shooting; gunnery techniques.

TANDOKU RENSHU

A style of Judo training that relies only on grappling and groundwork techniques and uses no striking techniques.

TANG LANG

See Praying Mantis.

TANG SOO

An early empty hand martial art in Korea. It is also called "Tang Hand," or "Chinese Hand," indicative of the influence of Chinese martial arts, in particular Kempo. Also called Tang Su.

TANG SOO DO

A modern Korean martial art with a forerunner in Subak, the ancient Korean martial art. Tang Soo Do means "the art of the knife hand" or "the way of the Chinese hand." It contains characteristics of Chinese internal methods and Japanese striking styles. Founded by Kee Hwang, a Subak practitioner.

TANG SOO DO MOO DUK KWAN

A school of Tang Soo Do emphasizing the "way" aspect of the martial arts, not the physical or sport aspect.

TAO YIN

Little is known about this art except that it included Ji Gong breathing exercises, which are now part of Tai Chi Chuan.

TAN SHENG MEN

See Monkey Style.

TEGUMI

An style of Okinawan wrestling with few rules. Like Sumo, participants grapple with each other and try to push each other down.

TENDO-RYU

A school of naginata (halberd). It is one of the three modern art or "do" schools of the naginata. The other two are Toda Buko and Jikiden Kage ryu. It emphasizes realistic fighting situations.

TENJIN SHIN-YO

A school of Jujutsu based on methods of holding and vital point attacking. The founder, Yanagi

Sekizai Minamoto no Masatari (later known as Iso Mataemon), had thousands of students. The school also taught resuscitation skills. The founder of Judo, Kano Jigoro, studied this method. Also called Tenshin Shin-yo ryu.

TENSHIN SHIN-YO RYU

See Tenjin Shin-yo ryu.

TERELAK

A style of Bersilat. Breathing is stressed and muscular strength and power are necessary to perform its techniques.

TETSUBO-JUTSU

Techniques for using the iron staff. See Bugei.

THAI BOXING

Sometimes called Muay Thai Boxing or Thai Kickboxing, dating from the mid-16th century. It is best known for its shin strikes, which participants train for by kicking trees. Kicks are of primary importance. It is so difficult and dangerous that few boxers last more than four or five years. There are no forms. Practitioners learn about thirty basic techniques, mostly practiced by sparring. At one time, fighters would wrap their arms with bandages embedded with ground glass to cause greater damage to the opponent. In formal competition today, groin protectors and gloves are mandatory. It has an immense following in Thailand and Japan. It is called "the science of the eight limbs," for the successful fighter uses hands, elbows, feet, and knees.

Fig. 2.5 : Thai boxers.

THAING

A Burmese style of self-defense. There are nine major styles, each confined to one major ethnic group. Each style teaches the art differently. Though hundreds of years old, it was driven underground during the British occupation. During the later Japanese occupation, Thaing was nationally organized and systematized. Thaing is sometimes referred to as Bando, but that is only the biggest school.

TIBETAN WHITE CRANE

See White Crane.

TIEN GUNN

Literally, "celestial stem." The celestial stem refers to the body and its connection with higher planes. The school advocates exercises for health and self-defense adopted from Eight Trigram Boxing and Mind-Body Boxing.

TIGER CLAW

A style of Wushu. See Tiger Style.

TIGER SILAT

A style of Pentjak Silat practiced in Sumatra, based on the movements of the tiger. Crouching stances characterize the style.

TIGER STYLE

A style of Wushu emphasizing offensive techniques and power. There are three Tiger schools — red, white, and black — each emphasizing slightly different techniques and practice.

TIMBEI

An Okinawan martial art that taught the use of dagger and shield.

TODA BUKO RYU

A school of naginata (halberd). It is one of three modern art or "do" schools of naginata, a weapon used primarily by women.

TOMARI-TE

An ancient Okinawan martial art that is the forerunner of modern Karate.

TOMIKI AIKIDO

A school of Aikido that encourages competition. Unlike Ueshiba Morihei, the founder of Aikido, Tomiki thought competition in Aikido would create greater participation. Forms competition is done with partners, so that coordinated movement can be judged. Sparring competitions of various kinds also exist. In other respects, Tomiki Aikido adheres to the same principles and teaches the same techniques as traditional Aikido. See Tournaments in the General section.

TORITE-KOGUSOKU

See Kogusoku-jutsu.

TOSHU-KAKUTO

A martial art similar to Taiho-jutsu, a style that is used by the Japanese police. It focuses mostly on close range fighting techniques and is taught primarily to the Japanese military.

TOSHU-KAKUTO-KYOHAN TAIKEI

Same as Toshu-Kakuto. See Toshu-Kakuto.

TSAI-CHIA CHUAN

A Southern method of Chinese Boxing.

TSAI LI FU CHUAN

A Southern method of Chinese Boxing.

TSUI PA HSIEN

See Eight Drunken Immortals.

TUAN CHUAN

A style of short hand boxing, of which numerous schools exist.

TUNG PI

A style of Northern Wushu that is extremely popular. It focuses on quick and powerful techniques, with a relaxed upper body until the moment of impact. It relies on hand techniques, notably the backhand strike, the palm strike and the corkscrew punch. It is also called Tung Bi.

TWO SWORD SCHOOL

See Emmei-ryu.

TZU JAN MEN

A style of Southern Chinese Wushu, called "spontaneous" or "natural" boxing. The training is arduous and difficult, but the goal is to achieve a relaxed, natural technique.

TZU MEN

See Tzu Jan Men.

UCHI-NE

Techniques of throwing arrows by hand. See Bugei.

UECHI-RYU

A modern Okinawan style of Karate founded by Uechi Kanbum. He combined elements of the Pangai Noon (also called Pangen-nu) style with the techniques of the Phoenix Eye school. The style also incorporated the characteristics of animals, typical of Chinese Wushu, which the founder had studied. As in Pangai Noon, the style relies on circular motions plus the single knuckle punch that is used in the Phoenix Eye style. It is different from other Karate schools in that it includes grappling techniques with the striking techniques.

UKIDOKAN

A martial art style developed by Benny "the Jet" Urquidez, who was a famous martial artist of the 1960s and 1970s. The style combines Karate techniques with boxing, Judo and Aikido methods.

VAJRAMUSHTI

A ferocious form of Indian wrestling. See Science of Combat.

VIET LONG GUOM

The art of the Vietnamese sword, which originated in the 17th century and is now taught as part of Qwan Ki Do.

VO THUAT VIETNAM

A style of martial art founded in 1945 by Nguyen Loc (1912-1960). In 1951, he opened a school in Saigon. The method uses wrestling and the techniques of Judo.

VOVINAM VIET VO DAO

Same as Vo Thuat Vietnam. See Vo Thuat Vietnam.

WA-JUTSU

A martial art that combines several approaches. It takes methods from Judo, Aikido and Karate. Founded in 1983 by Jacques Quero, the name means "science of concord." Underlying the physical techniques are philosophical concepts of Zen and Taoism. It focuses on self-development and the search for "the way."

WADO-RYU

The "school of the way of harmony," it was founded by one of the students of Funakoshi Gichin, the father of Karate. This student, Otsuka

Hidenori, combined methods of Jujutsu with a strong focus on evasion through body shifting. Soft techniques are applied to sparring. The school has higher stances and shorter punches than traditional Shotokan Karate. Though it teaches its techniques through forms and sparring, the school strives to develop mental awareness. It is considered a spiritual discipline rather than an exclusively physical discipline.

WAI CHIA
Chinese external system. See External System.

WASHIN-RYU
A style of Karate whose founder is unknown. It has been practiced in some form or another for more than four centuries. The bo (staff) is the weapon of choice in this system. Students learn forms, sparring and self-defense training. The balance of mind, body and spirit is sought.

WAY OF ARCHERY AND HORSEMANSHIP
Same as Way of Bow and Horse. See Way of Bow and Horse.

WAY OF THE BOW AND HORSE
The forerunner of modern archery, Kyudo. Chinese archers have taught archery techniques from both foot and mounted positions since the 11th century. By the middle of the 12th century, however, the name "way of the bow and horse" had acquired the additional meaning of warrior ethics; that is, the qualities of loyalty, bravery and so on that a warrior needed to possess. This expression of warrior ethics preceded Bushido, which articulated similar ethics. Also called Kyuba.

WAY OF THE FIST AND ENERGY
See Qwan-Ki-Do.

WHITE CRANE BOXING
The Chinese call this extremely popular Northern style of Wushu "Pao-hao," "Pak Hok," "Bak Hok," or "Ba fan." It is from the Lama or Hop Gar style of Wushu, which emulates the movements of the crane. It focuses on repeating a rapid series of hand and foot techniques. The principle of "revolving force" is important. This means that using the opponent's force against him or her is essential.

Feints are used to deceive the opponent into a vulnerable position. Vital point attacks are taught using hands that resemble a crane's beak. The arm techniques, both long and short, are circular, stances are solid and footwork uses short steps. Little body contact with the opponent is maintained. Like Hop Gar, some training is done on the plum flower stumps (mui fa jeong). The practitioner is constantly moving and circling the opponent. The kicks are high, which is surprising in a Wushu art. The practitioner never initiates an attack, only defends one. The style also emphasizes the angles of attack. White Crane style cultivates both internal and external methods and has both empty hand and weapons forms. One variation is the Tibetan White Crane.

WHITE EYEBROW
The founder, Bak Mei, had completely white hair, including his eyebrows; thus the name. He was a revolutionary in Ching Dynasty China, who betrayed others to avoid certain death. Because of this, his art was not taught until many years later when the monk Jok Fat finally received permission to do so. He traveled throughout China in search of students. The style consists of quick, explosive techniques with short and middle range preferred. Five external elements (eyes, mind, hands, waist, stance) are paired with five internal elements (spirit, purpose, courage, internal power, force) to produce power. Redirection of the opponent's energy is essential. The phoenix eye fist is the only hand technique used. The practitioner waits for the opponent to make the first move, then counterattacks efficiently. The style emphasizes breathing exercises to increase force. Triangle footwork is used. A number of weapons are studied, including the chainwhip, the staff, spear, double-edged sword and butterfly knives.

WHITE TIGER
A style of Wushu founded in the 17th century at the Fukien Shaolin temple. The founder, Fung Do Duk, was one of the five elders and later founded Triad, the Chinese secret society. The school was

so named after a ritual at the Fukien temple. Once a monk demonstrated his martial art skill, he entered the main hall, where there sat a heated urn with the symbol of the pure dragon and the white tiger, the emblems of yin and yang. The monk embraced the urn, leaving a scar tattoo on his chest. This was the sign of his graduation.

WING CHUN

Literally, "beautiful springtime," or "radiant springtime." It is sometimes called "Wing Shun" or "Wing Tsun." This style of Wushu was the first martial art learned by Bruce Lee; his fame helped to increase its popularity and make it the best known style of Wushu in other parts of the world. There are actually three varieties: slant body, the type practiced by Bruce Lee; side body; and the lesser known pao fa lein, which uses many weapons including the sword, trident and staff. There are five ways of defeating the enemy, according to Wing Chun: striking, kicking, joint locking, throwing and weapons use. According to legend, Wing Chun originated at the Shaolin temple, a place of refuge for dissidents and rebels. Since the government wished to subdue the temple, government soldiers knew the martial arts of the Shaolin temple. As more and more people joined the temple, the monks decided they needed a new fighting method, as the others took many years to learn. The temple elders began to create a new method, but before they could finalize their system and begin training, government soldiers destroyed the temple, killing almost all the residents. One exception was a nun named Ng Mu, who had been a temple elder. In hiding, she completed work on the new fighting art. The legend says she taught the art to a young girl, who she renamed Yim Wing Chun. One story relates how the son of Yim Wing Chun, Fong Sai Yu, was killed by Ng Mui when he disrespectfully challenged her. For more than two centuries, the art was taught privately, until Yip Man offered the first public classes in Hong Kong.

The system emphasizes self-defense, focusing on methods that allow a block and an attack in the same movement. Flowing movements with the waist as the pivot point are taught. It is characterized by aggressive action and the redirection of the opponent's energy. The movements are not circular, but rather are direct and straight. More than half the techniques are hand techniques and the style is best known for its quick punches. Only low kicks are used. Traps and other kinds of controls are important as well. Trapping and speed are developed through the famous sticky hands training, which also teaches balance. The Wing Chun dummy, a wooden dummy used for repetitive striking drills, is also a famous training method. There are three forms used in the style and all Wing Chun techniques can be found in these: Sil Lum Tao, Chum Kil, and Bil Jee. The concepts of the immovable elbow and the centerline are stressed.

WRESTLING, BURMESE

A style of wrestling imported from India, where it is known as Naban. Its techniques and tactics are crude. It is practiced primarily by Himalayan tribesmen.

WRESTLING, CHINESE

A collection of various kinds of grappling and wrestling styles. See Chiao Ti, Chih Yu Hsi, Goti, Hsiang Pu (same as Xiang Pu), Jiaoli, Pai Chang, Shang Pu, Shuai Chiao, and Shuai-go.

WRESTLING, INDIAN

In Indian wrestling, practitioners train from their youth. Most are in their teens but some begin even at the ages of five or six. A special diet, body conditioning and training routines are followed. The contest itself varies, and has flexible rules. Wrestling contests can last for a long period of time — upwards of an hour. The goal is to pin the opponent's hips and shoulders at the same time. See Asura, Dharanipata, Mall-krida, Mallavidy, Mallayuddah, Nara, Niyuddah-kride, Science of Combat, and Yuddah.

WRESTLING, KOREAN

See Cireum.

WRESTLING, FILIPINO

See Dumog.

WU STYLE TAI CHI

Also called Wu Jian Quan. See Tai Chi Chuan.

WU-DANG PAI

A style of Wushu. It is derived from the Shaolin tradition and uses the Chinese sword as its major weapon. It emphasizes the internal method, or soft movements. Also called Wutang.

WUSHU

A Chinese term broadly encompassing "martial arts." In Western countries, the term Kung Fu is usually used to refer to the martial arts of China, but this is an incorrect use of the term. Kung Fu simply means a skill which can be applied to anything from chess to needlework. In China, Wushu is the official term, meaning "arts of war." Sometimes the term Chinese Boxing is given to represent Chinese martial arts. Over three hundred styles and schools of the martial arts, each distinct, exist in China. Some are little more than gymnastic exercises, while others are legitimately considered combat arts. Wushu has been popular in China throughout its lengthy history, sometimes serving political, religious or even criminal aims, as the secret societies show us. These secret societies advanced political, religious or criminal goals and taught certain martial art styles to their members.

The various schools are classified in different ways. The most common division is between Northern China and Southern China schools, Northern being "internal," that is, soft and under Buddhist influence, and Southern being "external," that is, hard and under Taoist influence. Internal methods study chi, the life energy, as well as medicine and vital points. The external methods focus on force, power, and speed. Some schools use weapons, especially swords, while others use unarmed techniques only. All schools have stances, hand and foot attacks. Students also practice forms. Work with partners is also characteristic. Students spar in three different ways to improve their

Fig. 2.6 : Wushu stylist.

techniques: unarmed; unarmed against armed; or armed against armed. Most styles encourage contests between participants.

Originally there were five Wushu methods practiced primarily in the south that came from the Fukien Shaolin temple. These are identified by the founding family's name: Hung Gar; Lau gar; Choy Gar; Li Gar; and Mok Gar. The word "gar" simply means family. These are all strictly fighting systems, quickly learned and applied to combat situations. Hung Gar is the only style that is still routinely practiced. There are numerous schools of Wushu; the following are mentioned in this book: Ba Ji Quan, Baksing Choy Li Fut, Cha Chuan, Chang Chuan, Chin Na, Cho Chiao, Chow Gar, Choy Li Fut, Chung Chuan, Chuan Shu, Chung Kuo Chuan, Ditang Chuan, E-Mei-Shan Pai, Eagle Claw Style, Eight Drunken Immortals, Eight Hexagram Boxing, Erlang Man, Fan Tzu Hao Chuan, Five Animals, Five Elders, Heron Style, Hong Quan, Hop Gar, Hou Chuan, Hsing-I, Hung Chia Chuan, Hung Chuan, Ji Gong, Jun Fan, Kung Li, Kuo Chuan, Leopard Style, Lian I, Li Chia Chuan, Lien Chuan, Lion Roar, Liu Chia Chuan, Liu He, Liu He Bafa, Liu Ho Chuan, Lo Han Chuan, Long Huan Quan, Mien Chuan, Mi Tsung I, Mo Chia Chuan, Monkey Style, Ng Mi Phai, Pa Chi Chuan, Pa Chuan, Pa Kua Chuan, Phoenix Eye, Pi Kua Chuan, Pok Khek, Praying Mantis, Sanhwang Pao Chui, Shaolin Chuan, Shaolin Temple Boxing, Shau Wan Chuan, Shoubo, Shui Lu Fu, Siu Lum, Six Combinations, Six Harmonies Eight Steps, Six Methods, Splashing Hands, Ta Cheng Chuan, Ta

Sheng Men, Tai Chi Chuan, Tai I Chuan, Tai Mantis, Tai Tsu Chuan, Tang Lang, Tan Tui, Ti Tang, Tibetan White Crane, Tien Gunn, Tongbei Quan, Tsai Chia Chuan, Tsai Li Fu Chuan, Tsui Pa Hsien, Tuan Chuan, Tung Pi, Tzujan Men, Tzu Men, Wah Kuen, White Crane Boxing, Wing Chun, Wu-dang Pai, Yihe Quan, Yueh San Shou, Yung Chuan, and Zuyan Men.

WUTANG
See Wu-dang Pai.

XIANG PU
Same as Hsiang Pu. See Hsiang Pu. See Wrestling, Chinese.

XING-YI QUAN
See Mind-Body Boxing.

YABUSAME
"The Way of the Bow and the Horse." A combined art of archery and horsemanship originally practiced as a form of entertainment. By the Kamakura period (1185-1333), its combat potential had been realized and it became part of the standard training for warriors. In contests, between seven and thirty-six participants ride down a hill, one after the other. Three targets four or five feet tall are placed along the way. Wooden-tipped arrows are loosed at the targets, and the participants attempt to show their skill in horsemanship and in accuracy of target shooting. Two schools in Japan still practice this art, the Edo and the Ogasawara. Now, however, the art has mostly a religious significance, not a military one. The contests are observed by Shinto priests, who are seated next to the judges. See Ba-jutsu, Togasagake, Ogasawara-ryu, Takeda-ryu, and Inu-oi-mono.

YADOME
Techniques of using the sword to defend against arrows.

YAGYU RYU
A school of Kenjutsu (swordfighting) and Jujutsu founded by Yagyu Muneyoshiiake Sekishusai in the 16th century. The school teaches some Ninja techniques plus the dagger, rope tying and the halberd. The practitioners wear samurai armor. It follows the teaching of Zen Buddhism. Same as Yagyu Shingan-ryu.

YAGYU SHINGAN-RYU
See Yagyu ryu.

YANAGI-RYU
Same as Yoshin-ryu. See Yoshin-ryu.

YARI-DO
The study of the lance or the halberd.

YAWARA
An old term used for unarmed combat methods in general. However, it is thought to have been a distinct martial art at one time. The techniques are considered to be the forerunner of the earliest form of empty-handed Jujutsu. In some styles of Yawara, weapons such as the stick and the staff were used.

YAWYAN
A style of Arnis, founded in the Philippines in the early-1970s by Napoleon Fernandez. It includes showy kicks but traditional Arnis hand techniques.

YEN CHING CHUAN
See Mi-Tsung-I.

YO-RYU
See Hojo-jutsu.

YOGA
The practice of meditating in static postures with controlled breathing patterns. It is derived from a Hindu religious practice, but as an art is known for its ability to improve flexibility and muscle tone. It also has slow moving forms, as in Tai Chi, and it has various schools, such as the Frog and Peacock, each with a slightly different emphasis.

YOSHIN AIKIDO
A style of Aikido that focuses on wrist hold almost exclusively. A student learns a tremendous number of these "controls." Shida Gozo, the founder, emphasizes extensive practice but otherwise differs little from the principles of traditional Aikido.

YOSHIN-RYU
Literally, "willow heart school" or "willow spirit school." This school, which combines techniques of Jujutsu (unarmed combat) and K e n j u t s u (swordfighting) has various stories concerning its

origins. Essentially, it is believed that early in the 18th century, a physician, Akiyama Shirobei Yoshitoki, traveled to China where he studied medicine, including Kappo, or resuscitation art. He also learned various martial arts. The school's name, referring as it does to the willow tree, is said to be so named because the willow is non-resistive; its branches bend in the wind and under the weight of snow and do not break. Techniques also focus on strikes to the vital points, as the founder's study of Kappo indicates.

YU-SOL

A Korean martial art of self-defense, a soft style that emphasized non-resistance. Practitioners waited for the opponent to make the first move and used throws as well as striking techniques. The school was extremely popular for about two centuries between the mid-12th and the mid-14th, but was no longer in practice at the turn of the century.

YUDDAH

The most vicious style of Indian wrestling, in which participants could be killed. See Wrestling, Indian.

YUDO

A Korean style of Judo with its own Korean characteristics.

ZHONGGUO QUAN

Literally, "Chinese fist." See Kempo.

ZUYANMEN

A style of internal Chinese Wushu derived from the Shaolin Temple.

FORMS AND TECHNIQUES

108 MOVEMENTS

These are techniques used with mook jong, a wooden dummy training device used in Wing Chun Wushu. These series of movements and combinations of techniques are designed to simulate every conceivable situation a practitioner might find him or herself in. In addition, numerous forms and exercises have 108 movements because this is considered a fortunate number. See Training Equipment in the General section.

360 KICK

This term refers to a complete revolution of 360-degrees and means any kick in which the body makes a complete revolution before striking the target. Such kicks are popular in Tae Kwon Do because the revolution adds power to the kick. They require skill and technique and are impressive to watch. See Spinning Techniques.

ABISE-TAOSHI

In Sumo, any technique in which the practitioner pushes against the opponent's chest to off-balance him when the opponent has grabbed the practitioner's shoulders. See Sumo Techniques.

ACCOMPANIMENT FORM

In Iaido (sword drawing art) the first form in the secret forms standing set. In Japanese it is called "yukizure." In this form, the practitioner must use strategy to eliminate two opponents. The four phases of drawing the sword, cutting with the sword, shaking the blood from the sword and resheathing it are practiced.

ADVANCED FOOT SWEEP

A sweep technique used in Judo. From the rear, the practitioner sweeps the opponent's front leg, causing the opponent to fall forward or to the side. The technique is usually done when the opponent is moving and must be completed before the opponent has finished the action.

ADVANCING TIGER

A Shaolin Kenpo form done without a partner. See Kenpo in the Schools and Styles section.

AGE-TSUKI

See Punch, Uppercut.

AGE-UKE

See Block, Rising.

AGE-ZUKI

Same as Age-tsuki. See Punch, Rising.

AI-GAMAE

See Stance, Fighting.

AI-KAMAE

Same as Ai-gamae. See Stance, Fighting.

AIKI-TAISO

Basic exercises in Aikido designed to improve flexibility and to teach fundamental techniques. These include kote-mawashi-ho, kote-gaeshi, tekubi shindo and others.

AIKIDO TECHNIQUES

Techniques in Aikido are widely divided into defenses against various kinds of holds, the arm and the wrist holds being the ones most widely studied; and the more offensive techniques of controlling an opponent. Aikido techniques almost always conclude with a strike to a vital point. See Arm Holds. See Collar/Lapel Holds. See Throws. See Immobilizations.

The twelve basic holds that the Aikido practitioner learns to defend against are as follows:

one hand hold to the wrist, same side (katate tori)

one hand hold to the wrist, opposite side (katate tori)

two hand hold on one arm (katate tori ryote mochi)

two hand hold on two arms (katate tori ryote mochi)

one hand hold to the shoulder (kata tori)

two hand hold to the shoulders (ryokata tori)

wrist hold from behind (ushiro tekubi tori)

elbow hold from behind (ushiro hiji tori)

shoulder hold from behind (ushiro kata tori)

neck hold from behind (ushiro kubi shime)

high body hold from behind (ushiro tori)

low body hold from behind (ushiro tori)

General Techniques:

Gokyo no nage waza. Refers to the use of an outstretched arm to block a strike from above or from the side.

Gyaku te-dori. A wrist lock performed by twisting the opponent's hand inward.

Hiji-waza. Any technique that targets the opponent's elbow.

Irimi-nage. A group of throwing techniques that are used to counter an opponent's attack, especially by using the opponent's own force against him or her. These are called Katate-ryote-dori, Shomen-uchi, Yokomen-uchi, Shomen-tsuki, Ushiro-ryote kubi dori and Ushiro ryo kata-dori.

Keri-goho. Punches and kicks specifically aimed at the opponent's vital ponts.

Koshi-nage. A series of hip throws that defend against basic grips.

Kote gaeshi. Techniques of self defense that are executed by grabbing the opponent's wrist and manipulating the joint.

Kote uchi. Any strike against an armed opponent that targets the opponent's forearm with the intention of causing him or her to drop the weapon.

Oshi-taoshi. An armlock executed by pushing on the opponent's elbow.

Tanto dori defense. Defensive techniques against short sword or knife attacks.

Te-hodoki. A series of basic defense movements using evasive techniques based on body shifting.

Controls:

These are the five basic immobilizations, sometimes called principles, of Aikido. Ikkyo control is called "the first principle," and it consists of various techniques used for immobilizing an opponent's arm. These are Ryo-te-dori, Kata-te-ryo-te-dori, Shomen-uchi, Shomen-tsuki, Ushiro-ryote-kubi-dori, Ushiro-tekuba-kubi-dori, and Ushiro-eri-dori (also known as Ude-osae). Nikkyo control (second principle) includes movements that use a wrist turn-in to immobilize the opponent. Sankyo control (third principle) is a series of techniques that involve elbow locks. Yonkyo control (fourth principle) is a series of techniques for applying pressure to the wrist. Gokyo control (fifth principle) consists of arm pinning techniques.

Defenses:

1. Arm Hold (Te-dori):

Dosoku te-dori. The practitioner immobilizes the opponent's arm and then strikes it.

Gyaku kata te-dori. The practitioner bends the opponent's free wrist, then pulls the opponent forward, off-balance.

Jun Kata Te-dori. The practitioner pulls the arm away and strikes.

2. Bear Hug:

Mae shitate kumi-tsuki. The practitioner digs his or her thumbs under the opponent's ears.

Mae-u-ate kumi-tsuki. The practitioner delivers a knee strike, then applies an arm lock to the opponent.

Ushiro u-ate kumi-tsuki. The practitioner strikes the opponent in the face with his or her head while pulling free, then steps and performs an elbow lock.

3. Belt Grab:

Kumi-tsuki. A series of self-defense techniques performed against holds of the belt.

Ushiro shitate kumi tsuki. The practitioner strikes with the heel to the opponent's abdomen. Then the practitioner strikes the opponent's hand, and performs an armlock.

Ushiro eri obi tori. The practitioner steps forward, then strikes a vital point in the opponent's side.

4. Combination Hold:

Ushiro kata te dori eri-jime. A defense against a combination neck hold and wrist grab. The practitioner strikes the opponent's instep.

5. Lapel Hold:

Eri-tori tsuki age. The practitioner grabs the opponent's punching hand, then forces the opponent's wrist up sharply.

Fig. 3.1 : Aikido practitioner preparing to defend.

Eri-tori yokomen uchi. The opponent grabs the practitioner's lapels. The practitioner strikes the opponent's arm, slips under the opponent's arms and strikes to the face.

Eri-tori. The name given for a complete series of defenses used to defend against lapel or collar holds.

Hiji nage mae eri-tori. The practitioner sweeps the opponent backwards and strikes to a vital point with the foot.

Hiji nobashi eri tori. The practitioner grabs his or her own clothing near the opponent's grip and pulls the opponent forward.

Ryo-te-eri-tori. A defense against a lapel hold when the opponent grabs both lapels. The practitioner steps and grips the opponent's elbow with the free hand and pulls downward.

6. Shoulder Grab:

Kata-dori. The practitioner counters the attack by pivoting and throwing the opponent to the ground.

7. Sleeve Hold:

Dosoku kata sode-tori. The second defense against a sleeve grab or hold. The practitioner steps away and uses his or her free hand to strike to the opponent's elbow, aiming for a vital point.

Jun kata sode-tori. The first defense against a sleeve hold. The practitioner grabs the opponent's free hand and performs an elbow strike to the side of the opponent's chest.

Ushiro eri kata sodetori. A defense against a collar or sleeve hold from the rear. The practitioner bends under the opponent's arm, then throws the opponent forward.

Ushiro ryo kata sode tori. A defense against a sleevehold from the rear. The practitioner steps away, and slides under the opponent's arm.

8. Wrist Hold:

Kaiten-nage. A series of throws used against wrist holds and punches to the face. These require a turning motion of the body.

Ryote kata-dori. The practitioner brings his or her hands together and steps forward, then forces both hands down and back up to escape the grip.

Ushiro oshi age te-dori. The practitioner steps forward and grabs the opponent's elbow with his or her free hand.

Ushiro ryote dori. The practitioner steps to the side, pivots and grips the opponent by the elbow.

AKUMABARAI

"Demon Cutting." See Four Directional Cutting V.

ALIVE HAND

In Escrima, the alive hand is the one that is not holding the escrima stick. The alive hand blocks, disarms and can wield a knife or other weapon. The alive hand, if it is empty, can strike or feint to off-balance or distract the opponent.

AM DUONG TAN

See Stance, Horse.

AMI-UCHI

A technique used in Sumo. From the rear, the practitioner slides his arms inside the opponent's arms. The technique is used to force the opponent forward. See Sumo Techniques.

AN LONG

See Strike, Elbow (downward).

AN LONG SON

See Strike, Backfist.

ANANKU

A form in Shorei-ryu Karate that was devised to develop physical beauty in the sense of fluidity of movement and technique. Balance, speed and power are emphasized. See Karate Forms.

ANGULAR SWORD FORM

In Iaido, sword drawing art, the fourth form in the basic drawing methods set. In Japanese it is called "shato." The practitioner learns the technique of striking the opponent's bare wrists to block, plus evasive movements. The four phases of drawing the sword, cutting with the sword, shaking the blood from the sword and resheathing the sword are all executed.

AO-MUKU-YOKO-SHIHO-GATAME

See Facing Upward Side Four Quarters. See Judo Techniques.

AO-MUKU-KAMI-SHIHO-GATAME

See Facing Upward Upper Four Quarters. See Judo Techniques.

AP HURYA CHAGI

See Kick, Hooking.

AP-CHAGI

See Kick, Front.

APPARENT CLOSE UP

This technique is used in the Tai Chi Chuan Eight Minute Form. While it has a self-defense application, it primarily tones the back. See Eight Minute Form.

ARIAKE

A technique used in Kyudo, (archery). Specifically, positioning oneself to the left of the bow. It is used to improve aim. See Kyudo Techniques.

ARM AROUND NECK HIP THROW

See Hip Throw (koshi-guruma).

ARM AROUND SHOULDER THROW

See One Arm Shoulder Throw.

ARM HOLDS

Refers to immobilizing the opponent's arm. Often this is done by applying a joint lock to the wrist or elbow. Aikido supplies several defenses against the arm hold:

Dosoku te-dori. The practitioner immobilizes the opponent's elbow and then strikes it.

Gyaku kata te-dori. The practitioner grabs the opponent's free wrist and pulls forward.

Jun Kata Te-dori. The practitioner frees the wrist by turning the wrist and pulling the arm away in a circular motion. The practitioner then strikes to the opponent's face. See Aikido Techniques.

ARM LOCKS

Various techniques for immobilizing the arm, usually by applying pressure on the elbow. Judo and Aikido practitioners favor these techniques.

Hiza gatame. In Judo, a technique in which the opponent's arm is immobilized when the practitioner uses his or her knee and thigh to apply pressure.

Juji-gatame. In Judo, a cross armlock. This is a technique of gripping an opponent's arm, and

Fig. 3.2 : Tae Kwon Do practitioner defends against wrist/ arm hold.

Fig. 3.4: The Tae Kwon Do practitioner twists her wrist free.

Fig. 3.5 : Kenpo armlock technique.

101

locking it across the practitioner's pelvic area.

Oshi-taoshi. In Aikido, an armlock executed by pushing on the opponent's elbow.

Oten-gatame. In Judo, executing an armlock through bending the opponent's arm.

Ude garami. In Judo, the practitioner applies pressure on the elbow, while the opponent is lying on his or her back. Called the "arm entanglement" or "figure four arm lock."

Ude gatame. In Judo, straight arm lock. The practitioner pulls the arm up, and rests it between shoulder and neck, placing pressure on the shoulder just below the elbow.

Ude Hishiga Hiza-gatame. In Judo, controlling the opponent's arm by stretching it across one's knee.

Ude-hishigi ude-gatame. In Judo, an armlock executed on an opponent's outstretched arm.

Ude-hishigi juji-gatame. In Judo an armlock executed in a cross shape.

See Joint Locks. See Aikido Techniques. See Judo Techniques.

AROUSING THE DRAGON

Beginner form in Ji Gong. Its purpose is to regulate the flow of chi, life energy, through the channels of the entire body. This combined with meditation and exercise brings strength to the body, including internal organs, clears the mind, and relieves stress.

ASHI HARAI

Same as Ashi barai. See Sweeps. See Judo Techniques.

ASHI-BARAI

See Sweeps. See Judo Techniques.

ASHI-GATAME

See Immobilizations. See Judo Techniques.

ASHI-GATANA

See Kick, Knife Foot.

ASHI-GURUMA

See Leg Wheel. See Judo Techniques. See Throws.

ASHI-NO-TACHI KATA

See Stance, Fighting.

ASHI-TORI

A technique used in Sumo to take down the opponent. Sometimes the technique is used to simply off-balance the opponent, in an effort to gain a better entry. In this technique, the practitioner grasps the opponent's leg with both hands and pushes his shoulder against the opponent's inner thigh. See Sumo Techniques.

ASHI-WAZA

In Karate, this term is used to denote any foot or leg technique. In Judo, the term means foot and leg techniques when they are used to sweep or hook the opponent's foot or leg. Generally, these are the easiest techniques to master and for this reason are taught to beginners. See Judo Techniques. See Karate Techniques.

ASHIBO KAKE UKE

See Block, Hooking.

ASHIBUMI

In Kyudo, this is the ready position of the archer. One faces the target squarely, feet planted a shoulder's width apart. The archer holds the bow under the left arm and the arrow under the right arm. The bow and arrow point toward each other.

ASHIKUBI KAKE UKE

See Block, Hooking.

ASSISTING AT SEPPUKU FORM

In Iaido (sword drawing art), this is the seventh form of the seated set. In Japanese it is called "kaishaku." In this form, the practitioner waits as a samurai prepares to commit seppuku, then completes the act. The four phases of drawing the sword, cutting with the sword, shaking the blood from the sword and resheathing it are all practiced.

ATEMI-WAZA

Techniques based on a knowledge of vital points and acupressure. The goal is to attack the vital points, which are the most vulnerable areas in the body.

In Wajutsu, a series of techniques that focus on seizing the opponent's wrist from various positions.

ATO-NO-SAKI

See Ato-no-sen.

ATO-NO-SEN

The ability to anticipate or perceive an attacker's intentions before they are performed. This allows one to block an attack and counter immediately. Cultivation of this ability is of great importance to martial artists and can only be acquired through practice, in particular, through sparring practice. See Sparring, Free Style.

ATO-UCHI

In Kendo (swordfighting art), a feinting technique used during offense.

ATTACK

When one takes the initiative to deliver a blow or strike to the opponent, not in response to a technique the opponent has used. The opponent may be struck by the attacking blow, in which case the practitioner will have gained an advantage, but the opponent might also block, evade or counter-attack. See Strategy in the General Information section.

ATTACK BY COMBINATION

These boxing-like movements in Jeet Kune Do employ various hand and foot techniques in a sequence of attacks and counters. The practice makes one react more quickly.

ATTACK BY DRAWING

In Jeet Kune Do, any technique that lures an opponent into position for a powerful strike.

ATTENTION STANCE

See Stance, Attention.

AWASE-SUKI

See Punch, U.

AWASE-ZUKI

Same as Awase-tsuki. See Punch, U.

AXE KICK

See Kick, Crescent.

AYUMI ASHI

See Footwork.

BACK HIP THROW

In Judo, a throw using the hip against the opponent's back, throwing to the rear.

BACK KICK

See Kick, Back.

BACK STANCE

See Stance, Back.

BACK SWEEPING FOOT THROW

See Minor Outer Reap.

BACKFIST BLOCK

See Block, Backfist.

BACKFIST STRIKE

See Strike, Backfist.

BACKHAND BLOCK

See Block, Backhand.

BACKWARD STEPPING

See Footwork.

BAI

A kneeling bow. See Salutation Techniques.

BAI SU

See Stance, Ready.

BAITO

In Qwan-Ki-Do, salutation techniques. See Salutation Techniques.

BALANCING CHI

An exercise in Tai Chi designed for the purpose of focusing on and developing the chi.

BANDO FORMS

These include forms that emphasize qualities of different animals. The deer form, for instance, develops awareness, while the cobra form teaches attacks to vital points in the upper body. The forms consist of Eagle Form, Deer Form, Boar Form, Cobra Form, Viper Form, Monkey Form, Paddy Bird Form, Panther Form, Python Form, Scorpion Form, Bull Form, and Tiger Form.

BANGAI NO BU

See Secret Forms Extra Set.

BANGO

In Tae Kwon Do, a general term for evasive or blocking action. See Block.

BANTAY KAMAY

Philippine term for "alive hand." See Alive Hand.

BANXIE-BO

See Stance, Crab.

BARA-TE

See Punch, Reverse.

BARAI MAKIKOMI

Same as Harai makikomi. See Sweeping Winding Throw. See Throws. See Judo Techniques.

BARAI

See Harai.

BARAI-TE

Same as Harai-te. See Strike, Palm.

BARAI MAKEKOME

Same as Harai makekome. See Sweeping Winding Throw. See Throws. See Judo Techniques.

BARAI-GOSHI

Same as Harai goshi. See Sweeping Hip Throw. See Throws. See Judo Techniques.

BARAI-TSURIKOMI-ASHI

Same as Harai-tsurikomi-ashi. See Sweeping Drawing Ankle Throw. See Throws. See Judo Techniques.

BASAI FORM

A form in Tang Soo Do as well as in Tae Kwon Do, where it also goes by the name Bal Sack.

BASAMI-JIME

See Hasami jime. See Judo Techniques.

BASAMI-TSUKI

Same as Hasami-tsuki. See Punch, Double Fist.

BASAMI-ZUKI

Same as Hasami tsuki. See Punch, Double Fist.

BASIC DRAWING METHODS

In Iaido (sword drawing art), these basic drawing methods are fundamental to sword proficiency, teaching correct drawing techniques and correct standing postures. The first seven forms teach basic drawing skills, and are collectively known as "batto ho no bu." Batto forms are found in almost all major sword systems. These forms are: Ordered Sword I and II, Pursuing Sword, Angular Sword, Four Directional Cut I and II, and Beheading Stroke. The secret forms drawing methods set is part of basic drawing methods but these are taught at an intermediate level. They introduce the student to three important aspects of swordsmanship: 1. Drawing from a walking motion; 2. Rising draws and cuts; 3. Fast methods of resheathing the sword. The intermediate forms are: Forward Inverse Cut, Multidirectional Cut, Rearward Inverse Cut, and Rearward Quick Draw.

BASIC HIP THROW

See Major Hip Throw.

BASSAI DAI

This Japanese Karate form is used in both Shorei-ryu and Shotokan. It is designed to develop mental and physical coordination. The name means "to penetrate a fortress" and it focuses on turning a disadvantage into an advantage by use of blocks and varying levels of power. See Karate Forms.

BASSAI-SHO

Literally, "the lesser bassai," a Japanese Karate form related to Bassai Dai. See Karate Forms.

BAT HO

See Strike, Elbow (backward).

BAT PHONG SON

See Strike, Hammer Fist.

BATTO HO NO BU

See Basic Drawing Methods.

BEAR CLAW

See Clamp Hand.

BEHEADING STROKE FORM

In Iaido (sword drawing art), the seventh form in the basic drawing methods set. It is called "zantotsuto." The practitioner blocks by cutting at the opponent's wrists, and then controls the opponent's sword. The four phases of drawing the sword, cutting with the sword, shaking the blood from the sword and resheathing the sword are all executed.

BELT GRIPS

In Sumo, practitioners grasp each other's belts and attempt to force each other out of the ring. The belt can be gripped in a variety of ways; with the left hand inside, with the right hand inside, with both hands, and with either the thumb or the fingers inside. See Sumo Techniques.

BENEATH THE DOOR WAY FORM

In Iaido (sword drawing art), the fourth form in the secret forms seated set. It is called "towaki." The form helps the practitioner gain experience in dealing with obstructions. The practitioner imagines he or she is seated in a doorway when attacked. The four phases of drawing the sword, cutting with the sword, shaking the blood from the sword, and resheathing the sword are performed.

BENEATH THE LEDGE FORM

In Iaido (sword drawing art), the sixth form in the secret forms seated set. In Japanese it is called "tanashita." In this form, the practitioner gains experience in dealing with obstructions. The practitioner imagines he or she is seated beneath a ledge, facing outward, with an opponent attacking. The four phases of drawing the sword, cutting with the sword, shaking the blood from the sword and resheathing the sword are practiced.

BERSILAT TECHNIQUES

This Malaysian martial art focuses on seven basic groups of techniques that are practiced faithfully and must be mastered by each practitioner. They are:

1. Salutation
2. Weapon forms
3. Avoiding attack
4. Side stepping (footwork)
5. Kicking or falling techniques
6. Stabbing techniques
7. Art of the warrior techniques

BETWEEN THE WALLS FORM

In Iaido (sword drawing art), the ninth form in the secret forms standing set, called "kabezoe." The form gives the practitioner experience in dealing with obstructions. The practitioner imagines that he or she is in an alley when an opponent attacks. The four phases of drawing the sword, cutting with the sword, shaking the blood from the sword and resheathing the sword are all practiced.

BIU SAU SWITCH

See Wooden Dummy Drills.

BIL JEE FORM

In Wing Chun Wushu, this set, the third taught, develops finger strikes. It is called "thrusting fingers" or "shooting fingers."

BIRD PERCHING

A movement used in The Great Circle, a long Tai Chi form consisting of 37 different series of techniques.

BIRD WITH FOLDED WING

A movement used in The Great Circle, a long form consisting of 37 different series of techniques, performed by Tai Chi practitioners.

BLOCK

This is any movement that prevents a strike from hitting the intended target area, including those movements that deflect the strike completely as well as those that merely interfere. Jamming and sweeping movements act as blocks. Not all evasive techniques, however, are blocks. Blocks can be performed with the arm, hand, knee, leg, foot or shin. In Tae Kwon Do, bango is a general term for evasive or blocking action. The term chudan uke kake is used in Karate to refer to any technique that is used to block an opponent's arm.

BLOCK, BACKFIST

With this technique, one blocks a punch by sweeping in an outward direction with the back of one's closed fist.

BLOCK, BACKHAND

One deflects a punch by sweeping in an outward direction with the back of an open hand.

Haishu-uke. In Karate, a circular block using the back of an open hand.

BLOCK, BOULDER

A forearm block executed at close range, used in Wushu.

BLOCK, C-HAND

In this block, the practitioner executes a high block, to defend against attacks to the head while simultaneously performing a forearm block to defend the middle area. This technique can be performed with open or closed hands.

Fig. 3.6 : C-hand block.

BLOCK, CRESCENT

Sokutei mawashi uke. In Karate, a block using the sole of the foot to defend against a punch to the chest. The block moves in a circular way. It is performed in the same way as a crescent kick.

BLOCK, ELBOW

Hiji suri uke. In Karate, a block using the outside of the forearm in which the arm slides up and forward. This is a combination block and strike.

BLOCK, FOOT

A block with the sole of the foot in a stomping motion.

BLOCK, FOREARM

Refers to a wide variety of blocking movements usually made with the fleshy part of the forearm. The arm usually moves in a horizontal sweep.

Double forearm block. A technique using both arms. One arm performs the actual block, the other augments the block, providing support for the block and a further guard. This technique can be performed in an inside to outside movement or from outside to inside. Usually used to defend the low and middle sections. The palm of the blocking arm faces up, with the elbow slightly cocked. The palm of augmenting or guarding arm faces up, covers the midsection (solar plexus), and rests against the elbow of the blocking arm to provide further support.

Haiwan nagashi uke. A block using the bottom of the forearm, near the elbow. The arm protects the high section by a block upward.

Mae-ude de-ai osae uke. A pressing block in Karate. Using the forearm to defend against a strike to the middle section, the block is delivered with a pressing movement into the opponent's attacking arm.

Soto-ude-uke. A block using the outside surface of the forearm. The block moves in a circular motion and can generate great power.

Sukui-uke. In Karate, a scooping block using the outside of the forearm to defend against middle or high section kicks.

BLOCK, HAMMER FIST

A block executed using the bottom of the fist, moving either inward or outward. This technique defends against attacks to the middle target area.

BLOCK, HIGH

Sometimes refers to inside-outside blocks and outside-inside blocks used to deflect kicks and punches aimed at the high target area, but generally refers to an upward block using the forearm that rises from the chest level to the head level. Sometimes called an upper block.

BLOCK, HOOKING

The term refers to any block that uses a hooking technique to defend or trap. These can be performed with arm or leg.

Ankle hooking block. Ashikubi kake uke. In Karate, a block with the ankle. The front of the ankle moves upward to block the opponent's technique. This block is usually used to defend against a front kick.

Leg hooking block. Ashibo kake uke. In Karate, a block with the leg. The shin blocks in an upward movement, usually to defend against a side kick.

Gedan kake uke. A downward block in Karate to defend against kicks using a hooking movement. The inner surface of the forearm is used as the blocking surface.

BLOCK, INSIDE-OUTSIDE

The forearm blocks the middle section by sweeping from the body outward. Also called outward middle block. Using the muscular part of the forearm, with the hand as a fist, the arm sweeps from inside, across the body outward.

BLOCK, KNIFE HAND

These blocks are performed with the open hand in the knife hand position. The fingers are held tightly together and the elbow is bent. This technique is used to block a blow to the middle section. Similar to an inside-outside or outside-inside block (which are executed with the hands

Fig. 3.8 : Knife hand block, middle section.

as fists). The rear hand, a fist, rests near the waist.

Double knife hand block. The leading arm, cocked at a 45-degree angle, makes the block. The rear arm covers the mid-section and guards the solar plexus. Both hands are in the knife hand position.

Fig. 3.9 : Knife hand block, low section. KITA PINAN NINAN

Kake-shuto-uke. A knife hand block that uses a hooking motion to deflect an attack to the side or to the front.

BLOCK, LOW

A block performed with the outside of the forearm to deflect punches and kicks delivered middle and low. The blocking arm travels from near the opposite shoulder down to the outside of the knee, in a sweeping motion across the chest area. One of the first techniques taught in Karate and Tae Kwon Do, it is a very important though basic one.

Fig. 3.10 : Low block. GODEN BARIA

BLOCK, MOUNTAIN

In Tae Kwon Do, it is called san teul maki. A double block to defend the high section. Both arms perform inside-outside blocks simultaneously at head level.

BLOCK, OPEN HAND

Chudan tegatana-uke. Any block performed with palm open instead of as fist. In Karate, one keeps an open palm, held at chest level, to defend against an opponent's attack.

Fig. 3.7 : C-hand block with open hands.

BLOCK, OUTSIDE-INSIDE

A technique in which the arm sweeps from outside to inside, deflecting kicks and punches to the middle section. The arm is bent and the forearm does the blocking. The hand is usually in a fist. Also called inward middle block.

Nagashi-uke. In Karate, this outside-inside block is executed with an open palm.

BLOCK, PALM

A block with the heel of the palm, moving downward or sideways. The block can defend the middle or high area.

Fig. 3.11 : Outside-inside block, also called inward middle block.

BLOCK, PRESSING

A block that can be performed with hand or leg. It simply indicates that instead of pushing or strik-

Fig 3.12: Palm block

ing to block, the blocking limb is used to press the attacking hand or foot away. Pressing blocks are also used in combination with traps; the attacking limb is trapped and the defender's hands or feet press together to break a bone or cause pain.

De-ai osae uke. A block executed while moving forward. The technique uses a pressing motion instead of a striking motion.

Fig. 3.13 : Pressing block with leg.

Osae-uke. In Karate, a pressing block using palm to defend against a punch to the abdomen or groin in a downward motion (also known as te osae uke).

Sokutei osae uke. A pressing block using the sole of the foot to defend against a kick to groin, moving down and outward.

Sokuto osae uke. In Karate a pressing knife foot block using the side edge of feet to defend against a kick to the groin.

BLOCK, RISING

A block with the fleshy part of the forearm, to deflect a blow to the high section. Similar to an upper block or high block, but performed with an open palm and with a pressing motion.

Age-uke. In Karate, an upward block using the outer surface of the forearm (the fleshy part) to defend against any attack to the face. The block travels upward and guards against strikes from the front.

Age-uke gyaku tsuki. In Karate, an upward block in which the rear foot blocks an opponent's attack, usually to a low or middle target.

BLOCK, SCISSORS

A simultaneous low block with one arm and inside outside block with the other arm, called ka wey maki in Tae Kwon Do.

Fig. 3.14 : Karate practitioners demonstrating scissors block.

BLOCK, SMOTHERING

A technique in which one raises the knee to block a target area with the knee or leg.

BLOCK, WEDGE

In Tae Kwon Do, a technique called hea chu maki. Both wrists are crossed in front of the chest, with fists shoulder level, palms in or out.

BLOCK, WRIST

Using the part of the hand near the wrist to block in an open hand sweeping movement.

Kakuto uke. A bent wrist block in Karate. The top of the wrist defends against a punch to the high section.

Tekubi kake uke. In Karate, a block with the back of wrist to defend against a punch to the chest, using a hooking movement.

Fig. 3.15 : Wrist block.

BLOCK, X

Also called a cross block, performed with crossed forearms (usually right over left) with strong thrusting movement. Upward to guard the high section, downward to guard the low section. The wrists are used to trap the attacking limb.

BLOCKED AT THE DOOR FORM

In Iaido (sword drawing art), the second form in the secret forms seated set, called "tozume." The practitioner gains experience in dealing with obstructions. The practitioner imagines he or she is seated in a doorway facing two opponents. The four phases of drawing the sword, cutting with the sword, shaking the blood from the sword and resheathing the sword are performed.

BLOCKED ON BOTH SIDES FORM

In Iaido (sword drawing art), the seventh form of the secret forms seated set. In Japanese it is called "ryozune." The practitioner gains experience in dealing with obstructions. The practitioner imagines that he or she is seated in a narrow hall when an opponent attacks. The four phases of drawing the sword, cutting with the sword, shaking the blood from the sword and resheathing the sword are executed.

BO

Word used in Wushu to refer to stances collectively. See Stance.

BO LINH

A basic form in the Vietnamese martial art Qwan-Ki-Do.

BO LINH HAI

A basic form in the Vietnamese martial art Qwan-Ki-Do.

BO LINH MOT

A basic form in the Vietnamese martial art Qwan-Ki-Do.

BO PHAP

Word used in Qwan-Ki-Do to refer to stances collectively. See Stance.

BOAR FORM

In Bando, this form emphasizes qualities such as courage, and movements such as rushing and hitting, plus elbow and knee strikes. The other Bando forms also emphasize animal qualities. Other forms include Eagle, Deer, Cobra, Viper, Monkey, Paddy Bird, Panther, Python, Scorpion, Bull and Tiger.

BODY DROP

In Judo, a technique in which the practitioner extends a leg, and pulls an opponent over the leg and hip to the front. Often used in competition. See Throws. See Judo Techniques.

BODY SHIFTING

Techniques for moving to avoid the entire force of an attack. Instead of retreating, one merely eludes the strike or turns slightly away from it, sometimes just by moving one's weight from one leg to another. In some martial arts, body shifting consists of moving the entire body forward quickly, with both legs off the ground simultaneously to close the gap between two opponents. It is called tenshin waza in Karate, and the techniques consist of tsuri-ashi, dragging the feet; fumi-dashi, lunge step; hineri, hip twist; oshi fumikikomi, push step; kosa-susu-mi, cross step; and yoko-ido, side step.

BOLIN HAI

Same as Bo Linh Hai. See Bo Linh Hai.

BOLIN MOT

Same as Bo Linh Mot. See Bo Linh Mot.

BOTH HANDS SHOULDER THROW

In Judo, a shoulder throw in which one uses both hands to grab the opponent and throw him or her over one's shoulder. See Throws. See Judo Techniques.

BOULDER BLOCK

See Block, Boulder.

BOW, CEREMONIAL

See Salutation Techniques.

BOW STANCE

See Stance, Bow.

BREAKFALLS

These are techniques for safely landing on the ground, as a result of a throw, sweep or other take down. Nearly all schools of martial arts introduce their students to breakfall techniques at the very start of their training. Teaching students to fall correctly is essential to their later success. In Judo, the breakfall techniques that are used are called "ukemi." Judo students learn to fall to the left and to the right (yoko-ukemi); backward (ushiro-ukemi); forward (mae-ukemi); and rolling (zempo-kaiten-ukemi). Other styles emphasize other possibilities. Two methods are commonly taught: those in which one rolls away to absorb the impact by distributing it all over, and those in which one remains static. In the latter, one falls to the mat, bearing the brunt of the weight on shoulder, hip and thigh; arm and hand should strike the mat at the same time. The head is always tucked. In Judo, with its emphasis on throws, a number of basic breakfalls are taught. They include the basic backfall, the basic sidefall, the standing backfall, the walking sidefall, rolling over, the forward roll, standing forward roll, rolling side fall, leaping roll, forward fall, forward leap, and for advanced practitioners, the leaping back fall and the leaping sidefall.

BREAKING WAVES FORM

In Iaido (sword drawing art), the sixth form in the half seated set, called "iwanami." In this form, the practitioner gains experience in dealing with unexpected situations. The practitioner imagines being seated when an opponent grabs his or her scabbard from the side. The four phases of drawing the sword, cutting with the sword, shaking the blood from the sword, and resheathing it are all practiced.

BREAKING TECHNIQUES

This refers to the practice of using a hand or foot strike to break a board or a brick. Breaking is commonly taught in Tae Kwon Do and in some Karate schools. The ability to break a board or brick on command demonstrates focus, and the ability to concentrate all one's energy at a specific point. For this reason, breaking is thought to develop the martial artist's chi, or life energy. Breaks are performed with basic techniques, such as a simple side kick, or with more spectacular techniques, such as a jump spinning heel kick.

BREATHING TECHNIQUES

The primary breathing technique is to inhale deeply and fully through the nose and into the stomach, then exhale slowly through mouth. During the performance of a technique or a series of exercises, when to inhale and when to exhale is among the first things taught to the martial arts student. Some styles have complete forms that consist of variations of breathing exercises. This not only helps to stimulate chi, it increases the lung capacity, and thus, endurance.

BROKEN RHYTHM TRAINING

The idea of rhythm is important to sparring, because it helps one to understand and anticipate an opponent's movements even before they are begun. But an individual with a predictable rhythm can by easily defeated, so a martial artists must train in non- or un-rhythmic movements. Broken rhythm training also deals with countering various unrhythmatic attacks and counter attacks. See Unbroken Rhythm Training.

BRUSH KNEE

A technique in the Tai Chi Chuan Eight Minute Form. It increases leg strength while also having self-defense applications.

BULL FORM

In Bando, this form emphasizes power techniques. It helps the practitioner develop charging and tackling skills, plus power striking techniques. Other Bando forms help practitioners develop other animal-like qualities. These forms include Eagle, Deer, Boar, Cobra, Viper, Monkey, Paddy Bird, Panther, Python, Scorpion and Tiger.

BUNGA

The formal etiquette demanded of a practitioner prior to training with a partner, but with elements of self-defense and awareness. That is, one may bow to the partner without lowering one's eyes. This reinforces the need to remain on guard. Some schools consider not lowering the eyes to be very discourteous.

CABECADA

In Capoeira, a head butt to the opponent's upper body.

Karate Breathing Exercises

Fig. 3.16

Fig. 3.17

Fig. 3.18

Fig. 3.19

Fig. 3.20

Fig. 3.21 and 3.22: Karate breathing control exercises.

CAT STANCE

See Stance, Cat.

CHA YUN SEH

A natural stance. See Stance, Natural.

CHAGI

Korean word for kick. See Kick.

CHAHNG DAI JYEUNG SWITCH

See Wooden Dummy Drills.

CHALLENGED STANCE

See Stance, Challenged.

CHANGING HIP THROW

In Judo, a counter executed by pulling the opponent to one's hip and throwing him or her off-balance. See Judo Techniques. See Throws.

CHAO MA TAN

See Stance, Walking.

CHARGING THE TIGER FORM

In Iaido (sword drawing art), the eighth form of the secret forms seated set, called "torabashiri." In this form, the practitioner gains experience in dealing with unexpected situations. The practitioner assumes a confrontation is over, but it is not and the opponent strikes again. The four phases of drawing the sword, cutting with the sword, shaking the blood from the sword and resheathing it are repeated.

CHESTNUT FIST

See Punch, Chestnut Fist.

CHI-SAO

See Sticky Hand Drill.

CHIBURI

Various techniques for flipping or shaking the blood off the sword before resheathing it. Used in Iaido (sword drawing art). Several major methods of chiburi exist.

CHIKI CHAGI

See Kick, Crescent.

CHIN'NA

See Devil's Hand.

CHINESE SWORD TECHNIQUES

Unlike the Japanese sword, which was used for thrusting, blocking and slicing, more than fifteen techniques are used with the Chinese sword. They include:

1. *Piercing*
2. *Hacking*
3. *Splitting (a slash)*
4. *Jabbing*
5. *Thrusting*
6. *Chiseling*
7. *Groping (pushing or blocking)*
8. *Throwing*
9. *Rushing*
10. *Deflecting*
11. *Hooking*
12. *Upholding*
13. *Spinning*
14. *Scraping*
15. *Poking*
16. *Whirling (a circular movement with the point)*

CHINTE

An advanced form in Shotokan Karate, meaning "small hands."

CHINTO

An old name for the Gankaku form. See Karate Forms.

CHIREU-GI

See Punch, Corkscrew.

CHO

In Viet Vo Dao, a term used indicating all types of elbow strikes. See Strike, Elbow.

CHOI-YOUNG FORM

An International Tae Kwon Do Federation form learned at the sixth dan black belt level.

CHOKU TSUKI

See Punch.

CHOKU ZUKI

Same as Choku tsuki. See Punch.

CHON-JI FORM

An International Tae Kwon Do Federation form learned at the tenth class or beginner (white belt) level. With 19 movements, it is performed in a square pattern and consists of basic movements such as low block, middle punch, inside-outside block, front stance and back stance. The name of the form literally translates as "heaven and earth." Thus, the form has two parts; the first part represents heaven and the second part represents earth. In Korea, this symbolizes the creation of the world and the beginning of human history. See Tae Kwon Do Forms.

CHONGI FORM

See Chon Ji Form.

CHONGUL JA SAE

Korean name for front stance. See Stance, Front.

CHOONG MOO

Same as Chung-mu. See Chung-mu.

CHOW

See Punch, Hook.

CHUAT SING

See Stance, Fighting.

CHUDAN-SOTO-UKE

In Karate, an outside-inside block to the middle. See Block, Outside-Inside.

CHUDAN-UCHI-UKE

In Karate, an inside-outside block to the middle. See Block, Inside-Outside.

CHUDAN UKE KAKE

In Karate, any technique used to block an opponent's arm.

CHUDAN NO KAMAE

An on-guard or fighting stance in Kendo. See Stance, Fighting.

CHUDAN TEGATANA-UKE

See Block, Open Hand.

CHUIN

See Punch, Straight.

CHUL-GI FORM

Same as Chon-ji form. See Chon-ji Form. See Tae Kwon Do Forms.

CHUM KIL FORM

The second set of techniques taught in Wing Chun Wushu. The form teaches defensive footwork, body shifting and closing techniques. The name means "searching for the bridge."

CHUN NO KON

A beginning form in Bojutsu (staff art). It consists of basic movements using thrusts and slanting strikes.

CHUNBEE

In Tae Kwon Do, ready position. See Stance, Ready.

CHUNG JANG

An International Tae Kwon Do Federation form learned at the fifth dan black belt level. See Tae Kwon Do Forms.

CHUNG KWON

A Tae Kwon Do Form for sixth dan black belt from the palgue series. See Tae Kwon Do Forms.

CHUNG SIK

In Wushu, a fighting stance. See Stance, Fighting.

CHUNG-MU FORM

An International Tae Kwon Do Federation form taught at the second class level. It has 30 movements. This intermediate form consists of movements such as spearhand strike, flying side kick, reverse kick, roundhouse kick, staff block and double forearm block. The form is named for the Admiral Yi Sun Sin, who allegedly invented the first armored battleship 1592. The pattern ends with a left hand strike to symbolize his regrettably early death.

CHUNG-GEUN FORM

An International Tae Kwon Do Federation form taught at the fifth class level. This intermediate form consists of movements such as ridgehand strike, pressing block, elbow strike, double knife hand block, double fist punch, and hammer fist strike. It is named after An Chung Gun, who assassinated the first Japanese governor-general of Korea, Hiro Bumi Ito, who had played a large role in forging the Japanese occupation of Korea. The 32 movements represent An Chung Gun's age when he was executed for his act. See Tae Kwon Do Forms.

CIRCLE STEP

See Footwork.

CIRCLE THROW

See Stomach Throw.

CLAMP HAND

Also called Bear claw. A knife hand with the fingers bent. See Strike, Knife Hand.

CLOUD BANK FORM

In Iaido (sword drawing art), the first form in the half-seated set. In Japanese it is called "yokogumo." The practitioner executes basic cutting techniques from the difficult half seated position. The four phases of drawing the sword, cutting with the sword, shaking the blood from the sword and resheathing it are practiced.

CLOUD HANDS IN HORSE STANCE

An exercise in Tai Chi designed to aid the gastrointestinal system and to ease arthritis.

COBRA FORM

In Bando, this form teaches techniques for attacking vital points in the upper body. One strikes like a cobra. Other Bando forms emphasize other qualities of other animals. They include Eagle, Deer, Boar, Viper, Monkey, Paddy Bird, Panther, Python, Scorpion, Bull and Tiger.

COLLAR/LAPEL HOLDS

One of the most common holds performed in Aikido. The practitioner learns to defend against this common attack in a variety of ways.

Eri-tori. The name given for a complete series of defenses used to defend against lapel or collar holds.

Eri-tori tsuki age. The practitioner forces the opponent's wrist up sharply.

Eri-tori yokomen uchi. The practitioner strikes against the opponent's arm, then slips under the opponent's arms and executes a strike to the face.

Hiji nage mae eri-tori. The practitioner steps behind the opponent then sweeps the opponent backwards.

Hiji nobashi eri tori. The practitioner grabs his or her own clothing near the opponent's grip and pulls the opponent forward.

Ryo-te-eri-tori. A defense against a lapel hold when the opponent grabs both lapels. The practitioner grips the opponent's elbow with the free hand and pulls downward. See Aikido Techniques.

COLLAR SHOULDER THROW

In Judo, one throws the opponent forward over one's shoulder. The technique is called Eri-seoi-nage. See Throws. See Judo Techniques.

COMMENCING TAI CHI/COMMENCE-MENT OF TAI CHI

A ready position. See Stance, Ready.

COMPANIONS FORM

In Iaido (sword drawing art), the second form in the secret forms standing set, called "tsuridachi." In this form, the practitioner gains experience with more than one opponent. The four phases of drawing the sword, cutting with the sword, shaking the blood from the sword and resheathing the sword are all practiced.

Fig. 3.23 : Iaido downward cut.

COMPLETE RESOLUTION FORM

In Iaido (sword drawing art), the third form in the secret forms standing set. In Japanese it is called "so makuri." In this form, the practitioner uses parrying and cutting techniques while standing. The four phases of drawing the sword, cutting with the sword, shaking the blood from the sword and resheathing the sword are practiced.

CONCLUSION OF TAI CHI

The last technique in the Tai Chi Chuan Eight Minute Form. This technique allows the practitioner to focus his or her mind and emphasizes the correct flow of chi, or life energy.

CONFRONTATION STANCE

In Aikido, a fighting stance. See Stance, Fighting.

CORNER DROP

In Judo, a technique in which the practitioner pulls the opponent's sleeve down while pushing on the opposite shoulder. See Judo Techniques. See Throws.

CORNER THROW

In Judo, the practitioner catches the opponent on the inner thigh with the foot and falls in a sacrifice throw. See Judo Techniques. See Throws.

COUNTER ATTACK

A technique or techniques launched in response to the opponent's attack. Once the opponent has attacked and has committed him or herself, the martial artist can more easily evaluate and respond to the situation and defeat the opponent. Counter attacks sometimes include an evasive or defensive technique such as a block and then a strike of the defender's own.

COUNTER THROW FORM

In Judo, a prearranged series of throws and counter throws. The attacker attempts to throw and the defender immediately responds with a counter throw. The Judo practitioner is expected to master these throw-counter-throw pairs:

Throw	Counter-Throw
o-soto-gari	o-soto-gari
hiza guruma	hiza guruma
o-uchi-gari	ko-soto-gari
de-ashi-harai	de-ashi-harai
ko-soto-gari	tai otoshi
ko uchi gari	harai tsurikomi ashi
kochi guruma	ushiro goshi
tsurikomi goshi	uki goshi
harai goshi	ushiro goshi
uchi mata	ushiro goshi
seoi nage	sumi gaeshi

CRANE

A movement used in The Great Circle, a long form consisting of 37 different series of techniques, performed by Tai Chi practitioners.

CRANE STANCE

See Stance, Crane.

CRESCENT KICK

See Kick, Crescent.

CROSS BLOCK

See Block, X.

CROSS HANDS

A technique in the Tai Chi Chuan Eight Minute Form. The technique tones the muscles in the arms and improves lung capacity, as well as having a self-defense application.

CROSSED BRANCHES

A movement used in The Great Circle, a long Tai Chi form consisting of 37 different series of techniques.

CROSSING KICK

See Kick, Crescent.

CROSSOVER STEP

See Footwork.

CROSS TIGER FIST FORM

A form used in Hung Gar Wushu, the oldest form extant. It focuses on breathing and power.

CROUCHING STANCE

See Stance, Crouching.

CUNG THU

Basic blocks in Qwan-Ki-Do, performed with either arms or legs. Such blocks can defend low, middle or high areas.

CUOC PHAP

In Qwan-Ki-Do, a phrase meaning kicking techniques in general.

CUONG DAO

Vietnamese phrase for knife hand. See Strike, Knife Hand.

DA BAT

Viet Vo Dao term for reverse kick. See Kick, Reverse.

DA MOC

Viet Vo Dao term for hooking kick. See Kick, Hooking.

DA THANG

Viet Vo Dao term for front kick. See Kick, Front.

DACHI

Word used in Karate meaning stance. See Stance.

DAGGER HAND

Same as knife hand. See Strike, Knife Hand.

DAHU YUAN JIAO

In Wushu, a reverse roundhouse kick. See Kick, Roundhouse.

DAI-RYEUN

Korean term for free-style sparring. See Sparring, Free-Style.

DAISAN

Same as Zanshin. See Zanshin.

DAKI-TE

A hand technique in Karate. The hand is formed into a hook shape for the specific purpose of attacking the vital points in an opponent's face.

DAM THANG

In Viet Vo Dao, a punch. See Punch.

DAN DO FORM

Called "Dagger Form," an International Tae Kwon Do Federation form. See Tae Kwon Do Forms.

DAN EN SHO

A form practiced in Shorei-ryu Karate that was devised to improve mental and physical coordination. See Karate Forms.

DAN GUN FORM

Same as Tan Gun form. See Tan Gun Form.

DAN-TSUKI

In Karate, a punch that is not the initial attack. That is, it is either used to counter an attack, or it follows another technique in a combination. See Karate Techniques.

DAN ZUKI

Same as Dan-tsuki. See Dan-tsuki.

DANCING BEAR

A movement used in The Great Circle, a long form consisting of 37 different series of techniques, performed by Tai Chi practitioners.

DANG MON FORM

A beginner form in Qwan-Ki-Do.

DARK LADY SPINS FLAX

A movement used in The Great Circle, a long form consisting of 37 different series of techniques, performed by Tai Chi practitioners.

DE-AI

A counter-attack which depends for success on the opponent becoming distracted or momentarily losing his or her alertness. This moment is capitalized upon to defeat the opponent. The ability to detect and act on this momentary lapse of

attention takes much training and experience.

DE-AI OSAE UKE

In Karate, a pressing block. See Block, Pressing.

DE-ASHI-BARAI

Same as De-ashi-harai. See De-ashi-harai.

DE-ASHI-HARAI

In Judo, called a foot dash or foot sweep. See Sweeping Foot Throw. See Sweeps. See Judo Techniques.

DEAD PATTERNS

A Jeet Kune Do term to describe martial arts training that leads to the perfunctory performance of set patterns, instead of leading to the appropriate response to the particulars of a given situation. Such training does not lead to an understanding of the opponent or the opponent's flow or rhythm and can therefore prove dangerous in an actual fighting situation.

DECAYED TREE THROW

In Judo, a throw executed by grabbing an opponent's heel and pulling up. Also called Dead Tree Fall. See Judo Techniques. See Throws.

DEER FORM

In Bando, this form emphasizes alertness, a quality that deer must have to survive. Other Bando forms emphasize other qualities of different animals. Other forms include Eagle, Boar, Cobra, Viper, Monkey, Paddy Bird, Panther, Python, Scorpion, Bull and Tiger.

DEFY THE DRAGON

A movement used in The Great Circle, a long form consisting of 37 different series of techniques, performed by Tai Chi practitioners.

DEFY THE LEOPARD

A movement used in The Great Circle, a long form consisting of 37 different series of techniques, performed by Tai Chi practitioners.

DEFY THE PANTHER

A movement used in The Great Circle, a long form consisting of 37 different series of techniques, performed by Tai Chi practitioners.

DESTRUCTIONS

Term used in Jeet Kune Do to refer to a pattern of movements that intercept and immobilize a technique thrown by an opponent, in essence thwarting or destroying the opponent's attack.

DEVIL'S HAND

In Chinese wrestling, a technique of holding the opponent's body so that a strike will have greater impact. Also called chin'na. See Schools and Styles section.

DI SON

In Qwan-Ki-Do, a reverse punch. See Punch, Reverse.

DING BO

In Wushu, a cat stance. See Stance, Cat.

DINH TAN

See Stance, Fighting.

DINHG TAN

Same as Dinh Tan. See Stance, Fighting.

DO JIME

In Judo, a scissors technique. The practitioner uses his or her legs to squeeze the opponent. It is a basic grappling skill, often taught to beginners.

DO TREO

In Viet Vo Dao, an x-block. See Block, X.

DO RA

In Viet Vo Dao, an outside-inside block. See Block, Outside-inside.

DO VO

In Viet Vo Dao, an inside-outside block. See Block, Inside-outside.

DO XUONG

In Viet Vo Dao, a low block. See Block, Low.

DO-SAN FORM

Same as Toe-san form. See Toe-San Form.

DOC HAN VU TAN

In Qwan Ki Do, a walking stance. See Stance, Walking.

DOLL RYE CHAGI

In Tae Kwon Do, a roundhouse kick. See Kick, Roundhouse.

DOONG QUYEN

In Viet Vo Dao, blocks using the shin. See Blocks.

DOSOKU KATA SODE-TORI

In Aikido, the second defense against a sleeve grab or hold. The practitioner steps away and uses his or her free hand to strike to the opponent's elbow, aiming for a vital point. See Sleeve Holds. See Aikido Techniques.

DOSOKU TE-DORI

In Aikido, a defense against an arm hold. The practitioner immobilizes the opponent's arm, then strikes it.

DOUBLE FIST PUNCH

See Punch, Double Fist.

DOUBLE FOREARM BLOCK

See Block, Forearm.

DOUBLE KNIFE HAND BLOCK

See Block, Knife Hand.

DOUBLE PALM CHANGE

See Palm Change, Double.

DOUBLE UPPERCUT PUNCH

See Punch, Uppercut.

DOZUKURI

In Kyudo (archery), the second stance the archer assumes. The archer's right hand makes a fist, which rests on the right hip. The left hand holds the bow and arrow away from the body. See Kyudo Techniques.

DRAGON FLAME

A movement used in The Great Circle, a long form consisting of 37 different series of techniques, performed by Tai Chi practitioners.

DRAGON-TIGER FORM

A basic form in Viet Vo Dao, called Long-ho.

DRAWING METHODS SET

See Basic Drawing Methods Set.

DROPPING DRAWING ANKLE THROW

In Judo, a technique where the practitioner blocks the opponent's ankle with his or her foot, then lifts the opponent's ankle, causing him or her to fall. See Judo Techniques. See Throws.

DRUNKEN MONKEY

A form in Monkey style Wushu that simulates the imbalance and broken rhythm of a drunk person. In reality the practitioner is alert and perfectly well aware; the off-balance stance is really very solid. The movements are evasive and deceptive. Because the practitioner is so unpredictable, he or she is quite difficult to strike. The practitioner can deceive opponents, is elusive and can swiftly counter-attack. He or she tumbles, rolls, squats and jumps. The practitioner can strike quickly, catching an opponent off-guard. Other styles of Wushu have drunken forms, all of which simulate the same situation. These are usually reserved for the highest levels of training. They are the hardest, but most powerful techniques. Some of these "drunken" forms are Drunken Praying Mantis, Drunken White Crane and Eight Drunken Fairies.

DRUNKEN PRAYING MANTIS

See Drunken Monkey.

DRUNKEN WHITE CRANE

See Drunken Monkey.

DUI QUAN

See Punch, Double Fist.

DUIT-CHAGI

Same as Dwet Chagi. See Kick, Reverse.

DWET CHAGI

In Tae Kwon Do, a reverse kick. See Kick, Reverse.

EAGLE FORM

In Bando, this form emphasizes the techniques of double hand blocking and striking. Many martial arts systems emphasize imitating animal actions and name their forms after animals whose qualities, either physical or spiritual, are sought. Other Bando forms include Deer, Boar, Cobra, Viper, Monkey, Paddy Bird, Panther, Python, Scorpion, Bull and Tiger.

In Wushu, an advanced form with flowing movements that weave and dip like a bird, with emphasis on hand techniques.

EI-DAN CHAGI

In Tae Kwon Do, jumping kicks. See Kick, Jumping.

EIDO ZUKI

Same as Eido-tsuki. See Punch, Double Fist.

EIDO-TSUKI

In Karate, a double fist punch. See Punch, Double Fist.

EIGHT DRUNKEN FAIRIES

A "drunken" form developed by Eagle Claw Wushu master Lau Fat Mang. See Drunken Monkey.

EIGHT MINUTE FORM

Known as the short form in Tai Chi Chuan. It contains the essence of the Long Form but can be completed in less than ten minutes. The Long Form takes 35 minutes. The Eight Minute Form includes such techniques as parting the wild horse's mane, white stork cools it wings, repulse the monkey, hold ball gesture, and bow stance. The movements have self-defense applications.

EIGHTFOLD FENCES

In Iaido (sword drawing art), the fifth form of the seated set, called "yaegaki." The practitioner gains experience in dealing with the unexpected. The practitioner thinks that he or she has defeated an opponent who has retreated, but the opponent returns to attack. The four phases of drawing the sword, cutting with the sword, shaking the blood from the sword and resheathing the sword are all practiced.

Fig. 3.24 : Movement from the Tai Chi Chuan Eight Minute Form.

ELBOW STRIKE

See Strike, Elbow.

EMPI

A Shotokan Karate form. The name means "flying swallow." The form varies between fast and slow movements, high and low body position and emphasizes the sudden reversal of body position. See Karate Forms.

EMPI SHO

A Shorei-ryu form that was devised to develop mental and physical coordination in a martial arts practitioner. See Karate Forms.

EMPI-UCHI

See Strike, Elbow.

EN-NO-IRIMI

In Aikido, a takedown technique that uses the opponent's own force against him or her. See Takedowns.

ENCIRCLED LEG FORM

In Iaido (sword drawing art), the second form in the secret forms seated set. In Japanese, it is called "sunegakoi." The practitioner learns to respond to an unexpected obstacle. In this case, the practitioner finds that something has caught his or her leg and he or she cannot rise to fight the opponent. The four phases of drawing the sword, cutting with the sword, shaking the blood from the sword and resheathing the sword are practiced.

ENTEKI

Known as distant target shooting, with the target at least 70 yards from the archer. Practiced to improve archery skill.

ENTERING THE GATE FORM

In Iaido (sword drawing art), the eighth form in the secret forms standing set. It is called "moniri" in Japanese. The practitioner continues to learn strategies for dealing with obstructions. The practitioner imagines that he or she is on one side of an entrance such as a gate with an opponent in front and one behind. The four phases of drawing the sword, cutting with the sword, shaking the blood from the sword and resheathing the sword are performed.

ERI-JIME

In Judo, one of the several strangulation techniques in which the lapels of the opponent's uniform are used as a weapon. See Strangulation Techniques.

ERI-SEOI-NAGE

See Collar Shoulder Throw. See Throws. See Judo Techniques.

ERI-TORI

In Aikido, the name given for a complete series of defenses, nine in all, used to defend against lapel or collar holds. See Collar/Lapel Holds. See Aikido Techniques.

ERI-TORI TSUKI-AGE

In Aikido, the seventh of the defensive technique used against a collar or lapel hold. The practitioner grabs the opponent's punching hand then forces the opponent's wrist up sharply. See Aikido Techniques.

ERI-TORI YOKOMEN UCHI

In Aikido, a defensive technique used against collar or lapel grabs. The practitioner strikes the opponent's arm and then slips under. See Aikido Techniques.

ESCRIMA TECHNIQUES

In Escrima, certain techniques are basic to the art. These generally involve two opponents, each of whom is using an escrima stick. These techniques include the cross block, which defends low, middle or high. The practitioner blocks and crosses the opponent's weapon, then follows with an outside-inside block to control the opponent's stick. The two step pass requires that the practitioner step back two steps to avoid and counter the opponent's stick. The one step pass is a variation of the two step pass. In this case only one step back is taken to evade and then control opponent's stick. In the flip block, the practitioner blocks an attack and then flips the stick to his or her free hand to counter. Techniques also include interceptions, where the practitioner intercepts the opponent's stick and flips his or her own stick over to check the opponent's arm. The inside-outside block is used to control the opponent's stick. See Angles of Attack in the General Information section.

EVEN STANCE

See Stance, Even.

FACE THE NORTH WIND

A movement used in The Great Circle, a long form consisting of 37 different series of techniques, performed by Tai Chi practitioners.

FACE THE SOUTH WIND

A movement used in The Great Circle, a long form consisting of 37 different series of techniques, performed by Tai Chi practitioners.

FACING FRONT FORM

In Iaido (sword drawing art), the tenth form of the half-seated set, called "makkoh." The practitioner performs the form in a half-seated position, practicing basic cuts. The four phases of drawing the sword, cutting with the sword, shaking the blood from the sword and resheathing the sword are performed.

FAKE

See Feinting Techniques.

FAN THROUGH BACK

A technique in the Tai Chi Chuan Eight Minute Form. This technique tones the muscles in the body and improves overall flexibility. It also has a self-defense application.

FAREWELL VISIT ONE FORM

In Iaido (sword drawing art), the 11th form in the secret forms standing set, called "itomagoi sono ichi." It has only slight variations from the other "farewell visit forms." The practitioner learns to expect attacks even from unlikely sources, in this case a public official. The four phases of drawing the sword, cutting with the sword, shaking the blood from the sword and resheathing the sword are all performed.

FAREWELL VISIT THREE FORM

In Iaido (sword drawing art), the 13th form in the secret forms standing set. In Japanese it is called "itomagoi sono san." It has only slight variations from the other "farewell visit forms." The practitioner learns to expect attacks even from unlikely sources, in this case a public official. The four phases of drawing the sword, cutting with the sword, shaking the blood from the sword and resheathing the sword are all performed.

FAREWELL VISIT TWO FORM

In Iaido (sword drawing art), the 12th form in the secret forms standing set, called "itomagoi sono ni." It has only slight variations from the other "farewell visit forms." The practitioner learns to expect attacks even from unlikely sources, in this case a public official. The four phases of drawing

the sword, cutting with the sword, shaking the blood from the sword and resheathing the sword are all performed.

FAST WAVE FORM

In Iaido (sword drawing art) the first form in the secret forms extra set, called "hayanami." In this form, the practitioner learns techniques for dealing with multiple assailants. The four phases of drawing the sword, cutting with the sword, shaking the blood from the sword and resheathing the sword are all performed.

FEINTING TECHNIQUES

Also called "fakes," these are maneuvers designed to try to convince the opponent that the practitioner is planning to do one thing while actually intending to mislead the opponent and do something else. Usually jabs or short kicks are attempted, to see how the opponent will respond. Once the opponent commits him or herself to blocking or responding to the feint, the intended strike can be delivered.

FIGHTING, FREE

See Sparring, Free Style.

FIGHTING, FREE STYLE

See Sparring, Free Style.

FIGHTING STANCE

See Stance, Fighting.

FIRE ELEMENTS FORMS

In Iaijutsu, a series of forms designed to improve speed and defense. These are for use against an opponent who is not in armor. The cuts are less powerful than in the Omote forms.

FISH SCALING FORM

In Iaido (sword drawing art), the form in the half-seated set, called "urokogaeshi." The practitioner practices the half-seated position and is attacked from the side. The four phases of drawing the sword, cutting with the sword, shaking the blood from the sword and resheathing the sword are all performed.

FIST PARRIES FIST

See Wooden Dummy Drills.

FIVE ESCAPING TECHNIQUES, THE

Ninja techniques or guidelines for possible hiding places for escaping from the enemy. They include using trees and grass, using fire, using the ground or walls, using metal objects or weapons for distraction, and using water escapes.

FIVE STEP SPARRING

See Sparring, Step.

FLASH PALM

In Wushu, an upward palm heel strike. See Strike, Palm Heel.

FLOATING CLOUDS FORM

In Iaido (sword drawing art), the fourth form of the half seated set. In Japanese, it is called "ukigumo." The practitioner learns to handle an unexpected kind of attack. The practitioner imagines that he or she is seated when an opponent grabs his or her sword handle. The four phases of drawing the sword, cutting with the sword, shaking the blood from the sword and resheathing the sword are all performed.

FLOATING DROP

In Judo, the practitioner drops to one knee, wheeling the opponent over the forward foot. See Throws. See Judo Techniques.

FLOATING HIP THROW

In Judo, the basic hip throw all others are based on. The practitioner uses the hip to pivot and throw the opponent. See Throws. See Judo Techniques.

FLYING KICKS

See Kicks, Flying. See Kicks, Jumping.

FLYING PIGEON

Exercise in Tai Chi designed to improve breathing.

FLYING WILD GOOSE

Exercise in Tai Chi designed to improve blood circulation.

FON SAU DRILL

See Wooden Dummy Drills.

FOOT IMMOBILIZATION ATTACK

In Jeet Kune Do, the practitioner takes the opportunity to immobilize the opponent's foot, perhaps by trapping a kick, then attacks.

FOOT SWEEPS

See Sweeps.

FOOTWORK

A mastery of footwork is fundamental to success in the martial arts. Footwork can be used to close the gap, evade an attack, feint, or confuse the opponent. The main, basic footwork techniques are forward and backward stepping, that is, getting into and out of trouble quickly, plus the triangle technique, where all foot movements stay in the pattern of a triangle.

Straight stepping: move in straight line to the target.

Pivot stepping: push off with front or rear foot and pivot in a circle toward or away from opponent.

Beat step: a leaping step. One replaces the position of the front foot with the rear foot.

Skip step: move the back foot to the front position.

Curved step: in a half squat, move forward with rear foot arcing around and landing in front of front foot. Also called circle step.

Crossover Step: in a horse stance, one steps over one foot with the other, then slides the stationary foot over to a new position.

Gliding Side Step: in a horse stance, sliding to one side or the other.

Shuffle: advance or retreat while remaining in the same stance. Move rear foot a half step forward, then move front leg forward. To retreat, one does the opposite.

Sidestepping: move body to left and right without losing balance, to avoid attacks from front.

Stepping Horse: in Wushu, a way to move in a circle while maintaining a horse stance, by pivoting on a planted foot.

Forward and backward stepping: move rear foot to front foot, move front foot forward. Do the opposite to retreat.

Close stepping: step to side with back facing opponent.

In Judo, footwork, called walking action or shintai, consists of two basic types. In ayumi ashi, each foot moves in turn ahead of the other. In tsugi ashi, one foot follows but does not pass the other. Feet must slide over the mat.

FOREARM BLOCK

See Block, Forearm.

FORMAL THROWS

In Judo, an individual aspiring to black belt must learn the 15 formal black belt throws and demonstrate them smoothly and flawlessly. These formal throws are: uki otoshi; seoi nage; kata guruma; uki goshi; harai goshi; tsurikomi goshi; okuri ashi harai; sasae tsurikomi ashi; uchi mata; tomoe nage; ura nage; sumi gaeshi; yoko gake; yoko guruma; and uki waza.

FORMS

A series of attacking and defending movements in a prearranged pattern performed against imaginary opponents (sometimes with a partner). Forms aid in the development and refinement of coordination, balance, timing and breath control. Some ancient combat schools rely only on forms to teach techniques. In Chinese arts, forms are sometimes called Dao (Tao); in Korean arts, sometimes forms are called Taegeug (Tao). This identification with Tao reveals the essence of the performance of the form — that is, learning to be at one with the technique. In Japanese arts they are called kata. In Tae Kwon Do, they are called poomse or hyung. In the Vietnamese arts, they are called quyen. In the Wushu arts, they are called kuens.

FORWARD CUT FORM

The first of Iaido (sword drawing art) sword methods, also the first form of the seated set. It is called "maegiri" in Japanese. A basic seated form. The practitioner performs basic cuts. The four phases of drawing the sword, cutting with the sword, shaking the blood from the sword and resheathing the sword are all performed.

FORWARD FORM

See Forward Cut Form.

FORWARD STANCE

See Stance, Front.

FORWARD INVERSE CUT

In Iaido (sword drawing art), the first of the basic drawing methods secret set, intermediate level, called "zeneteki gyaku to." In this basic form, the practitioner performs fundamental cuts. The four phases of drawing the sword, cutting with the sword, shaking the blood from the sword and resheathing the sword are all performed.

FORWARD AND REARWARD CUT

The second of the Iaido (sword drawing art) sword methods. This form is from the Mugai ryu style, and is called "zengogiri." The practitioner must finish two opponents. The four phases of drawing the sword, cutting with the sword, shaking the blood from the sword and resheathing the sword are all performed.

FOUR DIRECTIONAL CUT I

In Iaido (sword drawing art), the fifth form in the basic drawing methods set, called "shihoto sono ichi." The practitioner learns to handle multiple opponents. The Four Directional Cut forms vary slightly in details. Essentially, the practitioner imagines being surrounded by four assailants, and practices cutting in four directions. The four phases of drawing the sword, cutting with the sword, shaking the blood from the sword and resheathing the sword are all performed.

FOUR DIRECTIONAL CUT II

In Iaido (sword drawing art), the sixth form in the basic drawing methods set, called "shihoto sono ni." The practitioner learns to handle multiple opponents. The Four Directional Cut forms vary slightly in details. Essentially, the practitioner imagines being surrounded by four assailants, and practices cutting in four directions. The four phases of drawing the sword, cutting with the sword, shaking the blood from the sword and resheathing the sword are all performed.

FOUR DIRECTIONAL CUT III

The fourth Iaido (sword drawing art) sword method, called "shihogiri." It is from the Suio-ryu style. Essentially, the practitioner imagines being surrounded by four assailants, and practices cutting in four directions. The four phases of drawing the sword, cutting with the sword, shaking the blood from the sword and resheathing the sword are all performed.

FOUR DIRECTIONAL CUT IV

In Iaido (sword drawing art), the fifth form in the secret forms seated set, called "shihogiri." Essentially, the practitioner imagines being surrounded by four assailants, and practices cutting in four directions. The four phases of drawing the sword, cutting with the sword, shaking the blood from the sword and resheathing the sword are all performed.

FOUR DIRECTIONAL CUT V

Also called "demon cutting." In Iaido, the fourth form in the secret forms extra set. In Japanese it is called "shihogiri" or "akumabarai (demon cutting)." Essentially, the practitioner imagines being surrounded by four assailants, and practices cutting in four directions. The four phases of drawing the sword, cutting with the sword, shaking the blood from the sword and resheathing the sword are all performed.

FREE SPARRING

See Sparring, Free Style.

FREE STYLE SPARRING

See Sparring, Free Style.

FREE STYLE FIGHTING

See Sparring, Free Style.

FREE FIGHTING

See Sparring, Free Style.

FRONT INSTEP KICK

See Kick, Front Instep.

FRONT STANCE

See Stance, Front.

FRONT KICK

See Kick, Front.

FRONT SNAP KICK

See Kick, Front.

FRONT THRUST KICK

See Kick, Front.

FRONT PUSH KICK

See Kick, Front.

FUDO NO SHIDEI NO KATA

A Japanese phrase used to refer to the basic forms in all martial arts styles.

FUDODACHI

Same as Fudotachi. See Stance, Ready.

FUDOTACHI

See Stance, Ready.

FUGUL SEUG-GI

See Stance, Back.

FUJOSHI YO GOSHIN NO KATA

In Judo, self-defense techniques for women. See Judo techniques.

FUKUSHIKI KUMITE

A term used to denote two attacks at once during a fighting or combat form in Karate.

FUKYU I

A form taught in Goju-ryu Karate. This form and Fukyu II were developed in the late-1970s by Meitoku Yagi, the leading authority of this school. The two forms were designed for beginning students. The form emphasizes vertical punches, blocking with double hands, and fingertip striking. This is the second form learned by the beginner. See Karate Forms.

FUKYU II

A form taught in Goju-ryu Karate. This form and Fukyu I were developed in the late-1970s by Meitoku Yagi, the leading authority of this school. The two forms were designed for beginning students. The second form concentrates on the horse stance and slow blocking movements. It is the third form learned. See Karate Forms.

FULL STOP FORM

In Iaido (sword drawing art), the fourth form of the secret forms standing set. In this situation, the practitioner blocks an attacker three times before the attacker gives up. The four phases of drawing the sword, cutting with the sword, shaking the blood from the sword and resheathing the sword are all performed.

FUMI-DASHI

Lunge step. See Body Shifting.

FUMI-KIRI

A Karate phrase used to denote any strike that uses the knife edge or cutting edge of the foot.

FUMI KOMI

A stamping kick used in Karate. See Kick, Stamping.

FUMI-WAZA

In Karate, a crushing technique used as either a strike or block. Either the foot or the fist can be used. Any part of the opponent's body can be the target. See Karate Techniques.

FUMIKOMI AGE-UKE

See Block, High.

FUMIKOMI SHUTO-UKE

See Block, Knife Hand.

FUMIKOMI UDE-UKE

See Block, Forearm.

FURIKABURI

In Iaido (sword drawing art), the ready position for a downward cut, with the raised sword over the practitioner's head.

FUSEGI

A Karate phrase meaning defensive techniques in general.

GAMEN KAMAE

See Stance, Ready.

GAMEN-TSUKI

See Strike, Backfist.

GAMEN-ZUKI

Same as Gamen-tsuki. See Strike, Backfist.

GANKAKU FORM

An advanced form in Karate taught by the Shotokan school. Formerly called "Chinto," the name means "a crane on a rock." Balancing on one leg, the practitioner performs techniques such as side kick and backfist strike.

GARAMI

A term used in both Aikido and Judo to refer to any wrap-and-hold motion used to immobilize the opponent.

GASSHO-GAMA

A saluting stance in Shorinji Karate. See Salutation Techniques.

GE-BAEK

Same as Kae Beck. See Kae Beck. See Tae Kwon Do Forms.

GEDAN NO KAMAE

In Kendo, a low guard stance in which the sword is held in front with the tip lowered. See Stances.

GEDAN UKE

See Block, Low.

GEDAN KAKE UKE

See Block, Hooking.

GEDAN-BARAI

See Block, Low.

GEKISAI I and II

The fourth and fifth forms of the 14 learned in Goju-ryu Karate. The name means "to destroy" and "to demolish." Grandmaster Miyagi invented the forms around 1940, but there is a significant similarity to techniques used in Shuri-te, an ancient Okinawan martial art similar to Karate. As is appropriate for a hard-soft style, both linear and circular techniques are taught in these forms, as are breathing techniques. Both forms contain sanchin-dachi steps, front snap kicks, elbow strikes and backfist strikes. The first form ends with three punches in three directions. The second ends with roundhouse blocking performed in a cat stance. See Karate Forms.

GESA-GATAME

In Judo, called a scarf hold, a grappling technique in which the practitioner lies across the opponent's body. Varieties of scarf holds include kuzure-gesa gatame, ushiro gesa-gatame, makura gesa-gatame and hon gesa-gatame. Also spelled Kesa-gatame.

GIAO LONG CUOC

In Qwan-Ki-Do, a scissors take down. The practitioner, using his or her legs like scissors, off-balances the opponent and both fall to the ground. See Takedowns.

GI IN

A form in Karate that emphasizes strikes and blocks with the hands. The only foot technique used is a front kick. See Karate Forms.

GINGA

The basic footwork for Capoeira, requiring constant movement.

GIWAKEN

Also called tenchiken. A phrase used in Shorinji Karate to indicate basic offensive and defensive techniques the practitioner must master.

GLIDING SIDE STEP

See Footwork.

GO-NO-SEN KATA

Throws and counter-throws. See Judo Techniques.

GOBU NO TSUME

In Kyudo (archery), this refers to the final aspects of tensing the bow.

GOGYO

See Fire Elements Form.

GOHO

Literally, "hard method." This term, used in Shorinji Karate, refers to active techniques such as striking and blocking, in contrast to evasive techniques. See Juho.

GOHON-KUMITE

See Sparring, Five Step.

GOJUSHIHO DAI

The Greater 54 Directions, a Shotokan Karate form. See Karate Forms.

GOJUSHIHO SHO

The Lesser 54 Directions, a Shotokan Karate form. See Karate Forms.

GOKYO NO NAGE WAZA

In Aikido, this refers to using an outstretched arm to block a blow from above or from the side. In Judo, it refers to the five groups of throwing techniques performed from a standing position. Each group contains eight throws and mastery of the throws in each group is essential to rank promotions. The throws become progressively more difficult. See Aikido Techniques. See Judo Techniques.

GOLDEN COCKEREL STANDS ON LEFT LEG and RIGHT LEG

Techniques in the Tai Chi Chuan Eight Minute Form. Each has a self-defense application, but they also serve to strengthen the abdominal muscles and increase balance and coordination.

GONG-BO

Same as Gung Bo. See Stance, Bow.

GONIN-GAKE

In Karate, refers to one practitioner defending against attacks from five opponents.

GO-NO-SEN NO KATA

See Counter Throw Form.

GOPEI SHO

A form in Shorei-ryu Karate that was devised to develop mental and physical coordination. See Karate Forms.

GOSHI-GURUMA

Same as Koshi-guruma. See Hip Wheel.

GOSHIN-JUTSU

In Judo, a set of prearranged exercises also called "the Kodokan Goshin-jutsu." These exercises include defense against grabs, chokes and so on. The exercises are divided into two categories, those against an opponent with a weapon, such as a dagger, stick and gun (nine techniques) and those against an unarmed opponent (12 techniques). See Judo Techniques.

GOTON NO JUTSU

See Five Escaping Techniques.

GRAPPLING

Techniques of seizing and holding the opponent. Instead of executing strikes at a long or medium range, the grappler must move in close and attempt to control the opponent through holds, immobilizations, takedowns and groundwork techniques.

GRASP THE BIRD'S TAIL LEFT and RIGHT

Techniques in the Tai Chi Chuan Eight Minute Form. The techniques can be used in self-defense, but primarily they are used to strengthen the muscles of the back and abdomen, and to increase lung capacity.

GRASP THE OARS

A movement used in The Great Circle, a long form consisting of 37 different series of techniques, performed by Tai Chi practitioners.

GRASP THE WHEEL

A movement used in The Great Circle, a long form consisting of 37 different series of techniques, performed by Tai Chi practitioners.

GREAT CIRCLE, THE

A long form practiced by Tai Chi martial artists. It consists of 37 different movements repeated throughout the routine.

GROIN STRIKE

Any technique that targets the vulnerable groin area. See Strike, Groin. See Vital Ponts in the General Information section.

GUARDS

Another name for blocks. See Blocks.

GUM SAU SWITCH

See Wooden Dummy Drills.

GUNG BO

In Wushu, the bow stance, sometimes called the bow-and-arrow stance. See Stance, Bow.

GUNG GEE FOOK FU

See Cross Tiger Fist Form.

GWANG-GAE

Same as Kwang Gye. See Kwang Gye. See Tae Kwon Do Forms.

GYAKU TE-DORI

In Aikido, a wrist lock performed by twisting the opponent's hand inward.

GYAKU JUJU-JIME

See Reverse Cross Strangle. See Strangulation Techniques. See Judo Techniques.

GYAKU TSUKI NO ASHI

See Stance, Front.

GYAKU KATA TE-DORI

In Aikido, a defense against an arm hold. The practitioner bends the opponent's wrist, then pulls the opponent forward, off-balance. See Aikido Techniques. See Arm Holds.

GYAKU KESA-GARAMI

Same as Gyaku gesa-garami. See Gyaku gesa-garami. See Judo Techniques.

GYAKU MAWASHI-GERI

In Karate, a reverse roundhouse kick. See Kick, Roundhouse.

GYAKU TSUKI

See Punch, Reverse.

GYAKU OKURI ERI

In Judo, a strangulation caused by grabbing the opponent's lapels and twisting.

GYAKU KESA-GATAME

Same as Gyaku gesa-gatame. See Gyaku Gesa-Gatame.

GYAKU GAMAE

See Stance, Fighting.

GYAKU-GERI

In Shorinji Karate, refers to a traveling kicking technique. This is a kick that is begun at some distance from the target.

GYAKU GESA-GARAMI

In Judo, any act of pinning one's opponent to the ground by lying across his or her body.

GYAKU GESA-GATAME

The same as Gyaku gesa-garami. See Gyaku Gesa-Garami.

GYAKU-JUJI

In Judo, any immobilization technique in which the practitioner crosses the arms of the opponent.

GYAKU-UCHI

One of the 12 basic blocks and strikes in the stick arts Jodo and Jojutsu.

GYAKU-ZUKI

In Karate, the same as Gyaku-tsuki. See Punch, Reverse. Also one of the 12 basic blocks and strikes in the staff arts Jodo and Jojutsu.

GYAKU-ZUKI NO ASHI

See Stance, Front.

HA

In Iaido (sword drawing art), the second movement in nukisuke, drawing the sword. This is the actual drawing of the sword. The other two movements are jo, preparation, and kyu, sudden cut.

HAC TAN

See Stance, Crane.

HACHIJI TACHI

Same as Hachiji Dachi. See Stance, Natural.

HADAKA-JIME

In Judo, a strangulation technique performed by using one's arms instead of the opponent's lapels or clothing. Called "naked struggle," because no clothing is needed. See Strangulation Techniques. See Judo Techniques.

HAIR GRABS

Any technique in which a practitioner or opponent grabs the other's hair as a means of control.

HAISHU-UCHI

In Karate, a backhand strike. See Strike, Backhand.

HAISHU-UKE

In Karate, a backhand block. See Block, Backhand.

HAITO-UCHI

See Strike, Ridge Hand.

HAIWAN NAGASHI-UKE

See Block, Forearm.

HAKKO-DORI

In Wa-jutsu, a phrase used to describe any self-defense methods executed against a wrist grab. In practice, the opponent kneels and seizes the practitioner's wrists and the practitioner uses various techniques to release the grab.

HALF-SEATED SET

An extremely challenging set of forms in Iaido (sword drawing art). These are taught at the intermediate level, after considerable training. The half-seated position is easier to rise from than the regular seated position, but it is difficult to master. The forms develop leg muscles. In Japanese, it is called "tatehiza no bu." The ten forms are:

1. *Cloud bank*
2. *Tiger's step*
3. *Lightning*
4. *Floating clouds*
5. *Mountain wind*
6. *Breaking waves*
7. *Fish scaling*
8. *Returning waves*
9. *Waterfall*
10. *Facing front*

HAMMER FIST BLOCK

See Block, Hammer Fist.

HAMMER FIST STRIKE

See Strike, Hammer Fist.

HANARE

In Kyudo (archery), the seventh stance: releasing the arrow. The fingers release the bowstring without conscious effort or thought, when mind and body are in harmony. Once the release has been accomplished, the drawing arm rests in the backward position, and the stance is maintained for several seconds.

HAND IMMOBILIZATION ATTACK

In Jeet Kune Do, those techniques designed for immobilizing the opponent's hand, usually by intercepting and trapping, and then delivering a counter-attack. See Immobilizations.

HANE MAKEKOME

Same as Hane Makikomi. See Outer Winding Spring Hip Throw.

HANE-AGE

In Kendo (sword fighting art), the technique of raising and striking downward with the sword after having performed a feinting movement designed to force the opponent to lower his or her guard.

HANE-GOSHI

Known as Spring Hip Throw. Also called Spring Leg Throw. See Spring Hip Throw. See Throws. See Judo Techniques.

HANE-MAKI-KOMI

See Outer Winding Spring Hip Throw. See Throws. See Judo Techniques.

HANGETSU FORM

In Karate, a form that uses hangetsu-dachi, a stance in which the feet move forward in such a way as to create a semi-circle. The stance is similar to sanchin stance. The name means "half moon form."

HANGETSU TACHI

Same as Hangetsu-dachi. See Stance, Hourglass.

HANGETSU-DACHI

See Stance, Hourglass.

HANGING HORSE STANCE

See Stance, Crane.

HANMI

See Stance, Fighting.

HAPPO-GIRI

In Kenjutsu (swordfighting), a technique that involves using the sword to cut in eight directions.

HAPPO-UNDO

In Judo and Aikido, an exercise designed to teach a practitioner how to throw the opponent in eight directions.

HARAI MAKEKOME

Same as Harai Maki-komi. See Sweeping Winding Throw. See Throws. See Judo Techniques.

HARAI MAKI-KOMI

See Sweeping Winding Throw. See Throws. See Judo Techniques.

HARAI

Any sweeping or hooking technique in which the practitioner uses his or her leg or foot to take down the opponent.

HARAI-GOSHI

See Sweeping Hip Throw. Also called Sweeping Thigh Throw. See Throws. See Judo Techniques.

HARAI-TE

See Strike, Palm.

HARAI-TSURIKOMI

See Sweeping Drawing Ankle Throw. See Throw. See Judo Techniques.

HARIA-TSURIKOMI ASHI

See Lifting Sweeping Foot Throw.

HARMONIOUS FORM, THE

A basic form in Viet Vo Dao, called Trung Hao.

HASAMI-TSUKI

See Punch, Scissors.

HASAMI-ZUKI

Same as Hasami-tsuki. See Punch, Scissors.

HASEGAWA EISHIN RYU

A form in Iaido (sword drawing art), of the Muso Shinden-ryu. It consists of ten movements executed from a standing position.

HASEN KATA

In Karate, performing a series of forms, one after the other. See Karate Techniques.

HASSO NO KAMAE

In Kendo (swordfighting), a stance in which the sword is held vertically at shoulder level either on the right or left side.

HATAKI KOMI

In Sumo, a side-stepping evasive movement that causes the opponent to fall from his or her own momentum. This technique can also be assisted by placing a palm on the opponent's back. See Sumo Techniques.

HAYANAMI

See Fast Wave Form.

HEI-KEN

See Strike, Two-Finger.

HEIAN GODAN

A beginner form in Karate, used in particular in Shotokan style. The fifth and final form learned by the beginner. The form emphasizes balancing and jumping techniques. See Karate Forms.

HEIAN KATA

These are five basic forms that are learned in particular in Shotokan Karate. The forms must be learned in order to earn rank promotions. The name means "peaceful." The forms were once called by their Chinese name, "pinan," and some Karate schools do continue to use this name. Once the Heian forms are mastered, the practitioner moves on to Tekka forms. The Heian forms are designated Heian Shodan, Heian Nidan, Heian Sandan, Heian Yondan, and Heian Godan, or sometimes Heian I through V.

HEIAN NIDAN

A basic form in Karate, used in particular in Shotokan style. The second form learned by the beginner. The form emphasizes front kick and side kick plus quick direction changes. See Karate Forms.

HEIAN SANDAN

A basic form in Karate, used in particular in Shotokan style. The third form learned by the beginner. The form emphasizes forearm blocking and back fist strikes. See Karate Forms.

HEIAN SHODAN

A basic form in Karate, used in particular in Shotokan style. The first form learned by the beginner. The form emphasizes front stance, back stance and footwork patterns. See Karate Forms.

HEIAN YONDAN

A basic form in Karate, used in particular in Shotokan style. The fourth form learned by the beginner. The form emphasizes balance and a variety of techniques. See Karate Forms.

HEIKO DACHI

Sometimes called Parallel Stance. See Stance, Ready.

HEIKO-TSUKI

See Punch, Parallel.

HEIKO-ZUKI

Same as Heiko-tsuki. See Punch, Parallel.

HEISOTU-DACHI

See Stance, Attention.

HEISOKU TACHI

Same as Heisoku-dachi. See Stance, Attention.

HIDARI TEIJI-DACHI

See Stance, T.

HIDARI-ASHI-JIME

In Judo, a strangulation technique executed when the practitioner throws his or her leg over the opponent's throat. See Judo Techniques. See Strangulation Techniques.

HIDARI-DO

In Kendo (swordfighting art), any strike that lands on the opponent's left side.

HIDARI-YOTSU

In Sumo, grappling techniques that are performed with the practitioner's left arm on the inside. See Sumo Techniques.

HIGH BLOCK

See Block, High.

HIGH PAT ON HORSE

A technique in the Tai Chi Chuan Eight Minute Form. In addition to its self-defense application, the technique is designed to improve posture and invigorate the practitioner.

HIJI NAGE MAE ERI-TORI

In Aikido, a technique used to defend against a lapel hold. The practitioner sweeps the opponent backward and strikes to a vital point with the foot. See Aikido Techniques. See Collar/Lapel Holds.

HIJI NOBASHI ERI-TORI

In Aikido, a technique used against a lapel or collar hold. The practitioner grabs his or her own clothing near the opponent's grip, pulls the opponent forward, and strikes to a vital point in the opponent's face. See Collar/Lapel Holds. See Aikido Techniques.

HIJI WAZA

In Aikido, any technique that attacks the opponent's elbow.

HIJI SURI UKE

See Block, Elbow.

HIJI-ATE

See Strike, Elbow.

HIKI WAKE

In Kyudo (archery), the fifth stance. The practitioner brings the bow above the head, holding the string taught, and stands without moving. The goal is to reach maximum tension, which occurs just before release of the bow string.

HIKI OTOSHI

In Sumo, a technique executed when the opponent attempts a low attack. The practitioner avoids the attack and pushes down on the opponent's shoulders or back to force the opponent to the ground.

HIKI TATE

A phrase used in the martial arts referring to the act of drawing an opponent closer in order to gain more or better control over him or her.

HIKIKAKE

In Sumo, avoiding an attack by side stepping. The practitioner then grabs the opponent's arm and pulls him off-balance.

HINERI

A hip twist in Sumo, used to twist and pull the opponent off-balance.

HINERI-NAGASHI

In Karate, an evasive movement executed by turning inward to avoid the opponent's strike. See Body Shifting.

HINERI-UCHI

See Strike, Elbow.

HIP WHEEL

In Judo, a technique executed by holding the opponent around the neck and pulling him or her over the hip. See Judo Techniques. See Throws.

HIRAKI UKE

In Karate, an evasive movement executed by turning the body sideways. See Body Shifting.

HITSUI-GERI

See Strike, Knee.

HIZA GATAME

In Judo, a technique in which the practitioner uses his or her knee and thigh to immobilize the opponent's arm.

h Wa-jutsu, a series of movements demonstrating techniques that free one from wrist holds.

HIZA-GERI

Same as Hitsui-geri. See Strike, Knee.

HIZA GURUMA

See Knee Wheel. Also called Kneeblock Wheeling Throw. See Throws. See Judo Techniques.

HIZA JIME

In Judo, a strangulation technique performed with the knee. See Judo Techniques. See Strangulation Techniques.

HIZA TSUI

See Strike, Knee.

HO VI CUOC

See Kick, Reverse.

HOANH CUOC

See Kick, Roundhouse.

HOANH PHONG

A backward elbow strike. See Strike, Elbow.

HOANH WA

An inward or outward elbow strike. See Strike, Elbow.

HOLD BALL GESTURE

A technique in Tai Chi Chuan where the left hand rests at waist level with the palm up, and the right hand is at chest level with the palm down. The positions of the hands may be switched. A fundamental technique for the Eight Minute form.

HOLDS

See Immobilizations. See Arm Holds. See Collar/Lapel Holds.

HON TATE SHIHO GATAME

See Judo Techniques.

HON KAMI SHIHO GATAME

See Judo Techniques.

HON YOKO SHIHO GATAME

See Judo Techniques.

HOOK PUNCH

See Punch, Hook.

HOOKING KICK

See Kick, Hooking.

HORSE FORM

A beginner form in Wushu, especially Hop Gar and Choy Li Fut, in which a series of horse stances are assumed.

HORSE STANCE

See Stance, Horse.

HORSEBACK STANCE

See Stance, Horse.

HOURGLASS STANCE

See Stance, Hourglass.

HUA CHIN

In Mind-Body Boxing (Hsing-I) Wushu, the technique of being able to generate power without resorting to physical force.

HUEN DA PROGRESSION

See Wooden Dummy Drill.

HUGUAL JA SAE

In Tae Kwon Do, a back stance. See Stance, Back.

HUI BO

See Stance, Cat.

HUL-GOK FORM

See Yul-Kok Form. See Tae Kwon Do Forms.

HUO LUNG CHENG CHING GONG

See Arousing the Dragon.

HUZI TAIDU

See Stance, Fighting.

HWA-RANG FORM

An International Tae Kwon Do Federation form learned at the third class level. There are 29 movements in this intermediate form. It consists of techniques such as spearhand strike, c-hand block, roundhouse kick and x-block. The form is named after the Hwarang youth group which formed during the Silla Dynasty around 620 A.D. Hwarang youths became an important part of the movement to unify the three independent kingdoms of Korea.

HYONG

See Form.

HYUNG

See Form.

IAIDO SWORD METHODS

In Japanese, it is called "toho." These are a series of forms selected by the All-Japan Iaido Federation as representative of the various forms from the various traditional styles of swordsmanship. The difficulty of the forms increases as the practitioner moves from the first to the fifth. The forms are: 1. Forward Cut; 2. Forward and Rearward Cut; 3. Rising Cut; 4. Four Directional Cut (III); and 5. Tip Flip.

IAGOSHI

See Stance, Crouching.

IDORI

In Judo, a series of eight basic self-defense movements. These are Ryo-te-dori, Tsugake, Tsuriage, Yoko-uchi, Ushiro-dori, Tsukomi, Kirikomi, and Yoko-tsuki (also called Yokozuki). See Judo Techniques.

IKKYO CONTROL

In Aikido, this is called "the first principle," and it consists of various techniques used for immoblizing an opponent's arm. These are Ryote-dori, Kata-te-ryo-te-dori, Shomen-uchi, Shomen-tsuki, Ushiro-ryote-kubi-dori, Ushiro-tekuba-kubi-dori, and Ushiro-eri-dori (also known as Ude-osae). See Immobilizations. See Aikido Techniques.

IL BO DAE RYUN

In Tae Kwon Do, one-step sparring. See Sparring, Step (one-step).

ILYEO

A Tae Kwon Do form taught at seventh dan black belt. Part of the palgue series. See Tae Kwon Do Forms.

IMMOBILIZATIONS

These are various techniques for controlling the opponent's body or a limb, sometimes using a lock technique, sometimes using the weight of one's own body.

Aikido:

Controls. These are called the Five Principles and they consist of various techniques used for immoblizing an opponent.

> *First Control: These immobilize the opponent's arm.*
>
> *Second Control: These immobilize the opponent's wrist.*
>
> *Third Control: These immobilize the opponent's elbow.*
>
> *Fourth Control: Joint locks to the wrist.*
>
> *Fifth Control: Arm holds.*

See Aikido Techniques.

Jeet Kune Do:

Foot immobilization attack. The practitioner takes the opportunity to immobilize the opponent's foot, perhaps by trapping a kick, then attacks.

Hand immobilization attack. Those techniques designed for immobilizing the opponent's hand, usually by intercepting and trapping, and then delivering a counter-attack.

Judo:

Ashi-gatame. An immobilization technique used on the ground. The practitioner immobilizes or dislocates the opponent's leg by using both arms while wedging a foot under the opponent's chin.

Kuzure-gesa-gatame. A technique for immobilizing the opponent by trapping the opponent's arm.

Kuzure-tate-shiho-gatame. A technique for controlling the opponent by sliding an arm around the opponent and gripping the belt at the back, which secures the opponent's shoulder and arm.

Kuzure-kami-shiho-gatame. An immobilization performed by pinning the opponent's chest, and gripping the belt and collar.

Kuzure-kami-shiho-garame. A immobilization technique in which the practitioner controls both arms and legs of an opponent.

Kuzure-yoko-shiho-gatame. An immoblization from the side. The practitioner pins the opponent's chest and shoulder, then grips the belt.

Makura-kesa-gatame. A technique for immoblizing the opponent from the rear. The practitioner wraps his or her arms around the opponent's upper body and locks the hands together.

Mune-gyaku. A technique for controlling and immobilizing an opponent by holding and immobilizing the chest.

Ude garami henka-waza. A shoulder immobilization technique performed with opponent's arm partly bent.

See Judo Techniques.

INAZUMA

See Lightning Form.

INNERCUT THROW

See Major Inner Reaping.

INNER THIGH THROW

In Judo, a technique where the practitioner supports his or her weight on one leg and uses the other to sweep the opponent's inner thigh. See Judo Techniques. See Throws.

INSIDE LATERAL SACRIFICE THROW

See Corner Throw.

INSIDE-OUTSIDE BLOCK

See Block, Inside-outside.

INSIDE SWEEPING FOOT THROW

See Minor Inner Reaping Foot Throw.

INWARD BENT KNEE STANCE

See Stance, Inward Bent Knee.

IPIT-KAMAY

See Block, C-Hand.

IPPON KEN TSUKI

Chestnut fist. See Punch, Knuckle.

IPPON KEN ZUKI

Same as Ippon ken tsuki. See Punch, Knuckle.

IPPON SEOI NAGE

See One Arm Shoulder Throw. Also called Arm Around the Shoulder Throw.

IPPON-KUMITE

In Karate, a phrase used to indicate any attack that uses only one technique. According to most Karate strategy, the best attack is made with several techniques in succession.

IPPON YO GOSHIN NO KATA

In Judo, self-defense techniques for men. See Judo Techniques.

IRIMI

The method of using any opponent's force against him or her. Also called tenkan and o-irimi.

IRIMI NAGE

In Aikido, a group of throwing techniques that are used to counter an opponent's attack, especially by using the opponent's own force against him or her. These are called Katate-ryote-dori, Shomen-uchi, Yokomen-uchi, Shomen tsuki, Ushiro-ryote kubi dori and Ushiro ryo kata dori. See Aikido Techniques.

IRIMI-UKE

In Karate, a technique for evading an attack by stepping diagonally away from the opponent. See Footwork.

IRON HORSE FORM

See Naihanchi.

IRON HORSEMAN POSTURE

See Stance, Horse.

IRON THREAD FORM

In Hung Gar, the most advanced form for chi and stance training. It contains both hard and soft techniques.

ITOMAGOI SONO ICHI

See Farewell Visit I Form.

ITOMAGOI SONO NI

See Farewell Visit II Form.

ITOMAGOI SONO SAN

See Farewell Visit III Form.

ITSUTSU NO KATA

In Judo, a series of five techniques practiced in defense of various attacks, called the five principles. Each attack-and-defense technique is practiced in succession with a partner and then the techniques are repeated in reverse order to reinforce learning. See Judo Techniques.

IWANAMI

See Breaking Waves Form.

JA YU DAE RYUN

In Tae Kwon Do, free style sparring. See Sparring, Free Style.

JA SAE

In Tae Kwon Do, the name for stance. See Stance.

JAB

See Punch, Jab.

JIAO

A general term meaning foot techniques in Wushu.

JI TAE FORM

A Tae Kwon Do form taught at fifth dan black belt level. It is part of the palgue series. See Tae Kwon Do forms.

JI-GEIKO

See Sparring, Free Style.

JI-IN

A form used in Karate that was created and preserved by ancient Buddhist monks. See Karate Forms.

JI-ON

A form in Karate that was created and preserved by ancient Buddhist monks. This form emphasizes body shifting and complex footwork patterns. See Karate Forms.

JIGO HONTAI

Also Jigotai. See Stance, Fighting.

JIGOTAI

See Stance, Fighting.

JIJU UNDO

See Sparring, Step.

JIJU KUMITE

See Sparring, Free Style.

JIMAN

In Kyudo (archery), the sixth stance. The archer pulls the bow to complete extension. This step occurs just before release of the bow. The archer must not show any sign of strain. Also called Kai or Jindachi-zukuri. See Kyudo Techniques.

JINRAI

See Thunderclap Form.

JIU-KUMITE

See Sparring, Free Style.

JIYU-KUMITE

Same as Jiu-kumite. See Sparring, Free Style.

JIYU-IPPON-KUMITE

See Sparring, Step (one-step).

JIYU-RENSHU

See Sparring, Free Style.

JO

The first of the three aspects of nukisuke, or drawing the sword, in Iaido (sword drawing art). This is the preparation for drawing. The other two are ha, actual drawing, and kyu, the sudden cut.

JO-SOKUTEI

See Kick, Front.

JODAN NO KAMAE

In Kendo (swordfighting art), the act of holding the sword above one's head before striking with a downward cut, one of the basic techniques.

JODAN AGE UKE

In Karate, a high block. See Block, High.

JODO TECHNIQUES

In Jodo, or way of the stick, there are several basic blows and blocks. These are built upon to create more complex techniques. Most techniques are performed with the standard two-handed grip, though a reverse grip is also used. The stick is used to strike, block, thrust, press and push. In the Shindo-Muso school, which is the original style as conceived by Muso Gunnosuke, a total of 64 techniques are taught. These include the twelve original or basic techniques, plus variations.

JOINT LOCKS

These are techniques for immobilizing the various joints of an opponent, usually caused by pulling or pushing the joint in the direction opposite of its natural movement. Joint locks can include armlocks, finger locks, ankle locks, wrist locks, spine locks, knee locks and elbow locks. They are effective in preventing the opponent from using the limb so immobilized, but they are also painful techniques, which may cause the opponent to end the confrontation. See Immobilizations.

JOJUTSU TECHNIQUES
In Jojutsu (staff art), the basic blows are the same as in Jodo. See Jodo Techniques.

JOM SAU CHASING
See Wooden Dummy Drills.

JONG
See Punch, Uppercut.

JOONG-GUN FORM
See Chung-Guen Form.

JOSHI JUDO GOSHINHO
In Judo, self-defense techniques specifically designed for women by Judo masters. These techniques focus on countering typical attacks and escaping from grabs and holds. See Judo Techniques.

JU NO KATA
In Judo, a series of lessons consisting of basic movements, which the student must master to promote in rank. The lessons include techniques such as the upper cut punch, the spear hand strike, plus others. Five techniques are taught in each lesson and three lessons comprise the series. See Judo Techniques.

JU-IPPON KUMITE
A series of basic techniques, eight in all, practiced in the Shotokan style of Karate and used in counter-attacks against the high punch, middle punch, middle front kick, middle and high roundhouse kick, and reverse kick. See Karate Techniques.

JUDO TECHNIQUES
Judo training consists of self-defense, forms practice and sparring. See Throws. See Armlocks. See Immobilizations. See Strangulation Techniques.

Gokyo no nage waza. The forty original throwing techniques in Judo. Refers to the five groups of throwing techniques performed from a standing position. Each group contains eight throws and mastery of the throws in each group is essential to rank promotions. The throws become progressively more difficult.

Goshin-jutsu. In Judo, a set of prearranged exercises also called "the Kodokan Goshin-jutsu." These exercises include defense against grabs, chokes and holds. The exercises are divided into two categories, those against an opponent with a weapon, such as a dagger, stick and gun (9 techniques) and those against an unarmed opponent (12 techniques).

Idori. A series of eight basic self-defense movements. These are Ryo-te-dori, Tsugake, Tsuri-age, Yoko-uchi, Ushiro-dori, Tsukomi, Kirikomi, and Yoko-tsuki (also called Yokozuki).

Itsutsu no kata. A series of five techniques practiced in defense of various attacks, called the five principles. Each attack-and-defense technique is practiced in succession with a partner and then the techniques are repeated in reverse order to reinforce learning.

Ju no kata. A series of lessons consisting of basic movements, which the student must master to promote in rank. The lessons include techniques such as the upper cut punch, the spear hand strike, plus others. Five techniques are taught in each lesson and three lessons comprise the series.

Katame no kata. A formal series of techniques used for controlling an opponent, including strangulation and joint lock techniques, of which five each are performed.

Kime no kata. A series of exercises that consist of self-defense techniques performed while kneeling and while standing. The kneeling set has eight techniques and the standing set has twelve.

Seiryoku zen-yo kokumin tai-iku no kata. Formal exercises, of which there are 28 solo exercises that emphasize vital point attacks and 20 exercises designed to improve speed and decision-making processes. These exercises are based on the principles of efficiency.

Tachi-ai. A series of twelve defensive techniques performed while standing. The techniques include joint locks, holds and evasive movements.

Uchi komi. Repeated practice of a movement until it is perfected, done with a partner. There are two types, active and passive. In the passive types, the partner stands still and does not resist as the other practitioner attempts different throws without actually throwing the partner. In the active type, the two practitioners try to complete throws against each other as if they were having a contest. As a test of endurance, some practitioners have been known to complete five hundred throws of this kind without stopping.

Ashi-waza. All forms of throwing, grappling and vital point attack. In prearranged formal routines, Judo practitioners apply such techniques. The only armlocks allowed in contest are those that apply pressure to the elbow joint. Higher grade students can learn shoulder and wrist locks not used in competition.

The following forms are taught at the Kodokan:

> *nage no kata — throwing forms*
> *katame no kata — grappling and holding forms*
> *randori no kata — the nage no kata and the katame no kata together.*
> *go no sen no kata — throws and counter throws from a standing position.*
> *kime no kate — focus or desicion forms*
> *ju no kata — basic forms*
> *koshiki no kata — ancient forms*
> *kodokan goshin jutsu — Self-defense forms*
> *itsutsu-no-kata — Five Principle forms*
> *seiryoku senyo kokumin taiiku no kata — national physical education forms.*
> *fujoshi-yo goshin no kata — self-defense for women*
> *ippon yo goshin no kata — self-defense for men*

Other forms include more advanced the shobu-no-kata, the form of attacks, and the go-no-kata, the form of strikes and hardness.

Seven forms were created by Kano Jigoro, the founder of Judo:

The first emphasizes displacements (shintai) and body shifting (tai sabaki). It includes several basic throws.

The second consists of immobilizations, strangulations and dislocations.

The third has 12 throws, including some of the more spectacular such as the tai-otoshi, or body drop.

The fourth, also called shinken-shobi or the form of combat, teaches techniques against empty hand and weapons attacks. The practitioner performs techniques both from a sitting and a standing position.

The fifth form demonstrates the five principles. These are 1) the principle of concentration of energy, 2) the principle of non-resistance, 3) the principle of circular movement, 4) the principle of the pendulum and 5) the principle of inertia.

The sixth form teaches techniques of evasion and displacement.

The seventh form, originally from the old Kito-ryu school of Jujutsu, represents the foundation of Judo. It has 21 throws.

HOLDS

Ashi-gatame. Ankle Arm Lock. Immobilizing or dislocating the opponent's leg using both arms, while one foot is wedged under opponent's chin.

Four quarters holds. The most common, basic ones are:

Hon kami shiho gatame. A basic upper four quarters hold. The practitioner pins the opponent's chest and grabs the belt at the sides.

Hon tate shiho gatame. A basic vertical four quarters hold. The practitioner straddles the opponent, and locks the opponent's arm and head against his or her own head.

Hon yoko shiho gatame. A basic side four quarters hold. From the side, the practitioner pins the chest of the opponent, with one arm over the opponent's shoulders and neck and the other arm gripping the belt.

Gesa-gatame. Called a scarf hold, a grappling technique in which the practitioner lies across the opponent's body. Varieties of scarf holds include kuzure-gesa gatame, ushiro gesa gatame, makura gesa gatame and hon gesa gatame.

Gyaku Gesa-Garami/ Gyaku Gesa-Gatame. Any act of pinning the opponent to the ground by lying across his or her body.

Gyaku-juji. Any immobilization technique in which the practitioner crosses the arms of the opponent.

Kumi-kata. Grabbing the opponent by the lapel and the sleeve. This technique can either aid the practitioner's own attack or can interfere with the opponent's attack.

Kuzure-kami-shiho-gatame. An immobilization performed by pinning the opponent's chest, and gripping the belt and collar.

Kuzure-kami-shiho-garame. An immobilization technique in which the practitioner controls both arms and legs of an opponent.

Kuzure-kesa-gatame. A technique for immobilizing the opponent by trapping the opponent's shoulder and arm.

Kuzure-tate-shiho-gatame. A technique for controlling the opponent by sliding an arm around the opponent and gripping the belt at the back, which secures the opponent's shoulder and arm.

Kuzure-yoko-shiho-gatame. An immoblization from the side. The practitioner pins the opponent's chest and shoulder, then grips the belt.

Makura-kesa-gatame. A technique for immoblizing the opponent from the rear. The practitioner wraps his or her arms around the opponent's upper body and locks the hands together.

Mune-gyaku. A technique for controlling and immobilizing an opponent by holding and immobilizing the chest.

LOCKS

Hiza gatame. A technique in which the practitioner uses his or her knee and thigh to apply pressure to the opponent's arm.

Juji-gatame. A cross armlock. This is a technique of gripping an opponent's arm, and locking it across the practitioner's pelvic area.

Oten-gatame. Executing an armlock by bending the opponent's arm.

Ude garami. The practitioner locks the opponent's arm, usually while the opponent is lying on his or her back. Called the "arm entanglement" or "figure four arm lock."

Ude garami henka waza. A shoulder immobilization technique performed with the opponent's arm partly bent.

Ude gatame. A straight arm lock. The practitioner pulls the arm up, and rests it between his or her shoulder and neck, then places pressure on the shoulder just below the elbow.

Ude hishigi hiza-gatame. Controlling the opponent's arm by stretching it across one's knee.

Ude-hishigi juji-gatame. An armlock executed in a cross shape.

Ude-hishigi ude-gatame. An armlock executed on an opponent's outstretched arm.

THROWING TECHNIQUES

There are forty common throwing techniques used in Judo competition. Those that follow are among the most basic.

Ashi-guruma. Leg Wheel. A leg throw in which the opponent is thrown forward in a circle over the practitioner's extended leg. This technique is similar to Sweeping Hip Throw (harai-goshi).

Ashi-harai. Any of a variety of foot sweeps, which entail sweeping the opponent's feet out from under him or her, using one's own foot or feet. Also called ashi-barai.

Ashi-waza. Sweeping Loin. This term means foot and leg techniques when they are used to sweep or hook the opponent's foot or leg. Generally, these are the easiest techniques to master and for this reasons are taught to beginners.

De-ashi-harai. Called a foot dash or foot sweep. When the opponent steps forward, the practitioner catches the foot

Fig. 3.24 : Judo shoulder throw.

before it lands, pushes it away and pulls the opponent down.

Do jime. A scissors technique. The practitioner uses his or her legs to squeeze the opponent. It is a basic grappling skill, often taught to beginners.

Eri-seoi-nage. Collar shoulder throw. The practitioner, gripping the collar, throws the opponent forward over his or her shoulder.

Hane-goshi. Spring Hip Throw. A throw in which the practitioner steps in front of the opponent, then "springs" the opponent over the hips and thighs.

Hane-maki-komi. In the "outer winding spring hip throw," the opponent is pulled into tight body contact and is twisted or wound across the practitioner's leg and hip, and pulled forward.

Happo-undo. An exercise designed to teach a practitioner how to throw the opponent in eight directions.

Harai-goshi. Sweeping Hip Throw. Also called Sweeping Loin. A throw in which the practitioner places his or her hip against the opponent's abdomen and sweeps the opponent forward over the leg and hip.

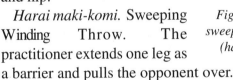

Fig. 3.25: Judo sweeping hip throw (harai-goshi).

Harai maki-komi. Sweeping Winding Throw. The practitioner extends one leg as a barrier and pulls the opponent over.

Hiza guruma. Knee Wheel. A technique in which the practitioner places a foot against the opponent's knee and pulls the opponent off-balance.

Ippon Seoi Nage. One Arm Shoulder Throw. Gripping the opponent's sleeve, the practitioner then throws him or her over the shoulder.

Kani basami. Scissors Throw. A technique that uses the practitioner's legs like scissors to unbalance the opponent, who falls to the side.

Kata guruma. Shoulder Wheel. A throw in which the practitioner lifts the opponent by sliding an arm between the opponent's legs and wheeling the opponent from one side of the shoulders to the other side.

Koshi-guruma. Hip Wheel. A hip throw assisted by holding the opponent around the neck.

Koshi-waza. Any of a series of hip throws. These are the most popular throws used in competition.

Ko-soto-gake. Minor Outer Hook. A technique used to hook the opponent's leg with one's foot to unbalance the opponent backward.

Ko-soto-gari. Minor Outer Reap. A hooking throw. The practitioner pulls the opponent's arm outward while sweeping his or her foot, which causes a backward fall.

Ko-uchi-gari. Minor Inner Reaping Throw. The practitioner catches the opponent's heel with his or her own foot and sweeps while pushing down.

Kote hineri. A hip throw performed by using an armhold around the opponent's neck.

Kukichi-daoshi. Decayed Tree Throw. Sometimes called Dead Tree Fall. A throw executed by grabbing the opponent's heel and pulling up.

Morote gari. Two-handed Reaping Throw. A throw where the practitioner drops into a squat and scoops the opponent's legs from behind, using both arms.

Morote-seoi-nage. Both Hands Shoulder Throw. A shoulder throw in which one uses both hands to grab the opponent and throw him or her over one's shoulder.

Nage-no-kata. An exercise with five techniques for throwing the opponent, three of which are executed while standing and two of which require a sacrifice throw, that is, the practitioner throws him or herself to the floor as well to execute the technique.

Nage waza. A category of Judo techniques. These are throwing techniques.

O-goshi. Major Hip Throw. A throwing technique in which the practitioner slides in front of the opponent and raises the opponent up and over the hip. This technique is used in training; rarely used in competition.

O-guruma. Major Wheel Throw. A throw performed by extending a leg across the opponent's thigh and pulling the opponent over.

O-soto-gari. Major Outer Reaping Throw. A throw executed when the practitioner steps alongside the opponent and brings one thigh into contact with the back of the opponent's thigh, then swings the opponent's leg away.

O-soto-guruma. Major Outer Wheel Throw. A throw in which the practitioner traps both of the opponent's legs and pulls him or her over while sweeping.

O-uchi-gake. Foot Trap. A technique for trapping the opponent's foot between the practitioner's feet, and pulling the opponent over.

O-uchi-gari. Major Inner Reaping Throw. A throw executed by sliding a leg between the opponent's legs and hooking.

Okuri-ashi-harai. Sweeping Ankle Throw. A technique where the practitioner sweeps both of the opponent's feet.

Sasae-tsuri-komi-ashi. Propping Drawing Ankle Throw. A technique where the practitioner blocks the opponent's ankle with his or her foot.

Seoi-otoshi. Shoulder Drop. A technique that uses both hands to pull the opponent over one's hip and shoulder.

Soto gake. Any hook to the outside of the opponent's leg.

Soto maki komi. Outer Winding Throw. A technique where the practitioner places a leg in front of the opponent, and with a quick movement causes the opponent to fall to the ground.

Sukui-nage. Scooping Throw. A technique where one raises the opponent by his or her thighs and leans, causing the opponent to fall backward.

Sumi-gaeshi. Corner Throw. The practitioner catches the opponent on the inner thigh with the foot and falls in a sacrifice throw.

Sumi-otoshi. Corner Drop. The practitioner pulls the opponent's sleeve down while pushing on the opposite shoulder.

Tai-otoshi. Body Drop. A technique in which the practitioner extends a leg, and pulls an opponent over the practitioner's leg and hip to the front. Often used in competition.

Tani-otoshi. Valley Drop. A sacrifice throw in which one places a foot behind the opponent's left heel and forces the opponent back.

Tomoe-nage. Stomach Throw. A sacrifice throw executed by falling backward and pulling the opponent by using a leg in the opponent's stomach.

Tsuri-goshi. Lifting Hip Throw. The practitioner pulls the opponent over the hip.

Tsuri-komi-goshi. Lifting Pulling Hip Throw. The practitioner squats, grips the sleeve and lapel of opponent and throws the opponent forward over the hip.

Uchi-mata. Inner Thigh Throw. A technique where the practitioner supports weight on one leg and uses the other to sweep the opponent's inner thigh.

Uki-goshi. Floating Hip Throw. The basic hip throw. The practitioner uses his or her hip to pivot and throw the opponent.

Uki-otoshi. Floating Drop. The practitioner drops to one knee, wheeling the opponent over the forward foot.

Ura-nage. Rear Throw. A backward throw. The practitioner wraps his or her arms around the opponent's body and falls back, bringing the opponent with him or her.

Ushiro-goshi. Rear Hip Throw. A throw in which one lifts the opponent and then slides an arm around the opponent's neck to turn and throw him or her.

Utsuri-goshi. Changing Hip Throw. A throw executed by pulling the opponent to one's hip and throwing him or her off balance.

Yoko gake. Side Body Drop. The practitioner blocks and hooks the opponent's ankle from the side, which causes the opponent to fall.

Yoko guruma. Side Wheel Throw. A sacrifice throw in which the practitioner reaches under the opponent's shoulders, grips the opponent's belt and throws.

Yoko otoshi. Side Drop. The practitioner blocks the opponent's movement with his or her thigh, then rolls away, taking the opponent down.

Yoko-wakare. Side Separation Throw. The practitioner blocks the opponent's movement with both legs and slides to the floor while pulling the opponent down as well.

STRANGULATIONS

Gyaku juji-jime. Similar to Nami-juji-jime. The practitioner kneels over the opponent, performing a strangulation.

Gyaku okuri-eri. A strangulation effected by grabbing the opponent's lapels and twisting.

Hadaka-jime. A strangulation technique performed by using one's arms instead of the opponent's lapels or clothing. Called "naked struggle," because no clothing is needed.

Hidari ashi-jime. A strangulation technique executed when the practitioner throws his or her leg over the opponent's throat.

Hiza-jime. Strangulation technique performed with the knee.

Kata-hajime. A strangulation technique used in conjunction with a shoulder hold.

Kata juji-jime. A strangulation technique using a cross grab. The practitioner grabs the opponent's collar with crossed arms, and pulls the opponent forward using a scissoring technique.

Koshi-jime. Hip Strangle. A strangulation technique in which the practitioner grasps the opponent's lapel and pulls it across the opponent's throat using the hip and shoulder to exert pressure.

Morote-jime. A strangulation technique executed by grabbing the opponent's lapels and rolling the clenched fists to create pressure on neck.

Okuri-eri-jime. A strangulation technique from the rear. The practitioner slides an arm under the opponent's arm and secures the grip. The practitioner then straightens his or her arm to create pressure on the opponent's neck.

Tsueikomi-jime. A strangulation technique executed by holding both lapels and pushing across the opponent's throat.

JUHO

A term, which means "soft method," used in Shorinji Karate to refer to passive techniques of evasion as opposed to active techniques of striking. See Goho.

JUJI-DOME

The two-sword techniques developed by Miyamoto Musashi. The two swords are crossed to form a wedge that cannot easily be attacked.

JUJI-GATAME

In Judo, a cross armlock. This is a technique of gripping an opponent's arm, and locking it across the practitioner's pelvic area. See Arm Locks. See Judo Techniques.

JUJI-UKE

A cross block. See Block, X.

JUJI-UKI

Same as Juji-uke. See Block, X.

JUMPING KICKS

See Kicks, Jumping.

JUN KATA TE-DORI

In Aikido, the first defensive technique against an armhold. The practitioner pulls the arm away and strikes. See Aikido Techniques. See Arm Holds.

JUN TSUKI

See Punch.

JUN KATA SODE-TORI

In Aikido, the first defense against a sleeve hold. The practitioner grabs the opponent's free hand and performs an elbow strike to the side of the opponent's chest. See Aikido Techniques. See Sleeve Holds.

JUN-TO SONO ICHI

See Ordered Sword One Form.

JUN-TO SONO NI

See Ordered Sword Two Form.

JUN-ZUKI

Same as Jun-tsuki. See Punch.

JUTTE

The collective name of ten hand forms taught in Shotokan Karate. These forms emphasize the use of the hips to generate power and also teach the use of the staff. See Karate Forms.

KABEZOE

See Between The Walls Form.

KAE BECK

An International Tae Kwon Do Federation form taught at the third dan black belt. See Tae Kwon Do Forms.

KAESHI-WAZA

In Judo and Aikido, this means a counter-attack. In Karate, it refers to a series of counter-attacks, and in Kendo, it means to deflect a blow by blocking with the sword.

KAGI-TSUKI

See Punch, Hook.

KAGI-ZUKI

Same as Kagi-tsuki. See Punch, Hook.

KAISHAKU

See Assisting At Seppuku Form.

KAITEN-NAGE

In Aikido, a series of throws used against wrist holds and punches to the face. These require a turning motion of the body. See Aikido Techniques.

KAKARI-GEIKO

In Aikido, Judo and Wa-jutsu, a variety of free style sparring used to test a practitioner or for training purposes. In Kendo, these are the basic attacking techniques.

KAKE-SHUTO-UKE

See Block, Knife Hand.

KAKE-UKE

See Block, Hooking.

KAKE-WAKE-UKE

See Block, X.

KAKIWAKE UKE

Same as Kake-wake-uke. See Block, X.

KAKUTO UKE

See Block, Wrist.

KAMI-SHIHO-GATAME

See Upper Four Quarters.

KAMI-TORE

In Jujutsu and Aikido, defense techniques (with several variations) used against hair grabs.

KANI BASAMI

See Scissors Throw.

KANKU KATA

In Karate, two forms on which the current Heian forms are based. The name means "sky viewing" or "to look at the sky." There are two forms, the great and the small. See Karate Forms. See Heian Kata.

KANKU DAI

A Karate form called the "great kanku." It emphasizes the variation of fast and slow techniques and jumping techniques. See Karate Forms. See Kanku Kata.

KANKU-SHO

A Karate form called the "small kanku." It is used to develop mental and spiritual awareness. See Karate Forms. See Kanku Kata.

KANSETSU-WAZA

In Judo, arm lock techniques. See Arm Locks. See Judo Techniques.

KARATE FORMS

There are over 50 different Karate forms taught with some frequency. Shotokan Karate recognizes 15 basic forms:

Heian 1 through 5
Tekki 1,2, and 3
Bassai dai
Kanku dai
Jion
Jutte
Empi
Hangetsu
Gankaku

Other commonly taught forms include the following: Sanchin, Saiha, Tsushibo, Seienchin, Hengetsu, Kitton 1, 2 and 3, Tai kyo ku 1, 2 and 3, Basai sho, Rou hai, Nisei shu, Sen-se-ru, Kyokushin, Yantsu, and Tensho.

KARATE TECHNIQUES

Karate uses numerous punches, strikes, blocks and kicks, as well as throws and immobilization techniques. See those headings for further information.

Ashi-waza. In Karate, this term is used to denote any and all foot and leg techniques.

Daki-te. A hand technique. The hand is formed into a hook shape for the specific purpose of attacking the vital points in an opponent's face.

Dan-tsuki. A punch that is not the initial attack. That is, it is either used to counter an attack, or it follows another technique in a combination.

Fumi-kiri. A phrase used to denote any strike that uses the knife edge or cutting edge of the foot.

Fumi-waza. A crushing technique used as either a strike or block. Either the foot or the fist can be used. Any part of the opponent's body can be the target.

Fusegi. A phrase meaning defensive techniques in general.

Hasen kata. Performing a series of forms, one after the other, as an exercise of endurance.

Ju-ippon kumite. A series of basic techniques, eight in all, practiced in the Shotokan style and used in counter-attacks against the high punch, middle punch, middle front kick, middle and high roundhouse kick, and reverse kick.

KARENSA
In Arnis, Kali and Escrima, a method of solo free style sparring using weapons.

KARI
See Sweeps.

KASUMI
See Mist Form.

KATA GURUMA
See Shoulder Wheel.

KATA HAJIME
In Judo, a strangulation technique used in conjunction with a shoulder hold. See Judo Techniques. See Strangulation Techniques.

KATA
A Japanese term for any prearranged series of movements, techniques and exercises designed to improve all martial arts performance; emphasized in some martial arts more than others but essential to all martial arts. See Forms.

KATA-DORI
In Aikido, a defensive technique used when the opponent grabs the practitioner's shoulder. The

practitioner counters the attack by pivoting and throwing the opponent to the ground. See Aikido Techniques. See Throws.

KATA GATAME
In Judo, a shoulder hold in which the opponent's arm is wedged between the practitioner's head and arm.

KATA-JUJI-JIME
In Judo, a strangulation technique using a cross grab. The practitioner grabs the opponent's collar, with crossed arms, one hand on each side, and pulls the opponent forward using a scissoring technique. See Judo Techniques. See Strangulation Techniques.

KATA-SUKASHI
In Sumo, a technique performed by wrapping one's arm around the opponent's shoulders and pushing him forward. See Sumo Techniques.

KATA ASHI
Ninja methods of traveling. See Ten Steps.

KATAME NO KATA
In Judo, a formal series of techniques used for controlling an opponent, including strangulation and joint lock techniques, of which five each are performed. See Judo Techniques.

KATATE-USHI
See Strike, Knife Hand.

KATATE-WAZA
In Kendo (swordfighting art), the ability to perform techniques while holding the sword in one hand, requiring much more muscular and joint strength in the arm and wrists than the usual two-handed grip.

KAWASHI
In Aikido and Karate, an evasive technique against an attack, executed by turning the body away. See Body Shifting.

KEE MAH SEH
In Tae Kwon Do, a horse stance. See Stance, Horse.

KEKOMI
See Kick, Front.

KEN-NO SEN

A phrase generally used in martial arts meaning to take the initiative in attacking.

KENJUTSU KATA

Carefully controlled training methods in the use of the wooden sword, the bokken. Two swordfighters attack and defend in a prearranged pattern.

KENTO

See Punch.

KENTSUI-KUCHI

See Strike, Hammer Fist.

KERI

In Judo, the act of pushing the opponent's knee with one's foot to knock him or her off balance. In Karate, the word refers to kicks.

KERI-AGE

See Strikes, Knee.

KERI-GOHO

In Aikido, punches and kicks specifically aimed at the opponent's vital points. See Aikido Techniques.

KESA-GATAME

Known as the scarfhold in Judo. Same as gesa-gatame. See Gesa-gatame.

KHOA GO

In Qwan-Ki-Do, techniques of joint locking. See Joint Locks.

KIBA-DACHI

In Karate, a horse stance. See Stance, Horse.

KIBITACHI

Same as Kiba-dachi. See Stance, Horse.

KICKS

Generally, any technique that uses part of the leg or the foot to strike. Karate and Tae Kwon Do kicks can be divided into straight and circular kicks. Direct or straight kicks are delivered in a straight line to the front side back or downward. Circular kicks are delivered usually by snapping the knee and swinging the hips. These kicks travel in a circular path before they hit their target. Some styles further divide their kicks into spinning kicks delivered with a revolution of the body, and

Fig. 3.26 : Thai boxing kick to the high section.

stamping/stomping kicks in which the kicks are delivered from close in by lifting the knee high and then driving the heel into the opponent's knee, shin, ankle or instep. These kicks can also be used to kick a downed opponent. Snap kicks are delivered by kicking and immediately withdrawing the foot with a sharp snapping motion of the knee. The practitioner can deliver a series of such kicks rapidly. Thrust kicks move in a straight line to the target. The kicking leg is sometimes locked for a moment to add power.

KICK, BACK

This technique is sometimes called a mule kick. Without changing the position or direction of one's body, one thrusts backward with heel of foot. The target area is the shin, knee, or groin.

KICK, CRESCENT

In Tae Kwon Do, called chiki chagi. In this kick, the striking surface is actually the sole of the foot, plus either the inner or the outer edge of the foot. The leg travels in an arc, either moving from outside the body, landing slightly inside, or from inside the body, landing slightly outside. The leg is swung as high up as possible and then brought sharply down. The axe kick is a variation of the technique, where the heel is the striking area.

KICKS, FLYING

These are kicks that are executed while the practitioner is in the air. Same as Jumping Kicks. See Kicks, Jumping.

Fig. 3.27 : Crescent kick.

Fig. 3.28 : Crescent kick performed as axe kick.

KICK, FRONT

In Tai Chi Chuan, shoes are worn and the front kick strikes with toes. In other martial arts, the ball of the foot is the striking area. The practitioner faces forward and brings his or her leg up and pushes forward with the foot. A snap front kick is executed with a sharp push. The snapped out leg returns to its cocked position before it is returned to the floor. With a thrust kick, the practitioner pushes hips forward to cover extra distance. A front push kick is used to push self away or push opponent away. The entire flat of the foot can be used, since the purpose is not to strike but to push. In Tae Kwon Do, the basic front kick is known as ap chagi.

Mae-geri-keagi. A front snap kick in Karate. The ball of the foot strikes the groin or abdomen with a snap; with this straight forward technique, the kicking leg must be pulled back instantly. In Tae Kwon Do, this kick is used to the high section as well.

Mae geri kekomi. In Karate, a front thrust kick. Heel or ball of the foot strikes the groin, chest or abdomen, with the hip driven into the kick, and the knee locked out for a second.

Nidan-geri. A double jump kick in Karate. The ball of the foot strikes the opponent's face or

Fig. 3.29 : Ryubu-kai Karate front kick.

Fig. 3.31 : Tae Kwon Do front kick, middle section.

Fig. 3.32 : Tae Kwon Do front kick, high section.

Fig. 3.33 : Hooking kick.

Fig. 3.34 : Flying or jumping side kick.

abdomen. Two quick kicks are delivered while jumping, one to the chest and one to the face.

KICK, FRONT INSTEP

A technique that is executed like a front kick, but with the instep of the foot targeting the groin area.

KICK, FRONT PUSH

See Kick, Front.

KICK, FRONT SNAP

See Kick, Front.

KICK, FRONT THRUST

See Kick, Front.

KICK, HOOKING

The practitioner stands with his or her side facing the target. The kicking foot travels parallel to the floor and snaps back to target making a hooking motion. The back of the heel is the striking surface. In Tae Kwon Do, this technique is called ap hurya chagi.

KICKS, JUMPING

These are also called flying kicks, though there is no real difference between them. The technique is executed while the performer is in the air. With these kicks, the practitioner covers more distance lengthwise; that is, a flying kick can be used to cover considerable distance between a practitioner and an opponent. Jumping or flying kicks generate more power than their standing counterpoints. Almost every kicking technique has a jumping counterpart. The kick can be executed with the foot that does the jumping, or with the opposite foot.

KICK, KNIFE FOOT

Any kick in which the side edge of the foot is used as the striking area. Often a slashing kick, in which the leg is used like a knife or sword.

Ashi gatana. A technique used in Karate, literally "sword foot." The foot, using its edge, strikes the target like a sword strikes a target.

KICK, OBLIQUE

A technique in which the inner edge of the foot

Fig. 3.35 : Oblique kick.

is used as the striking surface, usually aimed at a low target.

KICK, REAR

Similar to the back kick. The target is in the rear, and the practitioner throws the kick without changing the direction of his or her body.

Ushiro-geri-keage. A back snap kick in Karate. The heel of the foot strikes the groin or abdomen with a snap, traveling straight back. The leg is returned to its starting position immediately.

Ushiro-geri-kekomi. A back thrust kick in Karate. The heel strikes the opponent's groin, stomach or face. The kick is thrust straight back, with the hips pushed into the kick.

KICK, REVERSE

This term is used to refer to a reverse side kick, which is similar to a side kick, only the target is to the rear. The body pivots to the rear and the kick snaps out. Many kicks can be performed in reverse, such as the reverse hooking kick and the reverse roundhouse kick.

KICK, ROUNDHOUSE

The kick moves in a circular motion from outside the body to inside, striking the opponent with the instep of the foot. The kick is a sweeping, slapping technique that nonetheless can generate great power.

Fig. 3.36 : Roundhouse kick.

In Karate, the ball of the foot is sometimes used to strike. Striking with the ball of the foot is also called the breaking technique, since it is the foot formation used when the roundhouse kick is used to break boards.

Reverse. Gyaku mawashi-geri. In Karate, a circular kicking technique in which the foot travels in the opposite direction of the roundhouse kick. The striking area is the ball of the foot, and the target area is usually middle or low.

Short roundhouse kick. This is like a rising kick. The leg is moving toward the target while it travels in an arc to gain height.

Thrust roundhouse kick. One uses hips to thrust forward and add more power to the usual snap technique.

KICK, SCISSORS

A technique where the practitioner uses both legs in a scissoring movement to attack the opponent's body, one leg in the front and one leg in the back.

KICK, SIDE

The leg is drawn up and, as the supporting foot pivots, is thrust out. The edge and heel of the foot is the striking surface. There are numerous variations of this technique, which is a very basic one.

Limbering kick. The leg is swung as high as possible to loosen muscles.

Yoko geri kekomi. This is the traditional side thrust method in Karate. The hips are thrust into the kick for added power.

Fig. 3.37 : Side kick.

Yoko tobi geri. Jumping side kick. The target is the high section. The kick is pushed straight out while in the air. It is usually used as a surprise attack.

Rising side kick. The leg rises to its final position and is snapped out.

Side snap kick. The leg is cocked and the kick is snapped parallel to the ground. No rising motion is necessary.

KICK, SPINNING HEEL

Also called the spinning wheel kick. The practitioner spins backward, pivoting on one foot with the other leg extended straight out, knee

locked. The practitioner strikes the opponent to the high section with the heel of the extended leg. Also performed as a jumping kick, called topi-mikzuki-geri in Karate. Variations on spinning kicks, targeting different areas of the body, are present in many martial arts styles.

KICK, STAMPING/ STOMPING

Called fumi-komi in Karate. The heel of the foot strikes the opponent's leg or instep. The foot is thrust straight and down. The knee must be lifted high to generate sufficient power.

Fig. 3.38 : Stamping kick.

KICK, TORNADO

A jumping reverse crescent kick.

KICKBACK THROW

See Major Outer Reaping Throw.

KIHON KUMITE

The solo practice of basic attacking techniques, similar to shadow boxing.

KIHON KUMITE KATA

See Sparring, Step.

KIHON

The basic movements in a martial arts system. The practitioner repeats the basic movements until they can be performed perfectly without conscious thought or effort.

In Karate, a series of Karate forms which develop the practitioner's basic techniques.

KIM JA SAE

In Tae Kwon Do, a horse stance. See Stance, Horse.

KIMA SEUG-GI

See Stance, Horse.

KIMARITE

The original 48 techniques used in Sumo to throw the opponent. This group is also called Shijuhatte. See Sumo Techniques. See Shijuhatte.

KIME NO KATA

In Judo, a series of exercises that consist of self-defense techniques performed while kneeling and while standing. The kneeling set has eight techniques and the standing set has 12. See Judo Techniques.

KIRIAGE

See Rising Cut Form.

KIRI TSUKI

In Kendo and Iaido, any cutting action with the sword.

KIRIOROSHI

In Iaido, techniques for cutting with the sword.

KISSAKI GAESHI

See Tip Flip Form.

KIZAMI TSUKI

See Punch, Hook.

KIZAMI-ZUKI

Same as Kizami tsuki. See Punch, Hook.

KNEEBLOCK WHEELING THROW

See Knee Wheel Throw.

KNEE STRIKE

See Strike, Knee.

KNEE WHEEL THROW

In Judo, a technique in which the practitioner places a foot against the opponent's knee and pulls the opponent off-balance. Often, it is performed to give the practitioner an entry to execute another technique. See Judo Techniques. See Throws.

KNIFE HAND STRIKE

See Strike, Knife Hand.

KNIFE FOOT KICK

See Kick, Knife Foot.

KNIFE HAND BLOCK

See Block, Knife Hand.

KNUCKLE PUNCH

See Punch, Knuckle.

KO-DANG FORM

An International Tae Kwon Do Federation form taught at the seventh dan black belt. See Tae Kwon Do Forms.

KO-EMPI

In Karate, a backward elbow strike. See Strike, Elbow.

KO-SOTO-GAKE

See Minor Outside Hook.

KO-SOTO-GARI

See Minor Outer Reap. Also called Back Sweeping Foot Throw.

KO-UCHI-GARI

See Minor Inner Reaping Throw. Also called Inside Sweeping Foot Throw.

KOBUSHI

See Punch.

KODOKAN GOSHIN JUTSU

The Kodokan techniques of self-defense. See Judo Techniques.

KOKUSAN

The old name for the Kanku Dai form. See Kanku Dai.

KOKUTSU-DACHI

See Stance, Back.

KOKUTSU-TACHI

Same as Kokutsu-dachi. See Stance, Back.

KONG KEOK

In Tae Kwon Do, a standard punch. See Punch.

KONG KYEUK

Same as Kong Keok. See Punch.

KORYO FORM

A Tae Kwon Do form taught in the palgue series at the first dan black belt. It was the name given to a Korean dynasty by its founder, Wang Keon in 918 A.D. The dynasty was later renamed Korea by foreign traders.

KOSA SU SU MI

A cross step. See Body Shifting.

KOSHI-GURUMA

See Hip Wheel. Also called Arm Around the Neck Hip Throw.

KOSHI-JIME

In Judo, a strangulation technique, sometimes called the hip strangle, in which the practitioner grasps the lapel and pulls it across the opponent's throat using the hip and shoulder to exert pressure. See Strangulation Techniques. See Judo Techniques.

KOSHI-NAGE

In Aikido, a series of hip throws that defend against basic grips.

KOSHI-WAZA

In Judo, any of a series of hip throws. The hip is pushed against the opponent's abdomen and the opponent is raised and pulled over the hip. These are the most popular throws used in competition. See Judo Techniques.

KOSHIKI NO KATA

A series of ancient forms from the Kito-ryu school of Jujutsu and used in Judo. They are advanced forms that are intended to represent the connections among various martial arts. See Judo Techniques.

KOSOTO GAKE

See Minor Outer Hook. Also called Outer Cut Throw.

KOSOTO GARE

See Minor Outer Reaping.

KOTE-GAESHI

In Jujutsu, techniques of self-defense that are executed by grabbing the opponent's wrist and manipulating the joint.

In Aikido, a wrist turn out. An exercise done to increase flexibility and to learn basic techniques.

KOTE MAWASHI-HO

In Aikido, a wrist turn-in. An exercise done to improve flexibility and to learn basic movements.

KOTE NAGE

In Sumo, a forearm throw. The practitioner grabs the opponent's arm, grips the inside of the opponent's belt and twists the opponent over the hip.

KOTE UCHI

In Aikido, any strike against an armed opponent that targets the opponent's forearm with the intention of causing him or her to drop the weapon. See Aikido Techniques.

KOTEKI GYAKU-TO

See Rearward Inverse Cut Form.

KOTEKI NUKIUCHI

See Rearward Quick Draw Form.

KOTE HINERI

In Judo, a hip throw performed by using an armhold around the opponent's neck. See Judo Techniques.

KUEN

The Chinese word for form. See Form.

KUEN SIU KUEN

Any technique of punch interception that traps or holds the hand instead of simply blocking or deflecting it.

KUKICHI-DAOSHI

See Decayed Tree Throw.

KUM GANG FORM

A Tae Kwon Do form taught at the second dan black belt level. This form is in the palgue series. See Tae Kwon Do Forms.

KUMADE UCHI

See Strike, Palm.

KUMADE

See Strike, Palm.

KUM-KATA

In Judo, grabbing the opponent by the lapel and the sleeve. This technique can either aid the practitioner's own attack or can interfere with the opponent's attack. See Judo Techniques.

KUMI-TSUKI

In Aikido, a series of four self-defense techniques performed against holds of the belt. See Aikido Techniques.

KUMI-UCHI

In martial arts generally, refers to the technique of grabbing the opponent's clothing to enhance an attack or to interfere with one.

KUMITE

See Sparring, Step.

KUP

See Strike, Hammerfist.

KUP CHAKI

See Kicks, Jumping.

KUPCHAGI

See Kicks, Jumping.

KURE HARASHI

One of the 12 basic blocks and strikes in Jodo and Jojutsu, staff art. See Jodo Techniques.

KURE TSUKI

One of the 12 basic blocks and strikes in Jodo and Jojutsu. See Jodo Techniques.

KUREUNG-OPSI

See Sparring, Free Style.

KURU-RUN-FA

A very advanced form in Karate, the 12th of 14 learned in Goju-ryu. It consists of techniques of breaking and defense, including techniques such as open-hand blocks, side kicks to the knee, and hooking blocks from a cat stance. See Karate Forms.

KUSHANKU

An old name for Kanku Dai form. See Kanku Dai.

KUZURE-KESA-GATAME

In Judo, a technique for immobilizing the opponent by trapping the opponent's shoulder and arm. See Immobilization Techniques. See Judo Techniques.

KUZURE TATE SHIHO GATAME

In Judo, a technique for controlling the opponent by sliding an arm around the opponent and gripping the belt at the back, which secures the opponent's shoulder and arm. See Immobilization Techniques. See Judo Techniques.

KUZURE-GESA-GATAME

Same as Kuzure-kesa-gatame. See Kuzure-kesa-gatame.

KUZURE-KAMI-SHIHO-GATAME

In Judo, an immobilization performed by pinning the opponent's chest, and gripping the belt and collar. See Immobilization Techniques. See Judo Techniques.

KUZURE-KAMI-SHIHO-GARAME

In Judo, an immobilization technique in which the practitioner controls both arms and legs of an opponent. See Immobilization Techniques. See Judo Techniques.

KUZURE-YOKO-SHIHO-GATAME

In Judo, an immoblization from the side. The practitioner pins the opponent's chest and shoulder, then grips the belt. See Immobilization Techniques. See Judo Techniques.

KUZUSHI

See Throws.

KWANG-GYE FORM

An International Tae Kwon Do Federation form taught at first dan black belt level.

KWANSU

In Tae Kwon Do, a vertical spear hand strike. See Strike, Spear Hand.

KYASHI ZUKI

One of the 12 basic blocks and strikes in Jodo and Jojutsu, staff art. See Jodo Techniques.

KYO-JUTSU

In Karate and Kendo, any evasive movement followed by an attack.

KYOK PA

A name for breaking techniques. See Breaking Techniques.

KYOSHI NO KAMAE

A kneeling position used in Japanese martial arts. The thighs rest on the feet.

KYU

The third of the three aspects of nukisuke, drawing the sword, in Iaido (sword drawing art). This is the sudden cut. The other two are jo, preparation, and ha, actual drawing.

KYUDO TECHNIQUES

In classical archery, there are eight positions the archer takes that occur before, during and after shooting the bow. The first is positioning the feet (ashibumi). The second is steadying the bow (dozukuri). The third is holding the bow (yugamae). The fourth is raising the bow (uchiokoshi). The fifth is drawing the bow (hikiwake). The sixth is union with the bow (kai). The seventh is releasing the bow (hanare) and the eighth is the follow through (zanshin). Through these movements, the archer achieves a state of Zen enlightenment.

Ariake. A technique for taking aim, used to perfect the archer's aim. One positions oneself in such a way that one can see the whole target to the left of the bow.

Gobu no tsume. The final aspects of tensing the bow.

Reisha. A ceremonial drawing of the bow meant to celebrate the spiritual part of archery.

Te-no uchi. Gripping the bow.

Tsuri-ai. The balance between the hand holding the bow and the hand holding the bow string.

Tsuru-garami. Gripping the bowstring with the thumb, which is secured by the forefinger.

Yami. A way of aiming the bow that obscures the target completely and helps the practitioner achieve perfect aim.

LANGKAH

Refers to postures and footwork in Pentjak Silat.

LAOFU SHAN

An ancient form in the Shaolin style of Wushu. This form can be performed alone or with a partner. The name means "form of the old mountain tiger."

LAP TAN

In Qwan-Ki-Do, an attention stance. See Stance, Attention.

LATERAL SACRIFICE THROW

In Judo, a throw in which both practitioners land on the mat, to the side.

LAU-MA-BO

In Wushu, an X-stance. Called the Twisting Horse Stance. See Stance, Twisting Horse.

LEADING FINGER JAB

See Strike, Finger.

LEAPING DEER

A quick, springing upward high block used in Wushu. See Block, High.

LEFT FORM

In Iaido (sword drawing art), the third form of the seated set, called "hidari." The practitioner performs basic cuts from the seated position. The four phases of drawing the sword, cutting with the sword, shaking the blood from the sword and resheathing the sword are practiced.

LEG WHEEL

Ashi-guruma. In Judo, a leg throw in which one throws the opponent forward in a circle over one's extended leg. This technique is similar to Sweeping Hip Throw (harai goshi).

LENGTHWISE FOUR QUARTERS

In Judo, a hold executed when the opponent is on his or her back. The practitioner straddles him or her and then leans forward, sliding both arms under the opponent's neck and shoulder, and securing a grip.

LIEN HOA TAN

See Stance, Ready.

LIFTING HIP THROW

In Judo, a hip throw in which the practitioner pulls the opponent over the hip. See Throws. See Judo Techniques.

LIFTING PULLING HIP THROW

In Judo, the practitioner squats, grips the sleeve and lapel of an opponent and throws the opponent forward over the hip. See Judo Techiques. See Throws.

LIFTING SWEEPING FOOT THROW

In Judo, the practitioner lifts an opponent over the hip and sweeps his or her feet out.

LIFTING THE BALL IN FRONT OF THE SHOULDER

Exercise done in Tai Chi, designed to help clear the mind and relax the body.

LIGHTNING FORM

In Iaido (sword drawing art), the third form in the half seated set. In Japanese it is called "inazuma." The practitioner performs basic cuts from the half-seated stance. The four phases of drawing the sword, cutting with the sword, shaking the blood from the sword and resheathing the sword are practiced.

LIN SIL DIE DAI

In Wing Chun Wushu, a simultaneous block and strike. This economy of movement is characteristic of the Wing Chun style.

LOCKS

See Joint Locks.

LONG FORM

In Tai Chi Chuan, the original form for exercise and self-defense. The long form takes 35 minutes to complete, with 108 movements. In some Asian belief systems, 108 is considered a lucky number. In the early days of the People's Republic of China, a group of Tai Chi masters was gathered and together they shortened the long form, thus devising the Eight Minute or Short Form.

LONG HAND

A name applied to certain Wushu styles that are circular or internal in nature and rely on evasive movements.

LONG HAO

A basic form in Viet Vo Dao, called the Dragon-Tiger form.

LOOKING AT THE MOON BY TURNING THE BODY

Exercise in Tai Chi done to improve the movement of the blood and to improve the muscle tone of the lower body.

LOP SAU DRILL

See Wooden Dummy Drills.

LOST MONKEY FORM

An exercise in Monkey style Wushu useful for deceiving the opponent. The practitioner looks confused and vulnerable. The form, however, uses quick footwork that is difficult to anticipate.

LOW BLOCK

See Block, Low.

LOYAL RETAINER FORM

In Iaido (sword drawing art), the fifth form of the secret forms standing set, called "shinobu." The practitioner learns methods of stealth, by imagining he or she is stalking a guard. The four phases of drawing the sword, cutting with the sword, shaking the blood from the sword and resheathing the sword are practiced.

MA-BO

In Wushu, a horse stance. See Stance, Horse.

MA-UKEMI

See Breakfalls.

MAE

See Forward Form.

MAE GERI

In Iaido, see Forward Cut Form.
In Karate, see Kick, Front.

MAE HIJI-ATE

In Karate, a forward elbow strike. See Strike, Elbow.

MAE SHITATE KUMI-TSUKI

In Aikido, a defense against a bear hug. The practitioner digs his or her thumbs under the opponent's ears. See Aikido Techniques.

MAE EMPI-UCHI

Same as Mae hiji-ate. See Strike, Elbow.

MAE UDE HINERI UKE

See Block, Forearm.

MAE ASHI-GERI

See Kick, Front.

MAE GERI KEAGI

See Kick, Front.

MAE GERI KEKOMI

See Kick, Front.

MAE-TE

See Strike, Palm.

MAE-TOBI-GERI

In Karate, a jumping front kick. See Kicks, Jumping.

MAE-U-ATE KUMI-TSUKI

In Aikido, a defense against a bear hug. The practitioner delivers a knee strike, then steps back and applies an arm lock to the opponent. See Aikido Techniques.

MAE-UDE-DE-AI-OSAE-UKE

See Block, Forearm.

MAE-UKEMI

See Breakfalls.

MAJOR HIP THROW

In Judo, a throwing technique in which the practitioner slides in front of the opponent and raises the opponent up and over the hip. This technique is used in training; rarely used in competition. See Judo Techniques. See Throws.

MAJOR INNER REAPING THROW

In Judo, a technique for trapping the opponent's foot between the practitioner's feet, and pulling the opponent over. See Throws. See Judo Techniques.

MAJOR OUTER REAPING THROW

In Judo, a throw executed when the practitioner steps alongside the opponent and brings one thigh into contact with the back of the opponent's thigh, then swings the opponent's leg away. See Judo Techniques. See Throws.

MAJOR OUTER WHEEL THROW

In Judo, a throw in which the practitioner traps both of the opponent's legs and pulls him or her over while sweeping. See Judo Techniques. See Throws.

MAJOR WHEEL THROW

In Judo, a throw performed by extending a leg across the opponent's thigh and pulling the opponent over. See Judo Techniques. See Throws.

MAKGI

Term used in Tae Kwon Do meaning block. The same as maki or makki. See Block.

MAKI-OTOSHI

In Sumo, a throw in which one grabs the opponent under his or her shoulders.

In Jodo and Jujutsu, one of the 12 basic blocks and strikes. See Jodo Techniques.

MAKKOH

See Facing Front Form.

MAKURA-GESA-GATAME

Same as Makura-kesa-gatame. See Makura-kesa-gatame.

MAKURA-KESA-GATAME

In Judo, a technique for immobilizing the opponent from the rear. The practitioner wraps his or her arms around the opponent's upper body and locks the hands together. See Judo Techniques. See Immobilization Techniques.

MANJI NO KATA

A form in Ninjutsu that emphasizes throws.

MAO-BO

In Wushu, a cat stance. See Stance, Cat.

MARCHING BOUNCING BALL

An exercise done in Tai Chi designed to stimulate tired muscles.

MATAWARI

See Stretcing Exercises.

MAWASHI-EMPI-UCHI

See Strike, Elbow.

MAWASHI-GERI

See Kick, Roundhouse.

MAWASHI-TSUKI

A roundhouse punch in Karate. See Punch, Hook.

MAWASHI-UKE

See Block, Outside-inside.

MAWASHI ZUKI

Same as Mawashi-tsuki. See Punch, Hook.

MIGI

See Right Form.

MIGI-DO

In Kendo (swordfighting art), a strike to the right side of the opponent's chest, using the shinai, or bamboo sword.

MIGI-MEN

In Kendo (swordfighting art), a strike to the right side of the opponent's head, using the shinai, or bamboo sword.

MIGI-YOTSU

In Sumo, grappling with the right arm on the inside. See Sumo Techniques.

MIKAZUKI-GERI

In Karate, a crescent kick often used to block. See Kick, Crescent.

MING QUAN

In Wushu, a straight punch. See Punch.

MINOR INNER REAPING THROW

In Judo, the practitioner, facing the opponent, catches the opponent's heel with his or her own foot and sweeps while pushing down. See Throws. See Judo Techniques.

MINOR OUTER HOOK

In Judo, a hooking takedown. The practitioner controls the opponent's elbow, and hooks his or her leg from under. See Judo Techniques. See Throws.

MINOR OUTER REAPING THROW

In Judo, a hooking takedown. In this case, the practitioner controls the opponent's elbow by pulling it outward, then places a foot outside the opponent's foot and sweeps. See Sweeps. See Throws.

MINOR OUTSIDE HOOK

In Judo, a technique used to hook the opponent's leg with a foot to unbalance the opponent backward. See Judo Techniques. See Throws.

MISDIRECTION FORM

In Iaido (sword drawing art), the sixth of the secret forms standing set. In Japanese it is called "yuki chigai." The practitioner learns to handle more than one opponent. The four phases of drawing the sword, cutting with the sword, shaking the blood from the sword and resheathing the sword are executed.

MIST FORM

In Iaido (sword drawing art), the first form in the secret forms seated set, called "kasumi." The practitioner performs basic cuts while seated. The four phases of drawing the sword, cutting with the sword, shaking the blood from the sword and resheathing the sword are executed.

MITOKORO-ZEME

In Sumo, a throw executed by grabbing the opponent's thigh and hooking a leg around the opponent's other leg. See Sumo Techniques.

MOKUSO

See Stance.

MONIRI

See Entering The Gate Form.

MONKEY FORM

In Bando, this form emphasizes the development of agility, which requires flexibility, and confidence, which requires experience. Other Bando forms emphasize the characteristics of other animals. These forms include Eagle, Deer, Boar, Cobra, Viper, Paddy Bird, Panther, Python, Scorpion, Bull and Tiger.

MOO GI GONG

Offensive and defensive training of an intense variety. An advanced practitioner can use any available object as a weapon.

MOOK JONG FORM

Wooden dummy form. A series of prearranged techniques executed against the wooden dummy used particularly in Wing Chun Wushu.

MOONBEAMS FORM

In Iaido (sword drawing art), the ninth form of the seated set, called "tsukikage." The practitioner practices blocking by striking the opponent's bare wrists. The four phases of drawing the sword, cutting with the sword, shaking the blood from the sword and resheathing the sword are executed.

MOON MA

An International Tae Kwon Do Federation form, taught at eighth dan black belt. See Tae Kwon Do Forms.

MOROTE GARI

See Two-handed Reaping Throw.

MOROTE-JIME

In Judo, a strangulation technique executed by grabbing the opponent's lapels and rolling the clenched fists to create pressure on neck. See Strangulation Techniques. See Judo Techniques.

MOROTE-SEOI-NAGE

See Both Hands Shoulder Throw.

MOROTE UKE

See Block, Forearm (double).

MORAZASHI

In Sumo, grappling with both hands on the inside. See Sumo Techniques.

MOUNTAIN WIND FORM

In Iaido (sword drawing art), the fifth form of the half seated set. In Japanese it is called "oroshi." The practitioner learns to handle an unexpected situation. The practitioner imagines that he or she is seated when an opponent grabs the practitioner's sword handle. The four phases of drawing the sword, cutting with the sword, shaking the blood from the sword and resheathing the sword are executed.

MOUNTAIN BLOCK

See Block, Mountain.

MUKA-MAE

In Aikido, a natural stance. See Stance, Natural.

MULTI-DIRECTIONAL CUT

In Iaido (sword drawing art), the second form of the basic drawing methods secret set, of the intermediate level, called "tateki to." The practitioner cuts three different opponents. The four phases of drawing the sword, cutting with the sword, shaking the blood from the sword and resheathing the sword are executed.

MUNE-GYAKU

In Judo, a technique for controlling and immobilizing an opponent by holding and immobilizing the chest. See Immobilization Techniques. See Judo Techniques.

MUSUBI-DACHI

See Stance, Ready.

NAE GONG

Exercises that develop and control the chi, life energy. Specialized breathing, meditation and physical techniques are used. Advanced training develops the combat and healing applications of chi.

NAGASHI-TSUKI

See Punch, Hook.

NAGASHI-UKE

See Block, Outside-Inside.

NAGASHI-ZUKI

Same as Nagashi-tsuki. See Block, Outside-Inside.

NAGE-NO-KATA

In Judo, this is an exercise with five techniques for throwing the opponent, three of which are executed while standing and two of which require a sacrifice throw, that is, the practitioner throws him or herself to the floor as well to execute the technique. In Aikido, this is a group of ten throwing techniques. See Judo Techniques. See Aikido Techniques.

NAGE WAZA

A category of Judo techniques. These are throwing techniques.

NAIHANCHI

An old name for Tekki forms, which are the Karate forms learned after the beginner Heian forms. They are called "iron horse" forms, for their emphasis on horse stances. They also use high blocks and knife hand strikes. See Karate Forms.

NAIHANCHI I

A Karate form taught in particular in the Shorei-ryu style, which develops balance, speed and power, as well as perfection of technique. The first of the intermediate forms. See Naihanchi. See Karate Forms.

NAIHANCHI II

A Karate form taught in particular in the Shorei-ryu style, which develops balance, speed and power, as well as perfection of technique. The second of the intermediate forms. See Naihanchi. See Karate Forms.

NAIHANCHI III

A Karate form taught in particular in the Shorei-ryu style, which develops mental and spiritual awareness, as well as perfection of technique. The third of the intermediate forms. See Naihanchi. See Karate Forms.

NAKADATE IPPON-KEN TSUKI

See Punch, Knuckle.

NAKADATE IPPON-KEN ZUKI

Same as Nakadate ippon-ken tsuki. See Punch, Knuckle.

NAMI-GAESHI

In Iaido, see Returning Waves Form.

In Karate, the performance of several defensive techniques in sequence.

NAMI-JUJI-JIME

In Judo, a cross strangle in which the practitioner executes a cross grab with both hands. The practitioner pulls the opponent forward by using a scissor movement. See Judo Techniques. See Strangulation Techniques.

NAN DAN SHO

A form in Shorei-ryu Karate devised to develop the practitioner's mental and spiritual awareness. See Karate Forms.

NARANI SEUG-GI

In Tae Kwon Do, a ready stance. See Stance, Ready.

NATURAL STANCE

See Stance, Natural.

NAYASHI

In Kendo (sword fighting art), a defensive technique of pushing the opponent's sword toward the ground with the practitioner's own sword when the opponent has made a thrust to the high target area.

NE-WAZA

A term that means those techniques which are performed on the floor, usually called groundwork techniques. In Judo and Jujutsu, ground techniques include strangulations, immobilizations and armlocks.

NEKO ASHI-DACHI

See Stance, Cat.

NEKO-ASHI-TACHI

Same as Neko Ashi-dachi. See Stance, Cat.

NGANH PHAP

See Breaking Techniques.

NHAO LAN

See Breakfalls.

NHI TAN

See Stance, Back.

NICHO-NAGE

In Sumo, a hip throw that is performed by blocking the opponent's thigh and then pulling the opponent off-balance. See Sumo Techniques.

NIDAN-GERI

See Kick, Front.

NIHON KATANA

Techniques of fighting with two swords, perfected by the famous warrior Miyamoto Musashi.

NIHON NUKITE

See Strike, Two-finger.

NIHON KENDO KATA

Literally, "Japan Kendo formal exercise." This exercise, a series of prearranged Kendo techniques, is essential to all modern Kendo practice.

NIJUSHI-HO

A form in Karate, called "the 24 steps." With each step, the practitioner executes a different technique. See Karate Forms.

NIKKYO CONTROL

See Katame No Kata.

NIMAI-GERI

In Sumo, a technique for blocking an opponent's leg and pulling on his belt to produce a fall. See Sumo Techniques.

NINJA TECHNIQUES

Ninja relied on a variety of methods of fighting, disguise and escape to perform their duties. Of these, some of the most important techniques included horsemanship, stick and staff fighting, plus strategy, and deception. A knowledge of geography, disguise and impersonation were essential to escape and concealment. Methods of entering structures and special ways of walking, running and jumping were learned. Water training of all sorts, including swimming and underwater combat were necessary, as was a thorough knowledge of weapons. See Ten Steps. See Ninjutsu in the Schools and Styles section.

NOTO

In Iaido (sword drawing art), various methods for resheathing the sword.

NUKI-UCHE

In Iaido, see Sudden Draw Form.

In Karate and Kendo, a technique that blocks and strikes simultaneously.

NUKISUKE

In Iaido (sword drawing art), various techniques for drawing the sword. The goal is to be able to

Fig. 3.39 : Weapons use was an important part of Ninja training.

draw the sword and cut the opponent in one smooth movement before the opponent has the opportunity to draw his or her sword.

NUKITE

See Strike, Spear Hand.

O-GOSHI

See Major Hip Throw. Also called Basic Hip Throw.

O-GURUMA

See Major Wheel Throw.

O-MATA

In Sumo, throwing an opponent by grabbing his thigh and forcing him backward over one's own thigh. See Sumo Techniques.

O-SOTO-GARI

See Major Outer Reaping Throw. Also called Kickback Throw.

O-SOTO-GURUMA

See Major Outer Wheel.

O-UCHI-GAKE

See Major Inner Reaping.

O-UCHI-GARI

See Major Inner Reaping. Also called Innercut Throw.

OBLIQUE KICK

See Kick, Oblique.

OI TSUKI

See Punch, Lunge.

OI-ZUKI

Same as Oi-tsuki. See Punch, Lunge.

OIKAZE

See Tailwind Form.

OKU-IAI

A series of formal exercises in Iaido (sword drawing art), which consists of two parts. In the first part, eight forms are executed from a sitting position and 13 forms are executed from a standing position. All the forms include the techniques of drawing, cutting, shaking the blood from the sword and resheathing.

OKU IAI IWAZA NO BU

See Secret Forms Seated Set.

OKURI-ASHI-BARAI

See Sweeping Ankle Throw. Also called Side Sweeping Foot Throw.

OKURI-ASHI-HARAI

Same as Okuri-ashi-barai. See Sweeping Ankle Throw.

OKURI-DASHI

In Sumo, a technique of dodging an attack and from behind pushing the opponent. See Sumo Techniques.

OKURI-ERI-JIME

In Judo, a strangulation technique from the rear. The practitioner slides an arm under the opponent's arm and grabs the opponent's lapel. The practitioner then straightens his or her arm to create pressure on the opponent's neck. See Judo Techniques. See Strangulation Techniques.

OKURI-TAOSHI

In Sumo, forcing down on the opponent's back using both hands. The goal is to press the opponent to the ground. See Sumo Techniques.

OMORI-RYU

Also called Atari-to. A series of formal exercises in Iaido (sword drawing art) that consists of twelve basic movements necessary to master the art. These movements begin in a sitting position. All are composed of the four phases of cutting with the sword: drawing, cutting, shaking the blood off, and resheathing the sword.

OMOTE FORMS

A series of forms that train the Iaijutsu (sword drawing) practitioner in striking and thrusting. Endurance and quickness are essential. These are for use against armored opponents.

OMOTE KUMITACHI

Literally, "mutual attack." In Kenjutsu (swordfighting), a form of sparring in which partners defend and attack at the same time.

ON-GUARD STANCE

See Stance, Fighting.

ONE ARM SHOULDER THROW

In Judo, a throw over the shoulder that is popular in competition. See Throws. See Judo Techniques.

ONE-STEP PASS

In Escrima, stepping back one step, evading a strike and countering. See Escrima Techniques.

ONE-STEP SPARRING

See Sparring, Step (One-step).

OPENING THE CHEST

An exercise in Tai Chi designed to improve mental alertness.

ORDERED SWORD ONE FORM

In Iaido (sword drawing art), the first form in the basic drawing methods set, called "junto sono ichi." The practitioner performs basic cuts. The four phases of drawing the sword, cutting with the sword, shaking the blood from the sword and resheathing the sword are practiced.

ORDERED SWORD TWO FORM

In Iaido (sword drawing art), the second form in the basic drawing methods set, called "junto sono ni." It varies only slightly from Ordered Sword One form. The practitioner performs basic cuts. The four phases of drawing the sword, cutting with the sword, shaking the blood from the sword and resheathing the sword are executed.

OROSHI

See Mountain Wind Form.

OSAE-KOMI-TOKETA

In Judo, a defensive technique to escape from an immobilization hold.

OSAE-UKE

See Block, Pressing.

OSAE WAZA

In Judo, hold techniques in general.

OSHI-DASHI

In Sumo, a technique of pushing the opponent in the chest or under the arms, causing him or her to fall. See Sumo Techniques.

OSHI-TAOSHI

In Aikido, an armlock executed by pushing on the opponent's elbow. See Arm Locks. See Aikido Techniques.

OTEN-GATAME

In Judo, executing an armlock through bending the opponent's arm by twisting one's body to the side.

OTOSHI UKE

Blocking a technique with a push.

OTOSHI EMPI UCHI

See Strike, Elbow (Downward).

OUTER CUT THROW

See Minor Outer Hook.

OUTER WINDING SPRING HIP THROW

Hane-maki-komi. The opponent is pulled into tight body contact and is twisted or wound across the practitioner's leg and hip, and pulled forward. See Judo Techniques. See Throws.

OUTER WINDING THROW

In Judo, a technique where the practitioner places a leg in front of the opponent, and with a quick movement causes the opponent to fall to the ground. See Judo Techniques. See Throws.

OUTSIDE-INSIDE BLOCK

See Block, Outside-Inside.

OYAYUBI NUKITE

See Strike, Finger.

PADDY BIRD FORM

In Bando, this form emphasizes rapid flight — that is, the quick footwork required for swift advancing and retreating. Other animal forms emphasize other animal qualities. These include Eagle, Deer, Boar, Cobra, Viper, Monkey, Panther, Python, Scorpion, Bull and Tiger.

PAK HOK BO

See Stance, Crane.

PALGUE

The name for a series of Tae Kwon Do forms. Palgue 1-8 are designed for non-black belts. The first three are beginner forms and the remaining are intermediate. The series also includes other forms with specific names for black belts. See Tae Kwon Do Forms.

PALGYE

Same as Palgue. See Palgue.

PALM CHANGE, DOUBLE

Called "shuang huan chang." An exercise for learning how the body moves, taught in Pa Kua Wushu. Part of the Walking The Circle exercise.

PALM CHANGE, SINGLE

Called "tan huan chang," a technique for learning how the body moves. It is part of the walking the circle exercise in Pa Kua or Eight Trigram Wushu.

PALM HEEL STRIKE

The same as palm strike. See Strike, Palm.

PANDEA

See Kick, Roundhouse.

PANTHER FORM

In Bando, this form emphasizes footwork for circling as well as leaping and tearing techniques. Other animal forms emphasize other qualities. Other Bando animal forms are Eagle, Deer, Boar, Cobra, Viper, Monkey, Paddy Bird, Python, Scorpion, Bull and Tiger.

PAPER STRIKING EXERCISE

An exercise that develops complete control over hand techniques, used in Jeet Kune Do, as well as other martial arts. The practitioner hangs a piece of paper a few inches from the wall and strikes with full speed and power. The technique is repeated until the practitioner always hits the same spot and barely moves the paper. As control improves, the practitioner moves the paper closer to the wall. Eventually, the practitioner can strike the wall with full speed and power without injuring the hand. See Training.

PARRYING FORM I

In Iaido (sword drawing art), the sixth form in the seated set, called "ukenagashi." The practitioner performs parrying techniques from the seated position. The four phases of drawing the sword, cutting with the sword, shaking the blood from the sword and resheathing the sword are executed.

PARRYING FORM II

In Iaido (sword drawing art), the tenth form in the secret forms standing set, called "ukenagashi." The practitioner performs parrying techniques from a standing position. The four phases of drawing the sword, cutting with the sword, shaking the blood from the sword and resheathing the sword are executed.

PART THE NORTH WIND

A movement used in The Great Circle, a long form consisting of 37 different series of techniques, performed by Tai Chi practitioners.

PART THE SOUTH WIND

A movement used in The Great Circle, a long form consisting of 37 different series of techniques, performed by Tai Chi practitioners.

PARTING THE WILD HORSE'S MANE

A technique in the Tai Chi Chuan Eight Minute form. It energizes the nervous system, and strengthens neck and facial muscles. The technique has a self-defense application as well.

PATSAI

An old name for Bassai dai. See Bassai dai.

PECHURIN

Another name for Suparinpe. See Suparinpe Form.

PHAP

A Vietnamese word meaning "technique."

PHUONG DUC

In Qwan Ki Do, elbow strike techniques. See Strike, Elbow.

PI-GUA-QUAN

In Wushu, a series of strikes performed with arms and legs outstretched.

PIGEON TOE STANCE

See Stance, Pigeon Toe.

PINAN NIDAN KATA

Former name of Heian Nidan Form. See Heian Nidan Form.

PINAN GODAN KATA

Former name of Heian Godan Form. See Heian Godan Form.

PINAN YONDAN KATA

Former name of Heian Yondan Form. See Heian Yondan Form.

PINAN SANDAN KATA

Former name of Heian Sandan Form. See Heian Sandan Form.

PINAN SHODAN KATA

Former name of Heian Shodan Form. See Heian Shodan Form.

PLACING THE SPHERE LEFT and RIGHT

Movements used in The Great Circle, a long form consisting of 37 different series of techniques, performed by Tai Chi practitioners.

PLAYING THE HARP

A technique in the Tai Chi Chuan Eight Minute form that tones and develops the abdominal muscles and shoulder muscles. It has a self-defense application as well.

PO-EUN FORM

Same as Po-un form. See Po-un Form.

PO-UN FORM

An International Tae Kwon Do Federation form taught at second dan black belt.

POCK SAU DRILL

See Wooden Dummy Drills.

POOMSE

Korean name for forms. See Forms.

POSTURES

Another name for stances. See Stances.

POW

See Punch, Uppercut.

POWER PUNCH

In Jeet Kune Do, also called "floating punch." A technique used to increase the power of the practitioner's strikes.

PRAISE THE NORTH

A movement used in The Great Circle, a long form consisting of 37 different series of techniques, performed by Tai Chi practitioners.

PRESSING BLOCK

See Block, Pressing.

PROGRESSIVE INDIRECT ATTACK

In Jeet Kune Do, a strategy for achieving one's goals using alternate methods. That is, if one's goal, for instance, is to strike to the opponent's face, but one is too far away, one develops a plan of the techniques that will be necessary to move in close enough to execute the punch to the face.

PULLING DOWN STRAIGHT LEG THROW

See Floating Drop.

PUMSE

Same as poomse. Another name for forms. See Forms.

PUNCH

Punches are executed with palms, fingers, foreknuckles or the forefist. In the straight fist punch, the most commonly used technique, the fingers are rolled under and the thumb is folded

Fig. 3.40 : Double fist upperpunch, high target area.

across. The punch extends from the waist, forward, striking with the power of the shoulder and hips behind it. The forefist strikes to any target. The first two knuckles are the striking knuckles, except in some arts such as Jeet Kune Do, which uses the last three knuckles. Double fist techniques are simply performed with both hands, either one after the other or both at the same time. A double fist straight punch, for instance, simply means that both fists are launched usually in a scissoring movement, though sometimes to different target areas entirely. Most punching techniques can be performed with both or double fists.

PUNCH, CHESTNUT FIST

A punch delivered by a fist with one knuckle extended. See Punch, Knuckle.

PUNCH, CORKSCREW

Chireu-gi. A technique in Tae Kwon Do, in which the punch is delivered with a twist of the wrist. The fist begins palm up at the waist but strikes the target palm down. The added twist is thought to generate extra power.

PUNCH, CROSS

A straight punch from the rear hand. Often used in conjunction with a jab. It is similar to a reverse punch.

PUNCH, HOOK

This technique can be delivered with either the left or the right hand. The fist makes a horizontal arc and lands without fully extending. The shoulder moves and propels the arm, instead of the arm straightening out to deliver the strike.

PUNCH, JAB

Can be thrown with left or right hand, in which case the name indicates the hand used: left jab, right jab. This is a straight, short punch delivered with the lead hand, used to strike quickly. It is a feint used to distract or set up the opponent. The practitioner will often jab with one hand and then quickly perform a stronger punch with the other hand.

PUNCH, KNUCKLE

Any punch with any knuckles extended, including various fist positions. One, two or more knuckles may be extended. The knuckle punch is especially harmful when aimed at a vulnerable target such as the nose or throat.

Ippon ken tsuki. In Karate, a fist made with the knuckle of the index finger extending. A straight punch is performed.

Nakadate ippon-ken tsuki. The middle finger knuckle is extended.

PUNCH, LUNGE

A technique in which the practitioner steps or slides forward while striking. The punching hand is on the same side as the lead foot.

PUNCH, PARALLEL

In Karate, a simultaneous punch with fists striking the rib cage and the chest in straight movement.

PUNCH, PHOENIX EYE

See Punch, Knuckle.

PUNCH, RAM'S HEAD

A straight punch using the first two knuckles of the fist.

PUNCH, REVERSE

The most widely used technique in Karate and Tae Kwon Do. The fist strikes any target in a straight movement. The punching hand is on the opposite side of the forward foot.

Bara-te. In Karate, a reverse punch technique in which the fingers are used to strike.

PUNCH, RISING

In Karate, the forefist moves forward in a semi-circle, striking the opponent's face.

PUNCH, SCISSORS

Similar to a double fist punch. The forefists of both hands strike the target simultaneously, using

Fig. 3.41 : Reverse punch to middle section.

Fig. 3.42 : Reverse punch to high section.

a circular movement. The target areas are the front and back of the body.

PUNCH, U.

In Karate, the U-punch is performed with both hands as fists. Arms move in a straight line to the target; the forefists strike the face and the solar plexus at the same time.

PUNCH, UPPERCUT

Can be performed with one hand or two. A technique of hooking upward with the fist a short distance, usually targeted at the rib area. The shoulder does most of the movement, with the elbow joint remaining cocked for added power. Called age-tsuki in Karate.

Fig. 3.43 : Uppercut punch performed by Wushu stylist.

PUNCH, VERTICAL FIST

The fist strikes vertically to the face or solar plexus. This technique is useful at very close range.

PUNCH INTERCEPTION

Techniques used, especially in Jeet Kune Do, to intercept and trap an opponent's punch, instead of simply blocking or deflecting it.

PUNCHING IN HORSE STANCE

An exercise in Tai Chi designed to improve strength and supply energy.

PURSUING SWORD FORM

In Iaido, sword drawing art, the third form in the basic drawing methods set, called "tsuigekito." The practitioner uses basic techniques to block and cut the opponent. The four phases of drawing the sword, cutting with the sword, shaking the blood from the sword and resheathing the sword are executed.

PURSUIT FORM

In Iaido (sword drawing art), the eighth form in the seated set, called "tsukekomi." The practitioner practices rising from a seated position and practices basic sword cuts. The four phases of drawing the sword, cutting with the sword, shaking the blood from the sword and resheathing the sword are executed.

PUSH PALM

A palm heel strike technique in Wushu. See Strike, Palm.

PUSHING PALMS WHILE TURNING THE WAIST

An exercise in Tai Chi done to improve lower body strength.

PUSHING WAVE

An exercise done in Tai Chi to improve muscle tone in the lower body.

PYTHON FORM

In Bando, this form emphasizes gripping and grappling moves, crushing actions and strangulation techniques. Other Bando forms emphasize other animal qualities. These are Eagle, Deer, Boar, Cobra, Viper, Monkey, Paddy Bird, Panther, Scorpion, Bull and Tiger.

PYUNH AHN FORMS

See Tae Kwon Do Forms.

QUA

See Strike, Backfist.

QUA SHANG QUAN

See Punch, Reverse.

QUAN

See Punch.

QUYEN

A Vietnamese word for form. See Forms.

RAHASIA

Vital point attacks and defenses practiced in Pentjak Silat.

RAIDEN

See Thunder and Lightning Form.

RAINBOW DANCE

An exercise in Tai Chi designed to improve the function of the internal organs.

RAM'S HEAD PUNCH

See Punch, Ram's Head.

RANDORI

A form of free style sparring used in training in Judo. See Sparring, Free Style.

RASTEIRA

In Capoeria, a throw performed by hooking the opponent's leg as he or she kicks.

REACHING FOR LIMB

A movement used in The Great Circle, a long form consisting of 37 different series of techniques, performed by Tai Chi practitioners.

READY STANCE

See Stance, Ready.

READY WITH STAFF

A movement used in The Great Circle, a long form consisting of 37 different series of techniques, performed by Tai Chi practitioners.

REAPING THE WIND

A movement used in The Great Circle, a long form consisting of 37 different series of techniques, performed by Tai Chi practitioners.

REAR HIP THROW

In Judo, a counter attack in which the practitioner executes a hip throw assisted with an arm around the opponent's neck. See Throws. See Judo Techiques.

REAR KICK

Also known as a mule kick. See Kick, Rear.

REAR FORM

In Iaido (sword drawing art), the fourth form of the seated set, called "ushiro." The practitioner gains experience with attacks from the rear. The four phases of drawing the sword, cutting with the sword, shaking the blood from the sword and resheathing the sword are executed.

REAR THROW

In Judo, a backward throw. The practitioner wraps his or her arms around the opponent's body and falls back, bringing the opponent with him or her. See Judo Techniques. See Throws.

REARWARD INVERSE CUT

In Iaido (sword drawing art), the third form of the basic drawing methods secret set, intermediate level. In Japanese it is called "koteki gyaku-to." The practitioner must defeat two opponents. The four phases of drawing the sword, cutting with the sword, shaking the blood from the sword and resheathing the sword are executed.

REARWARD QUICK DRAW

In Iaido (sword drawing art), the fourth of the basic drawing methods secret set, intermediate level. In Japanese it is called "koteki nukiuchi." The practitioner gains experience with more than one opponent. It varies slightly from Rearward Inverse Cut. The four phases of drawing the sword, cutting with the sword, shaking the blood from the sword and resheathing the sword are executed.

RECEDING WAVES

A movement used in The Great Circle, a long form consisting of 37 different series of techniques, performed by Tai Chi practitioners.

REI

A bow. See Salutation Techniques.

REI NO JI-DACHI

An L-stance. See Stance, L.

REISHA

In Kyudo (archery), a ceremonial drawing of the bow meant to celebrate the spiritual part of archery. See Kyudo Techniques.

RENRAKU

In Judo, using several techniques in a series, with the goal of "opening" the opponent; that is, gaining an entry so that a successful throw can be executed.

RENSOKU-TSUKI

In Karate, a series of punching attacks.

RENSOKU-WAZA

In Jujutsu, a series of vital point attacks.

RENSOKU ZUKI

Same as Rensoku-tsuki. See Rensoku-tsuki.

RENSOKU-GERI

In Karate, a series of kicking attacks.

REPULSE THE MONKEY

A technique in the Tai Chi Chuan Eight Minute form designed to improve posture. It also has a self-defense application.

RETURNING WAVES FORM

In Iaido (sword drawing art), the eighth form in the half-seated set, called "namigaeshi." In this form the practitioner practices rising from the half-seated position, a difficult technique. The four phases of drawing the sword, cutting with the sword, shaking the blood from the sword and resheathing the sword are executed.

REVERSE CROSS STRANGLE

Gyaku juji-jime. In Judo, similar to Nami-juji jime. The practitioner kneels over the opponent, performing a strangulation.

REVERSE PUNCH

See Punch, Reverse.

REVERSE KICK

See Kick, Reverse.

REVERSE SCARFHOLD

In Judo, a technique used when the opponent is on his or her back. The practitioner sits, leaning across the opponent's chest, and grabs the belt by reaching under the shoulder and under the arm.

RIDGE HAND STRIKE

See Strike, Ridge Hand.

RIDING HORSE STANCE

See Stance, Horse.

RIGHT FORM

In Iaido (sword drawing art), the second form of the seated set. It is called "migi." The practitioner practices cuts from a seated position. The four phases of drawing the sword, cutting with the sword, shaking the blood from the sword and resheathing the sword are executed.

RIKEN-UCHI

See Strike, Backfist.

RISING CUT FORM

The third Iaido sword method. This, from the Shindo Munen-ryu style, is called "kiriage." The practitioner performs cuts from a standing position. The four phases of drawing the sword, cutting with the sword, shaking the blood from the sword and resheathing the sword are executed.

RISING BLOCK

See Block, Rising.

RITSUREI

A standing salutation. See Salutation Techniques.

RODA

In Capoeira, an exercise in which a circle of practitioners surround two martial artists who perform to music, gaining energy from the onlookers.

ROLLING ARMS

An exercise in Tai Chi designed to ease joint pain and improve breathing disorders.

ROTATING WHEEL IN A CIRCLE

An exercise in Tai Chi designed to ease stiffness and fatigue.

ROUNDHOUSE KICK

See Kick, Roundhouse.

ROWING THE BOAT IN THE CENTER OF THE LAKE

An exercise in Tai Chi designed to reduce headaches and backaches.

RYO-TE-ERI-TORI

In Aikido, a defense against a lapel hold when the opponent grabs both lapels. The practitioner grips the opponent's elbow with the free hand and pulls downward. See Collar/Lapel Holds. See Aikido Techniques.

RYOTE FORMS

In Iaijutsu (sword drawing), a series of forms that require two swords, used to develop an understanding of defense against a two-sworded opponent.

RYOTE KATA-DORI

In Aikido, a defense against a wrist hold. The practitioner brings his or her hands together and steps forward, then forces both hands down and back up to escape the grip. See Aikido Techniques.

RYOZUME

See Blocked on Both Sides Form.

SABAORI

In Sumo, a technique of forcing the opponent to the ground using his or her own weight as momentum. See Sumo Techniques.

SACRIFICE TECHNIQUES

Any technique in which the practitioner gives up his or her advantage to force the opponent into a greater disadvantage. In Judo, for instance, sutemi waza, sacrifice throws, are executed when the practitioner throws him or herself to the ground along with the opponent, as a way to force the opponent to the ground.

SAGI-ASHI-TACHI

In Karate, a crane stance. See Stance, Crane.

SAIFA KATA

A Chinese form, literally "tearing form." Though Chinese in origin, it is the sixth form of the 14 taught in the Goju-ryu Karate school. The techniques include hammer fist strikes, double punches and kicks executed while standing on one foot. See Karate Forms.

SALUTATION TECHNIQUES

Salutation is a sign of respect, usually performed at the beginning of a class, before a contest and

Fig. 3.44 : Salutation technique. Seated bows to the shomen, front of the room.

upon greeting one's senior belts and instructors. In Escrima, the escrima stick is used to perform a salute. In other arts, bowing from a standing or kneeling position is the appropriate show of respect. A kneeling bow, as is done in Karate, is sometimes performed with the palms placed on top of thighs. Sometimes the palms are pressed against the floor. In Qwan-Ki-Do, the student rests his or her head on the hands. Some schools insist on maintaining eye contact at all times, while others emphasize keeping eyes toward the floor as a show of respect.

Bai. A kneeling bow with hands placed palm down on the floor, in Qwan-Ki-Do.

Baito. In Qwan-Ki-Do, a collection of techniques used at different times to show respect. The kneeling bow, bai and the ready stance, bai su, are two of these.

Gassho-gama. A saluting stance in Shorinji Karate. The hands, joined together with palms facing each other, are raised to eye level.

Ritsurei. In Aikido, a standing salutation.

SAM BO DAE RYUN

See Sparring, Step (Three-step).

SAM-IL FORM

An International Tae Kwon Do federation form taught at sixth dan black belt level. See Tae Kwon Do Forms.

SAMBUT

Free-style sparring in Pentjak Silat.

SAN TEUL MAKI

See Block, Mountain.

SANBON KUMITE

See Sparring, Step.

SANCHIN KATA

Also called hangetsu, "crescent" or "half moon" form. A basic form in Karate. The first form taught in Goju-ryu and Uechi-ryu Karate. The practitioner moves slowly and matches breathing with movements. The muscles remain tense throughout the entire form. The emphasis on breathing exercises hardens the body. Once mastered, the practitioner is allegedly able to take kicks and

Figs. 3.45 and 3.46: Karate practitioner performs Sanchin Kata.

punches to any body target without pain or injury. It develops inner strength, proper stance, plus correct execution of blocks and punches. See Karate Forms.

SANCHIN DACHI

See Stance, Hourglass.

SANGO KEN

In Shorinji Karate, various techniques used to defend against and counter attack strikes to the chest.

SANKYO CONTROL

In Aikido, a series of techniques that involve twisting the opponent's wrist in a variety of situations. See Aikido Techniques.

SANREN-TSUKI

In Karate, three punching attacks delivered in a row.

SANREN-ZUKI

Same as Sanren-tsuki. See Sanren-tsuki.

SANSEIRYU KATA

An advanced form in Karate, the 11th of the 14 forms in Goju-ryu. It has 36 techniques, including slow-motion chest punches, performed with breath exercises and a right arm elbow strike simultaneous with a left hand punch. See Karate Forms.

SANSHU

In Wushu, practicing forms with a partner.

SAPPO

An ancient system of attacking weak, vulnerable areas of the body with the intent of subduing an opponent. Such methods were taught in Jujutsu systems, usually as hidden teachings.

SASAE-TSURI-KOMI ASHI

See Throw, Dropping Drawing Ankle.

SASHI-MEN

In Kendo (swordfighting art), a thrust with the point of the sword to the opponent's throat.

SAT TICH

See Strike, Knife Hand.

SCARFHOLD

Called Gesa-gatame. In Judo, any of several hold down techniques performed by throwing the opponent to his or her back and wedging the upper body between the thigh and the arm pit.

SCISSORS KICK

See Kick, Scissors.

SCISSORS THROW

In Judo, a technique that uses the practitioner's legs like scissors to unbalance the opponent, who falls to the side. See Throws. See Judo Techniques.

SCISSORS BLOCK

See Block, Scissors.

SCOOPING THE SEA WHILE LOOKING AT THE SKY

In Tai Chi, an exercise designed to promote relaxation.

SCOOPING THROW

In Judo, a technique where one raises the opponent by his or her thighs and leans, causing the opponent to fall backward. See Throws. See Judo Techniques.

In Sumo, a technique where the practitioner slides a leg between the opponent's legs and lifts the opponent by using a leg. See Throws. See Sumo Techniques.

SCORPION FORM

In Bando, this form emphasizes punching techniques and seizing attacks on vital points. Other Bando forms help develop other qualities associated with animals. These are Eagle, Deer, Boar, Cobra, Viper, Monkey, Paddy Bird, Panther, Python, Bull and Tiger.

SCORPION STRIKE

A backfist strike. See Strike, Backfist.

SE JONG FORM

An International Tae Kwon Do Federation form, taught at the 7th dan black belt level. See Tae Kwon Do Forms.

SEATED SET

In Iaido (sword drawing art), a series of forms called "seiza no bu." These forms teach techniques to move out of seiza (kneeling position) and into offensive or defensive positions. All of the major sword motions are found here. Balance and leg strength are developed. There are 11 forms to be mastered before the beginner can move on to other techniques.

1. *Forward Form*
2. *Right Form*
3. *Left Form*
4. *Rear Form*
5. *Eightfold Fences Form*
6. *Parrying Form*
7. *Assisting At Seppuku Form*
8. *Pursuit Form*
9. *Moonbeams Form*
10. *Tailwind Form*
11. *Sudden Draw Form*

SEATED STANCE

See Stance, Seated.

SECRET FORMS EXTRA SET

In Iaido (sword drawing art), a series of forms called "bangai no bu." These were created to help the practitioner learn to deal with large numbers of opponents. They are long forms, very advanced.

1. *Fast Wave Form*
2. *Thunder And Lightning Form*
3. *Thunder Clap Form*
4. *Four Directional Cutting (V). Also called Demon Cutting.*

SECRET FORMS STANDING SET

In Iaido (sword drawing art), a series of forms called "tachiwaza no bu." These are advanced techniques dealing with special situations requiring special methods of drawing, cutting or footwork. There are 13 forms in all.

1. *Accompaniment Form*
2. *Companions Form*
3. *Complete Resolution Form*
4. *Full Stop Form*
5. *Loyal Retainer Form*
6. *Misdirection Form*
7. *Sleeve Flip Form*
8. *Entering the Gate Form*
9. *Between the Walls Form*
10. *Parrying Form*
11.-13. *Farewell Visit I, II, and III Forms*

SECRET FORMS SEATED SET

In Iaido (sword drawing art), a series of forms containing advanced techniques. These techniques are designed to work when obstructions, such as doorways or narrow halls, prevent the usual execution of sword drawing techniques. There are eight forms.

1. *Mist Form*
2. *Encircled Leg Form*
3. *Blocked at the Door Form*
4. *Beneath the Doorway Form*
5. *Four Directional Cut Form*
6. *Beneath the Ledge Form*
7. *Blocked on Both Sides Form*
8. *Charging the Tiger Form*

SEIPAI KATA

A form in Karate, the ninth of 14 taught in the Goju ryu school. It consists of body twisting movements, plus a front kick, backfist strike and elbow strike. See Karate Forms.

SEIRYOKU ZEN YO KOKUMIN TAI-IKU NO KATA

A method of training in Judo. There are 28 solo exercises that emphasize vital point attacks and 20 exercises designed to improve speed and decision making processes. These exercises are based on the principles of efficiency. See Judo Techniques.

SEIRYU-TO

See Strike, Wrist.

SEIRYU-TO-UKE

See Block, Wrist.

SEISAN KATA

A Karate form that relies on sanchin-dachi and horse stances. It emphasizes quick punching techniques. It is the eighth of 14 forms taught in Goju-ryu Karate.

SEIYUNCHIN KATA

An ancient form in Karate, the 11th of 14 forms taught in Goju-ryu Karate. It is so old that its meaning is lost. It emphasizes breath control. All the movements are hand techniques. It is thought to be from the Chinese school of Mind-Body Boxing (Hsing-I). See Karate Forms.

SEIZA

A kneeling position in Iaido, sword drawing art. The practitioner performs "correct sitting" by resting the thighs on the heels.

SEIZA NO BU

See Seated Set.

SENKEN

In martial arts generally, a movement executed in anticipation of the opponent's movement or attack.

SENSITIVITY DRILLS

These are repetitions of exercises done to improve the student's reactions. See Paper Striking Exercises. See Wooden Dummy Drills. See Sticky Hand Drills.

SEOI-AGE

In Judo, shoulder throws executed by lifting the opponent and throwing him or her over the shoulders.

SEOI-NAGE

In Judo, shoulder throws.

SEOI-OTOSHI

See Shoulder Drop.

SEPARATING CLOUDS BY WHEELING ARMS

An exercise in Tai Chi designed to strengthen the lower body.

SERPENT DESCENDS

A movement used in The Great Circle, a long form consisting of 37 different series of techniques, performed by Tai Chi practitioners.

SET

The same thing as a form; that is, a prearranged pattern of techniques that allows the martial artist to perfect his or her skills without requiring a partner.

SHOULDER DROP

In Judo, a technique that uses both hands to pull the opponent over one's hip and shoulder. See Judo Techniques. See Throws.

SEUG-GI

In Tae Kwon Do, a name for stance. See Stance.

SHASHIN

A term meaning a feint. See Feinting Techniques.

SHATO

See Angular Sword Form.

SHIHOGIRI

See Four Directional Cut Form.

SHIHOTO SONO ICHI

See Four Directional Cut I.

SHIHOTO SONO NI

See Four Directional Cut II.

SHIKARE-WAZA

In Kendo (swordfighting art), a sudden attack by an opponent who is capitalizing on a lowering of the guard.

SHIME-WAZA

Methods of strangulation in Judo. See Strangulation Techniques.

SHIMEI

A strike to a vital point that could be dangerous or even fatal.

SHIMERU

In Kendo (swordfighting art), a strengthening exercise performed with the sword or staff.

Striking downward, the practitioner tenses the muscles of the arms when the weapon reaches its target. The exercise is performed sitting, standing or moving.

SHIN GONG

In martial arts generally, the study, development, and discipline of the mind.

SHINKO KATA

In Karate, a general term for advanced forms.

SHISEI

See Stance, Fighting.

SHISOCHIN

A typical Chinese form that is nonetheless used in Japanese Karate. It is the seventh form of the 14 learned in Goju-ryu. It includes finger strikes, palm strikes and cat stances. See Karate Forms.

SHITATE HINERI

In Sumo, a throw executed by gripping the opponent's belt under his or her arms with the inner hand and pulling. See Sumo Techniques.

SHITATE YAGURA-NAGE

In Sumo, a hip throw which relies on grasping the opponent's belt with one's arm under the opponent's arm. See Sumo Techniques.

SHITATE-NAGE

In Sumo, an inner arm throw, using an inner grip. See Sumo Techniques.

SHITSUI

See Strike, Hammerfist.

SHIZEN HONTAI

Same as Shizen-tai. See Stance, Natural.

SHIZEN-TAI

See Stance, Natural.

SHODAN NAGA NO KATA

In Judo, black belt formal throws. See Formal Throws.

SHODEN

Basic sword techniques in Kendo (swordfighting art).

SHOMEN

In Kendo (swordfighting art), a strike to the head.

SHOMEN-UCHI

A palm strike in Aikido. See Strike, Palm.

SHORT HAND

A name applied to certain styles of Wushu. It refers to styles that rely on linear, direct movements. See Long Hand.

SHOULDER WHEEL

Called Kata-guruma. In Judo, a throw in which the practitioner lifts the opponent by sliding an arm between the opponent's legs and wheels the opponent from one side of the shoulders to the other side. See Throws. See Judo Techniques.

SHUANG HUAN CHANG

See Palm Change, Double.

SHUJIHATTE

A set of traditional techniques in Sumo, 48 in all, that are the foundation of Sumo; there are however, countless moves and variations that Sumo wrestlers employ. The techniques can be divided into throws, trips, twists, or backward maneuvers. Some common Sumo techniques include: tsukidashi, sukuinage, tsukiotoshi, nodowa, oshidashi, kotenage, tottari, utchari, shitatenage, hatakikomi, sotogake, yorikiri, uwatenage, tsuradashi, uchigake, okuridashi. See Sumo Techniques.

SHUTO-UCHI

In Kendo (swordfighting art), a direct attack with the sword.

In Karate, see Strike, Knife Hand.

SHUTO-UKE

In Kendo (swordfighting art), a block with the back of the sword.

In Karate, see Block, Knife Hand.

SIDE BODY DROP

In Judo, the practitioner blocks and hooks the opponent's ankle from the side. See Judo Techniques. See Throws.

SIDE DROP

In Judo, a sacrifice throw. The practitioner brings his or her weight forward, blocking the opponent's movement with his or her thigh and pulling the opponent's sleeve. Then the practitioner rolls away, taking the opponent down. See Throws. See Judo Techniques.

SIDE FOUR QUARTERS HOLD

In Judo, a hold down executed when the opponent is on his or her back. From the side, the practitioner slides one arm under the opponent's neck and the other between the opponent's legs to grip the belt.

SIDE KICK

See Kick, Side.

SIDE SEPARATION

In Judo, the practitioner blocks the opponent's movement with both legs and slides to the floor while pulling the opponent down. Also called yoko-otoshi. See Judo Techniques. See Throws.

SIDE STANCE

See Stance, Side.

SIDE SWEEPING FOOT THROW

See Sweeping Ankle Throw.

SIDE WHEEL

In Judo, the practitioner reaches under the opponent's shoulders, grips the opponent's belt and throws. See Judo Techniques. See Throws.

SIDESTEPPING TECHNIQUE

See Footwork.

SIDEWAYS WALKING

A Ninja technique for leaving foot prints that would not show the direction the practitioner was actually moving.

SIL LUM TAO

"The way of the small idea," a Wing Chun Wushu form that contains techniques focusing primarily on breathing, balance and coordination as well as correct hand and arm positions. It is the first form taught to the beginner.

SILLA HANSOO

A Tae Kwon Do form that is taught at the sixth dan black belt level. It is part of the palgue series. See Tae Kwon Do Forms.

SINGLE WHIP

A technique in the Tai Chi Chuan Eight Minute form. It increases joint flexibility, but also has a self-defense application.

SIP JIN FORM

A Tae Kwon Do form for fifth dan black belt. Part of the palgue series. See Tae Kwon Do forms.

SITTING STANCE

See Stance, Seated.

SLEEVE FLIP FORM

In Iaido (sword drawing art), the seventh form in the secret forms standing set, called "sodesuri gaeshi." This form gives the practitioner experience with more than one opponent and a complicated situation. The practitioner imagines he or she is in a group of friendly associates when an opponent threatens. The four phases of drawing the sword, cutting with the sword, shaking the blood from the sword and resheathing the sword are practiced.

SLEEVE HOLDS

In Aikido, techniques to defend against sleeve grabs and holds are frequently practiced. There are several basic techniques used.

Dosoku kata sode-tori. The practitioner steps away and uses his or her free hand to strike to the opponent's elbow, aiming for a vital point.

Jun kata sode-tori. The practitioner grabs the opponent's free hand and performs an elbow strike to the side of the opponent's chest.

Ushiro eri kata sodetori. The practitioner bends under the opponent's arm, then throws the opponent forward.

Ushiro ryo kata sodetori. The practitioner steps away and slides under the opponent's arm.

See Aikido Techniques.

SMOTHERING BLOCK

See Block, Smothering.

SNAKE CREEPS DOWN LEFT SIDE and RIGHT SIDE

Techiques in Tai Chi Chuan Eight Minute Form. They increase flexibility and muscle tone, while having a self-defense application as well.

SNAKE STANCE

See Stance, Snake.

SOCHIN FORM

In Karate, a basic form in the Shotokan style used in Shito-ryu and Shotokai schools. The movements consist of basic stances and techniques of fundamental attack and defense. The form was once called hakko. The modern name is a combination of the word "so," meaning "violence" and "chin," which means "calm."

SOCHIN-DACHI

Same as Fudo-tachi. See Stance, Ready.

SODOME

See Full Stop Form.

SOKUTEI OSAE UKE

See Block, Pressing.

SOKUTEI MAWASHI UKE

See Block, Crescent.

SOKUTO GERI

See Kick, Side.

SUKUTO OSAE UKE

See Block, Pressing.

SOKUTO-KAEGE

See Kick, Knife Foot.

SON KYO

In Kendo, a ready stance. See Stance, Ready.

SONG DAI

See Sparring, Free Style.

SONG CUOC

See Kick, Side.

SOTAI-RENSHU

In martial arts generally, the study and practice of techniques with a partner.

SOTO GAKE

In Judo, a hook to the outside of the opponent's leg.

In Sumo, a technique in which the practitioner holds the opponent's belt under his or her arms and uses a leg to off-balance the opponent.

SOTO-KOMATA

In Sumo, grabbing the opponent's thigh underneath and attempting to off-balance him or her. See Sumo Techniques.

SOTO-MAKE-KOME

See Outer Winding Throw.

SOTO-MAKI-KOMI

Same as Soto-make-kome. See Outer Winding Throw.

SPARRING, FREE STYLE

In martial arts practice, partners practice fighting techniques without referees or judges; free style

Figs. 3.47 and 3.48 : Free style sparring practice.

sparring in competition is always conducted with referees and judges. In Karate, Jiyu kumite or free style sparring is the most advanced form of training. Partners move about exchanging kicks and strikes at will, using the various techniques of blocking, distancing, timing and strategy to score point to the partner's target area. In practice, this is a learning tool for students, who exert control over their techniques and pull their punches. There are many variations on this, including slow sparring, power sparring, kick sparring, and hand sparring, each of which develops different skills. Almost all schools of martial arts have practice periods in which techniques are attempted against one another without any prearrangement.

In Judo, randori is the training method where two Judo practitioners attack and defend at will. All techniques are used, including throws,

Fig. 3.49 : These Tae Kwon Do practitioners demonstrate three step sparring. The attacker low blocks while the defender assumes a ready stance.

Fig. 3.50 : Attacker punches while defender blocks with a knife hand block.

Fig. 3.51: Attacker punches a second time, while defender blocks.

Fig. 3.52: Attacker punches a third time and defender blocks and counter attacks this time with a punch to the solar plexus.

Fig. 3.53: The defender cocks his arm in preparation for another blow.

Fig. 3.54 : The defender finishes the attacker with a second punch, this one to the face.

strangulations and armlocks. The practitioners try to use the basic knowledge they have gained concerning methods of unbalancing the opponent and footwork. The goal is to practice and improve one's abilities without being concerned whether one is winning or losing. Such practice is done with numerous different partners so that the practitioner gains a wide variety of experience. A variation of this is done when the partners agree to offer less resistance than usual, or, in the case of Judo, when one stops short of the actual throw.

SPARRING, STEP

In Karate, the prearranged sparring methods are often called kihon kumite, basic sparring. The techniques of attack and defense are known ahead of time. There are a number of prearranged sparring methods.

Ippon kumite or one point sparring consists of participants facing each other from a fixed distance and taking turns in attacking and defending, again with prearranged routines. Usually one participant assumes a fighting stance while the defender remains in a natural or ready stance. As the attacker steps forward and delivers his attack, the defender steps away, blocks and counters. This is called one-step sparring in Tae-Kwon Do.

Gohon kumite or five-step sparring consists of one participant attacking five times in a row with the same technique. The partner blocks the attacks four times and after the last attack, counters with a powerful technique or series of techniques. In Tae Kwon Do, three-step sparring is the same thing, except only three attacks are launched. This is called sanbon sparring in Karate.

Jiyu ippon kumite is partially free style sparring, where perhaps the target or technique is known, but not all movements are prearranged.

Kihon kumite kata. Performing basic sparring patterns with a partner. The patterns are derived by breaking down a form.

Jiju Undo. Performing basic sparring patterns alone.

In Okinawan Goju-ryu Karate, there is no free style sparring (jiyu kumite). All sparring is done in prearranged exercises. In other martial arts, step or prearranged sparring is done in addition to free style sparring. See Sparring, Free Style.

SOTO-MUSO

In Sumo, a technique of blocking an opponent's thigh with a hand and then pushing on the opponent's shoulders to cause a fall. See Sumo Techniques.

SOTO-UDE-UKE

See Block, Forearm.

SOTO-UKE

See Block, Hammer Fist.

SPEAR FINGER STRIKE

See Strike, Spear Hand.

SPINNING TECHNIQUES

Used in the majority of Asian martial arts, these are techniques, usually kicks, which are performed with a partial or full revolution of the body. They are especially prevalent in Tae Kwon Do and Wushu. Many Karate systems avoid such techniques because the back must be turned to execute them. Spinning kicks can be performed from several positions including standing, crouching and jumping. The revolution adds power to the kick.

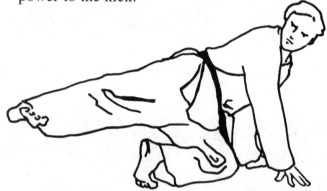

Fig. 3.55 : A low spinning back kick.

SPRING HIP THROW

In Judo, a throw in which the practitioner steps in front of the opponent, then "springs" the opponent over the hips and thighs in a circular motion. See Throws. See Judo Techniques.

SPRING LEG THROW

See Spring Hip Throw.

Figs. 3.56, 3.57 and 3.58 : A variety of Wushu stances.

STAMPING KICK/STOMPING KICK

See Kick, Stamping.

STANCE

This refers to various body positions used in the martial arts. These are sometimes called postures or steps. Stances generally concern foot placement and secondarily, arm placement. Basic stances include horse stance, front stance, back stance and natural stance.

STANCE, ATTENTION

All martial arts have a formal stance in which one comes to attention, perhaps to salute the instructor or to pay some other courtesy. Usually, one comes "to attention," that is, assumes that attention stance, when one is being addressed by an instructor or a senior belt. In many styles, the attention stance is performed with feet together and hands held flat at the side, although hands can be made fists sometimes. There are a few exceptions. In Escrima, for instance, one stands with hands at the sides and feet a shoulder width apart. Stances can be performed open toe or closed toe, but invariably the practitioner is expected to display unwavering focus and a rigid stance.

STANCE, BACK

A side facing stance. The back leg is bent deeply, bearing most of the weight. The front leg is slightly

Fig. 3.59 : Karate back stance.

Fig. 3.60 : Wushu back stance, also called empty stance.

bent with the heel off the ground. The front leg and foot can easily be lifted to block or strike. It is called hugul ja sae in Tae Kwon Do.

Kokutsu-dachi. In Karate, a stance with most of the weight resting on the back foot and less on the front foot. The front knee is slightly bent; the rear knee is more deeply bent. Legs are close together with the chest slightly forward, though that stance is sideways. A strong defensive stance.

STANCE, BOW

A stance used in Wushu, similar to a front stance, except the rear foot is at a 90-degree angle to the front foot. The forward leg is bent slightly and bears most of the weight. The rear leg is straight but the knee is not locked. The toes on the rear leg turn out at a 45-degree angle. Toes on the lead leg are straight forward. This is an important stance in Tai Chi Chuan.

STANCE, CAT

The cat stance is called neko ashi dachi in Karate and tuit bal seh in Tae Kwon Do. It is characterized by the narrow distance between the front and rear legs. The chest faces more forward than in a back stance. Almost all weight is on the back leg and the back foot is planted sideways for support.

Ding bo. In Wushu, most of the weight is on the back leg, and both feet face forward.

Hui bo. In Wushu, a modification of ding bo. The toes are parallel and face inward instead of to the front.

STANCE, CHALLENGED

A stance used in Tai Chi Chuan. It is similar to a ready stance. The legs are about a shoulder's width apart, and the knees are slightly bent.

STANCE, CONFRONTATION

See Stance, Fighting.

STANCE, CRANE

A popular stance in Wushu. The practitioner lifts one leg and places the foot to the back or side of the knee of the leg that is still standing. It is an excellent method for developing balance.

STANCE, CROUCHING

A stance in which one squats within inches of the ground with one leg extended parallel to the floor.

In Iaijutsu, a stance with one knee on the ground, the other raised.

STANCE, EVEN

Any stance in which the practitioner's weight rests evenly on both feet.

STANCE, FIGHTING

A basic stance used for attacking and defending. In most arts, it is a side-facing stance. The back leg is slightly bent and bears more weight than the front. Arms are bent to protect the body and hands are usually held about shoulder height. The body is evenly balanced so that weight can be easily redistributed as necessary. Sometimes weight is on the balls of the feet with the front of the body forward toward the target. Very similar to the back stance.

Jigotai. In Judo, a defensive stance, almost the same as a horse stance, used while waiting for an attack.

*Fig. 3.61 :
Bow stance.*

Fig. 3.62 : A Karate fighting stance.   *Fig. 3.63 : A fighting stance for full contact competition.*

Chudan no kamae. In Kendo, an on-guard stance in which one grips one's sword in both hands and aims it at the opponent's chest.

Gedan no kamae. In Kendo, a low guard stance in which the sword is held in front with the tip lowered.

Dinh tan. A basic stance used in Viet Vo Dao. The feet are in a natural position with the weight slightly forward. Arms are raised in a ready, on-guard position.

Ai-gamae (literally, confrontation stance). In Aikido the body faces the target with one foot forward, similar to a front stance, though the knees are not deeply bent. The stance is used as a fighting stance, while preparing to attack or defend.

Chung sik. In Wushu, a stance used in sparring. The weight is almost evenly divided between the two legs; the front or back leg kicks. Knees are bent with the front knee slightly raised.

Chuat sing. A variation of the Wushu fighting stance used for deflecting the opponent's momentum. The weight rests on the back leg. The heel of the front foot rests on the ground with the toes pointing up.

STANCE, FORWARD

See Stance, Front.

STANCE, FRONT

In Tae Kwon Do, the front stance called chun gool seh is one of the most important basic stances. The body faces front, legs are a shoulder's width or more apart, the front leg is forward and is bent 90-degrees. The back leg is locked and the toes on both feet face forward.

In Karate, an elongated front stance is zenkutsu dachi.

In Tae Kwon Do, a low stance, natchwoh seh, is an exaggerated front stance with a long distance between the front and rear leg. A short front stance is called pahn chun gool seh; the knees are not as bent.

Gyaku-zuki no ashi. In Karate, a front stance position with the upper body twisted toward the forward foot.

Zenkutsu-dachi. In Karate, an elongated front stance. It is the most commonly used Karate stance.

Also called a forward stance.

STANCE, HANGING HORSE

In Wushu, another name for crane stance. See Stance, Crane.

STANCE, HOOKING

In Wushu, a stance characterized by a forward lunging position.

Fig. 3.64 : Wushu stylist performs a horse stance.

STANCE, HORSE

The most fundamental martial arts stance. The entire body faces forward, with feet planted between a shoulder's width and two shoulders' width apart (depending on the style). The knees are bent, with the ideal position being a right angle between the thigh and calf. Since the stance is fundamental

Fig. 3.65 : Karate practitioners in horse stances.

Fig. 3.66: Karate practitioners doing horse stance exercise.

MARTIAL ARTS ENCYCLOPEDIA

and helps develop strong leg muscles, some martial arts styles pay great attention to perfecting the horse stance, devoting much time and training to it. Also called the horse riding stance, the horseback stance or the equestrian stance. In Karate, it is called kiba dachi.

Am duong tan. In Qwan-ki-do, a horse stance with hands resting on the thighs.

STANCE, HOURGLASS

Hangetsu-dachi. Also called Sanchin-dachi. A Karate stance where the feet and knees are turned in, sometimes called the "wide" hourglass stance. The weight is equally distributed and the front toes face forward while the rear toes turn inward 45 degrees. A defensive stance.

STANCE, INWARD BENT KNEE

Similar to an hourglass stance. The practitioner is in a horse stance, with toes forward and weight evenly distributed, then turns the knees inward.

STANCE, L.

An even stance with equal weight on each leg and knees bent as deep as in a horse stance. The toes on one foot face forward while the others point sideways, thus giving the shape of an "L."

STANCE, LOTUS

All lotus stances are similar, but the center of gravity shifts. The high lotus stance is similar to a front stance. The lead foot is slightly ahead of the back foot; the front knee is bent more than the back knee and weight rests more on the forward leg. In the low lotus stance, the back knee

Fig. 3.67 : Low lotus stance.

Fig. 3.68 : High lotus stance.

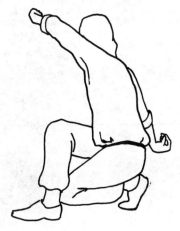

Fig. 3.69 : Sitting lotus stance, back view.

Fig. 3.70 : Sitting lotus stance, front view.

176

bends until it is about ankle height from the ground. It is turned in at a 45-degree angle. Sitting lotus stance is the same except that the rear knee rests on the ground.

STANCE, MOUNTAIN CLIMBING

Also called the bow-and-arrow-stance. The body is forward, the knees slightly bent. The front toes turn out at a 45-degree angle; the back toes face straight forward.

Fig. 3.71 : Mountain climbing stance.

STANCE, NATURAL

Hachiji dachi. A stance in Karate with weight evenly balanced between both legs. Legs are straight, with a slight bend in the knees. The toes are pointed outward about 45 degrees. This is a basic stance in Karate.

Shizentai. In Judo, a stance with the feet placed about a shoulder's width apart and the knees are bent slightly with the body straight and the weight evenly distributed. Similar to a horse stance. In right natural stance, called migi shizentai in Judo, the right foot is placed slightly forward while in left natural stance, the left foot is slightly forward. This is called hidari shizentai in Judo.

STANCE, PIGEON TOE

A stance with the knees and feet pointed inward, also called an inward stance. In Karate, it is called sanchin stance or hangetsu-dachi, and is known as

Fig. 3.72 : Pigeon toed stance, called sanchin-dachi.

the hourglass stance. It is one of the first stances learned by a beginner. See Stance, Hourglass.

STANCE, READY

Fudodachi. The position commonly assumed before the performance of a form or prior to taking the fighting stance in sparring. In Tae Kwon Do, arms are held waist high, with elbows slightly bent. Hands are fists, legs are relaxed, about a shoulder's width apart. In Karate, the practitioner's weight is equally distributed between both legs, with knees fully bent and tensed outward. The legs are wide apart and the front toes face forward, while the rear toes are at a 45-degree angle outward.

Commencing Tai Chi/ Commencement of Tai Chi. The practitioner prepares to perform a form. In this upright stance, the feet are together. The practitioner focuses his or her mind, and relaxes. Then he or she bring arms up, and presses down.

Musubi-dachi. A Karate stance with heels together and toes pointing outward.

Lien hoa tan. In Qwan Ki Do, a stance with the knees only slightly bent.

See photos next page.

STANCE, ROOSTER

The Wushu stance is similar to a crane stance. The body faces forward. One foot is lifted and the toes are placed on the side of the knee of the standing leg.

STANCE, SEATED

A stance in Wushu. A full squat with legs crossed.

Fig. 3.77 : Rooster stance.

STANCE, SIDE

In Tae Kwon Do, called yup seh. It is like a horse stance, only it is done when the opponent is on the side, not in front.

STANCE, SNAKE

In this narrow stance, one foot is placed directly in front of the other.

Fig. 3.73 : Karate practitioners preparing to begin class.

Fig. 3.74 : Judo ready stance.

Fig. 3.75 : Tae Kwon Do ready stance.

Fig. 3.76 : Commencing Tai Chi (ready stance).

STANCE, SQUARE

This stance is characterized by deeply bent knees, with weight equally distributed. Similar to a horse stance, except the toes face outward.

STANCE, SUMO

In Karate, an imitation of the stance Sumo wrestlers use, with toes pointed forward, and legs spread very wide apart. The knees are bent. The stance resembles an exaggerated horse stance.

STANCE, SWING

In Wushu, a stance similar to a deep leg squat.

STANCE, T

Hidari teiji-dachi. In Karate, a stance with the body facing forward and knees bent like a horse stance. The main difference is the toes on one foot face forward and on the other are at a 90-degree angle. The stance is the same for Tae Kwon Do. In Judo, the stance is used to prevent being thrown.

In Wushu, this is a half squat, with one leg flat on the floor, the other heel raised, and feet parallel.

STANCE, THREE ESSENTIALS

Called san tsai shih. In Wushu, a stance similar to the back stance, but more weight is on the forward foot.

STANCE, TIGER

In Wushu, a frequently used stance. The body faces forward, feet parallel. One knee is bent 45-degrees and the other foot extends all the way out from the side of the body. In other styles a forward facing stance. One leg remains flat, the other crosses over and slightly forward with knee bent and heel off ground.

STANCE, TWIST-ING HORSE

Called lau ma. Facing forward, the front leg is crossed

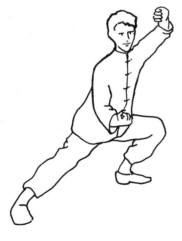

Fig. 3.78 : Tiger stance.

over the back with the front foot flat and the back heel raised.

STANCE, UNICORN

In Wushu, this stance is similar to a lotus stance. The body and legs face forward. The front leg is bent at a 45-degree angle with the back leg almost touching the ground.

STANCE, WALKING

A natural stance with knees relaxed and weight evenly distributed. *Chao ma tan.* A natural stance in Qwan Ki Do, where the knees are slightly bent but the practitioner is on his or her toes.

Fig. 3.79 : Unicorn stance.

STANCE, X

The body faces forward, and the front leg is crossed over the rear leg. The weight is carried on the balls of the feet, with slightly more weight on the forward leg.

STANDING MONKEY

See Tall Monkey.

STEP

Sometimes used to refer to stance, sometimes refers to footwork.

STEP, PARRY AND PUNCH TECHNIQUES

A technique in the Tai Chi Chuan Eight Minute Form. It strengthens the knee joints and increases flexibility in the hips while having a self-defense application.

STEP SPARRING

See Sparring, Step.

STEPPING HORSE

See Footwork.

STICKY HAND DRILL

This exercise is practiced mainly in Wing Chun Wushu. It helps develop speed, balance, and countering techniques. Two partners face each other, feet parallel. Both extend their hands with only wrists touching. Each partner rotates his or her arms counter clockwise, keeping pressure applied at the wrist. Each partner attempts to move the other from position. The drill is supposed to increase the student's balance and sensitivity; skilled practitioners can identify the opponent's intentions. Called chi sao.

STICKY FOOT

See Wooden Dummy Drills.

STOMACH THROW

In Judo, a sacrifice throw executed by falling backward and pulling the opponent by using a leg in the opponent's stomach. See Judo Techniques. See Throws.

STONE MONKEY

A form in Monkey style Wushu characterized by rolling and falling techniques, though the practitioners use powerful force against the opponent, rather than using evasion. Training requires a body resistant to punches and kicks.

STORK

A movement used in The Great Circle, a long form consisting of 37 different series of techniques, performed by Tai Chi practitioners.

STRAIGHT PUNCH DRILL

See Wooden Dummy Drill.

STRAIGHT STEPPING

See Footwork.

STRANGULATION TECHNIQUES

These are techniques for choking or holding the opponent around the throat to force his or her defeat in a contest. Mostly used in Judo.

Eri-jime. One of the several strangulation techniques in which the lapels of the opponent's uniform are used as a weapon.

Gyaku juji-jime. Similar to Nami-juji jime. The practitioner kneels over the opponent, performing a strangulation.

Gyaku okuri eri. A strangulation effected by grabbing the opponent's lapels and twisting.

Hadaka-jime. Performed by using one's arms instead of the opponent's lapels or clothing. Called

"naked struggle," because no clothing is needed.

Hidari ashi-jime. Executed when the practitioner throws his or her leg over the opponent's throat.

Hiza jime. Performed with the knee.

Kata hajime. Used in conjunction with a shoulder hold.

Kata juji-jime. A cross grab. The practitioner grabs the opponent's collar, with crossed arms, and pulls the opponent forward using a scissoring technique.

Koshi-jime. Hip Strangle. The practitioner grasps the lapel and pulls it across the opponent's throat using the hip and shoulder to exert pressure.

Morote-jime. Executed by grabbing the opponent's lapels and rolling the clenched fists to create pressure on the neck.

Okuri-eri-jime. The practitioner slides an arm under the opponent's grabs the opponent's lapel. The practitioner then straightens his or her arm to create pressure on the opponent's neck.

Tsukomi-jime. A strangulation technique executed by holding both lapels and pushing across the opponent's throat.

STRETCHING TECHNIQUES

Warming up and stretching cold muscles before beginning a martial arts workout is essential to maintaining flexibility and preventing injuries. Though it is important to stretch before a class, most martial arts classes

Fig. 3.80 : Karate practitioners warm up for class.

Fig. 3.81 : Karate practitioner stretches.

include instruction in stretching techniques during and after a session. Specific stretching exercises are performed in several martial arts styles. For others, with less specific guidelines, stretching techniques might include shoulder rotations, hurdler's stretches, trunk twists and others. To these are added crunches, leg lifts and pushups.

STRIKE EARS WITH BOTH FISTS

A technique in the Tai Chi Chuan Eight Minute form. It strengthens the arm muscles and increases flexibility in the back. It also has a self-defense application.

STRIKES

Used to refer to any attacking technique with any weapon that is intended to reach a target area on the opponent. The strikes that follow are all body techniques, that is, strikes using some part of the body. Punches, blows made with the fist, are not included in this heading, nor are kicks, which are strikes made with the leg or foot. Strikes can be linear or circular, though most hand strikes do follow a circular path to their target, mostly to generate power. Techniques are done with the fist, back of the fist, back of the hand, edge of the hand, elbow, ridge of the hand, fingertips, elbow, knees and so on. See Punches. See Kicks.

STRIKE, BACKFIST

This blow is delivered using the back of the fist. It requires a snapping motion of the arm to generate speed and power. It can be performed in an upward or downward motion, but most commonly the strike is delivered outward. An long son is the Vietnamese name. It is called ura-ken uchi in Karate. In Wushu, sometimes called a scorpion strike.

Fig. 3.82 : Backfist strike.

Gamen-tsuki. In Karate, a spinning backfist, executed by completing a full reverse revolution. This technique, though powerful, is also "blind," that is, one cannot always tell where it will land.

STRIKE, ELBOW

This technique, using the outside of the forearm or upper arm near the elbow can be executed backward, upward, downward, inward, outward. The backward elbow strikes starts in the front and is thrown to the rear. The upward starts at the side and is thrown up to strike the chin or face of the opponent. The downward starts

Fig. 3.84 : Inward elbow strike.

181

Fig. 3.85 : Hammer fist strike.

above the shoulder and is snapped down. Inward moves horizontally across the body from outside to inside, while the outward moves horizontally away from the body from inside to outside.

STRIKE, FINGER

Leading finger jab. A quick strike with the fingers folded together to prevent injury to the practitioner. Usually targeted at especially vulnerable areas such as the eyes.

Oyayubi nukite. A thumb strike. See Strike, Two-finger.

STRIKE, HAMMER FIST

Also called bottom fist. The practitioner uses the bottom of the fist to strike, usually with a downward motion. In Qwan-Ki-Do, it is called Bat phong son.

STRIKE, KNEE

A strike with the knee to any target area. The knee is usually thrust straight into the target. The technique is sometimes assisted by pulling the opponent into the knee. A close combat technique.

Front knee. When facing a target, the practitioner brings his or her knee up to strike.

Roundhouse knee. Bringing the knee from outside the target, like a roundhouse kick.

Fig. 3.86 : Knee strike.

STRIKE, KNIFE HAND

A strike delivered with the outer edge of the hand, with the elbow slightly bent and the hand open. The hand travels downward or from side to side

horizontally. Depending on the direction of the strike, the palm faces either up or down. It can be performed with fingers bent, called bear claw or clamp hand.

STRIKE, PALM

A blow made using the heel of the palm, usually thrust forward, though it can also go upward or downward. A hooking palm strike, rarely used, is a technique in which the hand comes across the body to strike.

Kumade uchi. Sometimes called the bear hand strike. In Karate, a palm strike executed with the fingers bent. The strike targets vulnerable areas such as the face.

STRIKE, RIDGE HAND

Also called inner edge strike. It is like the knife hand, only it uses the inner edge of the hand.

Haito-uchi. In Karate, an open hand strike, similar to a knife hand. The index finger side of the hand strikes any target. The circular strike can be done moving from the outside to the inside or the inside to the outside. The latter is sometimes called a reverse ridge hand.

STRIKE, SCORPION

A back fist strike. See Strike, Backfist.

STRIKE, SPEAR HAND

Sometimes called spear fingers. The tips of the fingers are held even with each other, and the hand is taut. Can attack with hand vertical, as in the Tae Kwon Do technique kwansu, or horizontally.

Fig. 3.87 : A downward knife hand

Fig. 3.88 : A horizontal knife hand strike.

Fig. 3.89 : Spearhand strike.

There are a number of variations, including those that use one finger, two or all five.

STRIKE, TEMPLE

A variation of the backfist technique. A snapping strike to the opponent's temple with the back of the closed hand.

STRIKE, TIGER CLAW

A palm heel strike with the fingers open like a claw.

STRIKE, TWO-FINGER

A straight strike with the index and middle finger extended usually aimed at the opponent's eyes.

Fig. 3.83 : Overhand temple strike.

STRONG RIGHT FIST

A movement used in The Great Circle, a long form consisting of 37 different series of techniques, performed by Tai Chi practitioners.

SUBURI

In Kendo (sword fighting art), the repetitive practice of sword strikes.

SUDDEN DRAW FORM

In Iaido (sword drawing art), the 11th form in the seated set, called "nukiuchi." The practitioner is seated, facing an opponent. As the opponent attacks, the practitioner finishes him or her with a downward cut. The practitioner shakes the blood from the sword and resheathes it.

SUIO RYU

See Four Directional Cut IV.

SUKUI-NAGE

See Scooping Throw.

SUKUI-UKE

See Block, Forearm.

SUMI-GAESHI

See Corner Throw. Also called Inside Lateral Sacrifice Throw.

SUMI-OTOSHI

See Corner Drop.

SUMO STANCE

See Stance, Sumo.

SUMO TECHNIQUES

There are four categories of Sumo techniques: throwing (nage), tripping (kake), bending (sori), and twisting (hineri).

Twelve each of the most common holds equals the 48 techniques of the shijuhatte. About 12 of these account for most wins.

Abise-taoshi. Pushing hands against an opponent's chest when his arms are wrapped around one's shoulders. The push is intended to off-balance the opponent.

Ami-uchi. From the rear, the practitioner slides his or arms through the opponent's arms. The technique is used to force the opponent forward.

Ashi-tori. A technique used to take down the opponent. The practitioner grasps the opponent's leg with both hands and pushes his shoulder against the opponent's inner thigh.

Hataki komi. A side-stepping evasive movement that causes the opponent to fall from his or her own momentum. This technique can also be carried out by placing a palm in the opponent's back.

Hidari-yotsu. Grappling techniques that are performed with the practitioner's left arm on the inside.

Hiki Otoshi. An evasive movement executed when the opponent attempts a low attack. The practitioner avoids the attack and pushes down on the opponent's shoulders or back to force him to the ground.

Hikikake. Avoiding an attack by side stepping. The practitioner then grabs the opponent's arm and pulls him off-balance.

Hineri. A hip twist, used to twist and pull the opponent off-balance.

Kata-sukashi. A technique performed by wrapping one's arm around the opponent's shoulders and pushing him forward.

Kote nage. A forearm throw. The practitioner grabs the opponent's arm, grips the inside of the opponent's belt and twists the opponent over the hip.

Migi yotsu. Grappling with the right arm on the inside.

Mitokoro-zeme. A throw executed by grabbing the opponent's thigh and hooking a leg around the opponent's other leg.

Morazashi. Grappling with both hands on the inside.

Nicho-nage. A hip throw that is performed by blocking the opponent's thigh and then pulling the opponent off-balance.

Nimai-geri. A technique for blocking an opponent's leg and pulling on the belt in an attempt to produce a fall.

O-mata. Throwing an opponent by grabbing either thigh and forcing him backwards over the practitioner's own thigh.

Okuri-dashi. A technique of dodging an attack and, from behind, pushing the opponent.

Okuri-taoshi. Forcing down on the opponent's back using both hands.

Oshi-dashi. Pushing the opponent in the chest or under the arms, causing him or her to fall.

Sabaori. Forcing the opponent to the ground using his or her own weight as momentum.

Shitate-nage. An inner arm throw, using an inner grip.

Shitate yagura-nage. A hip throw which relies on grasping the opponent's belt under the opponent's arm.

Shitate hineri. A throw executed by gripping the opponent's belt with the inner hand and pulling.

Soto gake. A technique in which the practitioner holds the opponent's belt under an arm and uses a leg to off-balance the opponent.

Soto-komata. Grabbing the opponent's thigh underneath and attempting to off-balance him or her.

Sukui-nage. Scooping Throw. A technique where the practitioner slides a leg between the opponent's legs and lifts the opponent by using that leg.

Suto-muso. Blocking an opponent's thigh with a hand and then pushing on the opponent's shoulders to cause a fall.

Suso-harai. Sweeping the opponent's foot with the practitioner's own foot.

Suso-tori. Sweeping the opponent's ankle with the practitioner's hand.

Tottari. A throw performed by completing an arm lock against an opponent and forcing the opponent forward.

Tsuppari. Several palm strikes or slapping techniques in succession against an opponent's chest to off-balance him or push him out of the ring.

Tsuki-dashi. A pushing technique which uses both hands against the opponent's chest.

Tsuki-otoshi. A twisting action with an arm thrust that forces the opponent to fall to the side.

Tsuma-tori. A block against an opponent who is trying to lift a leg. The practitioner grabs the opponent's leg and pushes forward.

Tsure-dachi. Gripping the opponent's belt with the intention of lifting and pushing the opponent out of the ring.

Uchi-gake. A technique in which the practitioner wraps a leg on the inside of the opponent and grips the belt under the opponent's arms to push him or her out of the ring.

FORMS AND TECHNIQUES

Uchi-muso. A throw made by gripping the opponent's thigh and forcing him back.

Uwate hineri. A throw executed by grabbing the opponent's belt while pulling with the outer hand.

Uwate-dashi-nage. Using one hand to grab the opponent's belt and cause a loss of balance.

Uwate yagura-nage. Throwing an opponent by using one's thigh to lift the opponent's thigh while gripping the opponent's belt.

Uttchari. An evasive technique executed by pivoting and throwing the opponent by lifting him by his belt. When the practitioner is about to be forced out of the ring, he bends backward and lifts the opponent off the ground and throws him out of the ring.

Watashi-komi. A push against the opponent's chest while one hand grips the opponent's thigh.

SUN WHEEL

A movement used in The Great Circle, a long form consisting of 37 different series of techniques, performed by Tai Chi practitioners.

SUNE-GAKOI

See Encircled Leg Form.

SUP YING

See Ten Forms Form.

SUPARINPE KATA

With 108 techniques, one of the most advanced and most difficult Karate forms. It is the 13th of 14 forms learned in Goju-ryu. It emphasizes open hand techniques, plus breath control. The focus is on varying slow and fast, hard and soft techniques. Also called Pechurin.

SUPPLICATION

A movement used in The Great Circle, a long form consisting of 37 different series of techniques, performed by Tai Chi practitioners.

SURIAGE-WAZA

In Kendo (swordfighting art), a technique in which the practitioner lifts the opponent's sword with his or her own sword to create an opening for an attack.

SUSO-HARAI

In Sumo, sweeping the opponent's foot with one's own foot. See Sumo Techniques.

SUSO-TORI

In Sumo, sweeping the opponent's ankle with one's hand. See Sumo Techniques.

SUTEMI-WAZA

A general term for sacrifice techniques in Judo. See Sacrifice Techniques.

SWEEPING ANKLE THROW

In Judo, a technique where the practitioner sweeps both the opponent's feet. The practitioner also uses his or her hands to assist the throw. See Judo Techniques. See Throws.

SWEEPING DRAWING ANKLE THROW

In Judo, a sweeping technique in which the practitioner sweeps the opponent's ankle and lifts the opponent forward, to off-balance him or her. See Judo Techniques. See Throws.

SWEEPING FOOT THROW

In Judo, when the opponent steps forward, the practitioner catches the foot before it lands, pushes it away, and pulls the opponent down.

SWEEPING HIP THROW

In Judo, also called Sweeping Loin. A throw in which the practitioner sweeps the opponent forward over the leg and hip.

SWEEPING THIGH THROW

See Sweeping Hip Throw.

SWEEPING WINDING THROW

In Judo, a sweeping and winding technique in which the practitioner extends one leg as a barrier and pulls the opponent over. See Throws. See Judo Techniques.

SWEEPS

These are techniques in which the opponent's feet are hooked, pushed or otherwise swept out from under, resulting in a takedown or throw.

Ashi-harai. In Judo and Karate, a sweep technique in which the practitioner sweeps the opponent's leading foot out by using his or her own foot or feet. Also called ashi-barai.

De-ashi-harai. In Judo, called a foot dash or foot sweep. When the opponent steps forward, the practitioner catches the foot before it lands, pushes it away and pulls the opponent down.

Kosoto gare. Minor outer reaping. In Judo, a hooking takedown. In this case, the practitioner controls the opponent's elbow by pulling it outward, then places a foot outside the opponent's foot and sweeps.

Ko-soto-gari. Minor outer reap. In Judo, a hooking throw. The practitioner pulls the opponent's arm outward while sweeping his or her foot, which causes a backward fall.

SWOOPING BIRD PARRY

Circular soft blocks used in Wushu to deflect an attack by using the attacker's own momentum. These blocks are executed with the forearm, and the hand can be open, in a fist, or in a claw. Double arm blocks are sometimes used.

SWORD HAND STRIKE

See Strike, Knife Hand.

SWORD FOOT STRIKE

See Kick, Knife Foot.

TAI CHI FAST FORM

Same as the Eight Minute form. See Eight Minute Form.

T-STANCE

See Stance, T.

TACHI

In Karate, a term for stance. See Stances.

TACHI-AI

In Judo, a series of 12 defensive techniques performed while standing. The techniques include joint locks, holds and evasive movements.

In Sumo, the first attack in a match.

TACHI SON

See Strike, Backfist.

TACHI-OYOGI

An ancient technique in which warriors learned to swim in armor. They moved through the water in a standing position.

TACHI HIZA GATAME

A basic form in Wa-jutsu which shows defensive techniques against wrist holds. The form ends with a strike to vital points at the rib cage and neck.

TACHI-WAZA

A category of Judo techniques, the standing techniques.

TACHI WAZA NO BU

See Secret Forms Standing Set.

TACHI REI

A standing bow. See Salutation Techniques.

TAE BAEK FORM

A Tae Kwon Do form for third dan black belt. This is part of the palgue series. See Tae Kwon Do Forms.

TAE GEUK FORMS

Forms studied by Tae Kwon Do students below the rank of black belt, designed to instruct the student in self-discipline and spiritual growth. The name Tae Geuk means "Tao" in Korean. These are the only forms sanctioned by the Korean Tae Kwon Do Association for rank advancement. See Tae Kwon Do Forms.

TAE GEUK EIGHT FORM

An intermediate form in Tae Kwon Do, recognized by the Korean Tae Kwon Do Association. Called "put jong." The techniques include the jump front kick and elbow strike. See Tae Geuk Forms. See Tae Kwon Do Forms.

TAE GEUK FIVE FORM

An intermediate form in Tae Kwon Do, recognized by the Korean Tae Kwon Do Association. Called "o-jong." The techniques include the hammer fist strike, x-stance, and elbow strike. The personal qualities it develops are self-understanding and the principles of Tae Geuk. See Tae Kwon Do Forms. See Tae Geuk Forms.

TAE GEUK FOUR FORM

An intermediate form in Tae Kwon Do, recognized by the Korean Tae Kwon Do Association. Called "sa jong." The techniques include the spear fingers, rising block, and side kick. The form emphasizes self-confidence and the tenet of indomitable spirit. See Tae Geuk Forms. See Tae Kwon Do Forms.

TAE GEUK ONE FORM

An beginner form in Tae Kwon Do, recognized by the Korean Tae Kwon Do Association. Called "el jong." The techniques include the punch, low block, high block and front kick. It emphasizes the principles of balance and creation. See Tae Geuk Forms. See Tae Kwon Do Forms.

TAE GEUK SEVEN FORM

An intermediate form in Tae Kwon Do, recognized by the Korean Tae Kwon Do Association. Called "chil jong." The techniques include the tiger stance, back fist, double knife hand block, scissors block, uppercut punches and crescent kick. It teaches working toward a goal, the tenet of perseverance. See Tae Geuk Forms. See Tae Kwon Do Forms.

TAE GEUK SIX FORM

An intermediate form in Tae Kwon Do, recognized by the Korean Tae Kwon Do Association. Called "yook jong." The techniques include the knife hand block, palm heel block and double low block. The form emphasizes gentleness and flexibility while teaching the tenet of integrity. See Tae Geuk Forms. See Tae Kwon Do Forms.

TAE GEUK THREE FORM

An beginner form in Tae Kwon Do, recognized by the Korean Tae Kwon Do Association. Called "sam jong." The techniques include the knife hand block and knife hand strike. See Tae Geuk Forms. See Tae Kwon Do Forms.

TAE GEUK TWO FORM

A beginner form in Tae Kwon Do, recognized by the Korean Tae Kwon Do Association. Called "e-jong." The techniques include the inside-outside block and walking stance. It emphasizes the principle of mental focus and happiness. See Tae Geuk Forms. See Tae Kwon Do Forms.

TAE-RIG-GI

In Tae Kwon Do, a straight punch. See Punch.

TAE KWON DO FORMS

The association founded by General Choi, the father of modern Tae Kwon Do, uses a series of forms for rank promotion in Tae Kwon Do. These are known as the International Tae Kwon Do Federation Forms. They begin at white belt, 10th keub (10th class):

Chonji, 10th keub
Tan Gun, 9th keub
Toe San, 8th keub
Won Hyo, 7th keub
Yul Kok, 6th keub
Chung Gun, 5th keub
Toi Gye, 4th keub
Hwa Rang, 3rd keub
Chung Mu, 2nd krub
Kwang Gye, 1st dan (black belt)
Po Un, 2nd dan
Kae Beck, 3rd dan
Yu Shin, 4th dan
Chung Jang, 5th dan
Ul Gi, 5th dan
Sam Il, 6th dan
Choi Jong, 6th dan
Ko Dan, 7th dan
Se Jong, 7th dan
Tong Il, 8th dan
Moon Ma, 8th dan

Schools that do not follow International Tae Kwon Do Federation Forms may follow other forms, such as the kibon hyung 1,2,3 for beginners, or the Pyung Ahn form for non-black belts:

Pyung ahn cho dan #1
Pyung ahn yi dan #2
Pyung ahn sam dan #3
Pyung ahn sa dan #4
Pyung ahn oh dan #5

The Chul ki forms are also taught to non-black belts:

Chul ki cho dan #1
Chul ki yi dan #2
Chul ki sam dan #3

The World Tae Kwon Do Federation has also sanctioned a series of forms for rank advancement, for both non-black and black belt levels. These forms are used predominately, as the World Tae Kwon Do Federation is generally recognized as the Tae Kwon Do organization of authority. These are the palgue forms, consisting of palgue one through eight (il chang, yi chang, sam chang, sa chang, oh chang, yook chang, chil chang, pal chang) for non-black belts, plus the following for black belt levels:

Koryo, 1st dan
Kum Gang, 2nd dan
Tae Back, 3rd dan
Pyung Won, 4th dan
Sip Jin, 5th dan
Ji Tae, 5th dan
Chung Kwon, 6th dan
Silla Hansoo, 6th dan
Il Yeo, 7th dan

The Tae Geuk forms are the only forms recognized by the Korean Tae Kwon Do Association for non-black belt rank advancement. These include Tae Geuk forms one through eight (el jong, e-jong, sam jong, sa jong, o-jong, yook jong, chil jong, put jong).

In addition, there are numerous not-so-common forms taught by various Tae Kwon Do schools, including: ro hai, ban wol, jin do, ahm hak, ja eun, so lim chang kwon, dan do hyong (dagger form), ba sai (bal sack), sip soo, yun moo, and kong sang goon (kwang kong).

TAI ATARI
One of the 12 basic blocks and strikes in Jodo and Jojutsu, staff art. See Jodo Techniques.

TAI HAZUSHI UCHI
One of the 12 basic blocks and strikes in Jodo and Jojutsu, staff art. See Jodo Techniques.

TAI-OTOSHI
See Body Drop.

TAI-SABAKI
In marital arts generally, a pivot or turning movement used to evade an attack. See Body Shifting.

TAIDU
See Stance, Fighting.

TAIKYOKU NO KATA
In Karate, a series of six forms emphasizing absolute control of body movement. They are called Taikyoku Shodan, Nidan, Sandan, Judan, Gedan, and Chudan. See Karate Forms.

TAILWIND FORM
In Iaido (sword drawing art), the tenth form of the seated set, called "oikaze." In this form, the practitioner practices drawing from a standing position. The four phases of drawing the sword, cutting with the sword, shaking the blood from the sword and resheathing the sword are practiced.

TAISO
A Japanese word meaning stretching exercises. See Stretching Techniques.

TAKEDOWN TECHNIQUES
A general term referring to all techniques that cause an opponent to fall from a standing position. These include throws, sweeps and other such movements.

En-no-irimi. In Aikido, a takedown technique that uses the opponent's own force against him or her. This technique is an advanced turning technique that causes the opponent to fall.

Giao long cuoc. In Qwan Ki Do, a scissors take down. The practitioner, using his or her legs like scissors, off-balances the opponent and both fall to the ground.

Fig. 3.90 : Tae Kwon Do students practicing takedowns.

TAKE THE BLOSSOM
A movement used in The Great Circle, a long form consisting of 37 different series of techniques, performed by Tai Chi practitioners.

TAKE THE PATH TO LEFT and RIGHT
Movements used in The Great Circle, a long form consisting of 37 different series of techniques, performed by Tai Chi practitioners.

TAKI-OTOSHI

See Waterfall Form.

TALL MONKEY

A form in Monkey style Wushu also called Standing Monkey. The form is especially suitable for tall people, as there is less falling and rolling than in other monkey forms. Arm and hand techniques and strong stances characterize this style.

TAMESHI-GIRI

A training exercise in Kenjutsu, swordfighting, and Iaijutsu, sword drawing, in which one cuts bamboo or straw to check one's swordstroke.

TAMESHIWARI

See Breaking Techniques.

TAN PHAP

Stances in Viet Vo Dao. See Stances.

TAN-GUN FORM

An International Tae Kwon Do Federation form taught at the ninth class level. It has 21 movements and is a beginner form. It is performed in an "I" pattern and consists of basic movements such as knife hand block, middle punch, high punch and low block. The form is named after Tan Gun, the legendary founder of Korea in 2333 B.C.

TAN HUAN CHANG

See Palm Change, Single.

TANASHITA

See Beneath the Ledge Form.

TANI-OTOSHI

See Valley Drop.

TANINZU-DORI

In Aikido, a training method in which attacks from various opponents come in succession. See Aikido Techniques.

TANTO DORI DEFENSE

In Aikido, defensive techniques against the short sword or knife attacks. See Aikido Techniques.

TAO PHONG CUOC

In Qwan Ki Do, techniques for sweeping an opponent off balance. See Sweeps.

TATE SHIHO GATAME

See Lengthwise Four Quarters.

TATE SHUTO

In Karate, when the striking hand is pulled back, the non-striking hands moves forward as a counter-balance. Counter-balance techniques are important in all striking arts.

TATE SHUTO UKE

See Block, Knife Hand.

TATE-HIJI

See Strikes, Elbow.

TATE-EMPI

See Strike, Elbow.

TATE-EMPI-UCHI

In Karate, an upward elbow strike. See Strike, Elbow.

TATE TSUKI

See Punch, Vertical Fist.

TATE ZUKI

Same as Tate tsuki. See Punch, Vertical Fist.

TATEKI TO

See Multi-Directional Cut Form.

TE-DORI

In Aikido, the name of a series of defenses against arm holds. See Aikido Techniques.

TE-GURUMA

In Judo, a hip throw that relies on the hands to execute. See Judo Techniques.

TE-HODOKI

In Aikido, a series of basic defense movements using evasive techniques based on body shifting. See Aikido Techniques.

TEKUBI SHINDO

In Aikido, wrist-shaking. An exercise designed to develop flexibility and improve the understanding of basic techniques.

TE-NO UCHI

In Kyudo (archery), this refers to gripping the bow. See Kyudo Techniques.

TE-WAZA

In Judo and Tae Kwon Do, refers to hand techniques.

TEGATANA

A form in Karate, taught in Shorei-ryu style, that was devised to help develop the mental and spiritual awareness of the practitioner. See Karate Forms.

TEIJI-DACHI

Same as Teiji tachi. See Stance, T.

TEIJI TACHI

See Stance, T.

TEISHI-ZUKI

Same as Teishi-tsuki. See Strike, Palm.

TEISHI-TSUKI

See Strike, Palm.

TEISHO AWASE UKE

See Block, Palm

TEISHO UKE

See Block, Palm.

TEISHO UCHI

See Strike, Palm.

TEKKI KATA

A general name given to three advanced forms in Karate (Tekki Shodan, Tekki Nidan and Tekki Sandan). These were once called Naihanchi. They can be performed alone or with a partner. Because they were once performed on horseback, they rely on the horse stance. See Naihanchi. See Karate Forms.

TEKKI NIDAN

The second of three advanced forms in Karate. This emphasizes grasping and hooking blocks. See Tekki Kata. See Karate Forms.

TEKKI SANDAN

The third of three advanced forms in Karate. This form emphasizes continuous middle section blocks. See Tekki Kata. See Karate Forms.

TEKKI SHODAN

The first of three advanced forms in Karate. This one emphasizes horse stances. See Tekki Kata. See Karate Forms.

TEKUBI KAKE UKE

See Block, Wrist.

TEKUBI WAZA

In Aikido, a general term for wrist techniques.

TEMPLE STRIKE

See Strike, Temple.

TEN CHARACTERS FORM, THE

A basic form in Viet Vo Dao, called Thap Tu.

TEN FORMS FORM

An advanced form in Hung Gar Wushu, which includes qualities of the five animals (tiger, crane, dragon, leopard, and snake) such as strength and spirit, plus qualities of the five elements (metal, wood, fire, earth and water) such as powerful attacks and counters.

TEN SEEDS OF CHOY LI FUT

In Choy Li Fut Wushu, there are ten hand techniques that serve as the foundation of the art. These are: 1. Backfist; 2. Hook punch; 3. Overhand strike; 4. Darting strike, a diagonal strike intended to off-balance the opponent; 5. Seizing hand (grabbing hair or clothes), and so on; 6. Straight punch; 7. Hammer fist strike; 8. Piercing punch, using the momentum of the body to add power; 9. Upper cut punch; 10. Crushing strike, a shortened uppercut.

TEN STEPS

These are the Ninja methods of traveling.

stealthy step — nuki ashi

rub step — suri ashi

tight step — shime ashi

flying step — tobi ashi

one step — kata ashi

big step — o ashi

little step — ko ashi

small step — kokizami

proper step — wari ashi

normal step — tsune ashi

TENKAN

Pivoting movements, especially at the waist and hips, as applied to Aikido, but fundamental to all martial arts.

TENSHIN WAZA

Refers to body shifting movements. See body shifting.

TENSHO

A Karate form that, like sanchin kata, focuses on breathing exercises. It is called "revolving hands," and was developed as a soft way of breathing. These techniques are supposed to harden the body so that kicks and punches will not cause pain or injury. The form also contains many blocking movements. It is the last of 14 forms taught in Goju-ryu Karate. In Shorei-ryu Karate, it is thought that this form can develop mental and spiritual awareness. See Karate Forms.

TENSHO UKE
See Strike, Palm.

TETSUI-UCHI
See Strike, Hammer Fist.

TETSUI-UKE
See Block, Hammer Fist.

TAN XA SON
See Punch, Uppercut.

THAN PHAP
A basic form in Qwan Ki Do.

THAP TU
A basic form in Viet Vo Dao, called the Ten Characters.

THE DOI LUYEN
In Qwan Ki Do, a series of five step exercises including blocks, stances and evasions. It also exists in a three step simplified version.

THE THU
See Stance, Fighting.

THIET GIAC
See Strike, Elbow.

THREE ESSENTIALS STANCE
See Stance, Three Essentials.

THREE STEP SPARRING
See Sparring, Step (three step).

THROWS
Techniques for pushing, pulling, tripping, and sweeping, with the objective of throwing the opponent to the ground. There are three stages in Judo: breaking the opponent's balance (kuzushi); entry into a position that prevents the opponent from regaining his or her balance (tsukuri) and the actual throw itself (kake).

Ashi-guruma. A leg throw in which one throws the opponent falls forward in a circle over the practitioner's extended leg. This technique is similar to Sweeping Hip Throw (harai goshi).

Eri-seoi-nage. A throw forward over one's shoulder.

Hane-goshi. Spring Hip Throw. A throw in which the practitioner steps in front of the opponent, then "springs" the opponent over the hips and thighs in a circular motion.

Hane-maki-komi. In the "outer winding spring hip throw," the opponent is pulled into tight body contact and is twisted or wound across the practitioner's leg and hip, and pulled forward.

Harai maki-komi. Sweeping Winding Throw. A sweeping and winding technique in which the practitioner extends one leg as a barrier and pulls the opponent over.

Harai-goshi. Sweeping Hip Throw. Also called Sweeping Loin. A hip throw in which the practitioner sweeps the opponent forward over the leg and hip.

Also, a sweeping technique in which the practitioner sweeps the opponent's ankle as the opponent steps back.

Hiza guruma. Knee Wheel. In Judo, a technique in which the practitioner places a foot against the opponent's knee and pulls the opponent off-balance.

Ippon Seoi Nage. One Arm Shoulder Throw. A throw over the shoulder that is popular in competition.

Kani basami. Scissors Throw. A technique that uses the practitioner's legs like scissors to unbalance the opponent, who falls to the side.

Kata guruma. Shoulder Wheel. A throw in which the practitioner lifts the opponent by sliding an arm between the opponent's legs and wheels the opponent from one side of the shoulders to the other side.

Kata-dori. In Aikido, a defensive technique used when the opponent grabs the practitioner's shoulder. The practitioner counters the attack by pivoting and throwing the opponent to the ground.

Ko-uchi-gari. Minor inner reaping throw. In Judo, the practitioner catches the opponent's heel and sweeps while pushing down.

Koshi-guruma. Hip Wheel. In Judo, a technique where the practitioner performs a hip throw, assisted by holding the opponent around the neck.

Ko-soto-gake. Minor Outside Hook. In Judo, a technique used to hook the opponent's leg.

Kukichi-daoshi. Decayed Tree Throw or Dead Tree Fall. In Judo, a throw executed by grabbing opponent's heel and pulling up.

Morote gari. Two-Handed Reaping Throw. A throw where the practitioner drops into a squat and scoops the opponent's legs from begin, using both arms.

Morote-seoi-nage. Both Hands Shoulder Throw. A shoulder throw in which the practitioner uses both hands to grab the opponent and throw him or her over the shoulder.

O-goshi. Major Hip Throw. A throwing technique in which the practitioner slides in front of the opponent and raises the opponent up and over the hip. This technique is used in training; rarely used in competition.

O-guruma. Major Wheel Throw. A throw performed by extending a leg across the opponent's thigh and pulling the opponent over.

O-soto-gari. Major Outer Reaping Throw. The practitioner steps alongside the opponent and brings one thigh into contact with the back of the opponent's thigh, then swings the opponent's leg away.

O-soto-guruma. Major Outer Wheel. A throw in which the practitioner traps both of the opponent's legs and pulls him or her over while sweeping.

O-uchi-gake. In Judo, a technique for trapping the opponent's foot between the practitioner's feet, and pulling the opponent over.

O-uchi-gari. A throw executed by sliding a leg between the opponent's legs and hooking.

Okuri-ashi-barai. A technique where the practitioner sweeps both the opponent's feet. The practitioner also uses his or her hands to assist the throw.

Sasae-tsuri-komi-ashi. Dropping Drawing Ankle Throw. A technique where the practitioner blocks the opponent's ankle with his or her foot.

Seoi-otoshi. A technique that uses both hands to pull the opponent over the practitioner's hip and shoulder.

Soto make-kome. Outer Winding Throw. A technique where the practitioner places a leg in front of the opponent, and with a quick movement causes the opponent to fall to the ground.

Sukui-nage. In Judo, a technique where one raises the opponent by his or her thighs and leans, causing the opponent to fall backward. Used when the practitioner is being held from behind. In Sumo, a technique where the practitioner slides a leg between the opponent's legs and lifts the opponent by using his or her leg.

Sumi-gaeshi. Corner Throw. The practitioner catches the opponent on the inner thigh with the foot and falls in a sacrifice throw.

Sumi-otoshi. Corner Drop. A technique in which the practitioner pulls the opponent's sleeve down while pushing on the opposite shoulder.

Tai-otoshi. Body Drop. A technique in which the practitioner extends a leg, and pulls opponent over leg and hip to the front.

Tani-otoshi. Valley Drop. A sacrifice throw in which one places a foot behind the opponent's left heel and forces the opponent back.

Tomoe-nage. Stomach Throw. A sacrifice throw executed by falling backward and pulling the opponent by using a leg in the opponent's stomach.

Tsuri-goshi. Lifting Hip Throw. A hip throw in which the practitioner pulls the opponent over the hip.

Tsuri-komi-goshi. Lifting Pulling Hip Throw. The practitioner squats, grips the sleeve and lapel of the opponent and throws the opponent forward over the hip.

Uchi-mata. Inner Thigh Throw. A technique where the practitioner supports weight on one leg and uses the other to sweep the opponent's inner thigh.

Uchi mata. A throw performed by sliding a leg between the opponent's legs and lifting that leg while pulling the opponent's uniform.

Uki-goshi. Floating Hip Throw. The basic hip throw all others are based on. The practitioner uses hip to pivot and throw the opponent.

Uki-otoshi. Floating Drop. The practitioner drops to one knee, wheeling the opponent over the forward foot.

Ura-nage. Rear Throw. A backward throw. The practitioner wraps his or her arms around the opponent's body and falls back, bringing the opponent with him or her.

Ushiro-goshi. Rear Hip Throw. A counter attack in which one lifts the opponent with one's hips and then slides an arm around the opponent's neck to turn and throw him or her.

Utsuri-goshi. Changing Hip Throw. A counter executed by pulling the opponent close and throwing him or her off-balance.

Yoko gake. Side Body Drop. The practitioner draws the opponent towards him or her by grabbing the opponent's sleeve, while blocking and hooking the opponent's ankle from the side.

Yoko guruma. Side Wheel. The practitioner reaches under the opponent's shoulders, grips the opponent's belt and throws.

Yoko otoshi. Side Drop. A sacrifice throw. The practitioner blocks the opponent's movement with his or her thigh and pulls the opponent's sleeve.

Yoko-wakare. Side Separation Throw. The practitioner blocks the opponent's movement with both legs and slides to the floor while pulling opponent down as well. Also called yoko otoshi. See Aikido Techniques. See Judo Techniques. See Sumo Techniques.

THU PHAP
A basic form in Qwan Ki Do.

THUMB STRIKE
See Strike, Finger.

THUNDER AND LIGHTNING FORM
In Iaido (sword drawing art), the second form of the secret forms extra set, called "raiden." The practitioner learns to deal with more than one opponent and to handle the unexpected. The practitioner imagines walking in a group of opponents, one of whom grabs his or her scabbard. The four phases of drawing the sword, cutting with the sword, shaking the blood from the sword and resheathing the sword are practiced.

THUNDER CLAP FORM
In Iaido (sword drawing art), the third form in the secret forms extra set. It is called "jinrai." The practitioner learns to handle a complex confrontation; the group the practitioner is walking with is mixed, including both friends and opponents. The four phases of drawing the sword, cutting with the sword, shaking the blood from the sword and resheathing the sword are practiced.

TI-GYE FORM
See Toi-gye Form. See Tae Kwon Do Forms.

TIDE COMES IN AND OUT
A movement used in The Great Circle, a long form consisting of 37 different series of techniques, performed by Tai Chi practitioners.

TIEU TAN
See Stance, Cat.

TIGER CLAW STRIKE
See Strike, Tiger Claw.

TIGER FORM
In Bando, this form emphasizes hand techniques of clawing and ripping. Other Bando forms emphasize other animal qualities. These are Eagle, Deer, Boar, Cobra, Viper, Monkey, Paddy Bird, Panther, Python, Scorpion and Bull.

In Wushu, an intermediate form that emphasizes hand techniques. It is supposed to resemble the actions of a confined tiger, clawing at the cage. Tiger claw strikes and knife hand strikes are performed in a cat stance.

TIGER'S STEP FORM
In Iaido (sword drawing art), the second form in the half seated set, called "toraisoku." The practitioner performs cuts from the half-seated position. The four phases of drawing the sword, cutting with the sword, shaking the blood from the sword and resheathing the sword are practiced.

TIGER STANCE

See Stance, Tiger.

TIP FLIP FORM

The fifth form in "Iaido sword method." It is called "kissaki gaeshi," and it is from the Hoki-ryu style. The practitioner performs a complex parrying and cutting movement. The four phases of drawing the sword, cutting with the sword, shaking the blood from the sword and resheathing the sword are practiced.

TIT SIEN

See Iron Thread Form.

TOBI-GERI

See Kick, Jumping.

TOBI-KOMI TSUKI

See Punch, Lunge.

TOBI-KOMI ZUKI

Same as Tobi komi-tsuki. See Punch, Lunge.

TOE-SAN FORM

An International Tae Kwon Do Federation form, taught at the eighth class level. A beginner form with 24 movements, it is performed in an "I" pattern. The form consists of basic movements such as high block, front kick knife hand strike, middle punch, and horse stance. The pattern is named for the patriot Ahn Chang Ho who helped educate Koreans and pursued the nationalistic movement. See Tae Kwon Do Forms.

TOHO

See Iaido Sword Methods.

TOI-GYE FORM

International Tae Kwon Do Federation form taught at the fourth class. It has 37 movements and is an intermediate form. It is performed in a "+" pattern. It consists of movements such as groin strike, low block, forearm block, and spear hand strike. The form is named after the pseudonym of Yi Hwang, a Korean scholar of neo-Confucianism. The 37 movements refer to his birthplace on the 37th parallel and the shape of the pattern, "+," means "scholar."

TOKUI-WAZA

In the martial arts, a favorite technique.

TOMOE-NAGE

See Stomach Throw. Also called Circle Throw.

TONG-IL FORM

An International Tae Kwon Do Federation form taught at eighth dan black belt level. See Tae Kwon Do Forms.

TOPI-MIKZUKI-GERI

See Kick, Spinning Heel.

TORA-BASHIRI

See Charging the Tiger Form.

TORAISOKU

See Tiger's Step Form.

TORNADO KICK

See Kick, Tornado

TOTTARI

In Sumo, a throw performed by completing an arm lock against an opponent and forcing the opponent forward. See Sumo Techniques.

TOUCH THE EAST WIND

A movement used in The Great Circle, a long form consisting of 37 different series of techniques, performed by Tai Chi practitioners.

TOUCH THE SOUTH WIND

A movement used in The Great Circle, a long form consisting of 37 different series of techniques, performed by Tai Chi practitioners.

TOWAKI

See Beneath the Doorway Form.

TOZUME

See Blocked at the Door Form.

TRAM TACH

See Strike, Knife Hand.

TRAM XA

See Strike, Knife Hand.

TRUNG BINH TAN

See Stance, Horse.

TSOP

See Punch, Straight.

TSUE SHO

A form in Shorei-ryu Karate that was devised to develop balance, speed, power and technique. See Karate Forms.

TSUIGEKITO

See Pursuing Form.

TSUKE KOMI

See Pursuit Form

TSUKI

See Punch.

TSUKI-DASHI

In Sumo, a pushing technique which uses both hands against the opponent's chest. See Sumo Techniques.

TSUKI-OTOSHI

In Sumo, a twisting action with an arm thrust that forces the opponent to fall to the side. See Sumo Techniques.

TSUKI-WAZA

See Punch.

TSUKI-KAGE

See Moonbeams Form.

TSUKOMI-JIME

In Judo, a strangulation technique executed by holding both lapels and pushing across the opponent's throat. See Judo Techniques. See Strangulation Techniques.

TSUMA-TORI

In Sumo, a block against an opponent who is trying to lift a leg. The practitioner grabs the opponent's leg and pushes forward. See Sumo Techniques.

TSUPPARI

In Sumo, several palm strikes or slapping techniques in succession against an opponent's chest to off-balance or push him or her out of the ring. See Sumo Techniques.

TSURE DACHI

See Companions Form.

TSURE-DACHI

In Sumo, gripping the opponent's belt with the intention of lifting and pushing the opponent out of the ring. See Sumo Techniques.

TSURI-AI

In Kyudo (archery), the balance between the hand holding the bow and the hand holding the bow string. See Kyudo Techniques.

TSURI-GOSHI

See Lifting Hip Throw.

TSURI-KOMI-GOSHI

See Lifting Pulling Hip Throw.

TSURI ASHI DACHI

See Stance, Crane.

TSURU-GARAMI

In Kyudo (archery), gripping the bowstring with the thumb, which is secured by the forefinger. See Kyudo Techniques.

TU VE

A general term in Qwan Ki Do for self-defense techniques.

TURN AND CHOP WITH FIST TECHNIQUE

A technique in Tai Chi Chuan Eight Minute Form. It tones the muscles at the waist and has self-defense applications as well.

TURNING THE WHEEL

A movement used in The Great Circle, a long form consisting of 37 different series of techniques, performed by Tai Chi practitioners.

TWISTING HORSE STANCE

See Stance, Twisting Horse.

TWO-STEP PASS

A technique in Escrima where the practitioner takes two steps back to avoid a strike and then immediately counters. See Escrima Techniques.

TWO FINGER STRIKE

See Strike, Two-Finger.

TWO-HANDED REAPING THROW

In Judo, a throw where the practitioner drops into a squat and scoops the opponent's legs from behind, using both arms. See Judo Techniques. See Throws.

UCHI KOMI

In Judo, repeated practice of a movement until it is perfected, done with a partner. There are two types, active and passive. In the passive types, the partner stands still and does not resist as the other practitioner attempts different throws without actually throwing the partner. In the active type, the two practitioners try to complete throws against each other as if they were having a contest. As a test of endurance, some practitioners have been known to complete five hundred throws of this kind without stopping. See Judo Techniques.

UCHI-GAKE

In Sumo, a technique in which the practitioner wraps a leg on the inside of the opponent and grips the belt under the opponent's arms to push him or her out of the ring. See Sumo Techniques.

UCHI-MATA

See Inner Thigh Throw. Also called Upper Innercut Throw.

UCHI-MUSO

In Sumo, a throw made by gripping opponent's thigh and turning him or her onto his or her back. See Sumo Techniques.

UCHIOKOSHI

In Kyudo (archery), the fourth position of the archer who lifts the bow overhead. Also called kikitori. See Kyudo Techniques.

UCHIOTOSHI WAZA

In Kendo, a technique in which the practitioner pushes the opponent's sword down and attacks in the same movement.

UDE GARAMI

In Judo, the practitioner locks the opponent's arm, applying pressure on elbow, usually while the opponent is lying on his or her back. Called the "arm entanglement" or "figure four arm lock." See Arm Locks. See Judo Techiques.

UDE GATAME

In Judo, a straight arm lock. The practitioner pulls the arm up, and rests it between his or her shoulder and neck, placing pressure on the arm just below the elbow. See Arm Lock. See Judo Techniques.

UDE HISHIGI HIZA-GATAME

In Judo, controlling the opponent's arm by stretching it across a knee. See Arm Locks. See Judo Techiques.

UDE GARAMI HENKA-WAZA

In Judo, a shoulder immobilization technique performed with opponent's arm partly bent. See Judo Techniques. See Immobilization Techniques.

UDE-HISHIGI UDE-GATAME

In Judo, an armlock executed on opponent's outstretched arm. See Arm Locks. See Judo Techniques.

UDE-HISHIGI JUJI-GATAME

In Judo, an armlock executed in a cross shape. See Arm Locks. See Judo Techniques.

UDE-UKE

See Block, Forearm.

UKE

In Judo and Aikido, the name given to person who attacks and is thrown. In Karate, see Block.

UKE-NAGASHI

See Parrying Form I and II.

UKEMI

Judo falling techniques. See Breakfalls.

UKETE

See Block.

UKE-WAZA

In martial arts generally, defensive techniques, evasive actions and counter attacks.

UKI-GOSHI

See Floating Hip Throw.

UKI-OTOSHI

See Floating Drop. Also called Pulling Down Straight Leg Throw.

UKI-WAZA

See Lateral Sacrifice Throw.

UKIGUMO

See Floating Cloud Form.

UL-GI FORM

An International Tae Kwon Do Federation form taught at fifth dan black belt level. See Tae Kwon Do Forms.

UNBROKEN RHYTHM TRAINING

Teaches various steady rhythms for sparring, useful for beginners who are uncertain of their techniques and reactions. The practitioner who relies too much on unbroken rhythm, however, become predictable and can easily be defeated. Thus, broken rhythm training is also used. See Broken Rhythm Training.

UP CHIGI

In Tae Kwon Do, a front kick. See Kick, Front.

UPPERCUT PUNCH

See Punch, Uppercut.

UPPER FOUR QUARTERS

In Judo, called kami-shiho-gatame. A hold down used against an opponent on his or her back. From above, one grabs the opponent's belt with both hands, one arm tucked under the opponent's shoulder, and one's head resting on the opponent's chest.

UPPER INNER CUT THROW

See Inner Thigh Throw.

URA-GERI

See Kick, Rear.

URA-GOSHI

See Back Hip Throw.

URA-KEN UCHI

See Strike, Backfist.

URA-NAGE

See Rear Throw.

UROKOGAESHI

See Fish Scaling Form.

USHIRO-ASHI-BARAI

In Karate, a reverse foot sweep. The practitioner sweeps the non-kicking foot of an opponent as he or she attempts to kick.

USHIRO U-ATE KUMI-TSUKI

In Aikido, a defense against a "bear hug." The practitioner strikes the opponent in the face with his or her head while pulling free, then steps away and performs an elbow lock. See Aikido Techniques.

USHIRO ERI OBI TORI

In Aikido, a defense against a belt grab. The practitioner steps forward, then strikes a vital point in the opponent's side. See Aikido Techniques.

USHIRO KATA TE DORI ERI-JIME

In Aikido, a defense against a combination neck hold and wrist grab. The practitioner strikes the opponent's instep. See Aikido Techniques.

USHIRO GERI

See Kick, Rear.

USHIRO ERI KATA SODETORI

In Aikido, a defense against a collar or sleeve hold from the rear. The practitioner bends under the opponent's arm, stands and throws the opponent forward. See Aikido Techniques.

USHIRO KESA GATAME

See Reverse Scarfhold.

USHIRO OSHI AGE TE-DORI

In Aikido, a defense against a wrist hold. The opponent grips both hands from the rear. The practitioner steps forward grabs the opponent's elbow with his or her free hand. See Aikido Techniques.

USHIRO EMPI-UCHI

A backward elbow strike in Karate. See Strike, Elbow.

USHIRO SHITATE KUMI TSUKI

In Aikido, a defense against belt grab. The practitioner strikes with the heel to the opponent's abdomen. Then the practitioner strikes a vital point in opponent's hand, turns and performs an armlock. See Aikido Techniques.

USHIRO RYOTE DORI

In Aikido, a defense against wristhold. The practitioner steps to the side, lifting his or her hand and grips the opponent by the elbow, striking to a vital point in opponent's face. See Aikido Techniques.

USHIRO RYO KATA SODE TORI

In Aikido, a defense against a sleevehold from the rear. The practitioner steps away and slides under the opponent's arm. See Aikido Techniques.

USHIRO-GERI-KEKOMI

See Kick, Rear.

USHIRO-GERI-KEAGE

See Kick, Rear.

USHIRO-GOSHI

See Rear Hip Throw.

USHIRO-MAWASHI-GERI

See Kick, Roundhouse (reverse).

USHIRO

See Rear Form.

UTSURI GOSHI

See Changing Hip Throw.

UTTCHARI

In Sumo, an evasive technique executed by pivoting and throwing the opponent by lifting him by the belt. When the practitioner is about to be forced out of the ring, he bends backward and lifts the opponent off the ground and throws him out of the ring. See Sumo Techniques.

UWATE YAGURA-NAGE

In Sumo, throwing an opponent by using a thigh to lift the opponent's thigh. See Sumo Techniques.

UWATE-DASHI-NAGE

In Sumo, using one hand to grab the opponent's belt and cause a loss of balance. See Sumo Techniques.

UWATE-HINERI

In Sumo, a throw executed by grabbing the opponent's belt and pivoting him or her while pulling with the outer hand. See Sumo Techniques.

VALLEY DROP

In Judo, a sacrifice throw in which one places a foot behind the opponent's heel and forces the opponent back. See Judo Techniques. See Throws.

VAT

In Qwan Ki Do, a general term meaning throws.

VIEW TO THE NORTH

A movement used in The Great Circle, a long form consisting of 37 different series of techniques, performed by Tai Chi practitioners.

VIPER FORM

In Bando, this form emphasizes techniques for attacking vital points in the lower part of the body. Other Bando forms emphasize other animal qualities. These are Eagle, Deer, Boar, Cobra, Monkey, Paddy Bird, Panther, Python, Scorpion, Bull and Tiger.

WAKI-GAMAE

In Kendo (sword fighting), holding the sword horizontally either to thrust or to sweep.

WALKING ACTION

See Footwork.

WALKING THE CIRCLE

The primary formal exercise in Pa Kua or Eight Trigram Wushu. The student learns how the body moves, rotates and revolves. One walks in a continuous circle, focusing on an imaginary opponent.

WALKING STANCE

See Stance, Walking.

WAN SU

In Shorei-ryu Karate, a form devised to develop physical technique, balance, speed, power and grace.

WATASHI-KOMI

In Sumo, a push against the opponent's chest while one's other hand grips the opponent's thigh. See Sumo Techniques.

WATERFALL FORM

In Iaido (sword drawing art), the ninth of the half seated forms, called "takiotoshi." The practitioner sits in a half-kneeling position as an opponent approaches from the rear and grasps the end of the practitioner's scabbard. The four phases of drawing the sword, cutting with the sword, shaking the blood from the sword and resheathing the sword are practiced.

WAVE HANDS LIKE CLOUDS

A technique in the Tai Chi Chuan Eight Minute form that emphasizes calmness. The technique also has a self-defense application.

WAZA

In general, means a technique.

WEDGE BLOCK

See Block, Wedge.

WHIPPING BRANCH

In Wushu, a quick, snapping high or upward block. See Block, High.

WHITE STORK COOLS ITS WINGS

A technique in the Tai Chi Chuan Eight Minute form that teaches the hold ball gesture. The technique also stretches the chest and back muscles and has a self-defense application.

WINGS OPEN AND CLOSE

A movement used in The Great Circle, a long form consisting of 37 different series of techniques, performed by Tai Chi practitioners.

WON-HYO FORM

An International Tae Kwon Do Federation form taught at the seventh class level, an intermediate form. It is performed in an "I" pattern and consists of movements such as c-hand block, temple strike, uppercut punch, and spear block. The pattern is named after the monk who introduced Buddhism to Korea during the Silla Dynasty, in 686 A.D.

WOOD MONKEY

An exercise in Monkey style Wushu that teaches the importance of aggression and persistence against an opponent. Unlike the other monkey exercises, movements here are more controlled, though also more physically overwhelming.

WOODEN DUMMY DRILLS

A variety of techniques can be performed using the Wing Chun wooden dummy. The dummy has extensions that simulate the limbs of an opponent and many prearranged exercises have a series of techniques that are to be executed against the dummy. Some of these prearranged exercises are:

fist parries fist
huen da progression
jom sau chasing
invisible kick
straight punch
lop sau/fon sau switch
chahng dai switch
biu sau switch
pock sau switch
gum sau switch
sticky foot
mook yan joang
fot yut ling bot

WORK SHUTTLES BOTH SIDES

A technique in the Tai Chi Chuan Eight Minute Form in which the knees are strengthened. The technique has a self-defense use as well.

WUSHU TECHNIQUES

The enormous variety of Wushu styles makes it impossible to list the techniques of all Wushu arts here, but the techniques are practiced in the following exercises: Empty handed exercises done solo; exercises with weapons, divided into long, short, double and composite weapons; exercises with partners, including grappling. Group exercises involving three or more people can be practiced with weapons or empty handed. Common exercises include five step exercises — five basic movements in a series. Combination exercises combine hand techniques plus footwork and stances in a short series. See photos next page. Sparring with partners is practiced in the following ways: empty hand against empty hand; empty hand against weapon; weapon against weapon.

Common forms follow:

1. *Chop with fist in bow step*
2. *Swing fist in bow step*
3. *Thrust fist in bow step*
4. *Push palm in bow step*
5. *Strike with back of fist in bow step*
6. *Parry with crossed hands (x-block) in bow step*
7. *Parry upward in empty step*
8. *Block in empty step*
9. *Raise knee and hook hand*
10. *Clap hands in bow step*
11. *Flash palm and kick sideways (see sidekick)*
12. *Kick forward (see front kick) with fists in hips*

X-BLOCK

See Block, X.

X-STANCE

See Stance, X.

XA TAN

See Stance, Snake.

XIONG QUAN

A palm strike with a bear hand. See Strike, Palm.

YAEGAKI

See Eightfold Fences Form.

YAKI CHIGAI

See Misdirection Form.

YAKUSOKU KUMITE

See Sparring, Step.

YAMA-TSUKI

See Punch, U.

Wushu Techniques

Fig. 3.91

Fig. 3.92

Fig. 3.93

Fig. 3.94

Fig. 3.95

YAMA-ZUKI

Same as Yama-tsuki. See Punch, U.

YAMI

In Kyudo (archery), a way of aiming the bow that obscures the target completely and helps the practitioner unaided perfect aim. See Kyudo Techniques.

YANG-MA-BO

See Stance, Hourglass.

YEOP SUDO

In Tae Kwon Do, a ridge hand strike. See Strike, Ridge Hand.

YOKO EMPI-UCHI

See Strike, Elbow.

YOKO GAKE

See Side Body Drop.

YOKO-GERI

See Kick, Side.

YOKO GUMO

See Cloud Bank Form.

YOKO GURUMA

See Side Wheel.

YOKO HIJI-ATE

See Strike, Elbow.

YOKO KEKOMI

See Kick, Side.

YOKO OTOSHI

See Side Drop.

YOKO GERI KEKOMI

See Kick, Side.

YOKO GERI KEAGE

See Kick, Side.

YOKO SHIHO GATAME

See Side Four Quarters.

YOKO TOBI GERI

See Kick, Side.

YOKO-WAKARE

See Side Separation.

YONHON NUKITE

See Strike, Spear Hand.

YONKYO CONTROL

In Aikido, the fourth method of control, by applying pressure to the wrist. See Aikido Techniques.

YU SHIN

An International Tae Kwon Do Federation form taught at fourth dan black belt level. See Tae Kwon Do Forms

YUAN JIAO

See Kick, Crescent.

YUGA-MAE

In Kyudo, archery, the third position of the archer. This consists of holding the bow and notching the arrow. The archer should show superiority over the opponent in the way this is done. See Kyudo Techniques.

YUL-GOK

See Yul-Kok Form.

YUL-KOK FORM

An International Tae Kwon Do Federation form taught at the sixth class level. It has 38 movements and is intermediate. It is performed in a "+" pattern and consists of movements such as front kick, side kick, elbow strike, horse stance, open hand c-block. The form is named after the pseudonym of the philosopher Yi I, who was called the Confucius of Korea. The 38 movements refer to his birthplace on the 38th parallel the shape of the pattern, "+", means "scholar."

YUP CHAGI

In Tae Kwon Do, a side kick. See Kick, Side.

ZANSHIN

In Kyudo (archery), the eighth and final position, after release of the arrow. The archer waits, allowing the muscles to relax before returning to the ready position. See Kyudo Techniques.

ZANTOTSUTO

See Beheading Stroke Form.

ZENETEKI GYAKU TO

See Forward Inverse Cut Form.

ZENGOGIRI

See Forward and Rearward Cut Form.

ZENKUTSU-DACHI

See Stance, Front.

ZENKUTSU-TACHI

Same as Zenkutsu-dachi. See Stance, Front.

W E A P O N S

Weapons are routinely divided into several categories: bladed; stick and staff; projectile; and composite weapons. Bladed weapons include of course swords and knives, but also weapons like halberds, which achieve their damage through the use of a blade. In this category, throwing or thrown weapons are not included even if they are bladed. Sticks and staffs, on the other hand, are not usually bladed and depend on striking or blocking to achieve their purposes. Lances and spears, even though they sometimes have blades, however, do fall into the staff and stick category for they have long shafts. Projectile weapons include all weapons that are thrown or shot at their target, such as arrows, firearms, and shuriken (throwing stars). Composite weapons combine several of these qualities or else achieve their goal through entirely different means. Weapons such as nunchaku and chainwhips fall into this category. These four categories are addressed here, with an additional general section that lists the weapons common to various countries.

GENERAL INFORMATION

A weapon is any implement of war or combat, such as a gun, or a sword. In fact, any means that may be used against an adversary can be considered a weapon. Chinese martial artists, for instance, routinely used chopsticks to strike or threw coins to distract the enemy. Parts of the body, such as fists, can be called weapons. Environmental weapons also exist; a rock or a telephone can block or strike as needed.

Short range weapons are those under two feet in length and include knives, sai, kama, clubs, tonfa, and others. Medium range are weapons that range in length from two to four feet, and include weapons such as the short staff, nunchaku, swords, and so on. Long range weapons measure five feet or more and consist of staffs, spears and lances. Projectile weapons are also considered long range weapons.

Weapons develop in a variety of ways. The terrain, for instance, can vary from one province to another. Long-handled weapons that may work on open plains do not work so well in heavily wooded areas. The physical traits of the martial artists who use the weapons must also be taken into consideration. Shorter and taller people, heavier and thinner, stronger and weaker, all require different kinds of weapons. The local culture and lifestyle, even the political climate, will influence the kind of weapons that develop.

CHINESE WEAPONS

In China, the most common weapons are generally considered those 18 weapons that a martial arts master was expected to be able to use. Because a master could be challenged by anyone to fight with any weapon, he or she had to be familiar with all of them. The original 18 weapons changed as new weapons were added and old ones fell into disuse. The following are the weapons considered essential to the martial artist during the earliest period, the Spring and Autumn Period:

THE EIGHTEEN CHINESE WEAPONS:

spear (chiang)
halberd (ghi or ge)
long rod (gunn)
iron bar (tieh)
trident (char)
horse fork, also called tiger fork (tang)

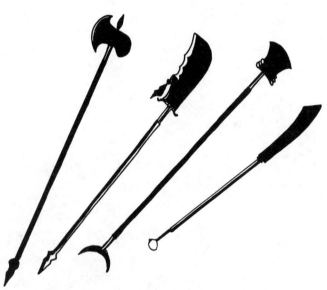

Fig. 4.2 : Wushu weapons.

Fig. 4.1 : Chinese calligraphy for various weapons.

鏟 AXE

把頭 LONG-HANDLED CLAW

筆 BRUSH or PEN

佛手 BUDDHA HAND

鈀 RAKE

鋤頭 HOE

流星鎚 WEIGHTED CHAIN

暗器劍 FLYING DART

鋼鞭 STEEL WHIP

鐵鎚 HAMMER

hook (gau)

ring (huan)

sabre (dau)

sword (jen or jiang)

axe (fu)

whip (bian)

sai (gen)

hammer (chuai)

short staff (barn)

bow and arrow (kurn gen)

long-handled battle axe (yueh)

long-handled claw (chua)

cross bow (neu)

lance (mao)

shield (dun)

When weapons are taught in most Chinese martial arts now, they are used mostly as props, not as fighting implements.

JAPANESE WEAPONS

In Japan, the crowning glory of Japanese weapons was the Japanese sword, though samurai or warriors also carried daggers and knives. The bow and arrow were also important, as were the naginata, spear and staff. The Ninjutsu resorted to less noble weapons, such as blinding powders and shuriken.

THE FIVE SCHOOLS

In Japanese sword smithing, the Five Schools, also called the five traditions, were very important. These schools of swordmaking smiths were located in five different provinces. They produced almost all swords during the Old Sword (Koto) Period, from 900 to 1530. This period is generally considered the time in which Japanese swordmaking art reached its zenith. The five schools were comprised of Bizen, Yamashiro, Yamato, Soshu (sometimes called Sagami) and Mino. The Bizen school was probably founded by Tomonari around 1100. The Yamashiro school was founded by Munechika in 987. The Yamato school developed because various religious sects needed weapons, and these were made at temples throughout this region. In Soshu province, the first shogunate was established and therefore smiths were in great demand. The Mino school is

believed to have been established by smiths from the Soshu school. Blades were very good at first in this school but became poorer over time.

SWORD PERIOD

The various Japanese sword periods are also of importance. The Ancient Sword Period, called Chokuto or Ken period, lasted until 900 A.D. These early swords were made of steel, and were not tempered well. They were usually straight bladed, in imitation of Chinese blades. In fact, high ranking Japanese officials would only wear Chinese blades.

The Old Sword Period, called Koto, lasted from 900 — 1530. During this period, a new samurai class

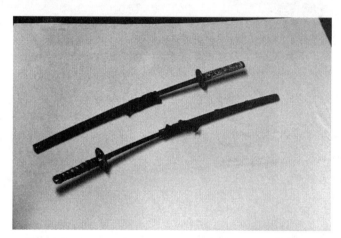

Fig. 4.3 : Japanese modern period sword. These remain partially sheathed because it is considered insulting and discourteous to unsheathe a blade entirely.

arose, demanding better weapons. Longer swords, over four feet in length, were often used. This period is the Golden Age of Japanese swordmaking. The blade became curved, to withstand more stress, and the blades were much better tempered. The Five Schools operated during this period.

The New Sword Period, called Shinto, is generally given as 1530 — 1867. When the numerous Japanese civil wars ended, the sword lost most of its functional value and so the distinctive methods of the different schools were lost. Inferior quality blades were produced, mostly for decorative purposes.

The Modern Period, called Shin Shinto, is that period after 1868, when swords could no longer be worn. After a time, the swordmaking art was revived, but during this period, most swords were mass produced and of very poor quality. Now, more smiths are recovering the old forging methods and compete to earn grades, and produce much higher quality swords.

KOREAN WEAPONS

In Korea, few weapons ever developed; the sword never went beyond a primitive stage. Most Korean martial arts systems are empty hand; however, in addition to the Korean sword, there is a staff, spear and bow.

OKINAWAN WEAPONS

In Okinawa, on the other hand, many non-weapons were turned into weapons. Farming tools, for instance, could turn into deadly weapons. The nunchaku, which was derived from the flail, and the kama, which was derived from the sickle, are characteristic of this country.

VIETNAMESE WEAPONS

In Vietnam, a variety of weapons developed. Probably the most significant of these was the Vietnamese sword, which was taught from the 17th century on. The weapons of Vietnamese martial arts, including staffs, flails, swords, daggers, halberds, lances and sickles, are together called co vo dao.

BLADED WEAPONS

AIKUCHI

A short dagger without a guard, often carried by samurai, especially in places where they could not wear swords, such as royal courts. See Dagger.

ARIT

An Indonesian sickle. See Sickle.

AXE

A wide bladed tool with a long handle, sometimes used in battle. A shorter version is used in some styles of Wushu, singly or in pairs. Also called t-uan ful and ono. See Mattock.

Fig. 4.4 : Chinese axe.

BADIK

See Dagger.

BALARAU

A knife similar to a dagger that is used in the Philippines. See Knife.

BALISONG

A fan knife originating in the Philippines but especially popular in the U.S. See Knife, Butterfly.

BARONG

A popular sheath knife used in the Philippines and Indonesia. See Knife.

BELT COMPANION

The name for the shorter sword or dagger worn in the belt by samurai. See Sword, Japanese.

BISEN-TO

A Japanese halberd, similar to the naginata. It has a short, thick, hooked blade attached to a long staff. See Halberd.

BOLO

A heavy knife used in the Philippines for ritual as well as practical purposes. See Knife.

BOSHI

The tempered lines on a sword. See Sword, Japanese.

BROADSWORD

A sword with a broad blade from which it derives its name. The Chinese broadsword has one cutting edge, and evolved from long-handled knives. It is a long-handled weapon with a sword-like head mounted to a staff. Though extremly heavy, it is used in many styles of Wushu, especially in the performance of forms. The broadsword was formerly used in horse-to-horse fighting. Some broadswords have hooked blades, some have narrower blades. Called da dau in Chinese. See Sword.

BUKE-ZUKURI

A sword characteristic of the New Sword Period. See Sword Periods. See Sword, Japanese.

BUNDI

An Indian dagger. See Dagger.

CAU LIEM

See Sickle.

CHIEN

A double-edged sword, ordinarily used by members of the Chinese military and others. See Sword, Chinese.

CHU-KISSAKI

A medium point on a blade. See Sword, Japanese.

CUTLASS

A short, broad curving sword used by European sailors. Similar to a machete. See Sword.

DA DAU

Chinese term for broadsword. See Broadsword.

DAGA

Refers to a dagger in the espada y daga style of the Philippine martial art Arnis. It evolved from a Spanish method of fighting. In practice, these are usually wooden sticks or wooden daggers used to perform Arnis techniques. See Dagger.

DAGGER

The dagger was the central bladed weapon in India for many years, and in other Asian countries as well. The samurai carried several varieties of daggers. These short knives are used in Chinese Wushu, but for practical purposes, daggers are excellent short defensive weapons, especially since they can be used in short range fighting as well as long range fighting (because they can be thrown).

Aikuchi: Short for aikuchi tanto, a short, ornate, guardless dagger, popular in Japan during the Kamakura period. It was used especially for situations when the sword could not be used. Both a thicker version and a smaller version, sharpened on both sides, were also used. See Sword, Japanese.

Badik: A type of dagger with only one cutting edge. It has a straight blade and is easily hidden. It was a favored weapon of rebels against the Dutch.

Bundi: A Indian dagger of vicious design. Much longer and wider than a conventional dagger, used singly or in pairs.

Dirk: A dagger with a long straight blade.

Hera: A short wooden dagger sometimes used for practice. Similar to the daga used in Arnis.

Piao: A Chinese short dagger resembling a spear head, used to thrust. It could also be thrown.

Yoroi-doshi: An armor-piercing dagger carried by the samurai.

DAI DO

Same as Daito. See Sword, Japanese.

DAISHO

The pair of swords, one long, one short, carried by the samurai. See Sword, Japanese.

DAITO

A long Japanese sword. See Sword, Japanese.

DARNKIM

See Sword.

DAU

A Chinese sabre. See Sabre.

DIRK

A long, straight-bladed dagger, often very ornate. See Dagger.

DOUBLE HOOK SWORD

A Chinese weapon. A sword with hooked blades on each end, often used in Wushu forms. See Sword.

DUAN GUOM

A type of Vietnamese sword. See Sword.

ESPADA

Term meaning, literally, sword, from the espada y daga style of the Philippine martial art Arnis. Originally based on a Spanish method of armed fighting, in practice a wooden stick or wooden sword is generally used. See Sword.

FUCHI

The metal pommel on a sword. See Sword, Japanese.

FUKURA-KARERU

A sword with a straight edge point. See Sword, Japanese.

FUKURA-TSUKU

A sword with a curved edge point. See Sword, Japanese.

FUNAGATA

A tang shaped like the bottom of a ship. See Sword, Japanese.

FURI-SODE

A tang shaped like the sleeve of a kimono. See Sword, Japanese.

GAMA

Same as Kama. See Sickle.

GE

Same as Ghi. See Halberd.

GHI

A Chinese halberd. See Halberd.

GUANDO

Same as Kwan-do. See Halberd.

GUNTO

A military style mounting. See Sword, Japanese.

GUOM

See Sword.

HA

The tempered edge of a blade. See Sword, Japanese.

HABAKI

The collar on a hilt. See Sword, Japanese.

HACHIMAN

A kind of sword. See Sword.

HALBERD

A wooden pole with a pointed metal head and a flat crosspiece that can double as a blade. Similar to an axe in contruction.

Ghi or Ge: A Chinese halberd, of which there are two kinds. One has a two or three pronged head; the other is a flat-headed rod of metal. They are used for stabbing, thrusting and sweeping the opponent.

Kwan-do: A Chinese weapon similar to the naginata, but it is heavier than the Japanese version.

Naginata: A Japanese weapon that consists of a long wooden staff with a shorter curved blade.

Bisen-to and kich are also names for halberds. See Naginata.

HA-MACHI

The notch marking the beginning of the sharpened blade. See Sword, Japanese.

HAMON

The pattern on the blade edge. See Sword, Japanese.

HERA

A short wooden dagger. See Dagger.

HIRA-MUNE

The back of a sword when it is flat. See Sword, Japanese.

HOOK SWORD

A double-edged sword with a hook at the tip, used in Wushu. Similar to double hook sword. See Double Hook Sword.

ICHI-MAI

A solid tempered line on a sword. See Sword, Japanese.

IKARI-O-KISSAKI

A long, curved point on a sword. See Sword, Japanese.

JEN

The Chinese name for sword. See Sword, Chinese.

JENGOK

A knife used in the Philippines, characterized by a sharply angled tip. See Knife.

JIANG

Chinese word for sword. See Sword, Chinese.

JINDACHI-ZUKURI

The name for a long sword from the Old Sword Period. See Sword Periods. See Sword, Japanese.

JIZO

Tempered lines in a sword that form the shape of a head. See Sword, Japanese.

JU-I

See Sword.

KAERI-ASASHI

A short turnback in the tempered lines in a sword. See Sword, Japanese.

KAERI-FUKASHI

A long turnback in the tempered lines in a sword. See Sword, Japanese.

KAERI-TSUYOSHI

A straight turnback in the tempered lines in a sword. See Sword, Japanese.

KAIGUNTO

A factory made mounting for naval swords. See Sword, Japanese.

KAIKEN

A small sword or dagger carried by Japanese women for self-defense or for seppuku, ritual suicide. It could easily be hidden in clothing. See Sword, Japanese.

KAKUMUNE

The back of a sword when it is flat. See Sword, Japanese.

KAMA

An Okinawan farming tool used as a weapon. See Sickle.

KATANA

The famous long sword, the primary weapon of the samurai. See Sword, Japanese.

KELEWANG

An Indonesian sword. See Sword.

KEN

The earliest type of sword known in Japan, it had a straight edge instead of the characteristic curve of the classic Japanese sword. See Sword, Japanese.

KICH

See Halberd.

KIEM

See Sword.

KIJIMOMO

A pheasant thigh tang; that is, a sword tang in the shape of a bird leg. See Sword, Japanese.

KISSAKI

The point of a sword. It can come in many shapes and sizes, including small, medium and long, curved and straight and so on. See Sword, Japanese.

KNIFE

A knife is any instrument for cutting, with at least one sharp-edged blade and usually with a point, set in a handle. Shorter than a sword, it can often be used like one.

In the Philippines, there are literally dozens of kinds of knives. Among these the most common are the balarau, banjal, bangkon, barong, bolo, gayang, gunong, jengok, kalis, lanot, laring, lcampilan, mandau, panabas, parang, pira, punal, and utak. Those knives without a special name are simply called pisau. Since most Indonesians carry knives, they are selected with special care, to reflect the personality of the owner. The balarau is a dagger-type knife. The barong is also used in Indonesia. Because it is over a foot in length, it is sometimes classified as a type of sword. It is a heavy sheath knife, highly valued by owners. The bolo is another heavy bladed long knife. It is used in ritual dance, but also for other practical purposes. The jengok is a long knife with a sharply angled tip. The mandau and parang are long, straight-edged knives of great practical utility and are highly valued.

Fig. 4.5 : Butterfly knives, various Philippine knives and shuriken.

The butterfly knife, also called the fan knife, is used in many different countries. In the Philippines, it called a balisong. It is similar to a switchblade in that the knife blade remains hidden in the handle until it is snapped open and locks into place. These knives, in pairs, are used in Wushu, where they are called butterfly double knives.

Chinese knives are given names based on the shape of the blade. The Chinese willow leaf knife, for instance, is shaped like a willow leaf and has less curvature than usual. The ghost head knife is an extremely heavy weapon that requires two hands, more like a sabre or a sword than a knife. Both kinds are sometimes used in Wushu. Chinese knives are made to cut and slash instead of thrust and jab.

The deer horn knife, called lu jyau do, is used in Pakua, Eight Trigram Boxing. Two sickle-shaped blades, crossed, provide excellent defense.

KO-GATANA

Same as Kozuta. See Sword, Japanese.

KO-KISSAKI

A small point on a sword. See Sword, Japanese.

KO-MARU

Tempered lines in the shape of a small circle. See Sword, Japanese.

KOZUKA

A small knife affixed to the scabbard of a sword for additional protection. See Sword, Japanese.

KOGAI

Same as Kozuka. See Sword, Japanese.

KOTO

See Sword Periods.

KOUGI

A dagger that slipped into the scabbard of a sword. It was usually poisoned and used for close range fighting. See Sword, Japanese.

KRIS

An important weapon in Indonesia and Malaysia. It is used in the Phillipines as well. It has an unusual wavy blade that is much wider at the base than the point. In some ways; it is like a guardian spirit to its owner, warning of danger. It has voodoo-like qualities, being thought capable of killing from a distance. The marks of forging are considered symbolic of the weapon's qualities. Since the blade takes on the personality of its owner, blades and owners are most carefully mated. The smith, called a "pande," is a mystic with supernatural powers.

KUSARI-GAMA

A weapon with a weighted chain attached to a sickle. See Sickle.

KWAN-DO

Also Kwan-tao. See Halberd.

KWAN-TAO

Same as Kwan-do. See Halberd.

KYU GUNTO

A regular military mounting. See Sword, Japanese.

LIAN

Chinese name for sickle. See Sickle.

LU JYAU DO

A type of knife used in Wushu. See Knife.

MA DAO

See Sword.

MANDAU

A long, single-edged knife that is similar to an axe or machete. See Knife.

MARU-MUNE

The back of a blade when it is round. See Sword, Japanese.

MATTOCK

A tool for digging or loosening the soil. It has a flat blade similar to an axe and resembles a pickaxe. See Axe.

MEKUGI-ANA

The rivet hole in a sword where the handle attaches to the blade. See Sword, Japanese.

MIDARE-KOMI

A flame shaped tempered line on a sword. See Sword, Japanese.

MITSU-MUNE

A double back on a sword. See Sword, Japanese.

MUNE

The name for the back of a sword. See Sword, Japanese.

MUNE-HIKUSHI

A low back on a sword. See Sword, Japanese.

MUNE-MACHI

The notch that marks the top of the tang, on the side opposite to the ha-machi, which marks the beginning of the sharpened blade. See Sword, Japanese.

MUNE-TAKASHI

A high back on a sword. See Sword, Japanese.

NAGAKAMA

A version of the naginata, a halberd with a long handle and shorter curved blade. The nagakama has a shorter handle and a longer blade and is used more often by men than by women, who prefer the naginata. See Naginata.

NAKAGO

The tang of a sword. See Sword, Japanese.

NAGASA

The measure of the length of the blade. See Sword, Japanese.

NAGINATA

A Japanese halberd-like weapon. A curved blade with a single cutting edge is attached to a long handle. It resembles a sword affixed to the end of a pole, with the blade one to five feet long and the staff five to nine feet long. The butt sometimes has metal fittings for jabbing. It was used by foot soldiers, where it replaced the bow and arrow for close fighting by the tenth century. Wives of samurai and Buddhist monks were also trained in its use. For training, a bamboo blade is substituted for the live blade. There are several styles of the art of the naginata, which is mostly studied by women. It is among the oldest bladed weapons. Its techniques are mostly circular slashes. It is also an excellent defensive weapon against the sword; today, Kendo practitioners routinely participate in contests with those who are skilled in naginata-do. The nagakama is a version of this halberd.

NINJA-TO

A sword used by Ninja. Its versatility allowed it to be used as a ladder, and the scabbard could work as a club, snorkel, blow gun and other tools. See Sword.

O-DACHI

A very long sword used by warriors on horseback. See Sword, Japanese.

O-KISSAKI

A long point on a sword. See Sword, Japanese.

O-MARU

Tempered lines that form a large circle. See Sword, Japanese.

ONO

See Axe.

PARANG

A heavy long bladed knife used for utility purposes in the Philippines. Also taught in most styles of Pentjak-Silat. See Knife.

PATA

An ancient Indian sword. See Sword.

PAIO

A short Chinese dagger. See dagger.

PISAU

An Indonesian term for any knife that does not have a specific name. See Knife.

PUN GUNG BI

A special weapon used in Pakua, Eight Trigram Boxing. A six-inch needle, sharp at both ends, attached to the fingers by a ring.

SABRE

A sword with a broad and heavy blade, used by the cavalry in Europe. The Chinese sabre, called dau, is a single piece of metal, with a blade at least 1½ inches wide, which distinguishes it from other kinds of swords. The back edge is usually dull except near the tip. The upper portion of the blade is sharper than the lower portion, and each side of the blade has a blood groove. The sabre is used for foot fighting, and its techniques include blocking, stabbing and cutting. See Sword.

SAYA

A scabbard. See Sword, Japanese.

SCIMITAR

A broad and heavy sword like a sabre which has a curved blade. The edge is on the convex side. This weapon was used mostly by Turks and Arabs. See Sword.

SEPPA

Spacers or washers between the collar and the guard on the hilt of a sword. See Sword, Japanese.

SHIKOME ZUE

A mounting from after the Meiji Restoration, having no value. See Sword, Japanese.

SHIN GUNTO

A new style mounting which began to be produced in the late-1930s. See Sword, Japanese.

SHIN NO MUNE

Same as mitsu-mune. See Sword, Japanese.

SHIN NO TACHI

A ceremonial sword worn by Japanese nobles. See Sword, Japanese.

SHINAI

A bamboo sword used for practice in sword fighting. It is the primary weapon used in the art of Kendo. See Sword.

SHINOGI

The ridge line of a sword. See Sword, Japanese.

SHINOGI-HIKUSHI

The ridge line of a sword when it is flat. See Sword, Japanese.

SHINOGI-JI

The upper surface of the ridge area. See Sword, Japanese.

SHINOGI-TAKASHI

A raised ridge line on a sword. See Sword, Japanese.

SHIRA-SAYA

A plain wood mounting with no guard. See Sword, Japanese.

SHIRAZAYA TACHI

A ceremonial sword reserved for Japanese nobles. These had decorative fur covered scabbards. See Sword, Japanese.

SHOTO

The short sword in the pair that Samurai carried. See Daisho. See Sword, Japanese.

SHOU LI JEN

Chinese name for sleeve sword. See Sword, Sleeve.

SHOZOKU TACHI

Same as shin-no-tachi. See Sword, Japanese.

SICKLE

A weapon with a crescent shaped blade and a handle attached at one end. Actually a farming tool used for reaping, it can also be used for chopping, hooking, striking, and blocking. Though it is usually considered an Okinawan weapon, where it is called kama or gama, it is also known in China, where it is called lian. The sickle is difficult to counter, but it is also extremely difficult to master, which is why sickle art is a dying art.

Arit: A short-handled Indonesian tool. Unlike most Indonesian bladed weapons, this one often requires both hands.

Kama: Okinawan tool. The kama is used by itself or in pairs. A short, sharp blade is set at right angles to the handle and the blade is less curved than an ordinary sickle.

Kusarigama: A sickle with a weighted chain attached to the handle. This chain was used to entangle other weapons, particularly the sword, while the sickle was used for in-close fighting.

Shinobigama: A smaller version of the kusarigama, used by the Ninja.

SO-NO-MUNE

Same as maru-mune. See Sword, Japanese.

SONG DAO

A type of Vietnamese sword. See Sword.

SORI

The measure of the curve on a sword. See Sword, Japanese.

SWORD

A sword is a hand weapon having a long blade usually made of steel. It can be straight with a sharp point for thrusting, or it can be curved to add strength, or it can have a point and sharp cutting edges for slashing. The blade is attached to the handle by a tang. There are many kinds of swords, including the broadsword, cutlass, darnkim, double hook sword, duan guom, espada, guom, hachiman, ju-i, kelewang, ken, kiem, ma dao, ninja-to, pata, sabre, scimitar, shinai, and viet long guom.

The Burmese sword is pointed but not so light and long as a sabre. It is used

Fig. 4.6 : Chinese sword.

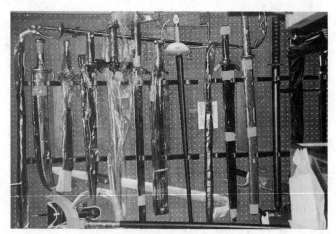

Fig. 4.7 : Collection of swords.

for cutting or thrusting, and, since it is not as heavy as a European or Japanese sword, it is easier to use.

The Chinese sword is called chien, jen or jiang. It is characterized by a narrow, straight, double edged blade. The blade is less than 1½ inches wide. The so-called scholar sword is lighter and shorter than the martial sword. It was a primary weapon used for piercing, thrusting, hacking, splitting, jabbing, deflecting, hooking, and so forth. The tao sword is like a broadsword, only the blade is s-shaped.

The ju-i is a ritual sword.

In India, the sword of choice is called pata. It has a hollow handle, and is very flexible and light.

The Indonesian sword, the kelewang, though shorter, is more swordlike than knife-like. It has a notch near the tip. It is used in the martial art system of Pentjak-Silat.

The Ninja sword, ninja-to, is extremely versatile. The scabbard, which is longer than the blade, could be used as a club, snorkel, blow gun, or even a rung for a ladder. The hand guard on the sword itself could work as a foothold if the sword were leaned up against a wall. An attached cord could pull the sword up. The cord could serve as a tourniquet.

In Vietnam, the sword is called song-dao. The kiem, another kind of Vietnamese sword, has a straight and narrow blade.

Japanese sword: It is considered a soul weapon.

The sword is seen as a divine symbol, and even a badge of honor, especially since it signified noble ancestry. The earliest swords were made of stone and wood but in the second century B.C., metal came to Japan.

Amakuni, who lived around 700, is traditionally called Japan's first swordsmith, and is credited with giving the Japanese blade its characteristic curve. The tsurugi, one of earliest swords in Japan, possibly from Korea, had a straight, double-edged blade. It was used by archers on horseback. The term ken refers specifically to a two-edged sword made before the ninth century. Since the eighth century, the Japanese sword has been curved with one cutting edge. Straight blades, it was discovered, weren't strong enough to withstand

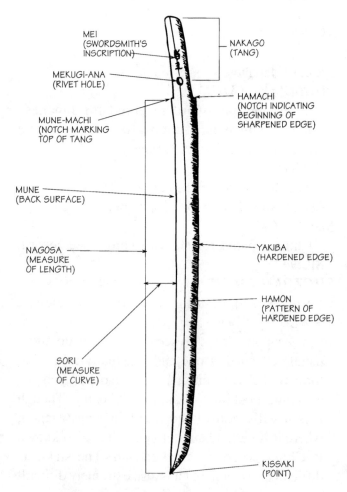

Fig. 4.8 : The parts of a Japanese sword.

214

battles. By the ninth century, Japanese swords had improved, though Korean and Chinese swords had already been much improved for a long period of time. This indicates that the forging of swords in Japan was influenced by other Asian countries. However, those Japanese smiths who worked in the Heian, Kamakura and Muromachi periods, the early-14th through mid-16th century, were unsurpassed by any other smiths. The Five Schools of swordmaking, responsible for most sword production, were established during this period.

Many weapons experts feel the Japanese sword was the best ever made, owing to the superior quality of the steel, and the sophistication of the smiths. The sword was thus the spiritual essence of the warrior class. In Japan, swordmaking had a ceremonial, semi-religious nature, and smiths were Shinto priests.

Sometimes swords were called kami vessels, that is, places of lodging for Shinto spirits. Each smith or school had its own techniques, special sources of raw materials and so on. Trade secrets were jealously guarded, but even so, forgery was widespread. A review board was especially created in the ninth century to stem this problem. The character of the smith was believed to enter the blades he crafted. Blades made by outstanding smiths were highly prized. For this reason, the sword-viewing ceremony was created. The smith inscribed his name in Chinese characters on the portion of the sword blade covered by the handle.

A variety of sword styles existed. The tachi was worn from the belt, and had a strong curve, as well as being quite long. The Yefu-no-tachi were special swords reserved for high-ranking nobles and palace guards. The ceremonial swords worn by nobles were called shozuko-tachi or shin-no-tachi. Shirizaya tachi were also worn by noble warriors; these were notable in that they had fur-covered scabbards. Soon though, the to sword became popular. This had a smaller curve, and fit easily into the belt. The high-ranking samurai could have two swords, one long and one short (daito and

shoto). The pair was called daisho. A very long sword, o-dachi, was used by warriors on horseback. Daggers were also among the array of short swords. Of these, the aikuchi tanto was the most popular. Among smaller swords, the kaiken was used by women, who could carry it concealed in their clothes.

Other small swords and knives were part of the samurai's arsenal. Small knives fixed to the scabbard of a sword are called kozuka or kogai. A kougi was a dagger that fit into the scabbard and was usually poisoned. The katana, a long sword, was the primary weapon of the samurai. Short swords, 16-20 inches long, were used in hand-to-hand combat, and in places where long swords were forbidden. These short swords were used for seppuku, ritual suicide.

Japanese swords can be classified by length: long = daito; medium = wakizashi; short = tanto. They can also be classified by mountings. Earlier mountings tend to be more valuable. The term jindachi-zukuri indicates a mounting on a long sword of the Old Sword Period. The term buke-zukuri indicates a mounting from the New Sword Period. Shira-saya refers to a plain wood mountng with no guard. Gunto refers to army and navy mountings, with kyu gunto referring specifically to regular military mountings of no value. Shin gunto are new military mountings from about 1937. Kaigunto refers to mountings on a naval sword, factory-made, with no value. Shikome zue are mountings made after the Meiji Restoration, which have no value.

The point is called kissaki. The pattern of the edge is called hamon, while the hardened edge is yakiba. The measure of blade length is nagasa and the measure of curve is sori. The back surface is called mune. The notch marking the beginning of the sharpened edge is ha-machi, and the notch marking the top of tang is mune-machi. The tang itself is nakago, while the rivet hole where the handle attaches to the tang is mekugi-ana. The smith's signature or other inscription is called mei.

The guard is known as tsuba. These are the major parts of the sword, though there are other components.

The kissaki is difficult to forge and polish. It comes in a wide variety of shapes and sizes. A straight edge is fukura-kareru. A curved edge is fukura-tsuku. A small point is ko-kissaki, a medium point is chu-kissaki and a long point is o-kissaki.

Swords have tempered lines, and these, too, come in a variety of shapes. Tempered lines are called boshi. Lines in the shape of a large circle is called o-maru. A small circle is ko-maru. A head shape is jizo. Wavy is midare-komi, flame is kaen, and solid is ichi-mai. No turnback at all is called yaki-zume; a straight turnback is called kaeri-tsuyoshi; a long turn back is kaeri-fukashi, and a short turnback is kaeri-asashi. The dividing line between the surface and the point is called the yokote. The ridge line, called shinogi, can be raised, shinogi-takashi, or flat, shinogi-hikushi.

The upper surface ridge area is known as shinogi-ji. The surface of the blade is decorated and this surface decoration can consist of grooves, carvings, inscriptions, and so on. The back, mune, can be low, in which case it is called mune-hikushi or high, in which case it is mune-takashi. The back can be double, known as mitsu-mune or sometimes shin-no-mune. It can be round, maru-mune or sometimes so-no-mune. It can be flat, called hira-mune, or sometimes kakumune. The curvature, sori, can be deep or shallow.

The tang, called nakago, where the blade fits into the hilt, can take on different shapes, such as pheasant thigh (kiji-momo), kimono sleeve (furi-sode), ship bottom (funa-gata), or fish-shaped (tanago-bara). The shape of the tip of the tang also varies, and there are various file markings on the tang. A rivet hole in the tang attaches the handle. The smith puts his inscription on the tang. This inscription can contain the name of the smith, the place, the date, the name of the sword owner, a

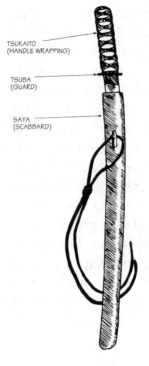

Fig. 4.9 : The parts of a sword scabbard.

good luck saying and so on.

The mountings include all the fittings exclusive of the blade, such as the scabbard (saya), the guard, the hilt or handle (tsuka), the collar (habaki), spacers or washers (seppa). The metal sleeve or pommel is called fuchi and hilt ornaments, of which there are many kinds, are called menuki. A tachi is a blade for a sword worn with the edge down, and a katana is a blade for a sword worn edge up.

Ha is the tempered edge of the blade. Aikuchi is used to describe all sword mountings in which threre is no guard between hilt and scabbard.

See Sword Periods. See Five Schools. See Dagger.

SWORD, SLEEVE

A Chinese weapon. A straight short sword with both edges sharpened. A hidden spring can expand it to twice its length, which makes it an appropriate weapon for a surprise attack at close range. The sword can be hidden in a sleeve; thus, its name.

TACHI SWORD

A very long sword with a strong curve, worn from the belt of a samurai. See Sword, Japanese.

TANAGO-BARA

A tang shaped like a fish. See Sword, Japanese.

TANTO

A short sword. See Sword, Japanese.

TAO

A Chinese broadsword. See Sword.

TO

A small sword with a small curve that could fit into belt. See Sword, Japanese.

TSUBA

The guard on the hilt of a sword. See Sword, Japanese.

TSUKA

The handle or hilt of a sword. See Sword, Japanese.

TSURUGI

Mountings on the earliest swords in Japan. See Sword, Japanese.

TUAN FUL

A Chinese short axe. See Axe.

TWINHOOK SWORD

Same as double hook sword. See Sword. See Double Hook Sword.

VIET LONG GUOM

A sword used in Vietnam. See Sword.

WAKIZASHI

A medium length sword. See Sword, Japanese.

YAKIBA

The hardened edge of a sword. See Sword, Japanese.

YAKI-ZUME

The tempered lines of a sword when they have no turnback. See Sword, Japanese.

YEFU NO TACHI

A sword reserved for high ranking nobles and palace guards. See Sword, Japanese.

YOKOTE

The dividing line between the surface and the point in a sword. See Sword, Japanese.

YOROI-DASHI

An armor-piercing dagger. See dagger.

YUE

A Chinese weapon made of metal, resembling a crescent. The multiple cutting edges could be used in a variety of ways.

STAFF AND STICK WEAPONS

BAR

Chinese term for trident. See Trident.

BARBED POLE

A long staff with barbs or short spikes set in one end.

BARN

A Chinese term for a kind of long staff. Similar to a barbed pole. See Staff, Long.

BO

The five or six foot staff used in the Japanese art of Bojutsu. See Staff.

BOKEN

See Bokken.

BOKKEN

A wooden sword formerly called bokuto, used for training in sword fighting.

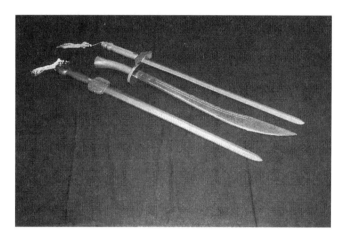

Fig. 4.10 : Wooden swords called bokken. These are used for training in swordfighting.

BOKUTO

See Bokken.

BONG

See Staff.

CHI

A hooked spear used in Chinese Wushu. See Spear.

CHUA

See Claw, Long-handled.

CLAW, LONG HANDLED

A Chinese weapon consisting of a metal or wooden rod that has a metal "hand" with sharp "fingers" attached. It was usually used in battle by rows of soldiers, not being practical for simple self-defense.

CRUTCHES

This weapon is like a crutch — and was derived from crutches used by injured and handicapped individuals. A handle is attached crosswise to a staff, and it is used as a Chinese martial arts weapon.

ESCRIMA STICK

A Philippine short stick similar to a jo, made of hardwood. It is used in the martial art Escrima to strike and block. See Stick.

FEROZUE

A hollow bamboo stick or staff enclosing a chain with an iron ball attached. Either staff or chain could be used as a weapon. See Stick.

FORKED STAFF

This weapon is sometimes called a tiger fork. It is a long trident that can be used to pin or hold a person. Originally, it was used to kill tigers. Eventually, the forked staff became a Wushu weapon. See Staff.

GIAU CHIZ

Chinese term for a tapered rod. See Rod, Tapered.

GUNN

Chinese term for long rod. See Rod, Long.

HAMBO

Same as Hanbo. See Staff.

HANBO

See Staff.

HOKO

An ancient lance from Japan, forerunner of the naginata. See Naginata. See Lance.

IRON BAR

An iron staff or truncheon used like a short staff or stick. See Stick. See Staff.

IRON RULER

In China, this weapon is called tieh tzu. It consists of a flat metal rod with or without a separate handle. It is used like a night stick and is similar to an iron bar.

ISHI-JO

Stone sticks that were the forerunner of the Bo and Jo staffs. See Staff.

JITE

A Japanese weapon. A short iron or steel rod attached to a long hilt. A hook is attached at the hilt. It is like a truncheon and was used mostly by the Japanese police force.

JO

A short staff used in the Japanese art of Jojutsu. See Staff.

KAMA-YARI

A Japanese sickle-spear similar to a halberd. See Spear.

KARASIK

A spear used in the Philippines. See Spear.

KEIBO

See Staff.

LANCE

A spear-like weapon with a long wooden staff and a metal spearhead. The hoko is from prehistoric Japan. It is probably the oldest bladed weapon, existing as early as 2000 B.C. Like a sword or knife, lances are often equipped with a guard and a scabbard. Thuong is the Vietnamese name for a lance.

LATHI

An Indian staff made of cane or bamboo of about five feet. See Staff.

MAO CHIANG

Chinese name for snake spear. See Spear, Snake.

MONKEY STAFF

Called Tai sing moon. The only weapon used in monkey style Wushu; the practitioner can use the staff to defend and attack, and can climb it to evade attack.

NABOOT

A long pole. See Staff.

ROD, LONG

A Chinese weapon from five to eight feet long. It was made of hardwood, brass or iron. It was used as a defensive weapon against a sword or knife. The techniques used were brushing or sweeping and striking. Called Gunn. See Staff.

ROD, TAPERED

A Chinese weapon. It is like a lance, but with tapered ends. It could be used by fighters on horseback and it was also used to attack a horse's legs. There are three lengths — long (8 feet or more, called shuo); medium (less than 8 feet, called shi) and short (about four feet, called giau chiz). See Staff.

ROKUSHAKUBO

A staff with tapered ends, similar to a tapered rod. See Staff.

SAN CHET KWON

See Three Section Staff.

SHAN CHAR

A Chinese term for trident. See Trident.

SHI

Chinese name for tapered rod. See Rod, Tapered.

SHORT STAFF

Also called Jo. See Staff.

SHUO

Chinese word for tapered rod. See Rod, Tapered.

SPEAR

Spears can be used to thrust, slice or throw. In India, for instance, most spears are projectile. Over 700 different types of spears exist in Asia. There are straight spear blades, hooked blades, curved blades, plus blades with projections. Some spears are double-headed. Spears were used by religious groups as well as warriors. They are second in importance for fighters only to the bow and arrow. Asian spears include the chi, kama-yari, karasik, vita and yari.

In China, spears are used primarily to thrust, hook or slice. The eyebrow spear is a specialized spear with sickle-shaped blade. The karasik is the spear used in the Philippines. The vita is a projectile spear usually thrown from horseback. A cord is attached to the spear and tied to the thrower's wrist or saddle. The Yari is a spear used in Japan. The head is different from the hoko, or lance.

SPEAR, SNAKE

A Chinese spear with a wavy head. It is sharp on both sides, which gives it greater cutting ability. Called mao chiang. See Spear.

STAFF

The best known staffs are the Japanese Bo and Jo. The Bo staff is made of hardwood and is five or six feet in length. Its practice is called bojutsu. The Jo staff is more appropriately a stick, as it is much shorter. Its art is called Jojutsu. Staffs are used to defend against swords and to thrust and strike and to sweep. Chinese staffs can be used with some spear techniques. Staffs in Asia are known by the various names of barn, bong, forked staff, hanbo, lathi, naboot, rod, short staff, tabak, tambo, tanbo, tekken, three section staff, and tien-bong. The walking cane was often converted to use as a staff, especially among monks who were otherwise unprotected.

The barn is a Chinese long staff. It is similar to the long rod, but has a heavy metal fitting at one end, sometimes with serrated edges, as on a wolf teeth staff.

Fig. 4.11 : Various spearheads.

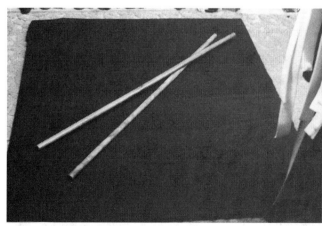

Fig. 4.12 : Bo staffs.

The lathi is an Indian staff, made of cane or bamboo, up to five feet long. For practice, the lathi is cushioned with leather.

The naboot is a long pole-like staff.

The rokushakubo is a staff with tapered ends, like a tapered rod. The force of the blow centers on a specific point in the opponent's body.

The three-section staff is a Chinese weapon constructed from three pieces of wood connected by metal rings. The lengths of sections are about equal, measuring about a yard in length and with a diameter of about an inch. It can be folded together and used as a short stick or staff to strike and parry, or one end can be held and the staff swung.

STICK

The stick is a shorter version of the staff, between one and three feet in length. It is used to block and strike and is variously a club, escrima stick, ferozue, nightstick, tabak, tchaa, tonfa, and truncheon. The ishi-jo are stone sticks, the forerunner of the Japanese jo and bo staffs. Tanbong is the Korean name for the short staff, like a jo. The tabak is used in the Philippines; it is a short, pointed hardwood stick.

TABAK

A Philippine stick. See Stick.

TAI SING MOON

The monkey staff used by Wushu practitioners. See Monkey Staff.

TAMBO

Same as tanbo. See Staff.

TANBO

See Staff.

TANBONG

Korean name for jo, the short staff. See Staff.

THREE-SECTION STAFF

A wood staff consisting of three sections joined by metal rings.

THUONG

Vietnamese name for lance. See Lance.

TIEH TZU

Chinese name for iron ruler. See Iron ruler.

TIEN BONG

See Staff.

TIGER FORK

Same as forked staff. See Forked Staff.

TONFA

An Okinawan farming tool. Originally the handle of a rice mill, it is a short staff about two feet long, with a rounded handle attached at a right angle. It could be used to stop a sword attack or to defend against other sticks or staffs. The skill of using the tonfa is a very difficult one to aquire. It is also called the tui-fa. See Stick.

TRIDENT

A Chinese weapon called shan char or bar. It consists of a three-pronged or tined metal head attached to a staff. Originally a hunting tool, similar

Fig. 4.13 : Various Jo sticks.

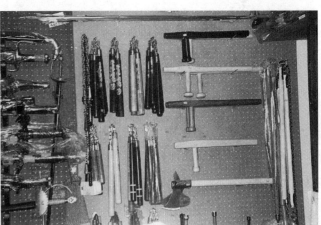

Fig. 4.14 : Tonfa and nunchaku.

to a forked staff or tiger fork, it could be used to block and lock an opponent's weapon. It could also be used to scare off evil spirits.

TUI FA

Same as tonfa. See Tonfa. See Stick.

VITA

A throwing spear. See Spear.

YARI

In Japan, spears in general. See Spear.

PROJECTILE WEAPONS

ARQUEBUS

A crude gun that worked with a spring mechanism. Used in Japan from the early-16th century.

ARROWHEADS

Arrows can have many different points. In martial arts, arrowheads can be of an infinite variety. Some are forked. Some are made to produce a whistling sound that frightens evil spirits. Known as kabura-ya, this arrowhead is shaped like a turnip. The samurai used iron tips of various design; each warrior family had a preference. Some were like sword points, some were triangular, some flat, and needle-like, some concave. Some were more fanciful, shaped like kites, willow leaves or dragon's tongues.

ARROW

Arrows for martial artists come in a variety of sizes. Most are made of bamboo with metal heads. Some arrows were made of iron in different shapes. The double hook arrow, which the Chinese called shunn gou shih, consists of a sharp metal head and two sharp hooks on either side of the arrow shaft. Such arrows could be thrown by hand. Certain arrows produce a whistling sound to frighten away evil spirits. These are kabura-ya. The arrow in Kyudo, called ya, is more than three feet long. The shafts are made of bamboo. The points are shaped in different ways. See Arrowheads. For the archer, arrow length is determined by the distance between the middle of the chest and the fingertips (with arm outstretched). This method of determining arrow

length is called yazuka. In Kyudo, an arrow with a wooden ball instead of a point, that is a muffled tip, is often used to prevent injury. This is called hikime.

ARROW, SLEEVE

This is a small version of the arrow, easily hidden in the sleeve, thus its name. It is thrown, not shot. It is called sui-jian.

ARROW, BACK

This is a Chinese weapon with an 18-to-24 inch arrow. The arrow is loaded into a tube with a spring. The tube is strapped to the practitioner's back. The arrow is triggered when one bows. It is a surprise weapon with a distance of about 20 yards.

BLOW PIPE

This projectile method is used by forest people, who also used poisoned arrows. Blowpipes were also a favorite weapon of the Ninja.

BO-SHURIKEN

A throwing weapon. See Shuriken.

BOW

The long bow used in Kyudo is called yumi. It can be six or more feet in length. Other bow-and-arrow arts use shorter bows. The hankyu is a half bow, that is, a miniature bow and arrow which could be hidden in clothing. It was used sometimes for defense and sometimes to send messages.

BOW AND ARROW

All Asian countries used the bow and arrow, especially on horseback. The Chinese bow and arrow was called kun gen and resembles the Western kind. The materials used were bamboo at first and then stronger wood and finally metal. The Ninja used short bows and poisoned arrows. The hankyu, called a half bow, was a miniature bow and arrow set.

CROSSBOW

The crossbow is used to shoot arrows, stone, and so on. It consists of a short bow mounted crosswise on a stock. The Chinese cross bow (neu) could fire three, four, or five arrows simultaneously.

DARTS

Used by Chinese fighters, these are sharp, pointed throwing weapons. A good martial artist could throw five at a time. Called Fri Bau.

FRI BAU

Chinese term for throwing darts. See Darts.

FUKIYA

Poisoned projectiles used in blowguns.

FUKUMI-BARI

Throwing weapons. See Shuriken.

GUN

See Arquebus.

HANKYU

A half bow, used by Ninja to send messages or to defend themselves. See Bow.

HARQUEBUS

Same as arquebus. See Arquebus.

HIKIME

An arrow with a muffled tip, used in archery practice. See Arrow.

KABURA-YA

A special arrow with a special arrowhead used to frighten away evil spirits. Used in Shinto and other ceremonies. See Arrow.

KUN GEN

Chinese term for bow and arrow. See Bow and Arrow.

NEU

Chinese word for crossbow. See Crossbow.

PAKU

A small, sharp throwing weapon used in Indonesia. See Shuriken.

SEMBAN-SHAKEN

A throwing weapon. See Shuriken.

SHAKEN

A throwing weapon. See Shuriken.

SHUNN GOU SHIH

A double hook arrow. See Arrow.

SHURIKEN

Any of a variety of throwing weapons used by the Ninja. They were made of steel, with sharpened edges. Sometimes the edges were poisoned. They could be thrown one at a time or

several simultaneously. Used for distracting or harrying, they could be dangerous if they struck a vital point. Throwing stars were called shaken. Dagger shaped ones were called bo-shuriken and those with a hole in the middle were called semban-shaken. Small needle-shaped weapons were called fukumi-bari. These could be held in the mouth and blown. The most famous ones were star-shaped, from which they get the name "throwing stars." Nine shuriken were often carried, since nine is a lucky number. Also could be used as a digging tool.

STARS, THROWING

A throwing weapon. See Shuriken.

TONKI

Any small metal throwing weapons, like dirks and daggers. See Shuriken.

YA

Japanese name for arrow. See Arrow.

YUMI

Japanese word for bow. See Bow.

YURI

See Bow.

COMPOSITE

BA

A rake-like tool that could be used to sweep or strike an opponent. See Rake.

BA TAOU

Chinese term for hoe. See Hoe.

BANKOKU-CHOKI

An ancient Japanese non-noble weapon used mostly by peasants, criminals and Ninja. It consists of a metal ring with spikes projecting from it. It was used to strike vital points and could be easily concealed.

BI

See Brush or Pen.

BIEN TZU CHIANG

Chinese term for steel whip. See Steel Whip.

BRUSH or PEN

A Chinese weapon called bi. It is made of metal or bamboo, with a very sharp point. It resembles a pen or brush used by scholars. It could be used effectively for stabbing. Also refers to a weapon used for horseback fighting. In this case, it refers to a wood or metal staff with a metal hand affixed. Attached to the hand is a very sharp metal pen. This longer pen was used for chopping and sweeping. A variation, called the Buddha hand (fu sou), is constructed without the pen. These weapons were used by priests for non-deadly self-defense.

CALTHROP
A small metal ball with spikes, thrown to injure or distract an opponent. They could also be tossed on the ground to prevent quick pursuit. Used mostly by Ninja.

CHAINWHIP
Same as steel whip. See Steel Whip.

CHAN
Chinese term for shovel or spade. See Shovel or Spade.

CHIGIRIKI
A Japanese weapon which consists of a wooden staff with a weighted chain attached. At one time used by peasants to disarm warriors or thieves. It could entangle a weapon or strike an opponent.

CLAW, FLYING
A Chinese weapon that consists of a length of chain or rope with a claw-like object attached to one end, used much like a whip.

FAN
A war fan, called gumbaiuchiwa. It was used by commanders to direct their armed forces but it

Fig. 4.15 : Chinese fan for leading armies and for self-defense.

could also protect the bearer. It was made of bamboo, wood or metal with an extremely sharp outer edge. Spring loaded darts could be hidden in the ribs. The fan could be used to cut, strike, or slide and did not have to be concealed, as it was an ordinary object. Called san in Chinese.

FLAIL
Originally, this was a hand threshing tool, a farming implement consisting of a wooden handle with a shorter stick attached by a cord at the end. The handle could swing freely. The tool became a weapon on Okinawa. See Nunchaku.

FU SOU
Chinese phrase meaning "Buddha hand." See Brush or Pen.

HAMMER
A short, thick stick of wood with a metal ball on one end, used in Wushu. The size of the ball varies. It is also called a mallet, or otsuchi.

HOE
Called a kue in Okinawa or ba taou in China. It resembles an ordinary hoe and can be used as a weapon.

KIYOKETSUSHIYOGE
A staff with a spike and hook attached to one end and a chain with a ring attached to the other end. This was used as a spear and could entangle a sword.

KUE
Okinawan name for hoe. See Hoe.

LIEN TZU CHIANG
Chinese name for steel whip. See Steel Whip.

LONG GIAN
See Nunchaku.

MALLET
Same as hammer. See Hammer.

MANRIKI-GUSARI
A long iron chain weighted at one end. The chain could be anywhere from two to twelve feet long. It was swung like a bola to entangle, immobilize or choke an opponent. It could also be used to defend against sword attacks.

METSU-BUSHI

Blinding powders carried by the Ninja to assist in escape.

NUMCHUK

See Nunchaku.

NUNCHAKU

A flail made of two short pieces of wood each the length of a forearm, attached by a short cord or chain. It was originally a farming tool, used for threshing. It developed in Okinawa into a formidable weapon. It can be used to crush, poke or jab, and it can deflect and parry other weapons. There are numerous blocking and striking techniques that can be performed by experts, though since it is a very difficult art, great masters are increasingly rare. The Vietnamese martial arts use longer nunchaku, with handles that are at least two feet long; other variants in China and Vietnam are very short. Also called long gian and tham thiet gian. In the Philippines, they are called tabak-toya.

NUNCHUK

See Nunchaku.

NUNTE

An Okinawan weapon, about a foot long, with a central prong and two tines, each pointing in different directions. It is similar to a sai and is used in the same way.

OTSUCHI

See Hammer.

RAKE

This Chinese weapon resembles a modern rake. It is a long wooden rod or staff with metal teeth attached. It was originally used in agricultural but could hold an enemy's weapon also. It was used to sweep or strike. It is called a ba.

RINGS

The metal ring, a Chinese weapon, ranges from 12-to-18 inches in diameter, and has sharp outer edges except for the area that is used as a grip. The ring can be used to block or slide an opponent's weapon away. A ring with spurs or short projections could be used to lock a weapon. They are used in some styles of Wushu. Rings are also used as a thrown weapon to distract an opponent.

ROPE DART

A Chinese weapon consisting of a long rope with a spearhead or dart attached. It is used like a whip.

SAI

A defensive weapon, probably of Indonesian origin. It resembles a dagger, being about a foot long, but it consists of a central prong with two shorter tines attached at the handle. It is used like a stick to block and parry and the tines can catch and trap a sword blade. The sai is an integral part of Karate. It is also found in various guises throughout Asia.

SAN

Chinese word for fan. See Fan.

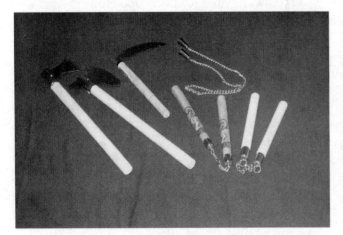

Fig. 4.16 : Nunchaku and axes.

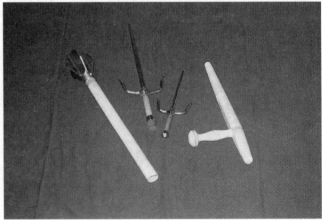

Fig. 4.17 : Sai and tonfa.

SHOVEL or SPADE

A tool with a flat metal head on the end of a metal rod or staff. The head could also be shaped like a crescent or a coin. This weapon is used by priests to bury the dead, but can also be used like a spear or rod in fighting.

SO-SETSU-KON

See Nunchaku.

STEEL WHIP

A Chinese weapon called bien tzu chiang or lien tzu chiang, made of links of chain. It can be wound up and easily hidden. It is used to strike, wrap or sweep the opponent. An expert can use one much as a sword or staff is used — to block, parry, disarm and perform other techniques.

Fig. 4.18 : Steel whip.

SURUCHIN

A primitive weapon from Okinawa. It consists of a short length of rope or chain weighted at both ends. The rope is swung and is used to strike at an opponent.

SURUJIN

Same as suruchin. See Suruchin.

TABAK-TOYA

Philippine name for nunchaku. See Nunchaku.

THAM THIET GIAN

Vietnamese name for nunchaku. See Nunchaku.

TITJIO

A Chinese version of the sai. See Sai.

TJABANG

An Indonesian weapon similar to the sai. See Sai.

TOHAI

A shield made of wood or leather with a peephole.

WHIP

See Steel Whip.

BIOGRAPHY

In Asia, the surname always precedes the given or first name whenever people are mentioned, unlike Western countries, in which the given name is first. Thus, in the name Funakoshi Gichin, the family name is Funakoshi, not Gichin. Since this is standard, in the following section, for Asian names, the last names are given first with no punctuation. In the case of westernized Asian names, names are given in American order; that is, while the last name is still first, a comma is used to show that it is the last name. Thus, Henry Cho is listed as Cho, Henry, while Funakoshi Gichin is listed as Funakoshi Gichin and not Funakoshi, Gichin or Gichen Funakoshi.

AHATI KILINDI IYI

Head instructor of African martial arts at the Tamerrian Martial Arts Institute, which is similar to the Kodokan in Japan.

AHN CHANG HO

(1876-1938). Korean patriot who devoted his life to furthering the education and educational opportunities of Koreans. He was also active in working toward the independence of the country from Japanese rule. A Tae Kwon Do form from the International Tae Kwon Do Federation system is named for him; Toe San, the form, is also his pseudonym.

AKIYAMA SHIROBEI YOSHITOKI

The physician credited with founding the Yoshin-ryu school.

AKO-NO-KAMI

The title for Asano Naganori, the legendary 18th century noble, who, after drawing his sword at court, was obligated by the demands of etiquette to commit seppuku, or ritual suicide. His samurai, believing he died wrongfully, plotted to avenge his death. The story, considered an example of true, noble samurai behavior is told in the *The Forty Seven Ronin*.

See *The Forty Seven Ronin* in the Literature section.

AMAKUNI

A legendary sword-maker, he is traditionally considered Japan's first swordsmith. He lived during the eighth century, and is said to have invented the characteristically curved blade of the Japanese sword.

AN CHUNG GUN

A Korean patriot who assassinated Hiro Bumi Ito, the first Japanese general governor of Korea. Hiro Bumi Ito was the target of anger for he played a significant role in the Korea-Japan merger. An Chung Gun was executed in 1910. A Tae Kwon Do form, Chung Gun, from the International Tae Kwon Do Federation system, is named after him.

ANZAWA HEIJIRO

(1887-1970). The first Kyudo (archery) master to teach his art to outsiders. He introduced Kyudo to Great Britain and France. He was influential in the development of Kyudo and helped create greater interest in the art throughout the world. He was awarded the rank of 10th degree black belt, the highest rank attainable in Kyudo.

ARAKI (MUJINSAI) MATAEMON MINAMOTO HIDETSUNA

See Minamoto Hidestsuna.

ASHIKAGA FAMILY

This noble family ruled Japan during the Ashikaga shogunate, which lasted more than two centuries. The Ashikaga were descended from the powerful ruling class family, the Minamoto (also known as the Genji family). The family produced 15 shoguns, or military rulers, who governed in place of the emperor. Their rule ended in 1573, when the general Oda Nobunaga defeated Ashikaga Yoshiaki.

ASHIKAGA TAKAUJI

(1308-1358). The first shogun from the Ashikaga noble family, thus beginning a family rule that lasted two hundred years. His appointment came after internal conflicts overwhelmed the Kamakura Shogunate, which had previously been in place. See Ashikaga Family.

ASHIKAGA YOSHIAKI

Best known as the last member of the Ashikaga family to serve as shogun. He was defeated by Oda Nobunaga in 1573.

BAK MEI

Founder of White Eyebrow Wushu, so-called because his hair, including his eyebrows, was entirely white. Because of his part in the betrayal of revolutionaries to the Ching dynasty, his art was lost for many years until one monk, Jok Fat, received permission to teach it.

BIMBA

A Capoeira master who helped legitimize Capoeira as a martial art early in the 20th century.

BODHIDHARMA

(c. 460 - 534 A.D.). A buddhist religious teacher, a patriarch of the dhyana or pure meditation sect of India. He created Chan Buddhism, known as Zen. Leaving India to proselytize in China, he arrived at the famous Shaolin Temple, where he is said to have taught martial arts to the monks, thus establishing the Shaolin Temple as the origin of martial arts in Asia. A famous story tells how he stared at a wall for nine years without moving from his seated position in an attempt to gain enlightenment. Allegedly, he wrote *I Chin Ching, (Muscle Changes Classic).* See Shaolin in the General Section. See *Muscle Changes Classic* in the Literature section.

BOW SIM MARK

A Wushu stylist credited with bringing Wushu to the Western world. She is a legendary performer in China and Hong Kong, and promotes Wushu in the United States. She teaches at Boston University.

CASILLAS, GRACIELA

(1956 -   ). An accomplished martial artist who was fundamental in establishing a professional division for female competitors in full contact Karate. In 1979, she became the first woman world champion in full contact Karate. She also won a number of world champion boxing bouts. She studied the Korean arts of Tae Kwon Do and Hwarang-do and now teaches the Philippine art Kali. She is retired from competition.

CHAN, JACKIE

(1954 -   ). A famous Chinese martial artist and movie star, Chan is beloved throughout Asia for his comic characters and stunning martial arts moves. He has acted since he was eight years old, and has set a number of box office records. Well-known to Hong Kong audiences, he has recently begun filming in America.

CHAN HUENG

(1806-1875). A Chinese Wushu master, the founder of the Choy Li Fut system, who was persuaded to move to San Francisco to teach martial arts to the Chinese community.

CHANG CHUNG CHIH

See Chang San Feng.

CHANG SAN FENG

(1279-1368). A Taoist priest, the legendary founder of Tai Chi Chuan, which came to him in a dream.

CHATAN YARA

An Okinawan who studied Wushu in China and founded a school which used weapons as well as empty-hand techniques, but emphasized the precise execution of forms. The forms he created are now part of the teaching at Shorinji-ryu schools.

CHAU QUAN KHI

(1895-1969). A Chinese martial arts master who fled to Vietnam during one of the many wars in China. In Vietnam he created a martial arts school based on Chinese styles. This is his adopted Vietnamese name, which he wished to be remembered by.

CHENG SAN FEN

See Chang San Feng.

CHIBA SHUSAKO

(1794-1855). Founder of the Hokushin-itto ryu school of Kenjutsu (swordfighting). This school emphasized the spiritual aspect of the art. The school originated contests between men armed with the shinai and women wielding the naginata (Japanese halberd). Such contests are still popularly practiced in Japan.

CHIBANA CHOSHIN

(1885-1969). A Karate master who taught the police his martial arts methods. He was student of the Okinawan "te" styles, and developed his own school, called Shorin-ryu. He developed two forms which are still widely used. He also founded an association of all Okinawan Karate styles.

CHINTO

A Chinese martial arts master who lived in Okinawa and assisted in the development of Okinawan te.

CHO HEE IL

(1940 -   ). A Tae Kwon Do master who studied directly under General Hong Hi Choi, the founder of Tae Kwon Do. He emigrated to the U.S. and established an international reputation as an instructor, martial artist and supporter of the martial arts. He has written many books and filmed many videos on his techniques.

CHO, HENRY

(1934 -   ). A Tae Kwon Do master credited with developing Tae Kwon Do in the United States.

CHOI, GENERAL HONG HI

(1918 -   ). A ninth degree black belt in Tae Kwon Do, Choi is generally credited as the founder of modern Tae Kwon Do. He is also the founder of the International Tae Kwon Do Federation, an important governing body for this Korean martial art. Choi survived a remarkable life as an activist, including a stretch in prison for planning to overthrow the Japanese government of Korea. After World War II ended, he became a martial arts instructor for the Korean Army. Soon he had developed Tae Kwon Do and was actively demonstrating it throughout Korea. He has written numerous books on his art.

CHUJO NAGAHIDE

A swordsman who introduced the Chujo-ryu style of Kenjutsu (swordfighting) around 1400. His school was the basis for many later styles of Kenjutsu.

CONFUCIUS

(551 - 479 B.C.). Latinized form of the name K'ung Fu Tzu, meaning Master K'ung. Little is known about the founder of Confucianism; only his teachings remain. He felt that the moral and political problems in China could be resolved by preserving the culture and society of the founders of the Chou dynasty (1030 - 256 B.C.) whom he thought very wise. Of course, no royal court was willing to accept his ideas, so instead he began to teach moral, social and political wisdom and ethics. Confucianism, along with Taoism and Buddhism, was the fundamental philosophy in the evolution of Wushu (Kung Fu). Confucianism is essentially a humanist belief. Its contributed to the development of Wushu and thus other martial arts styles.

Nine books are based on his teachings: *Book of Changes*, *Book of Poetry*, *Book of History*, *Book of Ceremonies and Rites*, *Spring and Autumn Annals*, *Analects* (a collection of his sayings), *The Great Learning*, *Doctrine of the Mean* and *Book of Mencius*. See the Literature section.

DAIDOJI YUSAN

(1639-1730). A martial arts master who wrote *Budo-shoshi-su (Elementary Readings in Budo)*, which deals with the principles and ethics of the samurai.

DEOK MOO LEE

Wrote an early Korean martial arts textbook called *Mu Yei Do Bo Tong Ji* in 1790.

DILLMAN, GEORGE

One of the major American Karate forms competitors. Now a martial arts instructor, Dillman studied several forms of Karate as well as Wushu.

DRAEGER, DONN

Famous martial arts historian. A prolific writer, he was a weapons expert and had studied and earned black belts in numerous martial arts.

EISAI

(1141-1215). He is sometimes called the founder of Zen Buddhism in Japan, but actually he tried to give Zen a more independent position in the culture. The drinking of tea and the tea ceremony are in memory of him.

EISHIN

His full name is Eishin Hasegawa Chikara-no-Suke Hidenbou. An 18th century Iaijutsu (sword drawing) master, he founded an important school,

Hasegawa Eishin-ryu, which was later shortened to Eishin-ryu.

EISHIN HASEGAWA CHIKARA-NO-SUKE HIDENOBOU

See Eishin.

FA HSIEN

A Chinese explorer who in the fourth century A.D. traveled to India and returned with Buddhist writings.

FUJIWARA KAMATORI

The founder of Koden-ryu Jujutsu in the seventh century. He was a member of the Fujiwara family, an important martial arts family who ruled Japan from the ninth through the twelfth centuries.

FUKUDA KEIKO

(1913 -). The senior instructor at the Kodokan's women's section. Fukuda was the first woman to earn a sixth degree black belt in Judo and remains one of the highest ranked Judo practitioners in the world.

FUNAKOSHI GICHIN

(1869 - 1957). The founder of modern Karate, in particular the Shotokan style. He was famous as a writer, teacher and martial arts supporter. Funakoshi began his Karate training at a young age and studied under many of the best masters. He became famous for his Okinawan Karate demonstrations and was invited to Japan to instruct martial artists there. Soon Karate had spread throughout the world. Its popularity was only briefly interrupted by World War II. See Karate in the Schools and Styles section.

FURUMARU

The pen name of the warrior, Yamamoto Tsunetomo, who wrote *Hagakure* (*Hidden Beneath the Leaves*), a work on the martial arts and the ethical principle of self-sacrifice.

GENERAL CHOI

See Choi, General Hong Hi.

GENJI FAMILY

See Minamoto Family.

GRACIE FAMILY

Modern founders of a Brazilian style of Jujutsu called Gracie Jujutsu.

HALL, MARCIA

(1956 -). In 1978, Hall became the first American to win a gold medal in an international Tae Kwon Do competition. Hall trained in both Karate and Tae Kwon Do and though she has retired from competition, she continues to teach Tae Kwon Do.

HAYASHIZAKI JINSUE JINNOSUKE MINAMOTO SHIGENOBOU

A 16th century swordsmaster who created the Hojo school of Iaido (sword drawing art). The school achieved great acclaim under Eishin and was renamed for him, as Muso Jikiden Eishin-ryu.

HEIKI DANJO

The founder of Heiki-ryu, an early school of combat archery.

HIRONORI OHTSUKA

See Otsuka Hidenori.

HIUEN TSAING

A Chinese explorer who traveled to India in the fourth century and brought Buddhist scriptures back with him.

HOSHI TETSUOMI

A disciple of Ueshiba Morihei, the founder of Aikido, Hoshi created a form of Aikido called Kobu-jutsu, which is a system of pure self-defense.

HOSHINO KANZAEMON

A champion archery target shooter who was defeated in 1686 by Wasa Daiichiro, whose performance has never been equalled.

HUA TO

(190-265 A.D.). A famous physician who created a series of exercises based on the movements and qualities of the Five Animals (tiger, bear, bird, deer and monkey). This series of exercises was called Five Animals Play. It is thought that it formed the basis for Wushu styles that incorporate the movements of the Five Animals.

IIZASA CHOISAI IENAO

(1387-1488). A swordsman who created a school of Kenjutsu (swordfighting) and lance techniques (So-jutsu). His school, Tenshin Shoden Katori Shinto-ryu, is the oldest extant martial arts school in Japan.

IIZASA CHOISAI

See Iizasa Choisai Ienao.

INSOSANTO, DAN

(1936 -   ). A famous martial arts instructor who studied under both Ed Parker and Bruce Lee. He teaches Philippine martial arts, and is one of three people originally authorized by Bruce Lee to teach Jeet Kune Do.

ITSUSAI CHOZANSHI

(1659-1741). A martial artist who wrote a martial arts work, *Tengu Geijutsu-ron (Treatise on the Martial arts of the Tengu)*, which was influenced by Zen and Confucian philosophies.

ITTO ITTOSAI KAGEHISA

(1560-1653). Founder of the Itto ryu school of Kenjutsu (swordfighting). His school was known as the one-sword school because he used one sword held with both hands. This style had a great influence on Kendo.

IZASA IENAO

See Iizasa Choisai Ienao.

IZUMO NO KANJA YOSHITERA

Founded Shinden Fudo Ryu, a So-jutsu (lance art) school, in the mid-15th century.

JAE KA PARK

With Deok Moo Lee, he wrote an early Korean textbook on the martial arts, called *Mu Yei Do Bo Tong Ji* in 1790.

JHOON RHEE

(1932 -   ). A Korean martial arts master called the father of American Tae Kwon Do. A famous instructor, he has taught federal agents and police officers, and operates several dozen schools. He emphasizes the sport aspect of the martial arts, and is credited with teaching some of the finest martial artists in the United States.

JOK FAT

A monk who resurrected the White Eyebrows style of Wushu.

KANO JIGORO

(1860-1938). The famous founder of Judo. He studied martial arts all his life, first learning Jujutsu and then studying other arts. In 1882, he created his own school by combining various techniques from Jujutsu schools. His goal was to create a sport that was less dangerous than traditional martial arts, especially Jujutsu, and better able to meet people's needs. He was often sent to China and Europe to teach Judo. See Judo in the Schools and Styles section.

KANRYO HIGASHIONNA

(1851-1915). A Confucian scholar who was also an Okinawan Karate master of Naha-te. He is considered one of the most influential Karate instructors in Okinawan history. In his early teens, he traveled to China and spent many years training under the famous Chinese Kempo master, Liu Liu Ko. When he returned home, he introduced a new school of Karate, which combined hard and soft techniques into one system.

KHARLAMPIEV, ANATOLY

The founder of Sambo, a Russian form of wrestling. He studied Judo and wrestling before devising Sambo, which has become a Russian national sport rather than a method of self-defense.

KOIZUMI GUNJI GINGYO

(1885-1965) A follower of Kano Jigoro, the founder of Judo. As a child, he learned Jujutsu and Kenjutsu. Judo came late in life. In 1918, he opened a Judo school in London, which he called the Budokwai, The Way of Knighthood Society.

KOU TZE

Chinese Wushu master who founded the Monkey style around 1900. He developed his art during a long imprisonment, based on the movements of monkeys he observed.

K UNG FU TZU

See Confucius.

LAO TZE

He is also called Lao Tzu. A Chinese scholar and philosopher, he founded Taoism in the sixth century B.C. This philosophy greatly influenced martial arts. The book *Tao Te Ching* describes his philosophy. See *Tao Te Ching* in the Literature section.

LEE, BRUCE

(1940-1974). Famous martial arts practitioner who invented Jeet Kune Do, the way of the intercepting fist, which he also called the way of no way. Best known as a film actor, he was born in San Francisco, but was raised in Hong Kong, where he studied street fighting as well as martial arts. He migrated to the United States, where he continued to study and teach Wushu. He developed the Jun Fan school of Wushu derived from Wing Chun Wushu before developing his theories of Jeet Kune Do. Later, he returned to Hong Kong, where he began to act in Wushu (Kung Fu) movies, which were a great success. He died under unusual circumstances while making one of these films.

LEE, JAMES Y

(1920 - 1972). One of three original people authorized by Bruce Lee to teach Jeet Kune Do. He operated a Wushu studio with Lee and later owned a martial arts publishing firm.

LEWIS, JOE

(1944 -   ). A famous Karate competitor who developed full-contact Karate. He now teaches seminars and writes about martial arts.

MAKINO TORU

A martial artist who wrote a famous book on Kendo (sword art), called *Kendo Shugyo-no-shiori (Kendo Training)* in 1930. He emphasized the value of loyalty that martial arts could encourage.

MATSUMURA SOKON

(1809-1899). An Okinawan martial arts master who studied sword fighting and Kempo, then founded the Shuri-te style of Okinawan Karate.

MAUNG GYE

(1933 -   ). Founder of the American Bando Association.

MINAMOTO HIDETSUNA

(1584 - 1638). Founder of Araki-ryu, a school of Kendo (sword fighting). His school used round wooden swords, the forerunner of the shinai. He later changed his name to Araki Mujinsai.

MINAMOTO NO YOSHITSUNE

(1159 - 1189). A famous warrior who helped his brother, Minamoto no Yoritomo, establish the first shogunate. Minamoto's brother allegedly suffered from envy and attacked him. For this reason, Minamoto committed seppuku, ritual suicide. He is honored as the ideal samurai.

MINAMOTO NO MASATARI

Founder of the Tenjin Shinyo-ryu, an early-19th century school that emphasized vital point striking and resuscitation skills.

MINAMOTO NO MASAYOSHI

See Takeda Sokaku.

MINAMOTO FAMILY

A ruling family that established the first shogunate in 1192 under Minamoto no Yoritomo. The family produced many important military and political figures. They are related to the famous Ashikaga family as well. Often called the Genji Family.

MINAMOTO NO YORITOMO

Member of the Minamoto Family, a warrior clan, who established the first shogunate in 1192. He became the most famous warrior of his time. See Minamoto Clan and Minamoto no Yoshitsune.

MIYAGI CHOJUN

(1888 - 1953). In 1930, this Okinawan Karate master founded the important Karate school called Goju-ryu. This school emphasizes slow movements and correct breathing. As a result of his untiring efforts on behalf of Karate, it was recognized officially as one of the martial arts of Japan.

MIYAMOTO MUSASHI

(1584 - 1645). Probably the most famous samurai who ever lived. His father, who taught him the art of swordsmanship, was murdered by a member of a rival clan. Miyamoto Musashi waited and trained and when his skills were exceptional, he killed his father's murderer.

He created a school of sword fighting called Niten Ichi-ryu, the two-sword school. He is also the writer of the famous *Book of Five Rings* about the techniques and philosophy of the art of swordfighting.

MOMON-I SHUNZO

(1826 - 1886). A weapons expert who opened a martial arts school in Edo (Tokyo), where he taught many samuari who were opposed to the shogunate of Edo, which eventually led to the return of direct rule by the emperor.

NAKANO MICHIOMI

See So Doshin.

NAKAYAMA MASATOSHI

(1913 - 1987). A martial arts expert who studied Karate with Funakoshi Gichin. With Funakoshi, he created the Japan Karate Association, whose experts were sent to other countries to teach. After Funakoshi's death, he organized Karate championships, which Funakoshi had objected to all his life.

NG MU

A Shaolin temple elder who fled the destruction of the monastery. She taught her martial arts techniques to Yim Wing Chun, who then created Wing Chun Wushu.

NGO DONG

The Vietnamese founder of Cuong Nhu. After studying a number of martial arts, he founded this school in 1965. He was arrested by the Communist government in 1975, but he escaped to the United States in 1977 where he established numerous branches of his school.

NIGGEL, BARBARA

A famous Karate champion, renowned for winning forms competitions in both men's and women's categories.

NORRIS, CHUCK

(1940 -   ). Professional Karate competitor turned actor. In addition to his acting career in both television and movies, he has taught numerous students, has written a series of books and is the founder of the United Fighting Arts Federation.

ODA NOBUNGA

(1534 - 1582). A powerful warrior who defeated the Ashikaga family. He ruthlessly suppressed numerous monasteries (known for harboring rivals and rebels). Unable to fulfill his dream of ruling all Japan, he committed seppuku, ritual suicide.

OHTSUKA HIDENORI

See Otsuka Hidenori.

OTSUKA HIDENORI

(1892 - 1982). Founder of the Wado-ryu school of Karate. He studied under Funakoshi Gichin, the founder of modern Karate. Otsuka's style emphasizes soft, evasive motions as opposed to hard striking movements.

PARKER, ED

(1931 - 1990). Founder of one of the first commercial Karate schools in the United States. He is called the father of American Karate, and taught a special style of Kenpo.

PASTINHA

A Capoeira master, early in the century, who taught his martial art in schools and helped bring legitimacy to Capoeira.

P U-T I-TA-MO

See Bodhidharma.

SAIGO TAKAMORI

(1827-1877). An important samurai who helped restore the Emperor Meiji to power. However, he came to disapprove of government policies and retired from service. With several thousand students, he studied weaponry in secret. In 1877, he became a leader in the Satsuma Rebellion. He was defeated and was obliged to commit ritual suicide.

SAKA NO UEUTAMORO

Founder of Kazei-ryu Jujutsu, which he developed from Koden-ryu.

SAKAKIBARA KENKICHI

(1830-1894). A martial arts master who invented several important Kendo (swordfighting art) techniques. He toured Japan giving demonstrations to revitalize this formerly neglected art.

SEAGAL, STEVEN

(1952 -   ). Famous movie star and martial artist. As a young child, he trained in a variety of martial arts, including Aikido. When he was 17, he traveled to Japan to further his knowledge. Several years later, he opened a school there which was attended by students from all over the world. Eventually, he returned to the United States and opened a martial arts school in California, eventually moving to Hollywood, where he launched his acting career. He is now a seventh degree black belt in Aikido, and teaches seminars in addition to acting.

SEKISHUSAI
See Yagyu Muneyoshi.

SHIRAI TORU
(1783-1850). A famous martial arts master of Itto-ryu (sword fighting), he wrote a work on sword techniques called *Huoho Michi Shirube* (*Traveling the Way of the Sword*).

SHUN-TZU
See Sun Tzu.

SHUNZI
See Sun Tzu.

SO DOSHIN
(1911 - 1980). Founder of Shorinji Kempo, a religious sect that is also a martial art. He studied in both China and Japan, then adapted the methods he had learned. His real name is Nakano Michiomi.

SONSHI
See Sun Tzu.

SU IN HYUK
(1939 -   ). Founder of the Korean Martial Arts Association, known as Kuk Sool Won, a martial art style that has spread throughout the world.

SUN TZU
Fourth century B.C. military leader who was famed for his strategic abilities. According to tradition, he created the first techniques of military strategy and is also credited with recruiting and commanding an entirely female army, made of the king's concubines. His work on warfare, *Sun Tzu Bingfa* (*The Art of War*), is the oldest work on martial arts to survive. He emphasized victory through the use of strategy, not force or size.

SUN-TZE
See Sun Tzu.

TAI YUK
Founder of Dragon Style Wushu.

TAKEDA SOKAKU
(1852-1943). A swordsman whose adventures have become legendary. As a young man, he travelled throughout Japan, challenging opponents. The government eventually confiscated his sword, whereupon he opened his own martial arts school called the Daito-ryu.

TAKENOUCHI HISAMORI
The founder of a school of self-defense called Takenouchi-ryu, in the early 16th century. The school taught the use of short weapons and emphasized defense against warriors in light armor. The school also taught methods of Jujutsu and immobilization techniques.

TAKUAN
(1573-1645) A Zen monk who formulated many of the beliefs of the samurai, and who posited the existence of various states of consciousness that could be instrumental to the success of a warrior.

TAKY KIMURA
A martial arts instructor, one of three people originally authorized by Bruce Lee to teach Jeet Kune Do.

TAMO
See Bodhidharma.

TAN GUN
Legendary founder of Korea in 2333 B.C. A form in the International Tae Kwon Do Federation system of Tae Kwon Do is named after him.

TERAO KASTUNOBU
A follower of Miyamoto Musashi who helped him write his famous treatise on swordsmanship, *The Book of Five Rings*.

TOKUGAWA IEYASU
(1542-1616). The founder of a famous warrior family, he was named shogun in 1603, thus ushering in the era of the Tokugawa shogunate. He attempted to unify the country and was killed from wounds received while taking the last castle of his rivals. His family ruled until the restoration of the emperor in 1868.

TSUJI GETTEN SAKEMOCHI

(1650- 1729). A commoner who founded Mugai-ryu, a school of Kenjutsu (swordfighting) that emphasized the spiritual aspect of the art.

UESHIBA MORIHEI

(1883-1969). The founder of Aikido. As a child, he suffered many illnesses but became healthier through regular physical exercise. As a young adult, he took a martial arts course and continued studying under various masters. In 1908, he received his teacher's certificate and immediately opened a school. He met Takeda Sokaku in 1915, who taught him and gave him a master's diploma. Political intrigues followed, but in the 1920s, he returned to his studies and perfected his techniques. Still, his political activism caused him difficulty, including a governmental closure of his school. In 1938, he named his collection of techniques Aikido. In 1949, he was allowed to reopen a school in Tokyo. By the time of his death, he was universally respected and admired.

VAN DAMME, JEAN-CLAUDE

A Belgian martial artist and movie star who turned his kickboxing career into an acting career in the 1980s.

WALLACE, BILL

(1945 -   ). A famous Karate competitor, he is known by the nickname Superfoot, because of the speed of his kicks. Now retired, he has conducted seminars and has written several text books.

WANG TSUNG-YUEH

A master of Tai Chi Chuan, he formalized and systematized the techniques and added a philosphical underpinning that he acquired from Taoism.

WASA DAIICHIRO

(1663-1713). A Japanese archer who, in 1686, set a record for shooting the most arrows at a target correctly. The performance has never been equalled, though many attempts have been made.

WILSON, DON

(1954 -   ). Known as the Dragon, a famous American full-contact Karate competitor.

WON HYO

The monk who introduced Buddhism to the Silla dynasty in Korea in 686. An International Tae Kwon Do Federation form is named after him.

WONG LONG

Founder of Praying Mantis Wushu.

YAGYU MUNENORI TAJIMA NO KAMI

(1571-1646). A martial arts master who assisted the shogun Tokugawa Ieyasu (who ruled 1623-1657). Yagyu wrote several books on martial arts and with his father, Yagyu Muneyoshi, founded the Yagyu-ryu school of swordsmanship.

YAGYU MUNEYOSHI

Founder of Yagyu-ryu school of sword fighting. Also known as Sekishusai.

YAMADA JIROKICHI

(1863-1931). A martial artist who revitalized Kendo (sword fighting art) through his writings. He emphasized the importance of spiritual as well as physical exercise and attempted to demonstrate how Kendo could develop admirable qualities in any individual who took up the practice.

YAMAGE SOKO

(1622-1685). A samurai who followed Confucianism. He felt that the samurai, following Confucian principles, should rule the country. He founded a school of martial arts called Yamaga-ryu, which taught martial artists to be ethically and morally responsible.

YAMAMOTO TSUNETOMO

See Furumaru.

YANAGI SEKIZAI MINAMOTO NO MASTARI

See Minamoto no Masatari.

YANG LUSHAN

(1799-1872). Founder of the Yang style of Tai Chi Chuan, generally accepted as the most popular style of Tai Chi Chuan. He is credited with spreading T'ai Chi throughout China.

YANG LU-CHAN

See Yang Lushan

YI HWANG

A noted Korean scholar, an authority on neo-Confucianism who lived in the 16th century. The International Tae Kwon Do Federation Tae Kwon Do form Toi Gye (his pseudonym) is named for him.

YI I

(1536-1584). This great scholar was known as the Confucious of Korea. The International Tae Kwon Do Federation form Yul Kok (his pseudonym) is named after him.

YI SUN SIN

A Korean Admiral who is reputed to have invented the first armored battleship in 1592. This ship is considered the precursor of the submarine. The International Tae Kwon Do Federation form Chung Mu is named after him.

YIM WING CHUN

The legendary founder of Wing Chun Wushu, she created the style using techniques from the Shaolin nun Ng Mu.

YIP MAN

(? - 1972). Famous Wing Chun grandmaster who began training at age 13. He taught the police his martial arts methods but is most famous for instructing Bruce Lee in Hong Kong. He was the first Wing Chun master to teach his style publicly.

YOSHITSUNE

See Minamoto no Yoshitsune.

LITERATURE

The literature of the martial arts comprises philosophical as well as military treatises. Anyone who is involved in the study of combative arts should consider seriously the study of strategy in warfare. This goes beyond techniques and forms and allows the student to grasp the principles, tactics, theories and strategies of the martial arts. The study of Asian martial arts requires the study of Asian classics of theory and philosophy.

Fig 6.1 : Shelves of books about martial arts schools, philosophies and styles.

In classical Japan, noblemen learned the arts of conduct: music, archery, chariot driving, writing and arithmetic. There were four books on neo-Confucianism that were required for an orthodox education in Japan under martial rule. These were *The Great Learning*, *The Book of Mencius*, *The Doctrine of the Mean* (sometimes called *Balance in the Center*) and *Analects*. Together they were called the Four Books. These were ancient Chinese literary texts dealing with fundamental Confucian teachings. They were grouped together by the philosopher Chu Hsi in 1190. *The Great Learning* and *The Doctrine of the Mean* are chapters from the *Book of Rites*, mentioned below, but because of their importance were treated individually as well. The Five Classics were linked with the Four Books to create the canon of Confucianism, the underlying philosophy of all martial arts.

The Five Classics are ancient Chinese literary works that include the *Book of History*, *Book of Odes*, *Book of Changes*, *Book of Rites* and *Spring and Autumn Annals*. Since the second century B.C., these books were to the East what the Bible was to the West.

An Imperial university was established in 142 B.C. with five departments corresponding to the Five Classics, which public officials had to study. The Five Classics and the Four Books were basic to education and from 1313 to 1905 were the basis of civil service exams.

Indian literature was also important. Sanskrit literature contains the roots of religious, philosophical and scientific thinking in Asia. Sanskrit was the sacred language of the Brahmins in India. Indian literature consists of this Sanskrit literature plus Vedic literature. The *Rig Veda*, the best known text in Vedic literature, is the oldest document extant in Sanskrit literature. Vedic literature consists of important texts of Indian philosophy and religious beliefs. The *Rig Veda*, *Yajur Veda*, *Sama Veda* and *Atharva Veda* are the most important. These are the sacred books of India, comparable to the Bible in the West.

AKO-GISHI

See *The Forty Seven Ronin*.

ANALECTS

This collection of Confucius sayings is also called *Conversations*. The wisdom collected here concerns his teachings and is considered the most authentic collection of his thoughts and ethical discussions. The work was compiled shortly after his death in 479. It is one of the Four Books on neo-Confucian philosophy taught to young adults in China and Japan.

ART OF WAR, THE

The oldest extant book on the martial arts, it details military strategy and was written by the famous Sun Tsu. Called *Sun Tsu Bingfa*.

BALANCE IN THE CENTER

See *Doctrine of the Mean, The*.

BANSENSHUKA

See *Hundred Thousand Rivers, A*.

BIBLE OF THE SAMURAI, THE

A work for samurai written in the 17th century by an unknown author. It details the appropriate behavior of a warrior-philosopher. It is nicknamed the Bible of the Samurai, in reference to its importance as a guide to the way of the warrior. Called *Koyo-gunkan*.

BOOK OF CHANGES

Called the *I-Ching*. This ancient Chinese text, written in the Chou dynasty (1122- 255 B.C.) is a book of divination and wisdom. All the parts of life, and the actions of people are represented by 64 hexagrams, made by combining the signs for yin (- -) and yang (—).

Eight different trigrams are combined in pairs to indicate an interpretation of events. The trigrams stand for the qualities of creating, yielding, beginning, trouble, inertia, gentleness, discord and temptation. Any quality of a subject can be represented by these symbols.

The book is also a mathematical treatise and is the origin of many Tao and Confucian ideas. The book also includes texts of interpretation, philosophical commentary and explanations for events and human experience. It is one of the Five Classics taught to all young adults in China and Japan.

BOOK OF HISTORY

Called *Shu Ching*. Written about the first century B.C., it is a collection of historical documents and speeches from the remote past to the Chou Dynasty (1122-255 B.C). Confucius is thought to have made use of these documents. The collection describes the emperor watching wrestling, among other things of interest to martial artists. It is one of the Five Classics taught to all young adults in China and Japan.

BOOK OF FIVE RINGS, THE

This famous text is by Miyamoto Musashi,who also wrote the *Mirror of the Way* and the *Thirty-Five Articles of Strategy*. This, his major work, concentrates on sword fighting (Kenjutsu), in particular the two-sword school he founded. The

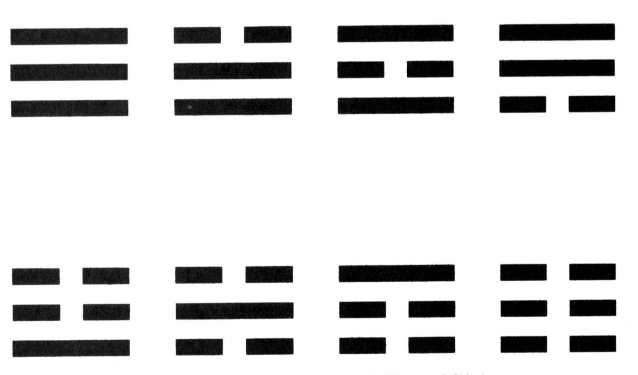

Fig 6.2 : The eight hexagrams from The Book of Changes (I-Ching).

five scrolls it is written on each have a name — "Concerning Earth," "Concerning Water," and so on. The five scrolls correspond with the Five Elements (earth, water, fire, wind, sky). These Five Elements are fundamental to Eastern philosophy. The book emphasizes the spirit of martial arts, instead of merely describing techniques.

BOOK OF MENCIUS

This book collects the teachings of Meng Tzu, a Confucian philosopher. It was written around 290 B.C. Meng Tzu was a great literary artist and philosopher who exalted Confucius. He describes virtue as the natural expression of four fundamental human feelings: compassion, reverence, modesty and moral discrimination. These fundamental feelings produce the virtues of benevolent love, rightness, proper conduct, and wisdom. He asserts the moral wrongness of war and suggests that heaven's will can be found in the will of popular opinion. It is one of the Four Books of neo-Confucian thought taught to all young people in China and Japan.

BOOK OF ODES

Known as *Shih Ching*, it is also called *Book of Songs*. It consists of hundreds of poems used in political and religious functions, each with moral significance. Confucius used these songs in his teachings. The book was written about the fourth century B.C. It is one of the Five Classics taught to all young adults in China and Japan.

BOOK OF RITES

This work dates from the Chou dynasty (1122-255 B.C.) in China. Also called *The Record of Ceremonies*. It is a collection of treatises on social ceremonies, religious rites, and etiquette and describes the principles underpinning them. It also contains martial arts information, as it mentions displays of archery, fencing and wrestling. Called *Li Chi*. It is one of the Five Classics taught to all young adults in China and Japan.

BUDO SHOSHINSU

See *Elementary Readings in Budo*.

BUKE SHO-HATTO

See *Rules of the Warrior Families*.

BUSHIDO

The complete title is *Bushido: the Soul of Japan*. It was written by Inazo Nitobe, in 1899. The term bushido was invented by the author to mean the way of the warrior. Nitobe was the primary teacher of Japanese customs to the West. His description of bushido lent it a romantic aura, and the idea of bushido led to the rise of nationalism in Japan. The book describes the essence of the way of the warrior, and the meaning of chivalry. It includes the seven virtues of justice, courage, benevolence, politeness, veracity, honor and loyalty.

CHRONICLES OF JAPAN, THE

This is a record of historical events in the order of their occurrence. There is little personal interpretation of facts and the writer is merely recounting events, not creating a literary work. These chronicles, from around the eighth century, are sometimes the only source of valuable information about this period in Japanese history. These chronicles describe displays of martial arts, including wrestling. The book is called *Nihongi*.

CHUN CHIU

See *Spring and Autumn Annals*.

CHUNG YUNG

See *Doctrine of the Mean, The*.

CHUSHINGURA

See *The Forty Seven Ronin*.

CLASSICS OF THE YELLOW EMPEROR

See Yellow Emperor, The.

CULLAVAGGA

This is an Indian Buddhist canonical text restricting martial arts practice by Buddhists.

DOCTRINE OF THE MEAN

A work containing 33 chapters of Confucian sayings. It discusses the proper balance of human actions that will bring humans into harmony with the underlying truth of the universe. It discusses human existence and the nature of the universe. It is ascribed to Confucius' grandson, Tzu Ssu. It is one of the Four Books of neo-Confucian thought taught to all young people in China and Japan. It is called *Chung Yung*.

ELEMENTARY READINGS IN BUDO

Written by Daidoji Yusan (1639-1730), this is a work on martial arts, but it focuses on bushido, or the way of the warrior (though it does not use this term itself). It deals with the virtues of loyalty and dignity, and preparation for death. It describes the principles of the samurai and is filled with neo-Confucianism philosophy. Called *Budo-Shoshinsu*.

FORTY SEVEN RONIN, THE

This is the true story of the ronin, masterless samurai, who avenged the death of their master. It is held as a classic example of the ethical code of bushido, or the way of the warrior, because it demonstrates how samurai should behave. It is also called *Ako-gishi* or *Chushinguru*. It recounts the tale of 47 warriors in service of Asano Naganori, lord of Ako. In 1701, in the court of the shogun at Edo (Tokyo), Asano was insulted by the behavior of another lord, whom he subsequently wounded at the palace. Since this action was discourteous (especially since he had unsheathed a weapon in the shogun's castle), Asano was obliged to commit seppuku, or ritual suicide. This left his 47 warriors without a master.

They vowed revenge on the person who had caused the tragedy by insulting their lord. They hid and prepared for two years, leaving their families, pretending to turn into drunkards to allay suspicions. Then, on December 14, 1702, they attacked the insulting lord's home and killed him, then surrendered themselves to authorities. They were ordered to commit seppuku, which they did, in front of their master's tomb. People called them heroes and they became symbols of courage and loyalty. People still place flowers on their tombs.

FUDOCHI SHIMMEIROKU

This book of wisdom was written by the Buddhist monk Takuan (1573-1645) for martial artist Yagyu Munenori (1571-1646). The book describes fudoshin, the calm and serene state of mind the warrior should have, according to Zen doctrine.

GEMPEI SEISUIKI

See *Record of the Rise and Fall of the Minoamoto and Taira*.

GLIMPSES OF ENTERTAINING THINGS

This book is similar to the *Chronicles of Japan*, except that it confines itself to events and activities of unusual interest, instead of recounting historical events as they happened. It was written about 1818 and describes Sumo wrestling in detail. It is called *Kiyushoran*.

GORIN-NO-SHO

See *Book of Five Rings, The*.

GREAT DOCTRINE OF ARCHERY, THE

This is the Japanese name of a Chinese work written during the Ming Dynasty (1374 - 1644), describing archery techniques; it considers Kyudo and Kyujutsu to be noble arts.

GREAT LEARNING, THE

This short treatise on the Confucian doctrine of education asserts that self-development, and harmony in the family, nation and world all stem from understanding gained through the investigation of things. Actively seeking knowledge, then, is both noble and ethical. One of the Four Books of neo-Confucian doctrine taught to young adults in China and Japan.

HAGAKURE

See *Hidden Beneath the Leaves*.

HAN BOOK OF ARTS

Written near the first century, this book describes important events and happenings in the Han Dynasty (206 B.C. to 220 A.D.) It describes martial arts tournaments among other events of interest.

HAN SHU

See *Han Book of Arts*.

HIDDEN BENEATH THE LEAVES

Written in 1716 by a samurai, Yamamoto Tsuentomo, this work deals with the spirit of bushido and the martial arts. It emphasizes the ideal of self-sacrifice in service to one's master. It is called *Hagakure*.

HISTORY OF THE T'ANG DYNASTY

This book, called *T'ang Yu Lin*, chronicles events of the T'ang dynasty and describes martial arts tournaments during this period.

HUANG DI NEI JING

See *Yellow Emperor, The.*

HUNDRED THOUSAND RIVERS, A

This book was written by Fujibayashi in 1676, a Ninja expert who belonged to the Iga-ryu school of Ninjutsu. It details the art of Ninjutsu, especially the physical and philosophical sides.

HYOHO-KYO

See *Mirror of the Way.*

HYOHO-SANJUGO

See *Thirty-five Articles on Strategy.*

I CHING

See *Book of Changes.*

I-CHING CHING

See *Muscle Changes Classic.*

KENDO RON

See *Treatise on Kendo.*

KIYUSHORAN

See *Glimpses of Entertaining Things.*

KOYO-GUNKAN

See *Bible of the Samurai.*

LI CHI

See *Book of Rites.*

LUN YU

See Analects.

MAHABHARATA

This Indian work of literature is one of two great classical Sanskrit epics of ancient India, the other being *Ramayana*. It is attributed to the poet Vyasa, but many people contributed to it. A long work, consisting of over 100,000 couplets in 18 books, it includes myths, folk tales, religious poems and a central narrative that involves a war. It collects theology and morality and is the most important source of information about Hindu ideals. It depicts the famous method of Indian wrestling.

MALLAPURANA

This is an Indian work written before 1650, which discusses the art of wrestling.

MANASOLLASA

This work was commissioned by the Indian king Someshvar (1124-1138). It gives details of Indian wrestling. It provides information on the etiquette, diet, and training of the professional caste of wrestlers.

MIRROR OF THE WAY

This treatise is by Miyamoto Musashi, whose most famous work is the *Book of Five Rings*. He also wrote *Thirty-five Articles on Strategy*. This classic, *Mirror of the Way*, deals with the art of strategy, especially the state of mind necessary for fighting.

MU YEI DO BO TONG JI

This early martial arts textbook on Korean styles was written by Deok Moo Lee and Jae Ka Park, and was published in 1790.

MUSCLE CHANGES CLASSIC

This book, called the *I-Ching Ching*, was reportedly written by Bodhidharma, the Indian monk who, according to legend, brought martial arts to China from India. The exercises in the book are calisthenics, not closely related to Chinese boxing.

NOHONGI

See *Chronicles of Japan, The.*

RAMAYANA

Literally, the adventures of Rama. It is one of India's two Sanskrit epics, the other being the *Mahabharata*. It consists of about 24,000 couplets and is ascribed to a single author, Valmiki. It honors Rama as an incarnation of the god Vishnu who rids the world of the demon Ravana. It depicts war and martial arts such as wrestling contests and asserts the virtue of loyalty and other qualities that the Japanese called bushido.

RECORD OF THE RISE AND FALL OF THE MINAMOTO AND THE TAIRA

A mid-13th century historical account of the two families, Minamoto and Taira. It includes many tales of wrestling plus other martial arts and war tales. Called *Gempei Seisuiki*.

RIG VEDA

One of the cornerstones of Vedic literature, that is, religious literature for ritual and philosophical use. It means literally *Book of Knowledge*, and is a book of hymns compiled before 1000 B.C. Over 1000 hymns are included for use in ritual. A related book, *Sama Veda*, is composed of chants for ritual. The *Yajur Veda* is prose formulas for sacrificial rituals. The *Atharva Veda* provides material for private religious use.

RULES OF THE WARRIOR FAMILIES

This text was composed on the order of the shogun in 1615, by the Zen buddhist monk Suden and others. This code emphasizes the study of literature, weapons, and so on, for the warrior class.

SHAGAKUSEIDO

See *Great Doctrine of Archery, The*.

SHIH CHI

See *Book of History*.

SHU CHING

See *Book of Odes*.

SHUYO SHOSEI RON

See *Treatise on the Education of the Mind and Instruction on Life*.

SPRING AND AUTUMN ANNALS, THE

This historical account of Confucius' native state of Lu, from 722-481 B.C., is brief and factual. It mentions archery, fencing and wrestling as performed by nobles. It is one of the Five Classics taught to young adults in China and Japan.

SUN TSU BINGFA

See *Art of War*.

TA HSUEH

See *Great Learning, The*.

TAO TE CHING

This is the canonical text of Taoism, the book of the way and of virtue. Originally written in reaction to Confucianism, it asserts that above the physical universe is a higher plane, the Tao, and that the spiritual must be experienced intuitively, not intellectually. Also called *Tao teh king*.

T'ANG YU LIN

See *History of the T'ang Dynasty*.

TENGU GEIJUTSU-RON

See *Treatise on the Martial Arts of the Tengu (Mythical Beings)*.

THIRTY-FIVE ARTICLES ON STRATEGY

This work is by Miyamoto Musashi, whose most famous work is the *Book of Five Rings*. He also wrote *The Mirror of the Way*, a book on military strategy. The *Thirty-five Articles* also deals with the art of strategy, especially the connection of mind and body, and mind and technique.

TREASURES OF THE FAITHFUL RETAINERS, THE

See *The Forty Seven Ronin*.

TREATISE ON THE MARTIAL ARTS OF THE TENGU (MYTHICAL BEINGS)

Written by a sword master, Itsusai Chozanshi, 1659-1741, this book describes martial arts. Its philosophy is a mixture of Zen and neo-Confucianism.

TREATISE ON THE EDUCATION OF THE MIND AND INSTRUCTION ON LIFE

Written by Yamada Jirokichi (1863-1931), a samurai who felt Kendo should be considered a noble art. In this writing he emphasized the necessity of individual and social morality. He also wrote *Treatise on Kendo*.

TREATISE ON KENDO

Written by a samurai, Yamada Jirokichi (1863-1931), who insisted that Kendo was a noble art. In this writing, he expressed the relationship of Zen and the sword, and emphasized that Kendo was a way of life, not a sport. He also wrote *Treatise on the Education of the Mind and Instruction on Life*.

UPANISHADS

This series of Indian texts deals with the nature of the universe and the human soul. These were the first written texts to develop the Hindu doctrine of rebirth and karma. They also speak of Yoga, as an aid to meditation. Written about 500 B.C.

YELLOW EMPEROR, THE

One of the earliest works on Chinese healing and holistic philosophy, written in 2697 B.C. It provides detailed descriptions of the action of chi.

YIJING

Same as *I-Ching*. See *Book of Changes*.

COUNTRIES OF ORIGIN

and became a means of self-defense. It relied primarily on leg techniques since the practitioner's hands were often chained. This development took place in Brazil, but the original dances can still be seen in Africa today.

AFRICA

Martial art:

Capoeira

The continent of Africa is comprised of numerous countries, most of which were at some time under the colonial rule of France, Great Britain, Belgium, Spain, Portugal or the United States. Prior to colonization, independent African kingdoms existed and trade flourished. African natives had contact with China as early as the 13th century. Islamic culture was prevalent in North Africa by this time as well. It had reached the continent in the eighth century and spread swiftly. During the Ming Dynasty, overland routes from Europe to China were cut off. Needing new trade routes, the Europeans explored Africa. The slave trade was established about 1530. Liberated slaves lived in colonies at Gabon, Sierra Leone and Liberia, on the African continent. A specifically African martial art — capoeira — developed from native dances. Originally, these dances were performed as religious rites, but as the brutality of the slave trade increased, the dance was adapted

From the beginning of colonial settlement, slaves were imported from Africa, which lead to the development of the famous Capoeira system of self-defense. The African native dances that gave rise to this system were brought to Brazil by slaves. Most of its techniques are kicking techniques for the slaves' hands were often chained together. Many techniques are performed from a handstand position. In Brazil, during the 17th century, a group of slaves formed their own republic, but were eventually defeated. Many fled to cities and villages where they spread this martial art. By 1972, it had become an official Brazilian sport, with official rules and regulations.

Other martial arts, including Jujutsu, have been introduced in modern times and have been adapted to suit the needs of Brazilians.

BRAZIL

Martial Arts:

Brazilian Jujutsu

Capoeira

Brazil is the largest country in South America both in land mass and in population. It is among the largest countries in the world. Though multiracial, Brazil is Portuguese in culture, for the Portugeuse began settling in the country in the early 16th century. Brazil became independent in 1822 and was proclaimed a republic in 1889. Since much of it borders the Atlantic Ocean, Brazil is a popular resort area, though it remains a poor country. Though it depends on agriculture, it is slowly becoming more industrialized. Physically, it has two contrasting land configurations, the lowlands and the highlands. Two enormous rivers, the Amazon and the Parana-Paraguay, occupy the lowland areas. The climate is mild, though it can be quite hot and humid in the summer.

BURMA (MYANMAR)

Martial Arts:

Burmese Boxing
Burmese Wrestling
Bando
Banshay
Thaing

Burma, now called Myanmar, is a country in Southeast Asia that shares borders with India, Bangledesh, China, Laos and Thailand. Mountains and hills on the west, north and east serve to isolate Burma from her neighbors. Like other Asian countries, Burma was colonized by the British, gaining independence late, in 1948. In 1962, the military overthrew the government and announced that the country would now follow Communism, albeit Burmese style. Many cultural and ethnic groups exist in Burma; in fact, less than 3/4 of the country can actually speak Burmese. The main religious groups are Buddhists, with Theravada Buddhism being the primary sect. In each large village, the Buddhist monastery has a recognized, important place.

Throughout its history, Burma has been at war with various countries and has been influenced by various others. For much of Burmese history, a two-sided influence existed, with India on one side and China on the other. In the martial arts, India had the greatest influence until about 1000 A.D. After that, contact with China increased and the Chinese influence was widely felt. The martial arts flourished throughout Burma's early history. The Mongols invaded in 1287 and Burma was divided into three kingdoms, the Shan Dynasty; the Mons, a Mongol group; and the kingdom of Toungoo, established by the ethnic Burmese. The country was not unified until the 16th century, when Tabinshwehti decisively defeated the Mons and the Shans. But the newly united country declined after Tabinshwehti's death. Centuries of war, especially with Thailand, devastated the country. Internal strife also contributed to the country's ills. Toward the end of the 19th century, the British invaded Burma on the pretext of the cruel treatment by Burmese authorities of some European merchants in Rangoon. Later, conflict over payments for teak concessions that had been negotiated with the independent Burmese kingdom of Ana again gave the British an excuse to invade. On January 1, 1886, Upper Burma was annexed by Great Britain. Later, Lower Burma would be added to the "province."

Eventually, independence from Great Britain was achieved. China became the primary source of aid. In order to solve a border dispute, Burma agreed to give up active relations with governments other than China. Internal conflict among communist, democratic and other groups continues to the present day.

CHINA

Martial Arts:

Wushu

Kempo

Chinese Wrestling

Tai Chi Chuan

Ruling Dynasties:

Hsia Dynasty--------------------1995 B.C. to 1523 B.C.

Shang (Yin) Dynasty----------1523 B.C. to 1028 B.C.

Chou (Zhou) Dynasty----------1027 B.C. to 256 B.C.

Chin Dynasty------------------ 221 B.C. to 206 B.C.

Han Dynasty-------------------- 202 B.C. to 220 A.D.

Three Kingdoms--------------- 220 A.D. to 265 A.D.

Chin (Tsin) Dynasty----------- 265 A.D. to 420 A.D.

Southern Dynasties------------ 420 A.D. to 589 A.D.

Northern Dynasties------------ 386 A.D. to 581 A.D.

Sui Dynasty--------------------- 581 A.D. to 618 A.D.

T'ang Dynasty------------------ 618 A.D. to 906 A.D.

Five Dynasties------------------ 907 A.D. to 960 A.D.

Ten Kingdoms------------------ 902 A. D. to 979 A.D.

Sung Dynasty------------------- 960 A.D. to 1279 A.D.

Yuan (Mongol) Dynasty--------1271 A.D. to 1368 A.D.

Ming Dynasty-------------------1368 A. D. to 1644 A.D.

Ching (Manchu) Dynasty-------1644 A.D. to 1912 A.D.

Republic of China (Taiwan)----1912 A.D. to Present

People's Republic of China-----1949 A.D. to Present

China is the world's largest country in terms of population. Since 1949, it has been split into two entities, the People's Republic of China, which is the communist mainland, and the Republic of China, which is Taiwan. Each claims legal jurisdiction over the other. Mongolia and Russia border the mainland to the north. To the east are Russia, Korea and the Pacific Ocean. In the south, the Pacific Ocean, Vietnam, Hong Kong, Burma and India border China. To the west, India, Pakistan, and Afghanistan are border countries.

Culturally, the Chinese are Taoists, Buddhists and Muslims. They absorbed and were greatly influenced by the tenets of Confucianism, which is the philosophical base of the culture. Confucius (551-479 B.C.) emphasized harmony, right conduct, and moral perfection. Even now, the political elite are expected to be morally superior. The Chinese have historically recognized three personal bonds of great importance: child-parent, husband-wife, and subject-ruler. During their long and violent history, the Chinese sought refuge in philosophy and not religion. The Cultural Revolution, which took place in 1949, was meant to reform the stagnant social system.

Led by Mao Zedong (Mao Tse Tung), the followers of the communist party turned temples into warehouses and the martial arts fell into disrepute. By the 1980s, however, the martial arts had regained their former popularity. The country has a rich martial arts history, and even the terrain played a part in the development of the martial arts. In the north, many mountains and canyons mark the land as do large tracts of forest. The weather is temperate, but floods and severe winter storms are not infrequent. The farmers and nobles were connected by the bonds of feudalism. The area was under constant threat of invasion. The north also contains Hunan province, the site of the original Shaolin Temple. This place is the legendary origin of martial arts.

According to legend, the monk Bodhidharma came to the Shaolin Temple from India in 522 A.D. He brought Zen Buddhism with him and introduced the martial arts to China. From Shaolin, the martial arts in various styles spread across all of Asia.

The southern part of China, however, is more isolated and was not constantly invaded. It is a thickly populated, subtropical area with heavy rainfall. The Fukien province is contained in southern China. This is where the second Shaolin temple was located after government troops burned the first for harboring dissidents and rebels. Throughout the history of China, secret societies were formed to benefit business people, farmers and religious or political groups. They functioned by protecting their members from being harmed by rivals. Partly this was in response to banditry, which existed on a large scale. Groups of criminals controlled vast areas of land and even entire towns. Sometimes they looted and took over temples, using them as their headquarters. Religious community members, then, had to protect themselves from such groups. Each group developed its own distinctive martial arts techniques. The idea of a monk or nun using spectacular methods of self-defense has interested countless generations of Westerners and Asians alike. From these beginnings, the martial arts spread through all levels of society in China.

EUROPE

Martial Arts:

Classical Greek Boxing
Pankration
Boxe Francais
Savate

Europe, the second smallest continent in the world, has no true indigenous martial arts. Several fighting methods have developed, as have several martial sports, but these were not derived from combat arts. Asian and European wrestling had early contact but the history of this relationship is obscure. Any records regarding it have been lost. The martial sports of Greek boxing, Pankration and Cornish Wrestling are old while the fighting methods are new and are confined to two systems — Savate and Boxe Francais — that originated in France. Savate is a method of streetfighting that was popular for a time among the upper classes; Boxe Francais is now mostly an exhibition sport. Judo was brought to Europe as early as 1901, and Jujutsu was introduced at the same time. Judo became extremely popular in Europe, especially in Germany and England. Karate was not introduced until the 1950s. Because of the European influence, some martial arts styles have changed and adapted, using the language of the country instead of the usual Japanese or Chinese.

INDIA

Martial Arts:

Indian Wrestling
Science of Combat

India is a large country in South Asia, the second most populous country in the world (behind China). The name "India" originally referred to the whole subcontinent but in 1947, at the time of independence, the country was divided into India and Pakistan. India is bordered on the north by China and Nepal and on the east by Burma and Bangledesh. In the south, the Indian Ocean borders India and in the west are Pakistan and the Arabian Sea. India is pocked with mountains, deserts and jungles, and this terrain served to isolate the country in many ways. Still, India was constantly invaded. It is the world's oldest continuous culture and survived these numerous incursions. The first known invaders were the Aryans (Indo-Europeans) who arrived around 1500 B.C. Their religion eventually became Hinduism. Later, an Islamic civilization evolved as well, around the Eighth century A.D. As Hinduism and Islam were completely irreconcilable, numerous conflicts resulted, leading finally to the creation of the two separate countries.

Modern India is troubled by severe economic problems plus border disputes with China and Pakistan. The country is still quite tribal as evidenced by the numerous languages and dialects spoken, including Hindi, English, Sanskrit, Bengali, and Urdu, among others. These have led to many religious and political conflicts.

Hinduism, which is followed by about 85% of the country, tolerates many philosophical ideas and has itself accumulated numerous beliefs and practices, some of which contradict each other, plus rigid rules for the most ordinary of activities. Hinduism has many sects or cults devoted to the veneration of different gods. Fundamentally, it is a religion in which the practioner seeks to grasp the "one reality." How this is achieved may vary. It is also a religion that places great emphasis on caste. One is born into a caste and this caste cannot change. It governs all aspects of life, from marriage to employment opportunities. Jainism is a religion that arose in response to Hinduism. It denies some aspects of Hinduism but accepts the doctrine of works and rebirth. Buddhism, which is also practiced in India, also denies some aspects of Hinduism. Sikhism, another important Indian religion, was founded in the 15th century. It is a monotheistic religion that opposes the caste system. Islam, which is followed by more than ten percent of the population, believes in one god, and the particular sect followed in India, Sufism, emphasizes the believer's relationship to God and downplays the importance of Islamic law. A tiny proportion of the society is Christian and these are divided into roughly equal numbers of Roman Catholic, Eastern Orthodox and Protestant believers. These religious differences have contributed to internal divisions in India.

The national sport of India is wrestling, and wrestling was popular even before Buddhism was introduced in 500 B.C. — in fact, wrestling was popular even before the Aryan invasion of India in 1500 B.C. The Islamic incursions brought Muslim wrestling, in particular the groundwork techniques that came to characterize later martial arts. India is considered the parent country of all martial arts. Indian monks are thought to have brought the martial arts to China and from there to other parts of Asia. The legendary Bodhidharma, who traveled to China to teach Zen Buddhism, is said to have brought the martial arts with him. He lived in the sixth century and is thought to have traveled to China in 520 A.D. By the 15th century A.D., Indian wrestlers and other martial artists held positions at court, where they frequently performed and were generously compensated. In the 17th century, a man named Ramdas traveled across India, encouraging Hindus to participate in athletics in order to pay homage to Hanuman, the god of strength and valor. Ramdas became known as the father of Indian athletics. The onset of British rule brought a decline to Indian martial arts from which they have never fully recovered.

INDONESIA

Martial Art:

Pentjak Silat

This island nation is home to more than 150 million people, of ten major ethnic groups with languages, religions and customs all their own. The major religious groups are Muslims, who account for 85% of the population, Christians, who are a little more than 5% of the population, plus animists, Buddhists and Hindus in approximately equal numbers. Over two hundred distinct languages and dialects are spoken. Major islands are Java, Sumatra, Borneo, and Bali. The islands stretch across the equator and have a tropical rain forest climate. Formerly, Indonesia was a Dutch colony referred to as the Dutch East Indies. The islands were occupied by Japan during World War II and though a republic was declared at the end of the war, the Dutch did not surrender possession until the end of 1949.

In addition to organized religious beliefs, Indonesians have, in general, a belief in a cosmic order that includes good and evil spirits. Rituals, including those showing respect for ancestors, are an important part of life, especially in rural areas. Culturally, although most Indonesians are Muslims, Islamic law is not emphasized. Women do not wear the veil and they have property rights, inheritance rights and can divorce their husbands. The people have also adopted much Hindu literature and have created a theatre similar to the Japanese Noh. Dance and theatre performances are done in groups, emphasizing the communal quality of Indonesian life.

Early in Indonesia's history, India had the greatest cultural influence, first in terms of trade and then in cultural and political developments. By the second century A.D., Indonesian city-states resembled Indian precursors. For the next few centuries, Indonesian city-states developed overseas trade and conquered territory. Late in the 15th century, Vasco de Gama, a Portuguese explorer, established military and trade bases in India. From there, the Portuguese moved into Indonesia. This formed the cornerstone of their spice trade. Late in the 16th century, the Portuguese injudiciously murdered an Indonesian sultan, thus sparking a war, which eventually drove them from the islands. The Dutch then gained their first foothold in 1641. They had a significant role, mostly negative, in the development of Indonesia. The Dutch policies in regard to the Indonesians were barbaric and exploitive. Over the course of the next two hundred years, nationalism among Indonesians grew until at the turn of the century, it exploded in acts of violence across Indonesia, which were viciously repressed on the part of the Dutch. Dutch control of Indonesia collapsed after the invasion of the Japanese. After World War II ended, Indonesia gained independence.

Throughout its history, the Indian influence on Indonesia led to the establishment of martial arts which acquired a native flavor. The centuries of Dutch rule led to great surges in the development of Pentjak Silat, as nationalists trained in the martial arts to achieve their desire for independence.

JAPAN

Martial Arts:
Aikido
Aikijutsu
Jujutsu
Kenjutsu
Naginata-do
Iaijutsu
Iaido
Kendo
Judo
Kyudo
Kyujutsu
Ninjutsu
Sumo

Japanese historical periods:
Ancient: to 537 A.D.
Asuka 538-644
Nara 645-781
Hakuho 645-710
Tempyo 711-781
Heian 782-1184
Jogan 782-897
Fujiwara 898-1184

Kamakura 1185-1332
Nambokucho 1333-1391
Muromachi 1392-1572
Momoyama 1573-1599
Edo (Tokyo, sometimes Tokugawa) 1600-1867
Meiji (modern) 1868- 1912

Japan, an island nation, was founded over 2,000 years ago. It is the oldest monarchy in the world. Isolated from other countries by the Pacific Ocean, the Phillipine Sea, the East Chinese Sea, the Sea of Japan and the Strait of Korea, Japan nonetheless has a strong Chinese heritage. In fact, all Japanese writing uses the application of Chinese script to Japanese words. The major religions are Shinto, Buddhism and Christianity. According to Shinto, harmony should always prevail. The culture places great emphasis on the interests of the group above the interests of the individual. Confucianism, which is not a religion, but a philosophy, had a less important role in Japan than in China. Buddhism, which co-exists with Shinto (virtually all Japanese are Shinto followers and about 85% are Buddhists), came to Japan from Korea in 552 A.D.

The culture stresses two kinds of relationships, reciprocal and asymmetrical. The first exists, for instance, between a husband and wife. Upon the marriage, each family exchanges gifts and assurances of mutual help and hospitality, thus fulfulling their reciprocal obligations to each other. Asymmetrical obligations, on the other hand, are those between an inferior and a superior. An obligation is created on the part of the inferior. Neither giver nor receiver expects the debt to be paid. This relationship exists when, for instance, a master artisan takes an apprentice. The apprentice can never hope to repay the artisan for this kindness. This relationship characterizes the one between the martial arts teacher and his or her student. The student is bound to the teacher and can never hope to repay the obligation.

Martial arts in Japan developed from the combat arts so beloved of the warrior class. During what is called the ancient period, the Japanese empire was established. In Japanese legend, before this time, two god-like creatures engaged in unarmed combat. Later, other such events happened. References to such struggles are prevalent in the literature of this early period. Buddhism was introduced in the sixth century brought by other Asian (Chinese and Korean) travelers. Japan's interest in Chinese culture started as early as the beginning of the seventh century as is shown by the official embassies that were sent from Japan to China starting in 607. China's T'ang dynasty, which began in 608, encouraged such contacts. One theory suggests that shipwrecked monks brought methods of Chinese self-defense to Japan. A more plausible theory suggests that Japanese citizens who studied Buddhism in China brought back some of the methods of Wushu (Kung Fu). Because Wushu and Buddhism were connected, such occurences were likely.

During the subsequent Nara period (630-793), Buddhism gained great popularity. And this had a profound influence on the development of the martial arts. The Taika family established the imperial family as the absolute rulers during this period. In the following era, the Heian period (794-1191), the capital was moved to Heian (now Kyoto). The Fujiawara family claimed power. Because of continued banditry, Buddhist monasteries took to hiring armed groups of warriors to deal with these problems. Rival temples even fought with each other. The government was forced to inteverne. Later, the shogunate, or military rule, was re-established during the Ashikaga (Muromachi) period (1337-1573). There were still many internal disputes and the Ashikaga family could not control the entire country. The classical age of Japanese martial arts began toward the latter part of this period.

The classical age is usually thought to have existed from about 1500 to 1868. Military commanders were often Buddhist monks, which shows the connection of religion with combat arts.

The following period, the Azuchi-Momoyama period (1574-1602) was notable in that Oda Nobunaga defeated the Ashikaga family with his assistant Toyatomi Hideyoshi. In 1592, Toyatomi Hideyoshi, by then a great warlord, had begun his "conquest" of China. For six years, until his death in 1598, he waged a completely unsuccessful war against China. It is thought that his soldiers, returning from China, brought Kempo with them, but though contact with China led to the development of Japanese unarmed martial arts, the relationship is not clear. During the Edo (Tokyo) period, sometimes called the Tokugawa period (1603-1867), the power shifted to Tokugawa Ieyasu and the Tokugawa clan. What followed was a peaceful period, though some historians believe that the weaponless martial art called Yawara was introduced during this time.

The modern period, which began with the restoration of the emperor, began in 1868. In 1876, the wearing of the sword was prohibited, completing the suppression of the samurai. Early in the 20th century, the Japanese asked the Okinawan Funakoshi Gichin to show them his method of Karate. He did so, thus sparking the beginning of modern Karate. All Karate in Japan is derived from Okinawan sytems. Though Karate was banned in Japan after World War II, after its restoration it resumed greater heights of popularity than before.

KOREA

Martial Arts:

Hapkido

Hwarang-do

Kum Do

Kuk Sool Won

Kwon Pup

Ma Sool

Tae Kwon Do

Tae Kyun

Tang Soo Do

Korea is situated on a peninsula in East Asia. Since 1945, it has been divided into a communist north and a non-communist south. It is bordered by China and Russia to the north and extends between the Yellow Sea and the Sea of Japan. Its modern name, Korea, derives from the Koryo dynasty which ruled from the tenth to the 14th century. Historically, both prior to the Koryo dynasty and subsequent to it, Korea was known as Choson, the land of the morning calm. Korea is a mountainous country with little farm land. Much Chinese cultural influence was exerted on Korea.

It was through Korea that Chinese culture was borrowed by Japan.

According to legend, Korea was founded by the holy Dan Gun, in 2333 B.C. Korea is known as the "hermit kingdom" for its isolationist policies. A unique array of fighting methods influenced by many cultures developed. Koreans were able to adapt to foreign ideas without losing their own cultural identity. They preferred projectile weapons and empty hand fighting. Bladed weapons were never as popular as in Japan. The Mongols, with whom the Koreans had significant contact, were primarily mounted and relied on the crossbow, not the sword. When the use of bladed weapons became available, no real development of a native swordfighting style happened. The Korean sword remained artistic with few practical qualities. By 108 B.C., the Chinese were ruling Korea, and with them brought the martial arts. Later, the Chinese colonies were destroyed and most of the country was ruled by three kingdoms, Koguryo (also spelled Kokoryo), Silla and Paekche (sometimes spelled Baekjae).

Though the Chinese colonies had been destroyed, the Chinese cultural influence continued. Certain martial ideas influenced each of the three kingdoms. Grappling styles were popular in Koguryo. Paekche, which had an inferior military, was indifferent to defense, concerning itself instead with developing cultural possibilites. Paekche became a center of culture where Buddhism flourished. The kingdom was defeated and razed. Silla emerged as the primary power in Korea during the fourth century, escaping Chinese occupation. Young members of the nobility received training as leaders as members of a group of young warriors known as the Hwarang. During 634-653, two queens inherited the throne and developed relations with the Chinese T'ang dynasty. Queen Songdok sent students to China to study Chinese methods of warfare, and sponsored military/religious schools for young nobles. Later, these developed a philosophical/martial code called Hwarang-do, which means the "way of the flower of manhood." This may be the pattern after which Japanese Bushido later developed. The ethical code centered on chivalry and patriotism. The heroic deeds of Hwarang warriors, memorialized in songs, helped bring about the successful unification of Korea under Silla rule. The Hwarang-do youths practiced martial arts. They followed five principles: loyalty to the country, loyalty to one's parents, loyalty to one's friends, never retreat and avoid killing when possible. During the flourishing of the Silla dynasty, Subaki tournaments were held. This martial art is considered the forerunner of Tae Kwon Do. By 780, however, the Hwarang warriors had become disorganized and ineffective. The king was assassinated and a series of struggles for the throne ensued. Later, the son of a Silla king organized a state called Later Koguryo, which in turn became Koryo, the origin of the name Korea. This kingdom ruled until the year 1392.

The influence of China was felt throughout the history of Korea. The empty hand arts of combat in Korea were called T'ang hand, that is "China hand," because of this influence. Like the sword, the staff was never highly developed. Partly this is owing to the unsuitable nature of Korean wood, much of which is soft and not suitable for the production of staffs. The Koreans, however, did favor the bow and arrow. The Mongol invasion of 1200-1250 introduced the bow and arrow as well as horsemanship techniques to Koreans. In 1592, the war with Japan weakened the Chinese Ming dynasty; soon, the Ching dynasty overthrew it. This preoccupied China, and Japan took the opportunity to widen her sphere of influence to Korea. Subsequently, Japan occupied Korea, forbidding the practice of native martial arts. By the start of World War II, the Japanese had re-established martial arts training for Korean youths, partly to prepare them for military training. After the end of the war, the United States encouraged sport applications of Korean

martial arts, and it was then that Tae Kwon Do developed as the national martial art of Korea.

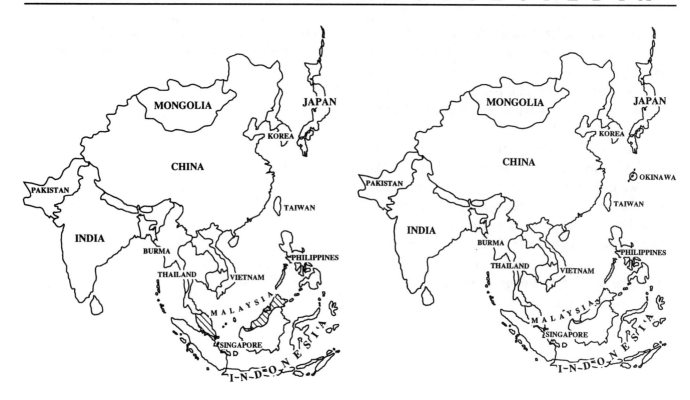

MALAYSIA.

Martial Art:

Bersilat

This country in Southern Asia is a federation of fourteen states that did not exist as a political entity until the 1960s. However, it has an ancient history as a region. It is extemely diverse, as a result of migration, with every group actually a minority. No language, religious or ethnic group has a majority. The largest ethnic group is the Malays, who are mostly Muslim. There are also Chinese, who are Confucianists as well as Buddhists, and Indians, who are mostly Hindus. A prosperous country, it is one of the richest in Southern Asia. Because of its rainy, wet climate and water-logged terrain, its martial arts developed numerous schools devoted to techniques for use on slippery ground. Around 1400, a Malay prince established a dynasty on the peninsula, which is about when the history of Malaysia begins. Later, Portugal conquered the country. It was controlled by the British until the end of the 18th century.

OKINAWA

Martial Arts:

Karate

Tegumi Wrestling

Timbei

Okinawa is the largest island in the Ryukyu archipelago south of Japan. The island is situated between Japan and Thailand. Although early in its history, independent kings ruled Okinawa, it paid tribute to China, who conquered it in the 16th century. By the mid-14th century, Okinawa had established relations with other Asian countries. It is thought that Okinawans visiting China brought back Kempo, and certainly the contact with China introduced elements of Wushu (Kung Fu) into the Okinawan martial arts. A permanent Okinawan community was organized in China during the Ming period (1386-1644), and later a Chinese community was established on Okinawa. This they called the Thirty Six Families. Chinese martial arts masters taught Wushu and Kempo to the Okinawans. The Japanese invaded in the 17th century, and the Okinawans were forced to pay tribute to both China and Japan. However, continual warfare in Japan forced many Japanese citizens to leave the country. Many arrived in Okinawa, bringing with them their martial arts skills. Okinawa was completely taken over by the Japanese in the 19th century and it is now part of the Japanese empire.

Both China and Japan banned the ownership of weapons by Okinawans, which lead to the development of empty hand techniques. Okinawans also developed ways to convert farming implements into deadly weapons. Different villages and regions developed their own styles. Three main branches of martial arts developed in Okinawa. Collectively they are known as Okinawa-te, "te"meaning "hand." These three were Shuri-te, Naha-te and Tomari-te. From these stemmed the art of Karate, which was called Karate-jutsu (China hand art) in respect for the three cultures: Okinawa, Japan and China. By the 18th century, modern Okinawan Karate had begun to emerge. In the late-1880s, the word "Karate" meaning "T'ang"or "China" hand was in u s e . In the early-20th century, Funakoshi Gichin brought Karate to Japan and then to the rest of the world. Judo and Kendo were introduced to Okinawa in the beginning of the 20th century.

y daga, "the "sword and knife" method of fighting. Native dances were used to practice forms. The United States later became involved in the governing of the Philippines. The Spanish-American war led to the "purchase" of the Philippines for $20 million dollars by President McKinley, which led almost inevitably to the Philippine-American war, which lasted from 1899 to 1901. Though the island was annexed, resistance continued until 1935, when the United States finally surrendered to the demands for self-rule.

PHILIPPINES, THE

Martial Arts:

Arnis (Northern Philippines)
Escrima (Central Philippines)
Kali (Southern Philippines)
Dumog Wrestling

The Philippines is an island country about 600 miles from the mainland of Asia. It is largely mountainous, which causes migration and overcrowding in the lowland cities. Filipinos are largely Christian, with about 85% of them Catholic. This is one cultural legacy of Spanish colonialism. About 4% are Muslim and a few are Protestant or animists. The fighting arts have always been important to this ethnically and culturally diverse society. Migration from central Asia and Malaysia brought weapons such as the kris and the stick, which characterize Philippine martial arts. The Chinese had the greatest influence early, establishing colonies in the Philippines, which brought Chinese martial arts. The Spanish arrived in 1570, which led to the suppression of the martial arts. However, the Spanish contributed a major system to the Filipino martial arts with the "espada

countries. It was started from within, through the benign influence of their kings, not imposed from without. This has led to fewer internal conflicts.

THAILAND

Martial Art:

Thai Boxing

Thailand was known as Siam for much of its existence. It is the only nation in the region that avoided colonial rule, which allowed Thailand to preserve its traditions, social, religious and cultural. Early warfare and martial arts were of a mass nature. Warriors rode war elephants, wore armor and devised shields made of hide. Many of the native dances still include the kris, the lance and the sword. Continual warfare with Burma, however, led to the continual destruction of records, so that much cultural and political history has been lost. In the 13th century, Thai leaders established an independent state. Mostly Buddhists, the Thai people owe much of their culture to China and India. Ethnic Chinese, however, are not considered Thai, and are the object of some suspicion. The Thai language is based on Sanskrit, which reveals the Indian influence on the country. Since the Thai people have always been self-governing, modernization was not as painful as it was for other Asian

VIETNAM

Martial Arts:
Viet Vo Dao
Vo Tu Do
Qwan Ki Do

In Vietnam, the oldest continuous civilization in Southeast Asia, martial arts are probably of Chinese origin. It is a country best known for a war, the field of battle of the Vietnam War. Vietnam was first conquered by China in 111 B.C. and was ruled by China for the next 1000 years. A notable event occurred in 39 A.D. when two sisters led the aristocracy in an uprising and restored Vietnamese independence. This was subsequently put down by the Chinese, but the warrior Trung sisters are still celebrated in Vietnam today. For hundreds of years, Vietnam served as a bridge from China to Southeast Asia. In the tenth century, Vietnam regained its independence and established a monarchy like that of China. Though there was much contact with China, most evidence suggests that indigenous Vietnamese martial arts were only established in modern times. In the 19th century, Vietnam was conquered by France. Under colonial rule little

was done to improve the conditions of the people and anti-French sentiment was publicly expressed in the 1920s. In 1945, a group of nationalists led by the Communist party, taking advantage of the Japanese occupation, seized the north. The French returned to subdue the rebels, but an eight year war ended in the division of Vietnam. In 1965, fearing a communist take over of the south, the United States sent troops to Vietnam. After a lengthy conflict, the United States withdrew and left the Vietnamese to their own devices. The majority of the Vietnamese are Buddhists who follow Confucianism and Taoism, along with ancestor worship. A minority is Catholic, from the French missionaries of the 17th century. Relations between the government and Catholics, who seem Western, are strained. Two major religious sects, native to Vietnam, also exist. Hoa Hao is a Buddhist sect and Cao Dai is a combination of many major religions.

SELECTED READINGS

Numerous martial arts publications exist, including an array of audio and video tape productions, plus monthly periodicals covering all styles of the martial arts. These are always an excellent source of information and can be found at any bookstore or library. The following list of books includes those that are worth looking for, as they should prove helpful to the martial artist who wishes to gain further insight into a discipline or training method. Nearly all of the books on the list are still in print and can be located by contacting the publisher. The few that are not should be available at libraries or used bookstores.

GENERAL INFORMATION

Corcoran, John. *The Martial Arts Sourcebook.* New York: HarperCollins, 1994.

Crompton, Paul. *Complete Martial Arts.* New York: Bantam, 1992

Draeger, Donn. *Weapons and Fighting Arts of the Indonesian Archipelago.* Rutland, Vermont: Charles E. Tuttle and Company, 1972.

Draeger, Donn and Robert W. Smith. *Comprehensive Asian Fighting Arts.* New York: Kodansha International, 1980.

Farkas, Emil and John Corcoran. *The Overlook Martial Arts Dictionary.* Woodstock, New York: Overlook Press, 1985.

Mitchell, David. *The Overlook Martial Arts Handbook.* Woodstock, New York: Overlook Press, 1987.

----. *The Young Martial Artist.* Woodstock, New York: Overlook Press, 1992.

Soet, John S. *Martial Arts Around the World.* Burbank, California: Unique Publications, 1991.

Villari, Fred. *The Martial Arts and Real Life: A Book of Fighting for the 21st Century.* New York: Morrow, 1985.

Yates, Keith. *Warrior Secrets: A Handbook of the Martial Arts.* Boulder: Paladin Press, 1985.

STYLES

Alexander, Howard et. al. *Pentjak-Silat: The Indonesian Fighting Art.* New York: Kodansha International, 1970.

Cho, Sihak Henry. *Korean Karate: Free Fighting Techniques.* Rutland, Vermont: Charles E. Tuttle and Company, 1968.

Conway, Frank and Jane Hallander. *Kajukenbo: The Ultimate Self-Defense System.* Burbank, California: Unique Publications, 1988.

Cuyler, P.L. *Sumo: From Rite to Sport.* New York: Weatherhill, 1979.

Funakoshi, Gichin. *Karate-do: My Way of Life.* New York: Kodansha International, 1981.

----. *Karate-Do Kyohan: The Master Text.* New York: Kodansha International, 1973.

Ho'o, Marshall. *Tai Chi Chuan.* Santa Clarita, California: O'hara Publications, 1986.

Insosanto, Dan. *The Filipino Martial Arts.* Burbank, California: Unique Publications, 1980.

----. *Jeet Kune Do: The Art and Philosophy of Bruce Lee.* Los Angeles: Know Now Publishing, 1980.

Lee, Bruce. *Tao of Jeet Kune Do.* Santa Clarita, California: O'hara Publications, 1975.

Park, Yeon Hee, et. al. *Tae Kwon Do: The Ultimate Reference Guide to the World's Most Popular Martial Art.* New York: Facts on File, Inc., 1989.

Presas, Remy. *Modern Arnis: Philippine Martial Art of Stick Fighting.* Manila: Modern Arnis Publishing, 1974.

Reay, Tony. *Judo: Skills and Techniques.* London: Crowwood Press, 1985.

Reilly, Robin L. *Japan's Complete Fighting System: Shin Kage Ryu.* Rutland, Vermont: Charles E. Tuttle and Company, 1989.

Rhee, Jhoon. *Chon-ji of Tae Kwon Do Hyung.* Santa Clarita, California: O'hara Publications, 1970. Plus other volumes in the series.

Saito, Morihiro. *Traditional Aikido: Volumes I-IV.* Tokyo: Minato Research and Publishing Co., 1973.

Sipe, Daniel. *Kickboxing.* Minneapolis: Capstone, 1994.

Smith, Kenneth A. *The Way of the Sun Dragon: Chinese Martial Art of Tai-Yang Lung Tao.* Fremont, California: Jain Publishing Company, 1993.

So, Doshin. *Shorinji Kempo: Philosophy and Techniques.* Tokyo: Japan Publications, 1970.

Spear, Robert. *Hapkido: The Integrated Fighting Art.* Burbank, California: Unique Publications, 1988.

Wiley, Mark V. *Filipino Martial Arts.* Rutland, Vermont: Charles E. Tuttle and Company, 1994.

Wong, Doc Fai and Jane Hallander. *Shaolin Five Animals.* Burbank, California: Unique Publications, 1987.

FITNESS, TRAINING AND SELF-DEFENSE

Canney, J. C. *Health and Fitness in the Martial Arts.* Rutland, Vermont: Charles E. Tuttle and Company, 1992.

Crowley, Brian and Esther. *Moving With the Wind: Magick and Healing in the Martial Arts.* St. Paul: Llewellyn Publications, 1993.

DePasquale, Michael. *Woman's Guide to Self-Defense.* New York: Cornerstone, 1980.

Gray, Brian. *Complete Iron Palm Training.* Burbank, California: Unique Publications, 1989.

Isnosanto, Dan. *Guide to Martial Arts Training.* Los Angeles: Know Now Publications, 1986.

Neff, Fred. *Lessons from the Western Warrior: Dynamic Self-Defense Techniques.* Minneapolis: Lerner Publications, 1987.

----. *Lessons from the Samurai: Ancient Self-Defense Strategy and Techniques.* Minneapolis: Lerner Publicatiions, 1987.

Urquidez, Benny with Emil Farkas and Stuart Sobel. *Training and Fighting Skills.* Burbank, California: Unique Publications, 1981.

FORMS AND TECHNIQUES

Chan, Poi. *Chinese Fatal Flute and Stick Forms.* Burbank, California: Unique Publications, 1985.

Cheung, William. *Advanced Wing Chun.* Santa Clarita, California: O'hara Publications, 1988.

----. *Wing Chun Bil Jee: The Deadly Art of Thrusting Fingers.* Burbank, California: Unique Publications, 1983.

DeMile, James W. *Bruce Lee's Power Punch.* Seattle, Washington: Tao of Wing Chun Do Publications, 1994.

Hibbard, Jack. *Karate Breaking Techniques: With Practical Applications for Self-Defense.* Rutland, Vermont: Charles E. Tuttle and Company, 1981.

Kim, Ashida. *Ninja: Secrets of Invisibility.* Boulder: Paladin Press, 1985.

Lam, Kwon W and Ted Mancuso. *Northern Sil Lum Form Number Seven: Plum Flower Fist.* Burbank, California: Unique Publications, 1984.

Peterson, Kirtland. *Mind of the Ninja. Exploring the Inner Power.* Chicago: Contemporary Books, 1986.

Seiji, Omoto. *Taijutsu Tactics: Ninja Close-Quarter Grappling.* Boulder: Paladin Press, 1987.

Yates, Keith. *Complete Book of Taekwon Do Forms.* Boulder: Paladin Press, 1988.

PHILOSOPHY

Christensen, Loren. *The Way Alone: Your Path to Excellence in the Martial Arts.* Boulder: Paladin Press, 1987.

Dang, Tri T. *Beyond the Known: The Real Meaning of the Martial Arts.* Rutland, Vermont: Charles E. Tuttle and Company, 1993.

Deshimaru, Taisen. *Zen Way to Martial Arts: A Japanese Master Reveals the Secrets of the Samurai.* New York: Viking Penguin, 1992.

Hyams, Joe. *Zen Martial Arts.* New York: Bantam, 1982.

Kauz, Herman. *The Path to Liberation: A Spiritual and Philosophical Approach to the Martial Arts.* Woodstock, New York: Overlook Press, 1991.

King, Winston L. *Zen and the Way of the Sword.* Oxford: Oxford University Press, 1993.

Morgan, Forrest E. *Living the Martial Way.* Fort Lee, New Jersey: Barricade Books, 1992.

Musashi, Miyamoto. *The Book of Five Rings.* Trans. Thomas Cleary. Boston: Shambhala Press, 1993.

Nelson, Randy, ed. *The Overlook Martial Arts Reader.* Woodstock, New York: Overlook Press, 1989.

Reid, Howard and Michael Croucher. *The Way of the Warrior: The Paradox of the Martial Arts.* Woodstock, New York: Overlook Press, 1991.

WEAPONS

Daniel, Charles. *Traditional Ninja Weapons and Ninjutsu Techniques.* Burbank, California: Unique Publications, 1986.

Gruzanski, Charles V. *Ninja Weapons: Chain and Shuriken.* Rutland, Vermont: Charles E. Tuttle and Company, 1991.

Hernandez, Cacoy. *Iron Butterfly — Balisong Knife.* Burbank, California: Unique Publications, 1985.

Huey, David. *Spearplay.* Burbank, California: Unique Publications,1986.

Imada, Jeff. *Advanced Balisong Manual.* Burbank, California: Unique Publications, 1986.

Sato, Kanzan. *The Japanese Sword.* Trans. Joe Earle. New York: Kodansha International, 1960.

Shiroma, Jiro. *Nunchaku.* Burbank, California: Unique Publications, 1989.

Suh, In H. *Fighting Weapons of Korean Martial Arts.* Burbank, California: Unique Publications, 1987.

Yamashita, Tadashi. *Advanced Tonfa.* Santa Clarita, California: O'hara Publications, 1987.

----. *Bo: The Japanese Long Staff.* Santa Clarita, California: O'hara Publications, 1986.

Yang, Jwing-Ming. *Introduction to Ancient Chinese Weapons.* Burbank, Calfornia: Unique Publications, 1985.

Yumoto, John. *The Samurai Sword.* Rutland, Vermont: Charles E. Tuttle and Company, 1958.

INDEX

Dayang, Apat, 30,
Dayang, Dalawa, 30,
Dayang, Isa, 30,
Dayang, Lima, 30,
Dayang, Pito, 30,
Dayang, Sampu, 30,
Dayang, Siyam, 30,
Dayang, Tatlo, 30,
Dayang, Walo, 30,
Dead Patterns, 116,
Dead Tree Fall, 137, 192,
De-Ai, 116,
De-Ai Osae Uke, 108, 116,
De-Ashi-Barai, 116,
De-Ashi-Harai, 115, 116, 136, 185,
Deer Form, 116,
Defy the Dragon, 116,
Defy the Leopard, 116,
Defy the Panther, 116,
Degree, 12, 28,
Delayed Death Touch, 12, 13,
Demon Cutting, 123,
Deok Moo Lee, 230, 232,
Dero Dohras, 12, 13,
Destructions, 116,
Devil's Hand, 117,
Dewanoumi, 37,
Dharanipata, 59,
Dhyana, 12, 49, 229,
Di Son, 117,
Dillman, George, 230,
Dim Mak, 12,
Ding Bo, 117, 174,
Dinh Tan, 117, 175,
Dinhg Tan, 117,
Dirk, 208,
Distance, 12,
Distance Death, 12,
Ditang Chuan, 59,
Di-Tang-Quan, 59,
Do, 13, 7, 27, 38, 64, 66, 73, 75, 87, 89, 90,
Do Jime, 117, 137,
Do Ra, 117,

Do Treo, 117,
Do Vo, 117,
Do Xuong, 117,
Dobo, 45,
Dobok, 13, 45,
Doc Han Vu Tan, 117,
Doces Pares Society, 13,
Doctrine of the Mean, 230, 240,242,
Dogi, 13, 46,
Dogu, 13, 46,
Dohras, 13,
Dohyo, 13, 31, 45,
Dohyo-Iri, 13, 42,
Dojang, 13, 45,
    Dojo, 13, 34,
    Dojo, Code, 13,
    Dojo, Defeat, 13,
    Dojo, Destruction, 13,
    Dojo, Oath, 13,
    Dojo, Pledge, 13,
    Dojo, Tempest, 13,
Doll Rye Chagi, 117,
Dong Jing, 18,
Doong Quyen, 117,
Do-San Form, 117,
Dosoku Kata Sode-Tori, 100, 117,
Dosoku Te-Dori**, 99, 117,
Dozukuri, 117, 149,
Draeger, Donn, 56, 230,
Dragon Flame, 117,
Dragon Style Wushu, 59, 235,
Dragon-Tiger Form, 117,
Dragon, The, 236,
Drawing Methods Set, 117,
Drunken Monkey, 117,
Drunken Praying Mantis, 118,
Drunken Style, 59,
Drunken White Crane, 118,
Duanguom, 208, 213,
Dui Quan, 118,
Duit-Chagi, 118,
Dumog, 59,
Dun, 206,

Kakumune, 210, 216,
Kakuto Uke, 108, 140,
Kalari Payat, 69, 83,
Kali, 53, 69, 72, 141, 229, 262,
Kama, 85, 204, 207, 210, 213,
Kamakura, 34, 53, 95, 215,
Kamakura Period, 256,
Kamakura Shogunate, 228,
Kama-Yari, 218, 219,
Kame, 19, 44,
Kami, 19, 34, 215,
Kamidana, 19, 35, 44,
Kamikaze, 19,
Kami-Shiho-Gatame, 140, 197,
Kami-Tore, 140,
Kamiza, 20,
Kancho, 39,
Kan-Geiko, 20, 43,
Kani Basami, 137, 140, 191,
Kan-Keiko, 20,
Kanku Dai, 140, 147, 149,
Kanku Kata, 140,
Kanku-Sho, 140,
Kano Jigoro, 21, 62, 67, 90, 135, 232,
Kanryo Higashionna, 232,
Kansetsu-Waza, 140,
Kan-Shu, 20, 44,
Kappo, 6, 20, 21, 96,
Kapu Luilua, 70,
Karasik, 218, 219,
Karate, 15, 16, 22, 29, 35, 36, 37, 38, 39, 41, 42,
    55, 58, 61, 62, 72, 74, 78, 79, 80, 82, 84, 85, 88,
    90, 91, 102, 105, 106, 107, 108, 109, 110, 113,
    115, 116, 118, 123, 124, 125, 126, 127, 128,
    129, 130, 132, 133, 140, 141, 142, 145, 146,
    147, 149, 151, 152, 154, 155, 160, 161, 164,
    165, 166, 167, 168, 169, 170, 172, 174, 175,
    177, 179, 181, 182, 185, 188, 189, 190, 197,
    198, 224, 229, 230, 231, 232, 233, 234, 236,
    253, 257, 260, 261
    Karate, American Freestyle, 53,
    Karate, Full Contact, 61, 72, 233, 236,
    Karate, Heian Forms, 140, 154,
Karate, Iron Horse Forms, 154,
Karate, Kenpo, 29, 72,
Karate, Knock-Down, 73,
Karate, Korean, 73, 87,
Karate, Okinawan, 62, 65, 76, 80, 82, 83, 84,
    85, 172, 233,
Karate, Professional, 42,
Karate, Semi-Contact, 42,
Karate, Shorei-Ryu Style, 154, 194,
Karate, Shorinji, 125, 126, 139, 164, 165,
Karate, Shotokan,
    85, 92, 112, 118, 124, 125, 128,129, 134, 139,
    140, 169, 231,
Karate, Tekki Forms, 154,
Karate-Do, 70,
Karate-Jutsu, 71, 261,
Karensa, 141,
Kari, 141,
Karma, 17, 20, 36, 245,
Karumi Jutsu, 56,
Karumi-Jutsu, 71,
Kasugano, 37,
Kasumi, 141, 153,
Kata, 122, 141,
Kata Ashi, 141,
Kata Gatame, 141,
Kata Guruma, 137, 141, 168, 191,
Kata Hajime, 139, 141, 180,
Kata Juji-Jime, 139, 180,
Kata Tori, 98,
Kata-Dori, 100, 141, 191,
Kata-Juji-Jime, 141,
Katame No Kata, 134, 135, 141,
Katana, 210, 215, 216,
Kataonami, 37,
Kata-Sukashi, 141, 184,
Katate Tori, 98,
Katate Tori Ryote Mochi, 98,
Kata-Te-Ryo-Te-Dori, 99,
Katate-Ryote-Dori, 99,
Katate-Ushi, 141,
Katate-Waza, 141,
Katayama Hokinokami Hisayasu, 63,